# Media
# Ethics

*Issues*
*&*
*Cases*

# Media Ethics

## *Issues & Cases*

**PHILIP PATTERSON**
OKLAHOMA CHRISTIAN UNIVERSITY
OF SCIENCE AND ARTS

**LEE WILKINS**
UNIVERSITY OF MISSOURI-COLUMBIA

Boston, Massachusetts   Burr Ridge, Illinois   Dubuque, Iowa
Madison, Wisconsin   New York, New York   San Francisco, California
St. Louis, Missouri

McGraw-Hill
A Division of the McGraw-Hill Companies

MEDIA ETHICS: ISSUES AND CASES

This book is printed on recycled, acid-free paper containing 10% postconsumer waste.

1 2 3 4 5 6 7 8 9 0 DOC/DOC 9 0 9 8 7

ISBN 0-697-32717-5

Publisher: *Phillip Butcher*

Sponsoring Editor: *Marge Byers*

Developmental Editor: *Valerie Raymond*

Marketing Manager: *Carl Leonard*

Project Manager: *Jane C. Morgan*

Production Supervisor: *Sandra Hahn*

Cover designer: *Z Graphics*

Compositor: *ElectraGraphics, Inc.*

Typeface: *10/12 Times Roman*

Printer: *R.R. Donnelley & Sons Company, Crawfordsville, IN*

**Library of Congress Cataloging-in-Publication Data**

Media ethics : issues and cases / [edited by] Philip Patterson, Lee
  Wilkins. — 3rd ed.
      p.    cm.
  Includes bibliographical references and index.
  ISBN 0-697-32717-5
  1. Mass media—Moral and ethical aspects.   I. Patterson, Philip.
II. Wilkins, Lee.
P94.M36   1997                                    97-8386
174—dc21                                          CIP

www.mhhe.com

*To Amy, Andrew, Miranda and Joshua*
*Four equally bright kids, unequally distributed between us*

# CONTENTS

## CHAPTER I
### AN INTRODUCTION TO ETHICAL DECISION MAKING   1

### CHAPTER 1 ESSAY

## CHAPTER II
### INFORMATION ETHICS: A PROFESSION SEEKS THE TRUTH   20

### CASES

# CHAPTER III
## PERSUASION ETHICS: WHAT'S FAIR IN ADVERTISING AND PUBLIC RELATIONS    60

### CASES

# CHAPTER IV
## LOYALTY: CHOOSING BETWEEN COMPETING ALLEGIANCES    92

### CASES

# CHAPTER V
## PRIVACY: LOOKING FOR SOLITUDE IN THE GLOBAL VILLAGE    119

### CASES

# CHAPTER VI
## THE MASS MEDIA IN A DEMOCRATIC SOCIETY:
## KEEPING A PROMISE    151

**CASES**

# CHAPTER VII
## MEDIA ECONOMICS: THE DEADLINE MEETS THE BOTTOM LINE    185

**CASES**

# CHAPTER VIII
## PICTURE THIS: THE ETHICS OF PHOTO AND VIDEO JOURNALISM   216

## CASES

# CHAPTER IX
## ETHICS IN CYBERSPACE: NEW QUESTIONS AND ROLES   264

## CASES

# FOREWORD

CLIFFORD G. CHRISTIANS
*Research Professor of Communication*
*University of Illinois, Urbana*

The playful wit and sharp mind of Socrates attracted disciples from all across ancient Greece. They came to learn and debate in what could be translated "his thinkery." By shifting the disputes among Athenians over earth, air, fire and water to human virtue, Socrates gave Western philosophy and ethics a new intellectual center (Cassier 1944).

But sometimes his relentless arguments would go nowhere. On one occasion, he sparred with the philosopher Hippias about the difference between truth and falsehood. Hippias was worn into submission, but retorted at the end: "I cannot agree with you, Socrates." And then the master concluded: "Nor I with myself, Hippias. . . . I go astray, up and down, and never hold the same opinion." Socrates admitted to being so clever that he had befuddled himself. No wonder he was a favorite target of the comic poets. I. F. Stone likens this wizardry to "whales of the intellect flailing about in deep seas" (Stone 1988).

With his young friend, Meno, Socrates argued whether virtue is teachable. Meno was eager to learn more, after "holding forth often on the subject in front of large audiences." But he complained, "You are exercising magic and witchcraft upon me and positively laying me under your spell until I am just a mass of helplessness. . . . You are exactly like the flat stingray that one meets in the sea. Whenever anyone comes into contact with it, it numbs him, and that is the sort of thing you seem to be doing to me now. My mind and my lips are literally numb."

Philosophy is not a semantic game, though sometimes its idiosyncracies feed that response into the popular mind. *Media Ethics: Issues and Cases* does not debunk philosophy as the excess of sovereign reason. The authors of this book will not encourage those who ridicule philosophy as cunning rhetoric. The issue at stake here is actually a somewhat different problem—the Cartesian model of philosophizing.

The founder of modern philosophy, René Descartes, preferred to work in solitude. Paris was whirling in the early seventeenth century, but for two years even Descartes's friends could not find him as he squirreled away studying mathematics. One can even guess the motto above his desk: "Happy is he who lives in seclusion." Imagine the conditions under which he wrote *Meditations* II. The Thirty Years' War in Europe brought social chaos everywhere. The Spanish were ravaging the French provinces and even threatening Paris, but Descartes was shut away in an apartment in Holland. Tranquility for philosophical speculation mattered so much to him that upon hearing Galileo had been condemned by the Church, he retracted parallel arguments of his own on natural science. Pure philosophy as an abstract enterprise needed a cool atmosphere isolated from everyday events.

Descartes's magnificent formulations have always had their detractors, of course. David Hume did not think of philosophy in those terms, believing as he did that sentiment is the foundation of morality. For Søren Kierkegaard, an abstract system of ethics is only paper currency with nothing to back it up. Karl Marx insisted that we change the world and not merely explain it. But no one drew the modern philosophical map more decisively than Descartes, and his mode of rigid inquiry has generally defined the field's parameters.

This book adopts the historical perspective suggested by Stephen Toulmin:

> The philosophy whose legitimacy the critics challenge is always the seventeenth-century tradition founded primarily upon René Descartes. . . . [The] arguments are directed to one particular style of philosophizing—a theory-centered style which poses philosophical problems, and frames solutions to them, in timeless and universal terms. From 1650, this particular style was taken as defining the very agenda of philosophy. (1988, 338)

The seventeenth-century philosophers set aside the particular, the timely, the local and the oral. And that development left untouched nearly half of the philosophical agenda.

> Indeed, it is those neglected topics—what I here call "practical philosophy"—that are showing fresh signs of life today, at the very time when the more familiar "theory-centered" half of the subject is languishing. (Toulmin 1988, 338)

This book collaborates in demolishing the barrier of three centuries between pure and applied philosophy; it joins in reentering practical concerns as the legitimate domain of philosophy itself. For Toulmin, the primary locus of ethics has moved from the study to the bedside, to criminal courts, engineering labs, the newsroom, factories and the ethnic street corners. Moral philosophers are not being asked to hand over their duties to technical experts in today's institutions, but rather to fashion their agenda within the conditions of contemporary struggle.

All humans have a theoretical capacity. Critical thinking, the reflective dimension, is our common property. And this book nurtures that reflection in communication classrooms and by extension into centers of media practice. If the mind is like a muscle, this volume provides a regimen of exercises for strengthening its powers of systematic reflection and moral discernment. It does not permit those aimless arguments that result in quandary ethics. Instead it operates in the finest traditions of practical philosophy, anchoring the debates in real-life conundrums but pushing the discussion toward substantive issues and integrating appropriate theory into the decision-making process. It seeks to empower students to do ethics themselves, under the old adage that teaching someone to fish lasts a lifetime, and providing fish only saves the day.

*Media Ethics: Issues and Cases* arrives on the scene at a strategic time in higher education. Since the late nineteenth century, ethical questions have been taken from the curriculum as a whole and from the philosophy department. Recovering practical philosophy has involved a revolution during the last decade in which courses in professional ethics have reappeared throughout the curriculum. This book advocates the pervasive method and carries the discussions even further, beyond freestanding courses into communication classrooms across the board.

In this sense, the book represents a constructive response to the current debates over the mission of higher education. Professional ethics has long been saddled with the dilemma that the university was given responsibility for professional training precisely at the point in its history that it turned away from values to scientific naturalism. Today one sees it as a vast horizontal plain given to technical excellence but barren in enabling students to articulate a philosophy of life. As James Carey concludes,

> Higher education has not been performing well of late and, like most American institutions, is suffering from a confusion of purpose, an excess of ambition that borders on hubris, and an appetite for money that is truly alarming. (1989, 48)

The broadside critiques leveled in Thorstein Veblen's *The Higher Learning in America* (1918) and Upton Sinclair's *The Goose Step* (1922) are now too blatantly obvious to ignore.

But *Media Ethics: Issues and Cases* does not merely demand a better general education or a recommitment to values; it strengthens the communications curriculum by equipping thoughtful students with a more enlightened moral awareness. Since Confucius we have understood that lighting a candle is better than cursing the darkness. Or in Mother Teresa's version, we feed the world one mouth at a time.

# PREFACE

As you glance through this book, you will notice its features—text, illustrations, cases, photos—represent choices the authors have made. I think it's as important to point out what's missing as what's there, and why.

First, you'll find no ethics codes in the book. Several media organizations have codes that are well thought out. Some media ethics texts include them. However, we agree with Anthony Insolia of *Newsday* when he says, "Rules and guidelines, unfortunately, cover only the pat situations." And with Arnold Rosenfeld, editor of the *Dayton Daily News and Journal-Herald,* when he says, "The decisions straight out of the book are easy. It is unfortunately the 2 to 3 percent for which there are no book rules that we earn our pay—and reputations." This book is for the tough situations where codes work only when combined with a knowledge of ethical theory and a deep sense of personal ethics.

Second, you'll find no media bashing in this book. There's enough of that already, and besides, it's too easy to do. This book is not designed to indict the media; it's designed to train its future employees. If we dwell on ethical lapses from the past, it is only to learn from them what we can do to prevent similar occurrences in the future.

Third, you'll find no conclusions in this book—neither at the end of the book nor after each case. No one has yet written the conclusive chapter to the ethical dilemmas of the media, and I don't suspect that we will be the first.

*What, then, is in the book?* You will find a diverse, up-to-date, and classroom-tested compilation of cases in media ethics. Authors from more than thirty institutions and media outlets contributed real-life and hypothetical cases to this text to help students prepare for the ethical situations they will confront in whatever area of the media they enter. The authors are convinced that case studies are the premiere teaching vehicle for the study of ethics, and this book reflects what we think are the best available written by the most qualified people.

Binding these cases together and providing a philosophical basis from which to approach them is the text. While it has intentionally been kept succinct, the text introduces students to the relevant ethical theory that will help eliminate "quandary ethics," which often results when cases are used as a teaching strategy. Deni Elliott's essay at the end of chapter 1 instructs students and professors on how to use case studies as an educational tool without bogging down into quandary ethics.

You will find built-in discussion starters in the questions that follow each case. These questions were written by the authors of each case, with the instructions that they were to be like concentric circles. The tightest circle—the micro issues—focuses only on the case at hand and the dilemmas it presents. The next circle—middle-range issues—focuses on the problem in its context, and sometimes manipulates the facts slightly to see if the decisions remain the same. On the most abstract level—the macro issues—the students are dealing with issues such as truth, equity, responsibility and loyalty. Properly used, the questions can guide the discussion from the particular to the universal in any case in a single class period.

The book may be used either as the main text for a media ethics course or as a supplementary text for ethics sequences found in courses in newswriting, media and society, advertising and public relations, and photojournalism. The book works well for teachers who like to use the Socratic method in their classes, or as resource material for lecture classes.

More than a third of the cases in this text are new to this edition. Also new is a chapter on the emerging ethical issues of cyberspace and an appendix that capsulizes some of the most historically significant media ethics "milestones" in this century.

Our approach in this text is best illustrated by an anecdote from a few years ago. One student in my class had the last hand up after the debate on a particularly heated case study. When I called on her, she asked, "Well, what's the answer?" I was surprised that she asked the question, and I was surprised that I didn't have a ready answer. I joked my way out of the question by asking if she wanted the Answer with a capital *A* or a lowercase one. If she asked today, I'd respond differently. I'd tell her that the answer exists within her, but that it won't emerge in any justifiable form without systematic study and frequent wrestling with the issues.

That's what this book is about. The chapters are an attempt to direct you in some systematic way through the philosophy that has explored these questions for centuries. The cases will make you wrestle with that knowledge in scenarios not unlike ones you might encounter while working. Together, they might not enable you to find *the answer,* but they might help you find *your answer.*

For the authors and contributors,
Philip Patterson

# ACKNOWLEDGMENTS

One's first lessons in ethics are learned by modeling ethical people, and I am grateful for parents who provided me with good, commonsense role models for the research and writing in ethics that I would do later in life.

No book of this type is a solo effort, and this book is certainly the result of hard work and encouragement by many people. To begin, Marty Linsky, Lou Hodges, Cliff Christians, Deni Elliott and others listened patiently to the idea in its many stages and offered advice along the way. In the past decade, I have been privileged to attend ethics workshops sponsored by the Poynter Institute, the Freedom Forum, and the University of Nebraska. To Bob Steele, Ed Lambeth, Steve Kalish and Robert Audi, I owe a debt of gratitude for helping me to continue to learn about ethics as I seek to teach my students. And every new edition brings a new group of people to get to know and to be deeply grateful to. This group of case study authors and photographers—forty-eight by my latest count—were all a pleasure to work with in meeting deadlines and writing excellent cases strictly for the love of the profession and the hope that their contribution could make a difference in the education of a future media professional.

Others on the Oklahoma Christian University campus deserve credit as well. Vicki Wendling entered much of the copy into the computer as it came in from several dozen sources. She also went above the role of duty and into the realm of friendship in the amount of work she put into making sure the details of this book were correct. Tamie Willis processed all of our requests for library acquisitions as we pursued books, articles, and other materials as source material for the chapters. Thank you both.

A special thanks goes to the Ethics and Excellence in Journalism Foundation for a grant to cover photographs and illustrations in this edition of the text. Thanks to the many instructors who responded to the questionnaire for the first edition of the text. The insightful comments were very useful to us as we revised the text. Thanks to our publishers for believing in the project enough to give it an expanded third edition. Finally, I thank Linda and our children Amy, Andrew, and Joshua: I love you all.

**p.d.p.**

When ethics entrepreneur Michael Josephson opens his public speeches, he asks audience members to think of the most ethical people they know. Those people set ethical standards for others, by who they are and by what they inspire. It's fair for readers of this book to know who's on my list.

First, my mother—whose sense of human connection and compassion has been only incompletely copied by her daughter. Second, my father, who is the most principled human being I have ever met. Third, my stepmother Carrie, who's managed to love the family she's married into—a feat worthy of far more than a Kantian sense of duty.

My dissertation advisor and friend Jim Davies affirmed for me the ethical connection between people and politics. My former colleagues at the University of Colorado—Russ Shain, Steve Jones, Sue O'Brien and Risa Palm—have proved that connection a very human one, as have my colleagues at the University of Missouri. They have also been willing to listen—*another ethical activity that too often goes unmentioned.* Barrie Hartman and the staff of the *Boulder Daily Camera* were wonderful reality checks.

There has been intellectual help as well. I've attended a number of conferences designed to teach me about ethics. The Hastings House, Gannett, the Poynter Institute, and the University of Nebraska have done their best to educate me in this field. The people connected with those efforts deserve special mention. Among them, Ed Lambeth, Ted Glasser, Deni Elliott, Cliff Christians, Lou Hodges, Martin Linsky, Roy Peter Clark, Don Fry, Sharon Murphy, Jay Black, Ralph Barney, Steve Kalish and Robert Audi have helped most profoundly. Many of them you will find listed in various ways on the pages that follow. All of them have a special place in my intellectual psyche.

Two sets of acknowledgments remain.

For the past twelve years, my students at the Universities of Missouri and Colorado have taught me much more about ethics than I have taught them. They have suffered through portions of this manuscript with me. Their questions and their insights are evident on every page of this book.

Then there are Miranda and David—my daughter and my spouse. For the smiles, the hugs, the reading of first drafts, the talking, the listening, the suggestions, the lecture about using "skin" names, the films, and all of the rest that being a family means. Love and thanks. I could not have done this without you.

**l.c.w.**

# CHAPTER I
## *An Introduction to Ethical Decision Making*

**At the end of this chapter, you should be able to:**

- **Recognize the need for professional ethics in journalism.**
- **Work through a model of ethical decision making.**
- **Be familiar with five philosophical principles applicable to mass-communication situations.**

## Making Ethical Decisions

Few people must make ethical decisions in public. Though all professionals make occasional ethical mistakes, only journalists have the courage or misfortune to display them to the public. And when those ethical decisions are faulty, public reaction is swift and critical.

Attempting to gain public acceptance or prevent public outcry isn't the only reason for advocating ethical professional practice—and it's not a very profound one at that. The most compelling reason for making ethical choices, other than internal personal satisfaction, is what ethical behavior can contribute to the profession. Ethical journalism is better journalism. Not only is it journalism that sustains reader confidence, an important consideration in these days of waning media credibility, but ethical journalism also sets a standard by digging deeper, including necessary context, and providing a variety of sources without undue regard to any particular set of special interests, including the journalists' own.

Too many books insist that ethics can't be taught. It's situational, they say—every message is unique, leaving no real way to learn ethics other than by daily life. This analysis is partially correct. Most of us, outside of church or parental teachings, have learned ethics by the choices we've made or seen others make.

Ethics, it is argued, is something you have, not something you do. But, while it's true that reading about ethics is no guarantee you will perform your job ethically, thinking about ethics is a skill anyone can acquire. It first requires some background about the study of ethics, which you will be introduced to in this chapter. Then you should learn a decision-making model that allows you to make ethical choices systematically. The model we've adopted was developed by philosopher Sissela Bok.

She has written about the ethical choices many professionals, among them lawyers, doctors and journalists, have to make.

While each facet of mass communication has its unique ethical quandaries, thinking about ethics is the same, whether you make your living writing advertising copy or obituaries. Each day at work, journalists make ethical choices, and some days those choices will have an influence far beyond a single broadcast or one newspaper's circulation area. An example is the controversy over how much coverage the media should give teenage suicides in the face of research that shows that a number of "copycat" suicides sometimes follow a well-publicized teen suicide. Such "suicide clusters" have occurred in communities around the world. The decision about whether and how to cover these events is a troublesome one indeed for editors in the communities involved, and such decisions influence people far beyond individual media markets.

Thinking about ethics won't make many of those choices easier, but, with practice, your ethical decision making can become more consistent. Ethics will then become not something you have, but something you do. A consistently ethical approach to your work as a reporter, photographer, or copywriter in whatever field of mass media you enter can improve that work as well.

Contemporary professional ethics revolves around these questions:

- What duties do I have, and to whom do I owe them?
- What values are reflected by the duties I've assumed?

Ethics takes us out of the world of "this is the way I do it" or "this is the way it's always been done" into the realm of "this is what I should do" or "this is the action that can be rationally justified." Ethics in this sense is "ought talk." The dual questions of duty and values can be answered a number of ways as long as they are consistent with each other. For example, if a journalist sees her primary duty as that of informing the public, she will place a high value on truth telling, tenacity in the pursuit of a story, etc. If a public relations practitioner sees his duty as promoting a cause, his choices would change accordingly.

It is important here to distinguish between **ethics,** which is a rational process founded on certain principles, and **morals,** which are in the realm of religion. For example, the Ten Commandments are a moral system in the Judeo-Christian tradition, and Jewish scholars have expanded this study of the laws throughout the Bible's Old Testament into the Talmud, a 1,400-page religious volume. The Buddhist Eightfold Path provides a similar moral framework.

But moral systems are not synonymous with ethics. *Ethics begins when elements within a moral system conflict.* Ethics is less about the conflict between right and wrong than it is about the conflict between equally compelling (or equally unattractive) values and the choices that must be made between them.

Immanuel Kant, the most influential philosopher of the eighteenth century, described this famous ethical dilemma: What should you do when a man carrying a gun arrives at your front door, asking the whereabouts of a second man (who is hiding in your closet) because he wants to kill him. Do you lie, or do you tell the truth? The Judeo-Christian moral system says that both killing and lying are wrong. Yet,

---

**A Word about Ethics**

The concept of ethics comes from the Greeks, who divided the philosophical world into three parts. *Aesthetics* was the study of the beautiful and how a person could analyze beauty without relying only on subjective evaluations. *Epistemology* was the study of knowing, debates about what constitutes learning and what is knowable to the human mind. *Ethics* was the study of what is good, both for the individual and for society. The Greeks were concerned with the individual virtues of courage, justice, temperance, and wisdom, as well as with societal virtues, such as freedom.

Two thousand years later, ethics has come to mean learning to make rational choices between what is good and bad, what is morally justifiable action and what is not. Ethics also means distinguishing among choices, all of which may be morally justifiable, but some more so than others. Rationality is the key word here, for the Greeks believed, and modern philosophers affirm, that people should be able to explain their ethical decisions to others. That ability to explain ethical choices is an important one for journalists, who, in the course of reporting a single story, may have to make separate ethical decisions when dealing with sources, colleagues, and, ultimately, the public. When an angry viewer telephones to ask why you broadcast the name of a rape victim, "It seemed like the right thing to do at the time" becomes a personally embarrassing and professionally unsatisfactory explanation.

---

you are being asked to make a choice between the two, and Kant's question is a surprising and perplexing one.

When elements within a moral system conflict, ethical principles can help you make tough choices. We'll review several ethical principles briefly after describing how one philosopher, Sissela Bok, says working professionals can learn to make good ethical decisions.

## Bok's Model

Bok's ethical decision-making framework was introduced in her book, *Lying: Moral Choice in Public and Private Life.* Bok's model is based on two premises: that we must have empathy for the people involved in ethical decisions and that maintaining social trust is a fundamental goal. With this in mind, Bok says any ethical question should be analyzed in three steps.

First, consult your own conscience about the "rightness" of an action. *How do you feel about the action?*

Second, seek expert advice for alternatives to the act creating the ethical problem. Experts, by the way, can be those both living or dead—a producer or copywriter you trust or a philosopher you admire. *Is there another way to achieve the same goal that will not raise ethical issues?*

Third, if possible, conduct a public discussion with the parties involved in the dispute. These include those who are directly involved, i.e., the reporter or the source, and those indirectly involved, i.e., a reader or a source. If they cannot be gathered, conduct the conversation hypothetically. The goal of this conversation is to discover: *How will my action affect others?*

Let's see how Bok's model works on the following sample scenario. In the section after the case, follow the three steps Bok recommends and decide if you would run the story.

> **How Much News Is Fit to Print?**   In your community, one of the major charities is the United Way. The annual fund-raising drive will begin in less than two weeks. However, at a late-night meeting of the board of directors at which no reporter is present, the executive director resigns. Though the agency is not covered by the Open Meetings Act, you are able to learn most of what went on from a source on the board.
>
> According to her, the executive director had taken pay from the agency by submitting a falsified time sheet while he was actually away on National Guard duty. The United Way board investigated the absence and asked for his resignation, citing the lying about the absence as the reason, though most agreed that they would have given him paid leave for Guard duty had he asked.
>
> The United Way wants to issue a short statement, praising the work of the executive director while regretfully accepting his resignation. The executive director will also issue a short statement citing other opportunities as his reason for leaving. You are assigned the story by an editor who does not know about the additional information you have obtained but tells you to "see if there's any more to it (the resignation) than they're telling."
>
> You call your source on the board and she asks you, as a friend, to withhold the damaging information because it will hinder the United Way's annual fund-raising effort that is just underway and jeopardize services to needy people in the community for years to come because faith in the United Way will be destroyed. Also, if you run the story, she says, you will ruin the ex-director's chances of a future career. What do you do?

## The Analysis

Bok's first step requires you to *consult your conscience.* When you do, you realize you have a problem. Your journalistic responsibility is to tell the truth, and that means providing readers with all the facts you discover. You also have a larger responsibility not to harm your community, and printing the complete story about the United Way director's actions might well cause at least some short-term harm. Clearly, your conscience is of two minds about the issue.

You move to the second step: *alternatives.* Do you simply run the resignation releases, figuring that the person can do no further harm to the community and therefore should be left alone? Do you run the whole story but buttress it with board members' quotes that such an abuse couldn't happen again, figuring that you have restored public trust in the agency? Do you sit on the story until after the fund-raising drive and risk the loss of trust from the readers if the story circulates around town as a rumor? Again, there do seem to be alternatives, but they are not without some cost.

In the third step of Bok's model, you will attempt to *hold a public ethical dialogue* with all of the parties involved. Most likely you won't ask the executive director, the story's source, average readers of the newspaper, a United Way donor and your editor into the newsroom for a lengthy chat about the issues involved when you are on deadline. Instead you can conduct an imaginary discussion among the parties involved. Such a discussion might go like this:

**Executive Director:** "I think my resignation is sufficient penalty for any mistake I might have made, and your article will jeopardize my ability to find another job. It's really hurting my wife and kids, and they've done nothing wrong."

**Reporter:** "But shouldn't you have thought about that *before* you decided to falsify the time sheet? This is a good story, and I think the public should know what the people who are handling their donations are like."

**Reader 1:** "Wait a minute. I am the public, and I'm tired of all of this bad news your paper focuses on. This man has done nothing but good in the community, and I can't see where any money that belonged to the poor went into his pocket. Why can't we see some good news for a change?"

**Reader 2:** "I disagree. I buy the paper precisely because it does this kind of reporting. It's stories like this that keep the government, the charities and everyone else on their toes."

**Publisher:** "You mean like a watchdog function."

**Reader 2:** "Exactly. And if it bothers you, don't read it."

**Publisher:** "I don't really like to hurt people with the power that we have, but if we don't print stories like this, and the community later finds out that we withheld the news, our credibility is ruined, and we're out of business." [To source] "Did you request that the information be off the record?"

**Source:** "No. But I never thought you'd use it in your story."

**Reporter:** "I'm a reporter. I report what I hear for a living. What did you think I would do with it? To use the same argument he used a minute ago, it's stories like these that allow me to support my family."

**Executive Director:** "So it's your career or mine, is that what you're saying? Look, no charges have been filed here, but if your story runs, I look like a criminal. Is that fair?"

**Publisher:** "And if it doesn't run, we don't keep our promise to the community. Is that fair?"

**Needy Mother:** "Fair? You want to talk fair? Do you suffer if the donations go down? No, I do. This is just another story to you. It's the difference in me and my family getting by."

The conversation could continue, and other points of view could be voiced. Your imaginary conversations could be more or less elaborate than the one above, but out of this discussion it should be possible to rationally support an ethical choice.

There are two cautions in using Bok's model for ethical decision making. First, it is important to go through all three steps before making a final choice. Most of us make ethical choices prematurely, after we've consulted only our consciences, an error Bok says results in a lot of flabby moral thinking.

Second, while you will not be endowed with any clairvoyant powers to anticipate your ethical problems, the ethical dialogue outlined in the third step is best when conducted in advance of the event, not in the heat of writing a story. For instance, an advertising copywriter might conduct such a discussion about whether advertising copy can ethically withhold disclaimers about potential harm from a product. A reporter might conduct such a discussion well in advance of the time he is actually asked to withhold an embarrassing name or fact from a story. Since it is likely that such dilemmas will arise in your chosen profession (the illustration above is based on what happened to one of the authors the first day on the job), your answer will be more readily available and more logical if you hold such discussions either with trusted colleagues in a casual atmosphere or by yourself, well in advance of the problem.

Bok's model forces you to consider alternatives. It's in the pursuit of these alternatives that journalistic technique improves.

## Guidelines for Making Ethical Decisions

Since the days of ancient Greece, philosophers have tried to draft a series of rules or guidelines governing how to make ethical choices. Obviously, in most ethical dilemmas such as the one above, you will need principles to help you determine what to do amid conflicting voices. While there are a number that work well, we will review five.

## Aristotle's Golden Mean

Aristotle, teaching in the fourth century B.C., believed that happiness—which some scholars translate as "flourishing"—was the ultimate human good. By flourishing, Aristotle meant to exercise "practical reason" in the conduct of any particular activity through the setting of high standards.

Aristotle believed that practical reason was exercised by individuals. The *phrenemos,* or person of practical wisdom, was that human being who demonstrated ethical excellence through daily activity. For Aristotle, the highest virtue was citizenship, and the highest form of citizenship was exemplified by the statesman, a politician who exercised so much practical wisdom in his daily activity that he elevated craft to art. In contemporary terms, we might think of a phrenemos as a person who excels at one of a variety of activities—flautist Jean Pierre Rampal, poet Maya Angelou, filmmakers George Lucas and Steven Spielberg. They are people who flourish in their professional performance, extending our own vision of what is possible.

*This notion of flourishing led Aristotle to assert that people and their acts, not particular sets of rules, are the moral basis of activity.* His ethical system resulted in the creation of what is now called *virtue ethics.* Virtue ethics flows both from the nature of the act itself and the moral character of the person who acts. In the Aristotelian sense, the way to behave ethically is that (1) you must know (through the exercise of practical reason) what you are doing; (2) you must select the act for its own sake—in order to flourish; and (3) the act itself must spring from a firm and unchanging character.

It is not stretching Aristotle's framework to assert that one way to learn ethics is to select heroes and to try to model your individual acts and ultimately your professional character on what you believe they would do. An Aristotelian might well consult this hero as an expert when making an ethical choice. Asking what my hero would do in a particular situation is not necessarily a poor form of ethical analysis. The trick, however, is to select your heroes carefully and still think for yourself rather than merely copy behavior you have previously seen.

Aristotle's philosophy is often reduced to the somewhat simplistic **"golden mean"**: *Virtue lies at the mean between two extremes.* Courage, for example, is a mean between foolhardiness on one hand and cowardice on the other. But to determine that mean for yourself, you have to exercise practical wisdom, act according to high standards and act in accordance with firm and continuing character traits. *In reality, therefore, the middle ground of a virtue is not a single point on a line that is*

CALVIN AND HOBBES copyright Watterson. Dist. by UNIVERSAL PRESS SYNDICATE.

**Figure 1.1**
*Aristotle's golden mean*

| Unacceptable behaviors | Acceptable behaviors | Unacceptable behaviors |
|---|---|---|

Cowardice  – – – – – – – – – – – – Courage – – – – – – – – – – – – – Foolhardiness

*the same for every individual.* It is instead a range of behaviors that varies individually, while avoiding the undesirable extremes, as shown in figure 1.1.

Continuing with the example of courage, this principle can be illustrated by considering two witnesses to a potential drowning. If one onlooker is a poor swimmer yet a fast runner, then it would be foolhardy for him to attempt to jump into the water and attempt a rescue, just as it would be cowardly for him to do nothing. For him, the courageous thing might be to run for help. If, on the other hand, the second onlooker is a good swimmer, it would not be foolhardy for her to attempt a rescue; in fact, it would be cowardly for her not to jump into the water. In each instance, both onlookers have done the courageous act, yet in radically different ways.

Seeking the golden mean implies that individual acts are not disconnected from one another, but rather that they form a whole that a person of good character should aspire to. In this age of questions about character, Aristotle's concept of virtue ethics has been rediscovered by a variety of professions.

## Kant's Categorical Imperative

Immanuel Kant's **categorical imperative** asserts that an individual should act on the premise that the choices one makes for oneself could become universal law. Furthermore, he states that you should act so that you treat humanity always as an end and never as a means only. Kant called these two maxims "categorical" imperatives, meaning that their demands were not subject to situational factors. Many readers will recognize the similarity between Kant's categorical imperative and the Bible's Golden Rule: Do unto others as you would have them do unto you. The two are quite similar in their focus on duty.

*Kant's ethical theory is based on the notion that it is the act itself, rather than the person who acts, in which moral force resides.* This theory of ethics is unlike Aristotle's in that it moves the notion of what is ethical from the actor to the act itself. This does not mean that Kant did not believe in moral character, but rather that people could act morally from a sense of duty even though their character might incline them to act otherwise.

For Kant, an action was morally justified only if it was performed from duty, and in Kant's moral universe there were two sorts of duties. The strict duties were generally negative: not to murder, not to break promises, not to lie. The meritorious duties were more positive: to aid others, to develop one's talents, to show gratitude. Kant spent very little time defining these notions, but philosophers have generally asserted that the strict duties (i.e., not to harm) are somewhat more morally mandatory than the meritorious duties (e.g., to render aid).

To some, Kant's ethical reasoning indicates that as long as you perform the right act based on what the categorical imperative and duty demand, the consequences of that act are not important. We prefer a somewhat less austere reading of Kant. While Kant's view is that the moral worth of an action does not depend on its consequences, those consequences are not irrelevant. For example, a surgeon may show moral virtue in attempting to save a patient through an experimental procedure. But the decision about whether to undertake that procedure requires taking into account the probability of a cure. This framing of Kantian principles allows us to learn from our mistakes.

The test of a moral act, according to Kant, is its universality—whether it can be applied to everyone. For instance, Kant would insist that the ethical person drive at a speed and in a manner that would be appropriate for everyone else on the same highway. Under Kant's categorical imperative, journalists can claim few special privileges, such as the right to lie or the right to invade privacy in order to get a story. Kant's view, if taken seriously, reminds you of what you give up—truth, privacy, etc.—when you make certain ethical decisions.

## Utilitarianism

The original articulation of **utilitarianism,** by Englishmen Jeremy Bentham and later John Stuart Mill in the nineteenth century, introduced what was then a novel notion into ethics discussions: *The consequences of actions are important in deciding whether they are ethical.* Under the utilitarian view, it may be considered ethical to harm one person for the benefit of the larger group. This approach, for example, is the ethical justification for investigative reporting, which may harm individuals but the results of which are printed or broadcast in the hope of providing a greater societal good.

With its focus on the consequences of an action, utilitarianism completes a cycle begun with Aristotle (see table 1.1). Aristotle, in developing the golden mean,

**TABLE 1.1  The Shifting Focus of Ethics from Aristotle to Mill**

| PHILOSOPHER | KNOWN FOR | POPULARLY KNOWN AS | EMPHASIZED |
|---|---|---|---|
| Aristotle | Golden mean | Virtue lies between extremes. | The actor |
| Kant | Categorical imperative | Act so your choices could be universal law; treat humanity as an end, never as a means only. | The action |
| Mill | Utility principle | An act's rightness is determined by its contribution to a desirable end. | The outcome |

focused on the *actor.* Kant, in his categorical imperative, focused on the *action,* while Mill, in his utilitarian philosophy, focused on the *outcome.*

Utilitarianism has been condensed to the ethical philosophy of the greatest good for the greatest number. While this pithy phrase is a very rough-and-ready characterization of utilitarian theory, it also has led to an overly mechanistic application of the principle: Just tally up the amount of good and subtract the amount of harm. If the remaining number is positive, the act is ethical. However, when properly applied, utilitarianism is not mechanical.

In order to do justice to utilitarian theory, it must be understood within a historical context. Mill wrote during the earliest years of the Enlightenment, when the principle of democracy was fresh and untried, and when the thought that the average person should be able to speak his mind to those in power was novel. Utilitarianism as Mill conceived of it was a profoundly social ethic; Mill was among the first to acknowledge that the good of an entire society had a place in ethical reasoning.

Mill was what philosophers call a *valuational hedonist.* He argued that pleasure—and the absence of pain—were the only intrinsic moral ends. Mill further asserted that an act was right in the proportion in which it contributed to the general happiness, wrong in the proportion in which it contributed to general unhappiness or pain. Utilitarianism can be subtle and complex. Mill acknowledged that the same act can make some happy but cause others pain. Mill insisted that both sets of consequences be valued simultaneously, a precarious activity but one which forces discussion of competing stakeholder claims.

Utilitarianism can be applied in both the specific and the general, what some philosophers have referred to as "act utilitarianism" as opposed to "rule utilitarianism."

For instance, one way of evaluating the ethical impact of investigative reporting is through the application of *act utilitarianism.* A producer might reason that an investigative report, while it would hurt the subject of the investigation, might further the general welfare. Crooks and cheats could be exposed, general societal problems aired. When the methods of obtaining information are ethical, investigative journalism can be justified because it contributes more to human happiness than it extracts in the pain it causes some individuals.

*Rule utilitarianism,* on the other hand, might be applied as follows. Take the assertion sometimes made that advertising itself is unethical. The rule utilitarian would note that in contemporary American culture, advertising provides needed information about a variety of products and services. It is also, sometimes, entertaining. And, advertising supports the media we enjoy. Of course, advertising sometimes can be in poor taste, it can be intrusive, and it can sometimes provide false or misleading information. When balancing the societal good against the societal harm, the rule utilitarian might well conclude that while the practice of advertising is ethical, certain forms of the activity—advertising products to children or advertising certain substances such as alcohol—should be regulated. Utilitarian theory does allow the sort of ethical reasoning that approves of particular activities while rejecting specific acts.

In utilitarian theory, no one's happiness is any more valuable than any one

## Kantian Principles

Applying Kant's categorical imperative can expand the journalistic ethical imagination. Tom French, a reporter for the *St. Petersburg Times,* had accepted the professional norm that reporters *never* show stories to sources prior to publication. But when he began a year-long effort to research contemporary high school life from the students' point of view, research he knew would result in public revelations of painful and sometimes private moments, he decided to treat his sources as individuals worthy of dignity, respect and moral autonomy. French knew that he was the first journalist many of the young people he was covering would get to know; he wanted both parties to emerge from the relationship with dignity.

After a year of observation, he showed his sources (and their parents and teachers) both the words and pictures he intended to print. He had promised to try to see that what he had written accurately reflected the students' point of view. While French didn't promise to change what he had written, he invited their comments. In one instance, he refused to change a detail, even though it was painful for the student. In others, he did alter what he wrote. Before the stories ran, he explained to both the young people and their parents that seeing themselves in the newspaper is *always* a shock.

The result was a series that was widely praised for its accuracy and depth. Both parents and students agreed that much of what French had published was private—emotional responses to divorce, students' sometime self-destructive methods of coping with the pressures of high school life, comments that were critical of the teachers and school administrators. But no one claimed invasion of privacy or inaccuracy. More importantly, French and his sources still speak to one another; they have come to value each other as people and to respect French's professional capacities.

Writer Janet Malcomb opened a widely discussed *The New Yorker* piece on journalism with the assertion that all journalists are professional users.

"Every journalist who is not too stupid or too full of himself to notice what is going on knows that what he does is morally indefensible," Malcomb wrote, "He is a kind of confidence man, preying on people's vanity, ignorance or loneliness, gaining their trust and betraying them without remorse" (Malcomb 1989).

French's response, which we view as an application of Kantian principle, negates much of the Malcomb critique. French's approach also allowed him to question the profession's conventional wisdom about the process of newsgathering, and to develop an innovative solution to a problem every reporter or editor encounters. It is through such application of principles that better professional practice emerges.

else's—quantity and quality being equal. In democratic societies, this is a particularly important concept because it meshes well with certain social and political goals. In actual application, utilitarianism uniformly applied has a way of puncturing self-interest; although critics have argued that, when badly applied, it can actually promote selfishness.

Utilitarianism also suggests that moral questions are objective, empirical, and even in some sense scientific. Utilitarianism promotes a universal ethical standard that each rational person can determine. However, utilitarianism is among the most criticized of philosophical principles because it is so difficult to accurately anticipate all the ramifications of a particular act. Different philosophers also have disputed how one calculates the good, rendering any utilitarian calculus fundamentally error prone.

While we recommend utilitarianism as a theory, we do caution you against exclusive reliance on it. Taken to extremes, the act of calculating the good can lead to an ethical gridlock, with each group of stakeholders having seemingly equally strong claims with little way to choose among them. Sloppily done, utilitarianism may bias you toward short-term benefit. And a view to the short term, in an ethical sense, can often be shortsighted.

## Pluralistic Theory of Value

Modern philosopher William David Ross (1930) bases his ethical theory on the belief that there is often more than one ethical value simultaneously "competing" for preeminence in our ethical decision making. In this, he differs from Kant or Mill, who proposed only one ultimate value. To Ross these competing ethical claims, which he calls duties, are equal, providing the circumstances of the particular moral choice are equal. Further, these duties do not gain their moral weight from their consequences, but from the highly personal nature of duty.

Ross proposed six types of duties:

1. Those duties that rest on previous acts of my own: duties of *fidelity,* based on my implicit or explicit promise, and duties of *reparation,* arising from a previous wrongful act;
2. Those duties of *gratitude* that rest on previous acts of others;
3. Those duties of *justice* that arise from the necessity to ensure the equitable and meritorious distribution of pleasure or happiness;
4. Those duties of *beneficence* that rest on the fact that there are others in the world whose lot we can better;
5. Those duties of *self-improvement* that rest on the fact that we can improve our own condition;
6. Finally, Ross stated one negative duty, the duty of *not injuring others.*

We would recommend two additional duties that may be implied by Ross's list but are not specifically stated:

7. The duty to tell the truth, *veracity*, (which may be implied by fidelity);
8. The duty to *nurture*, to help others achieve some measure of self-worth and achievement.

Ross's typology of duties works well for professionals who often must balance competing roles. It also brings to ethical reasoning some affirmative notions of the primacy of community and relationships as a way to balance the largely rights-based traditions of much Western philosophical theory.

Ross's concept of multiple duties allows the ethical decision maker to appreciate and consider important aspects of a situation without losing the value of following some rules. Like Kant, Ross divided his duties into two kinds. *Prima facie duties* are those duties that seem to be right because of the nature of the act itself. *Duty proper* are those duties that are paramount given specific circumstances. Arriving at your duty proper from among the prima facie duties requires that you consider what ethicists call the morally relevant differences.

Let's take an example using one of Ross's prima facie duties: keeping promises. In your job as a reporter, you have made an appointment with the mayor to discuss a year-end feature on your community. On your way to City Hall, you drive by a serious auto accident and see a young child wandering, dazed, along the road. You stop to help, knowing that as the first person on the scene, you must stay until the police arrive. You will certainly be late for your appointment and may have to cancel altogether. You have broken a promise.

But is that act ethical?

Ross would probably say yes because the specific aspects of the situation had a bearing on the fulfillment of a prima facie duty. You exercised discernment. You knew that your commitment to the mayor was a relatively minor sort of promise. Your news organization will not be hurt by postponing the interview, and your act allowed you to fulfill the prima facie duties of beneficence, avoiding harm, and nurturing. Had the interview been more important, or the wreck less severe, you could have analyzed the situation differently. Ross's pluralistic theory of values may be more difficult to apply than a system of absolute rules, but it reflects the way we make ethical choices.

Ross's concept of multiple duties "helps to explain why we feel uneasy about breaking a promise even when we are justified in doing so. Our uneasiness comes from the fact that we have broken a prima facie duty even as we fulfilled another. It helps explain why even the good consequences that might come from a failure to tell the truth or keep a promise do not always seem to us to justify the lie or breach of confidence" (Lebacqz 1985, 27).

## Communitarianism

Classical ethical theory places its dominant intellectual emphases on the individual and individual acts by emphasizing concepts such as character, choice, liberty and duty.

But contemporary politics points out the intellectual weakness in this approach. Consider the environment. On many environmental questions, it is possible for people to make appropriate individual decisions—today I drive my car—which taken together promote environmental degradation. My individual decision to drive my car doesn't matter very much; but when individual decisions are aggregated, the impact is profound. Furthermore, this environmental impact has consequences not for a single generation but for geologic time. Individual human beings cannot opt out of participation through daily living in the physical environment—unless they decide to live on the moon. While classical ethical theory acknowledges such problems, it provides little guidance for determining individual action or in understanding how individual actions fit within a larger whole.

Communitarianism, which has its roots in political theory, seeks to provide ethical guidance when confronting the sort of society-wide issues that mark current political and business activity.

Communitarianism spotlights society understood holistically and dynamically. Communitarianism returns to Aristotle's concept of the "polis"—or community—and invests it with moral weight. People begin their lives, at least in a biological sense, as members of a two-person community. Communitarian philosophy extends this biological beginning to a philosophical worldview. "In communitarianism, persons have certain inescapable claims on one another that cannot be renounced except at the cost of their humanity" (Christians et al. 1995, 14). In modern parlance, communitarians assert that when issues are political and social, community trumps individuals but does not trample them.

Communitarianism focuses on the outcome of individual ethical decisions, understood not as disconnected choices but analyzed as the impact of the sum of the choices on society. "Nurturing communitarian citizenship entails, at a minimum, a journalism committed to justice, covenant and empowerment. Authentic communities are marked by justice; in strong democracies, courageous talk is mobilized into action. . . . In normative communities, citizens are empowered for social transformation, not merely freed from external constraints. . . ." (Christians et al. 1995, 14).

Communitarianism asserts that social justice is the predominant moral value. While communitarians recognize the value of process, they are just as concerned with outcomes. They formally acknowledge one of history's more difficult lessons, that "good" process—for example, democratic elections or the writing of constitutions—can produce "bad" outcomes—for example, the 1933 takeover of Germany by a minority party headed by Hitler or the inclusion in the original American Constitution of the three-fifths clause (African-Americans were equal to three-fifths of a single European, Caucasian colonist for purposes of population count to determine the number of representatives each state would have in the U.S. Congress). Communitarians measure individual acts against the normative standard of their impact in creating a more just society.

Communitarian thinking allows ethical discussion to include values such as altruism and benevolence on an equal footing with more traditional questions such as truth telling and loyalty. Indeed, empirical testing of the concept of community through game theory has demonstrated that cooperation, one of the foundation stones of community, provides a robust (in other words, long-lived) rejoinder to competition (Axelrod 1984). Cooperation is particularly powerful when something called the "shadow of the future" looms sufficiently large. The "shadow of the future" means that people understand they will encounter the outcome of their decisions, in the form of their impact on others, in readily foreseeable time.

Communitarian philosophy lacks a succinct summation of its general propositions. Amitai Etzioni, one of the movement's leaders, suggests that communitarianism emphasizes responsibilities "to the conditions and elements we all share, to the community." Political theorist Michael Sandel arranges communitarianism as both an extension of and a counterpoint to traditional political liberalism. Like traditional political liberalism—as expressed in this book by the philosophy of John Rawls and, to a lesser extent, the utilitarians—a communitarian community would be manifest in the aims and values of its individual participants. But it would differ from a traditional community in the sense that community members would include, as part of their understanding of self, their membership in the community. "For them, community describes not just what they have as fellow citizens but also what they are, not as a relationship they choose (as in a voluntary association) but an attachment they discover, not merely an attribute but as a constituent of their identity" (Sandel 1982, 150). Communitarian community resembles family more than it resembles town.

We believe that communitarianism is most helpful in discussing ethical issues that revolve around the journalistic role.

Viewed this way, journalism cannot separate itself from the political and economic system of which it is a part. Communitarian thinking makes it possible to ask whether current practice (for example, a traditional definition of news) provides a good mechanism for a community to discover itself, learn about itself, and ultimately transform itself into a more just and cohesive entity. Communitarian reasoning allows journalists to understand their institutional role and to evaluate their performance against shared societal values. It mutes the competition among journalistic organizations while amplifying the collective effect that journalists and their organizations have on society and culture. Communitarian thinking can provide journalists with an effective justification for sometimes placing family before work, for including mobilizing information in a story about the local rape crisis center, or for inviting viewers and readers to help determine the sort of political stories in which they are most interested and then providing ample coverage of them.

Because communitarianism is a philosophy of ideals, it is difficult to find concrete journalistic examples of the theory in action. Many writers have linked communitarian philosophy with the civic journalism movement (discussed more extensively in chapter 6). But, we believe perhaps the best example of communitarianism at work is in the ethic of the Internet. That ethic, as it has evolved since about 1990, emphasizes equality of access, cooperation and sharing (particularly of software known as freeware), global communication, decentralized control and a fierce devotion to communication as an activity between equals in which all have a chance to participate and benefit. While it remains to be seen whether the cooperative community of electrons will survive the assault of media conglomerates and government supervision, the Internet itself is a working example of a community that comes before—is axiologically and ontologically prior to—(Christians et al. 1995, 14) its individual members.

## The "Science" of Ethics

Life in the twentieth century has changed how most people think about issues, such as what constitutes a fact and what does or does not influence moral certainty. We will explore those changes, and the changes they have led to in the lives of mass-communication professionals, in more detail in the next chapter. But for now, suffice it to say that ethical theory, with its apparent uncertainties and contradictions, appears to have taken a back seat to science in much of modern life. Part of the reason people have become so concerned with ethics in the late twentieth century is that they seek "the answer" to ethical dilemmas in the same way they seek "the answer" in science. In such an endeavor, the vagaries of ethical choice as contrasted with scientific knowledge seem unsatisfactory.

We'd like to offer you a different conceptualization of "the facts" of both science and ethics. Science, and the seeming certainty of scientific knowledge, have undergone vast changes in the past one hundred years. After all, before Einstein, most educated people believed that Sir Francis Bacon had accurately and eternally described the basic actions and laws of the physical universe. But Bacon was wrong. Scientific inquiry in the twentieth century has searchingly explored a variety of physical phenomena, almost always uncovering new relationships, new areas of knowledge, and most importantly, new and expanding areas of ignorance. What modern humanity regarded as the certainty of scientific truth has changed fundamentally in the last one hundred years, and humanity has every reason to expect similar changes in the next century. Science and certainty are not synonymous, despite our tendency to blur the two.

Contrast these fundamental changes in the scientific world view with the developments of moral theory. Aristotle's writing, more than two thousand years old with no fundamental changes, still has much to recommend it to the modern era, although, of course, there will continue to be new interpretations. The same can be said of utilitarianism and of the Kantian approach—both subject to more than one hundred years of critical review. Certainly, new moral thinking has emerged—for example, John Rawls's work on utilitarian theory, which we will introduce you to in the chapter on privacy. But such work tends to build on rather than radically alter the moral theorizing that has gone before. This is not to assert that ethical philosophers do not have fundamental debates but rather to suggest that these debates have, in general, tended to deepen and enlarge previous insights rather than to "prove" them incorrect in some epistemological sense.

From this viewpoint, there is a continuity in thinking about ethics that is lacking in the development of scientific thought. Further, thinking about ethics in a global way uncovers some striking areas of agreement. We are aware of no ethical system, for example, that argues that murder is an ethical behavior, or that lying, cheating and stealing are the sorts of activities that human beings ought to engage in on a regular basis. Applying the various ethical theories outlined in this chapter will deepen your understanding of these principles and the complexity of application, but they are unlikely to change your views about the ethical correctness of murder or lying.

When the average person contrasts ethics with science, it is ethics that tends to be viewed as changeable, unsystematic and idiosyncratic. Science has rigor, proof, and some relationship to an external reality. We would like to suggest that such characterizations arise from a short-term view of the history of science and ethics. In our view, ethics as a field has at least as much continuity of thought as developments in science. And while it cannot often be quantified, it has the rigor, the systematic quality, and the relationship to reality that moderns too often characterize as the exclusive domain of scientific thinking.

## Conclusion

We've all, of course, been raised with a variety of ethical principles. We've heard the Native-American proverb, "You can't know another man until you've walked a mile in his moccasins." Doctors take an oath to do no harm in the pursuit of healing. These axioms, and many others, have their roots in the more formal ethical principles. No principle is markedly superior to the others, although you may find that one of these points of view has more explanatory power for you than do the others. When you discover that one principle begins to accomplish more for you than the rest, you are ready for yet another step in your moral development—some formal study of philosophy.

But even without that formal study, what all the ethical principles we've discussed amount to is a plea for empathy, a compassionate understanding of one's fellows, and the capacity for rational, principled moral action. We believe that a systematic application of these principles will help you make better and more rational ethical choices. Just as important, we believe their daily application also will sharpen your journalistic insights.

## Suggested Readings

Aristotle. *The Nicomachean ethics.*

Bok, Sissela. 1978. *Lying: Moral choice in public and private life.* New York: Random House.

Christians, Clifford, Kim Rotzoll, and Mark Fackler. 1993. *Good News: Social ethics and the press.* New York: Oxford University Press.

Gert, Bernard. 1988. *Morality: A new justification of the moral rules.* New York: Oxford University Press.

Mill, John Stuart. *On liberty.*

## CHAPTER I ESSAY

## Cases and Moral Systems: An Essay

DENI ELLIOTT

*University of Montana*

Case studies are wonderful vehicles for ethics discussions. Some of their great strengths include helping discussants

1. Appreciate the complexity of newsroom decision making;
2. Understand the context within which difficult decisions are made;
3. Track the consequences of choosing one action over another;
4. Learn both how and when to reconcile and how and when to tolerate divergent points of view.

However, when case studies are misused, these great strengths become their fundamental weaknesses. Case studies are vehicles for an ethics discussion, not its ultimate destination. The purpose of an ethics discussion is to teach discussants how to "do ethics"; that is, to teach them processes by which they can practice and improve their own critical decision-making abilities. Each discussant should, through the use of the case-study vehicle, reach the end point: a reasoned response to the issue at hand.

When the discussion stops short of this point, it is often because the destination has been fogged in by one or more myths of media case discussions:

**Myth 1: Every opinion is equally valid.**

Not true. The best opinion (conclusion) is the one that is best supported by judicious analysis of fact and theory. In an ethics discussion, it is the one that best addresses the morally relevant factors of the case. An action has morally relevant factors if it is likely to cause some individual to suffer an evil that any rational person would wish to avoid (such as death, disability, pain, loss of freedom or pleasure), or if it is the kind of action that generally causes evil (such as deception, breaking promises, cheating, disobedience of law, or neglect of duty) (see Gert 1988).

**Myth 2: Since we can't agree on an answer, there is no right answer.**

It's tough to take into account all of the various points of view when working through a case. One way people avoid doing this is to refuse to choose among the different perspectives. But this retreat to fatalistic subjectivism is not necessary. It may be that there are a number of acceptable answers. But there will also be many wrong answers—many approaches that the group can agree would be unacceptable. When discussants begin to despair of ever reaching any agreement on a right answer or answers, it is time to reflect on all of the agreement that exists within the group concerning the actions that would be out of bounds.

**Myth 3: It hardly matters if you come up with the "ethical thing to do" since people ultimately act out of their own self-interest anyway.**

The point of ethical reflection is to find and deal with those situations when one should not simply do that which benefits oneself. Acting ethically means to refrain from causing unjustified harm, even when prudential concerns must be set aside.

Any institution supported by society, manufacturing firms and media corporations as well as medical centers, provides some service that merits that support. No matter what the service, practitioners or companies that act only in short-term interest, for instance to make money, will not last long. Free-market pragmatism, as well as ethics, dictates that it makes little sense to ignore the expectations of consumers and of the society at large.

The guidelines below can serve as a map for an ethics discussion. They are helpful to have when discussants are working through unfamiliar terrain toward their individual end points. They can also help discussants detour around the myths discussed earlier.

As the case is discussed, check to see if these questions are being addressed:

1. What are the morally relevant factors of the case?
   (*a*) Will the proposed action cause an evil, such as death, disability, pain, loss of freedom or opportunity, or a loss of pleasure, that any rational person would wish to avoid?
   (*b*) Is the proposed action the sort of action, such as deception, breaking promises, cheating, disobedience of law, or disobedience of professional or role-defined duty, that generally causes evil?
2. If the proposed action is one described above, is a greater evil being prevented or punished?
3. If so, is the actor in a unique position to prevent or punish such an evil, or is that a more appropriate role for some other person or profession?
4. If the actor followed through on the action, would he be allowing himself to be an exception to a rule that he thinks that everyone else should follow? If so, then the action is prudential, not moral. One way to test this out is for journalists to ask how they would react if a person in another profession did what they are thinking of doing. Would the journalists applaud the action, or would they write an exposé?
5. If, at this point, the proposed action still seems justified, consider if a rational, uninvolved person would appreciate the reason for causing harm. Are the journalists ready to state, explain and defend the proposed action in a public forum?

# CHAPTER II

## *Information Ethics: A Profession Seeks the Truth*

**By the end of the chapter, the student should be able to:**

- **Define both the Enlightenment and pragmatic constructions of truth.**
- **Understand the development and several criticisms of objective news reporting as a professional ideal.**
- **Understand why truth in "getting" the news may be as important as truth in reporting it.**
- **Begin to develop a personal list of ethical news values.**

## Introduction

Each of the traditional professions has laid claims to one of the central tenants of philosophy. Law, ideally, is equated with justice; medicine with the duty to render aid. Journalism, too, has a lofty ideal: the communication of truth.

But the ideal of truth is problematic. In routine interaction we consider truth a stable commodity: it doesn't change much for us on a day-to-day basis, nor does it vary greatly among members of a community. While we are willing to accept some cultural "lies," for example the existence of Santa Claus; we stand ready to condemn others, for example income tax evasion or fraud. Most of the time, we seem to know what the boundaries are, at least when we deal with one another face to face.

However, the concept of truth has changed throughout human history. At one level or another, human beings since ancient times have acknowledged that truth may vary depending on individual points of view. Since Plato's analogy of life as shadows on the wall of a cave 3,000 years ago, people have grappled with the amorphous nature of truth.

Compounding the modern problem of the shifting nature of truth is the changing media audience. When a profession accepts the responsibility of printing and broadcasting the truth, facts that are apparent in face-to-face interaction become subject to different interpretations among geographically and culturally diverse viewers and readers. Ideas that were once readily accepted are open to debate. The whole concept of telling the truth becomes not merely a matter of possessing good moral character but something that requires learning how to recognize truth and how to convey it in the least distorted manner possible.

## A Changing View of Truth

One pre-Socratic Greek tradition viewed truth—*aletheia*—as encompassing all that humans remember, singled out through memory from everything that is destined for Lethe, the river of forgetfulness (Bok 1978). Linking truth and remembrance is essential in an oral culture, one that requires information be memorized and repeated so as not to be forgotten. Repeating the message, often in the form of songs or poetry, meant that the accumulated ideas and knowledge were kept alive or true for subsequent generations. Homer's *Iliad* and the *Odyssey* or much of the Bible's Old Testament served this function.

This oral notion of truth as noted in table 2.1 was gradually discarded once words and ideas were written down. However, it has come to the fore again with the advent of television. Television allows viewers to hear the words of the president rather than wait for those words to be passed down orally or written down. When we see something on television, we assume that it closely corresponds to reality—that it is in some sense true. The maxim "Seeing is believing" reminds us that truth has somehow become tangled up with pictures and presence. It is an oral concept of truth that has been a dormant form of knowledge for hundreds of years.

While the other ancient Greeks tied truth to human memory, Plato linked truth to human rationality and intellect. In *The Republic,* Plato equated truth with a world of pure form, a world to which human beings had only indirect access. In Plato's vision, there was an ideal notion of a chair—but that ideal chair did not exist in reality. What people thought of as a chair was as similar to the ideal chair as the shadows on the wall of the cave are to objects illuminated by the fire. Truth was knowable only to the human intellect—it could not be touched or verified.

Plato's metaphor has had a profound influence on Western thought. Not only did Plato link truth to rationality, as opposed to human experience, but his work im-

**TABLE 2.1    A Philosophy of Truth Emerges**

| SOURCE | TRUTH EQUALS |
| --- | --- |
| Ancient Greeks | What is memorable and is handed down |
| Plato | What abides in the world of perfect forms |
| Medieval | What the king, Church, or God says |
| Milton | What emerges from "marketplace of ideas" |
| Enlightenment | What is verifiable, replicable, universal |
| Pragmatists | What is filtered through individual perception |

plies that truth is something that can be captured only through the intellect. Platonic truth is implicit within a thing itself; truth defined the "perfect form." Plato's concept of truth separated the notion of something as true from the external world in which that thing existed.

Subsequent centuries and thinkers adhered to Plato's view. Medieval theologians believed truth was revealed only by God or by the Church. The intellectual legacy of the Reformation centered on whether it is possible for the average person to ascertain truth without benefit of a priest or of a king. About two hundred years later, Milton suggested that competing notions of the truth should be allowed to coexist, with the ultimate truth eventually emerging (see table 2.1).

Milton's assertions foreshadowed the philosophy of the Enlightenment—from which modern journalism borrows its notion of truth. The Enlightenment cast truth in secular terms and developed what is now called a "correspondence theory" of truth. The correspondence theory asserts that truth should correspond to some external set of facts or observations. The Enlightenment concept of truth was linked to what human beings could perceive with their senses harnessed through the intellect. Truth acquired substance. It was something that could be perceived, and ultimately perception of truth was something that could be replicated.

This Enlightenment notion of truth has remained with us and is essential to what twentieth-century scholars refer to as the scientific method. Truth has become increasingly tied to that which is written down, to that which can be empirically verified, to that which can be perceived by the human senses, and to that which does not vary among people or among cultures. It is a truth uniquely suited to the written word, for it links what is written with what is factual, accurate, and important in the most profound of senses.

This Enlightenment notion of truth undergirds the journalistic ideal of objectivity. Objectivity has its intellectual roots in the previous three hundred years. While objectivity has many definitions, it may be considered, most simply, a mechanism that allows journalists to divorce fact from opinion. Journalists view objectivity as refusing to allow individual bias to influence what they report or how they cover it. It is a journalism in which all facts and people are regarded as equal and equally worthy of coverage. Culture, an individual sense of mission, and individual and organizational feelings and views do not belong in objective news accounts. An Enlightenment view of truth allowed objectivity to be considered an attainable idea.

However, philosophy was not the only reason, and some scholars have argued not even the most important reason, that objectivity became a professional standard in the early 1900s. The libertarian press of the Enlightenment was not really a mass press, and it garnered most of its financial support from political advertising and most of its readers through partisan political reporting. As the United States became urban in the late 1800s, publishers realized that to reach this large urban audience, they needed more support from a wider variety of advertisers. To convince potential advertisers that their advertising would be seen and possibly acted upon by a large audience, publishers had to make certain their publications would be read. Partisan publications could not assure that, for strong views offended potential readers.

What publishers of the day needed was a product that built on an Enlightenment philosophical construction that guaranteed that facts would be facts, no matter who was doing the reading. Opinion would be relegated to specific pages. Both facts and opinion could be wrapped around advertising. Objective news reporting was born (Schudson 1978).

Objectivity came along at an advantageous time for yet another reason. The mass press of the early 1900s was deeply and corruptly involved in yellow journalism. Fabricated stories were common; newspaper wars were close to the real thing. Although many of the specific events of the era (for example, the apocryphal story that William Randolph Hearst began the Spanish-American War so he would have something to photograph) have been exaggerated, the excesses in pursuit of circulation tarnished the profession's image. Objectivity was a good way to clean up journalism's act with a set of standards where seemingly none had existed before. It fit the cultural expectations of the Enlightenment that truth was knowable and ascertainable. And it made sure that readers of news columns would remain unoffended long enough to glance at the ads.

The Enlightenment view of truth also was compatible with democracy and its emphasis on rational government. People who could reason together, who could arrive at some shared "truth" of how their political lives ought to function, could govern themselves. Information was essential to such a form of government, for it allowed citizens to scrutinize government. As long as truth was ascertainable by the rational being, government could function. Under this view, information—written, logical, linear—provided the social glue as well as the grease of such a society. Citizens and government need information in order to continue their rational function. Information, and the notion that it corresponded in some essential way with the truth, carried enormous promise.

Twentieth-century pragmatists, most notably Americans John Dewey, George Herbert Mead, Charles Sanders Pierce, and William James, challenged the Enlightenment view of truth. They held that the perception of truth depended on how it was investigated and on who was doing the investigating. Further, they rejected the notion that there was only one proper method of investigation—i.e., the scientific method. Borrowing from Einstein's insights, pragmatists argued that truth, like matter, was relative.

Specifically, the pragmatists proposed that knowledge and reality were not *fixed by,* but instead were the *result of,* an evolving stream of consciousness and learning. Reality itself varied based on psychological, social, historical, or cultural contexts. Additionally, reality was defined as that which was probable, not as something intrinsic (the Platonic view) or something determined by only one method of observation (the Enlightenment view).

Pragmatism found a comfortable home in the twentieth-century United States. Under pragmatism truth lost much of its universality, but it was in remarkable agreement with the American value of democratic individualism. Soon pragmatism filtered through literature, science, and some professions, such as law.

Pragmatic notions of truth provided a philosophical basis to challenge objectivity. At roughly the same time that the journalistic community was embracing Enlightenment standards of objectivity, the culture itself was adopting more pragmatic notions of truth. That clash fueled criticism of objectivity on both a scholarly and a popular level. Several questions surfaced. If truth is subjective, can it be best obtained and reported by an impassive, objective, and detached reporter? Does such a reporter exist? Is truth a construct that relies on the context of the source, the message, and the receiver?

The last twenty years have added yet another level of complexity to the problem: the information explosion. Not only do we as a culture now question the meaning of the terms *fact* and *truth,* we literally cannot sort them all out. Facts and truth come to us quickly from all over the globe. Our ability to attend to these various messages, let alone construct rational meaning from them, is on the verge of being overwhelmed.

*In short, less than sixty years after it evolved, the concept of objectivity, which was once equated with printing the truth, has been deeply undermined by both philosophical shift and technological innovation* (Christians, Ferré and Fackler 1992). Telling your readers and viewers the truth has become a complicated business.

> Telling the "truth" therefore is not solely a matter of moral character; it is also a matter of correct appreciation of real situations and of serious reflection upon them. . . . Telling the truth, therefore, is something which must be learnt. This will sound very shocking to anyone who thinks that it must all depend on moral character and that if this is blameless the rest is child's play. But the simple fact is that the ethics cannot be detached from reality, and consequently continual progress in learning to appreciate reality is a necessary ingredient in ethical action. (Bok 1978, 302–303)

It is to the issue of learning to appreciate reality that we will now turn. First, we will review some of the scholarly findings about news coverage and what the news does and does not reflect. Then we will ask you to apply these scholarly findings, as well as a question or two, to case studies that deal with the links between news and the truth.

## Who's Doing the Talking, Anyway?

The pragmatic's critique of objectivity has called attention to the question of who writes the news. Journalists—who themselves are primarily male, Caucasian, well educated, and middle-to-upper class—are often asked to cover issues and questions for which their life experiences have not prepared them. Stephen Hess (1981) noted that journalists, in terms of their socioeconomic status, look a great deal more like the people they cover than the people they are supposedly writing for. While the eastern, elite press provides an extreme example of this tendency, other work on the national press corps has shown similar results (Weaver and Wilhoit 1986).

In the past ten years, almost every professional journalistic organization has developed programs specifically to attract and retain women and minorities. However, research and observation indicate that news organizations remain unsuccessful in

NON SEQUITUR     WILEY

© *1993, Washington Post Writers Group. Reprinted with permission.*

this endeavor, particularly in management positions (Sanders and Rock 1988). Journalism education itself still reflects this Caucasian, male reality (Beasley and Harlow 1988).

This lack of access to the engines of information has not been lost on a variety of minority groups—from religious fundamentalists, who have in some cases established their own broadcasting networks, to racial minorities, who fail to find themselves either as owners of media outlets, managers of those corporations, or in front of the cameras and with front-page bylines. They argue that the result is news about middle-class Caucasians, for middle-class Caucasians, about a political-economic system that systematically excludes everyone but middle-class Caucasians.

How individual journalists and the corporations they work for should remedy the situation is unclear. But many editors and publishers as well as their corporate bosses worry that as the demographics change us from a culture that is predominantly Caucasian to one that is not, the mass media, particularly newspapers, will play an increasingly minor role unless journalists find a way to report news that is of interest to the new majority of their readers. Some are changing as a result. For instance, Gannett, the nation's largest newspaper chain, initiated the Gannett 2000 project in the early 1990s, a mechanistic attempt to assure ethnic diversity and reader input in its news pages through formulas and heavy reliance on reader polls. The civic journalism movement is another reflection of such efforts.

## Seeing Isn't Believing

Another assumption embedded in the concept of objectivity centers on how the news is perceived. More than seventy years ago, journalist Walter Lippmann (1922) foreshadowed what modern psychology has now documented when he said, "For the most part, we do not first see, and then define, we define first and then see." He added that we tend to pick out what our culture has already defined for us, and then perceive it in the form stereotyped for us by our culture.

A New York journalism professor, blind since birth, performed an experiment in the 1970s on stereotyping with startling results (Rainville and McCormick 1977).

The professor, an avid football fan, wanted to see if he could predict the race of football players being described in the play-by-play sports commentary by what was being said about them. He theorized Caucasian athletes would be described as intellectually gifted, literally examples of heads-up play. African-American athletes would be praised for their physical prowess and described as physically gifted but not as smart. An experiment proved the professor correct. In a culture that values brains over brawn, African-American football players were the subject of repeated stereotypical insults—all couched as praise in the play-by-play.

Groups such as women, the elderly, and the gay community have conducted studies with similar results. Their conclusion has been that while journalists maintain that they are objective, they (like their readers and viewers) bring something to the message that literally changes what they see and, hence, what they report (Lester 1996).

Journalists also bring technology to the message, and the technology of television has led scholars to question the role of objectivity in news reporting. Two famous studies provide an indication of the questions scholars have asked in the past five decades.

The first study centered on the difference between the reality of a parade to welcome General Douglas MacArthur home from the Korean War and what people saw on television. The researchers stationed observers along the parade route to record what they saw. They saw what anyone would have predicted: several hours of waiting followed by a few minutes of excitement as the dignitaries passed. But television didn't present the event that way. On television, there were expectant crowds and little boredom, and the dignitaries did not pass from the screen in just a few minutes. And MacArthur returned to the United States in 1951 prior to a television era of videotape, sound enhancement, remote crews, and satellite feeds.

Any journalist who has ever covered a city council meeting can confirm these results. Council members yawning, digressing, or receiving endless explanations from earnest city staff members seldom make the newspaper pages. The event itself is condensed and packaged into an inverted pyramid. The reader can learn in five minutes what it took a reporter four hours to sift through.

All of this is accepted media practice. But, it also says something about journalistic notions of truth. Was the "mediated reality" people saw on television the truthful account of the parade? Or was the truthful account the eyewitness reports of the observers standing at the curb? Which standard is the objective one? Which standard is worth professional aspiration?

A second study shows how pictures can interact with the story in an unintended way. In 1960, when a relatively unknown Democrat from Massachusetts debated the current vice president of the United States during the presidential campaign, political scientists examined whether television itself would make a difference. They found two groups of people—one group who had heard the first Kennedy-Nixon debate only on radio and a second group who had watched the event on television. They made certain that the two groups were in all other ways similar to each other. Then they asked those who had seen and listened to the debates who won and discovered that the medium and not the message was what had made a difference.

Those who heard the debate on radio said that Richard Nixon won. They heard his words and the arguments of a practiced debater. People who saw the debate as well as heard it said that John F. Kennedy had won. They saw a tan young man who looked at the camera instead of at his opponent. They saw Nixon sweat. And the visual image—which conveyed information of a sort that is not easily put into words—was compelling. In an election that was decided by less than 1 percent of the total votes cast, television acquired enormous political power.

Years ago, Marshall McLuhan commented that the next war will be fought not with bullets but with images. He was proven right in 1991 when the U.S. Army packaged the visual images of the Persian Gulf War with the help of a New York public relations firm. Today, a variety of political rhetoric, from campaigning to revolutions, is being packaged for the media, attempting to tap into the enormous persuasive power of the supposedly objective news format.

## Defining and Constructing the News

News reflects certain cultural values and professional norms. Those values and norms, often at odds with an Enlightenment concept of truth, lend themselves to a pragmatic version of the news, provided you remember who's doing the writing and story selection.

One professional norm that plays an important role in shaping the news is the journalistic imperative to tell a story to make a point. Often this leads to predictable narratives, many of them centering on crisis and politics (Nimmo and Combs 1985; Bennett 1988). Sociologist Herbert Gans (1979) studied how stories became news at *Newsweek* and CBS and found that almost all news stories reflected these six cultural values: ethnocentrism, altruistic democracy, responsible capitalism, individualism, an emphasis on the need for and maintenance of social order, and leadership. These dominant values not only helped to shape which stories were printed, but also what they said.

News stories about middle-class or upper-class people, those who tend to successfully adopt the culture's values, made the news "budget," according to Gans, while stories about minorities, blue-collar Americans, and those sharply critical of governmental policy got lost on the cutting-room floor.

The goal of telling a "good story" also raises other ethical questions, specifically those that focus on packaging to highlight drama and human interest. Ethical questions about packaging began with newspapers but have intensified with television. Television demands video, and television's video imperative has been found to dominate both story selection and placement (for example, Epstein 1974). If television arrives at a disaster before print journalists, it's television that frames the stories for the written word (Smith 1992). Photo availability sometimes contradicts the classic notion of objectivity that each story should stand on its own merits, but it certainly reflects the professional norms of particular media. *USA Today*'s graphic impact on the newspaper industry has not been applauded by everyone. Some see the paper as a further indication of the trivialization of news, with an emphasis on packaging. Political ads have helped journalists to frame news stories about the same issue (Jamieson 1992) to some extent because of compelling visuals in the ads.

Journalists also need something to package, which has led to a professional drive to find an "event" to report and to be there first. The need to find an event has meant journalists have missed some important stories because they were not events but were historic developments with both a past and a future. For example, major social developments such as the women's movement (Mills 1989), the civil rights movement, and the anti-Vietnam War movement were undercovered until their leaders created events such as sit-ins and demonstrations for the media to report. More recently, director Michael Moore said he began his wickedly funny 1989 film *Roger and Me* about the devastation of General Motors layoffs on his hometown of Flint, Michigan, because he "didn't see on the silver screen or the television screen what happened to people like us. It was a story then (in the mid-1980s) and it's a story now and that's part of the reason I did the movie" (Smith 1992).

This preoccupation with events affects coverage of several types of stories. Science is most frequently reported as a series of discoveries and "firsts" rather than as a process of discovery (Nelkin 1987). We are treated to stories about the next cancer or AIDS cure without the necessary context to interpret the latest research results. The socioeconomic, scientific, and political causes of a disaster, such as the one that claimed thousands of lives in Bhopal, India, were seldom mentioned in news coverage that focused on the picture-friendly event (Wilkins 1987). Elections become horse races with one candidate the "front-runner" and the "rest of the pack" struggling to narrow the gap with each new poll. But reporting an election as a contest fails to focus on the policy issues, which is what democratic elections are supposed to be about. Finally, phenomena not linked to specific events, such as the greenhouse effect or the growth of an American underclass, often go unreported or underreported until an appropriate news peg arrives to supply the needed event the coverage requires.

The drive to get to the event first has led to another sort of horse race, one chronicled in the film *The Front Page* and later recounted in Timothy Crouse's book *The Boys on the Bus* (1974) and Sabato's *Feeding Frenzy* (1992). All emphasize journalistic excesses and an unwillingness to engage in independent thought that would disturb Enlightenment and pragmatic philosophers alike. Yet the twin problems of pack journalism and the scoop mentality still dominate much reporting and editing. Because of this, important stories have been killed, while some poorly researched stories have been aired or published.

Seymour Hersh's original reporting of the My Lai massacre for the *New York Times* is only one example of a story that was held up because no other reporter had a similar story and a particular media outlet was afraid to stick its neck out. In that story, Hersh documented that American troops had massacred civilian residents of a Vietnamese village. No other news organization picked up the story at the time.

On the other hand, the *New York Times* resorted to quoting the supermarket tabloid the *National Enquirer* in its coverage of the O.J. Simpson case largely in an effort to keep up with media competition. Equally significant, the *Enquirer* had the story right. The *Dallas Morning News* appears not to have fared as well in its coverage of accused Oklahoma City bomber Timothy McVeigh's alleged confession.

Truth is more than just a collection of facts. Facts have a relationship to one another and to other facts, forming a larger whole. Yet analytic coverage of American institutions, of science and technology, of politics, and of social movements is rare. If the role of the mass media is not only to detail events and issues, but to do so in a way that relationships among them are clear, is merely retelling a story sufficient? Or do we need to do it better?

Stephen Hess (1981) has argued that journalists need to engage in reporting that looks more like social science than storytelling. Gans argues for news that is labeled as originating from a particular point of view. If readers and viewers are alerted to the world view of those who have selected the news, just as they were during the era of the partisan press, they would be better able to place news in context. Other scholars argue for news that is analytic rather than anecdotal, proactive rather than reactive, and contextual rather than detached. And on a practical level, working reporters and editors insist that individual journalists need to do a better job of understanding their own biases and compensating for them.

These findings, from studies about how the media decide what is news to analyses of how individual audience members interpret the same news message, strike at the core of objectivity and its relationship to the complex truths of the twentieth century. Intellectually, we are living in a pragmatic era. But, professionally, we seem to be unable to develop a working alternative to the Enlightenment's view of truth.

## The Means to the End

In a profession that values the truth, is it ethical to lie to get a story? This seemingly simple question has layers of meaning. The first is generally phrased as, What if there is no other way to get the story? Some forms of journalistic deceptions, for example, serving time in a prison to do a story on conditions there, have resulted in real social good. On the other hand, the well-known Mirage Bar scam in which a Chicago newspaper set up a phony bar to document government corruption was denied a Pulitzer prize because of the methods used to obtain the story. In both instances, what journalists worry about is the impact such reporting methods have on the believability of news accounts and on journalists' ability to cover subsequent stories.

The second layer of questions revolves around the issue of whether it is ethical to lie to liars. If I know that a politician is going to lie to me, am I justified in lying to him or her, providing a larger social good is served? A second question is this: If we lie are we willing to be lied to? Or do we expect what Bok (1978) calls "free rider" status—gaining the benefits of lying without incurring the risks of being lied to?

Many philosophers have asserted that lying is a way to get and maintain power. Those in positions of power often believe they have the right to lie because they have a greater than ordinary understanding of what is at stake. Lying in a crisis (for instance, to prevent panic) and lying to enemies (for instance, to protect national security) are two examples. In both circumstances journalists can be, either actively or without their knowledge, involved in the deception. Do journalists have a right to counter this lying with lies of their own, told under the guise of the public's need to know?

Ethical thought leaves journalists with difficult choices. Bok asserts that a genuinely white lie may be excusable on some grounds, but that all forms of lying must stand up to questions of fairness and mutuality. Even lying to liars can have its down side.

> In the end, the participants in deception they take to be mutually understood may end up with coarsened judgment and diminished credibility. But if, finally, the liar to whom one wishes to lie is also in a position to do one harm, then the balance may shift; not because he is a liar, but because of the threat he poses. (Bok 1978, 140)

Since so many of the lies journalists are told emanate from powerful sources, the issue of telling some forms of lies to report a socially beneficial story remains a troubling and important one. Another ethical issue centers on exactly how much truth journalists ought to tell. Completeness and accuracy are sometimes used synonymously with truthfulness and objectivity, but important ethical distinctions can be made among the concepts. If truth itself is relative, then how should a journalist balance getting the story against providing his or her readers with the essential information needed to evaluate it? Again, the issue becomes one of the means to a specific end, both now and in the long run.

## Ethical News Values

In most mass media courses, you were presented with a list of things that, collectively, define news. Most such lists include proximity, timeliness, conflict, consequence, prominence, rarity, change, concreteness, action and personality. Additional elements may include notions of mystery, drama, adventure, celebration, self-improvement and even ethics. While these lists are helpful to beginning journalists, they probably will not help you decide how to recount the news ethically.

We suggest you expand your journalistic definitions of news to include a list of ethical news values. These values are intended to reflect the philosophic tensions inherent in a profession with a commitment to truth.

If news values were constructed from ethical reasoning, we believe the following elements would be emphasized by both journalists and the organizations for which they work.

**Accuracy**—using the correct facts and the right words and putting things in
context. Journalists need to be as independent as they can when framing
stories. They need to be aware of their own biases, including those they
"inherit" as social class, gender and ethnicity, as well as learned professional
norms. Their news organizations need to trust journalists when they report
independently rather than expect them to act as part of a pack.

**Tenacity**—knowing when a story is important enough to require additional effort, both personal and institutional. Tenacity drives journalists to provide all the depth they can regardless of the individual assignment. It has institutional implications, too, for the individual cannot function well in an environment where resources are too scarce or the corporate bottom line too dominant.

**Dignity**—leaving the subject of a story as much self-respect as possible. Dignity values each person regardless of the particular story or the particular role the individual plays. Dignity allows the individual journalist to recognize that news gathering is a cooperative enterprise including editors, videographers, designers and advertising sales staff where each plays a role.

**Reciprocity**—treating others as you wish to be treated. Too often, the journalistic enterprise is defined as "writing for the lowest common denominator." Reciprocity eschews the notion of journalism as a sort of benevolent paternalism—we'll tell you what we think is good for you—and recognizes that journalists and their viewers and readers are partners both in discovering what is important and in gleaning meaning from it.

**Sufficiency**—allocating adequate resources to important issues. On the individual level, sufficiency can mean thoroughness, for example, checking both people and documents for every scrap of fact before beginning to write. On an organizational level, it means allocating adequate resources to the news-gathering process.

**Equity**—seeking justice for all involved in controversial issues and treating all sources and subjects equally. Like the ethical news value of accuracy, equity assumes a complicated world with a variety of points of view. Equity demands that all points of view be considered, but that not all be framed as equally compelling. Equity expands the journalistic norms of "telling both sides of the story" to "telling all sides of the story."

**Community**—valuing social cohesion. On the organization level, a sense of community means that media outlets and the corporations that own them need to consider themselves as citizens rather than a mere "profit center." On the individual level, it means evaluating stories with an eye to social good first.

**Diversity**—covering all segments of the audience fairly and adequately. There appears to be almost overwhelming evidence that news organizations do not "look like" the society they cover. While management can remedy part of this problem through changing hiring patterns, individual journalists can learn to "think diversity" regardless of their individual heritages.

Like all lists, ours should not be considered inclusive or without some measure of internal contradiction. We believe those contradictions, however, provide an important continuum within which informed ethical choice can be made.

## Suggested Readings

Bennett, Lance. 1988. *News: The politics of illusion.* Longman: New York.
Gans, Herbert. 1979. *Deciding what's news: A study of CBS Evening News, NBC Nightly News, Newsweek and Time.* New York: Vintage.
Jamieson, Kathleen Hall. 1992. *Dirty politics.* New York: Oxford University Press.
Lester, Paul M. 1996. *Images that injure.* Westport, CT: Greenwood Press.
Lippmann, Walter. 1922. *Public opinion.* New York: Free Press.
Plato. *The republic.*
Sabato, Larry. 1992. *Feeding frenzy: How attack journalism has transformed American politics.* New York: Free Press.

## CHAPTER II CASES

## CASE II-A
## When Is Objective Reporting Irresponsible Reporting?
THEODORE L. GLASSER
*Stanford University*

Amanda Laurens, a reporter for a local daily newspaper, covers the city mayor's office where yesterday she attended a 4:00 P.M. press conference. The mayor, Ben Adams, read a statement accusing Evan Michaels, a city council member, of being a "paid liar" for the pesticide industry. "Councilman Michaels," the mayor said at the press conference, "has intentionally distorted the facts about the effects of certain pesticides on birds indigenous to the local area." Mr. Michaels, the mayor continued, "is on the payroll of a local pesticide manufacturer," and his views on the effects of pesticides on bird life "are necessarily tainted."

The press conference ended at about 5:15 P.M., less than an hour before her 6:00 P.M. deadline. Laurens quickly contacted Councilman Michaels for a quote in response to the mayor's statement. Michaels, however, refused to comment, except to say that Mayor Adams's accusations were "utter nonsense" and "politically motivated." Laurens filed her story, which included both the mayor's accusation and the councilman's denial. Laurens's editor thought the story was fair and balanced and ran it the following morning on the front page.

The mayor was pleased with the coverage he received. He thought Laurens had acted professionally and responsibly by reporting his accusation along with Michaels's denial. Anything else, the mayor thought, would have violated the principles of objective journalism. The mayor had always believed that one of the most important responsibilities of the press was to provide an impartial forum for public controversies, and the exchange between him and the councilman was certainly a bona fide public controversy. Deciding who's right and who's wrong is not the responsibility of journalists, the mayor believed, but a responsibility best left to readers.

Councilman Michaels, in contrast, was outraged. He wrote a scathing letter to the editor, chiding the newspaper for mindless, irresponsible journalism. "The story may have been fair, balanced, and accurate," he wrote, "but it was not truthful." He had never lied about the effects of pesticides on bird life, and he had "never been on the payroll of any pesticide manufacturer," he wrote. "A responsible reporter would do more than report the facts truthfully; she would also report the truth about the facts." In this case, Michaels said, the reporter should have held off on the story until she had time to independently investigate the mayor's accusation; and if the accusation had proved to be of no merit, as Michaels insisted, then there shouldn't have been a story. Or if there had to be a story, Michaels added, "it should be a story about the *mayor* lying."

By way of background: The effects of pesticides on bird life had been a local issue for nearly a year. Part of the community backs Mayor Adams's position on the harmful effects of certain pesticides and supports local legislation that would limit or ban their use. Others in the community support Councilman Michaels's position that the evidence on the effects of pesticides on bird life is at best ambiguous and that more scientific study is needed before anyone proposes legislation. They argue that pesticides are useful, particularly to local farmers who need to protect crops, and because the available evidence about their deleterious effects is inconclusive, they believe that the city council should not seek to further restrict or prohibit their use. The exchange between Mayor Adams and Councilman Michaels is the latest in a series of verbal bouts on the subject of pesticides and the city's role in their regulation.

## Micro Issues:

1. Did Laurens do the right thing by submitting her story without the benefit of an independent investigation into the mayor's accusations about Councilman Michaels?
2. Is the mayor correct in arguing that Laurens acted responsibly by providing fair and balanced coverage of both sides of a public controversy without trying to judge whose side is right and whose side is wrong?
3. Is the councilman correct in arguing that Laurens acted irresponsibly by concerning herself only with reporting the facts truthfully and ignoring the "truth about the facts"?

## Middle-range Issues:

1. Is it sufficient when covering public controversies to simply report the facts accurately and fairly? Does it matter that fair and accurate reporting of facts might not do justice to the truth about the facts?
2. Does the practice of objective reporting distance reporters from the substance of their stories in ways contrary to the ideals of responsible journalism?
3. If reporters serve as the eyes and ears of their readers, how can they be expected to report more than what they've heard or seen?

## Macro Issues:

1. What distinguishes facts from truth? For which should journalists accept responsibility?
2. If journalists know that a fact is not true, do they have an obligation to share that knowledge with their readers? And if they do share that knowledge, how can they claim to be objective in their reporting?

## CASE II-B
## The Doctor Has AIDS
DENI ELLIOTT
*University of Montana*

A practicing pediatrician admits to having tested positive for the AIDS virus; court documents contain his admission and his name. Should these facts be turned into a front-page story or should they be forgotten? This was the decision that Dallas-area news media faced in the fall of 1987.

Robert J. Huse, M.D., was one of only six pediatricians in the politically conservative suburb of Mesquite, Texas. He was a twelve-year veteran and was extremely popular—topping more than five thousand office visits a year for the past three years. Parents described him as a caring doctor, one who would treat a child knowing that no money was available to pay his bill.

Dr. Huse was also involved in a legal battle with his former roommate, Tyrone Sims. According to a request Dr. Huse filed for a temporary restraining order, Sims had told some of Huse's employees and patients that the doctor had AIDS. Furthermore, Sims was blackmailing Huse with threats of further disclosures, the court request revealed.

Soon after, reporters from local print and electronic media received telephone calls from an anonymous source who told them of Huse's request and alerted them to a September 11 hearing of the petition in open court. *Dallas Morning News* court reporter David Jackson said that he was so busy with criminal cases that he certainly would not have heard about this civil hearing if it hadn't been for the telephone call.

Jackson retrieved court documents before the hearing and found that the temporary restraining order had been granted and was signed on September 1. The order forbade Sims from initiating communication with Huse's patients, associates, or employees or with "any other person regarding the plaintiff's (Dr. Huse's) physical or medical condition." The September 11 hearing had been scheduled to provide Sims an opportunity to argue against a continuance of the restraining order.

Discussions then began in Dallas newsrooms about what, if anything, should be published. Three issues emerged as relevant prior to the hearing:

1. Civil cases are often settled or pushed back on the court calendar. The fact that the hearing was scheduled for September 11 carried no guarantee that it would be heard that day.
2. Dr. Huse was using the court system to seek privacy and protection.
3. People with AIDS are normally not identified without their consent.

Representatives from the electronic and print media attended the hearing Friday, September 11. Huse had, by then, extended his request for court protection to include sealing the records so that his name and the case would no longer be public record.

The court continued the restraining order against Sims but declined to seal the records or issue restraining orders against the news media. "The court proceeds from a strong commitment to First Amendment openness," said Judge John Mc-Clellan Marshall, who heard the case. "It's a bad policy for courts to seal things away."

*Author's note: A little more than two years after Dr. Huse saw his last patient, he was found dead in his bathroom, stabbed to death after what police described as a violent struggle with an unknown assailant. The* Dallas Morning News *quotes a friend as remembering him as "outspoken, kind-hearted and a stubborn human being. He never gave up. And I don't think that night he was killed that he ever gave up," the friend said. Dallas police have no suspects in the murder, but refused to rule out the possibility of a "vigilante" killing by relatives of a former patient.*

## Micro Issues:

1. What makes this story newsworthy?
2. Do the local news organizations have the responsibility to tell the community that a practicing pediatrician is HIV-positive?
3. Does the pediatrician have a right to keep this information private?
4. Should it make a difference (in the decision of whether to publish the story) if the anonymous caller was Sims?
5. Should news organizations refrain from publishing the story prior to the hearing? After the hearing?

## Middle-range Issues:

1. Does the judge's refusal to seal the records add weight to the argument that the story should be published?
2. How should the presence of Dr. Huse's name in the court records be balanced against his request that he not be identified in the decision whether to identify him in the news story?
3. Would it be unfair to the other doctors if Dr. Huse was identified in the story as "a Mesquite pediatrician"?
4. Should the presence of other news-media representatives at the hearing affect a news organization's decision whether to go with the story or whether to identify the doctor?

## Macro Issues:

1. Under what conditions should people with AIDS be identified in news stories?
2. Often a person who seeks court relief to guarantee privacy must do so through public court documents and hearings. Should news organizations shield the names of such people as they usually do with victims of rape or incest?

## CASE II-C
## Taste in Photojournalism: A Question of Ethics or Aesthetics?
LOU HODGES
*Washington and Lee University*

Photographer Garry Bryant, in his essay "Ten-Fifty P.I.: Emotion and the Photographer's Role," (1987) says his reaction over the years to a ten-fifty p.i. call—an accident with personal injury—had changed from one of thrill to one of wariness. He attributes the change to the drama he has witnessed at countless tragedies and the resulting hassles with crowds, police, and the reading public in obtaining and printing the photos.

Undoubtedly, John Harte of the *Bakersfield Californian* knows the feeling well. So does his editor, who after receiving the brunt of the public reaction to printing the photo that follows, says he has rethought his position on publishing photos of personal tragedy.

Photographer Harte took the photo after he responded to a call on the police scanner. He arrived at a lake northeast of Bakersfield, California, while divers were still searching for a drowning victim. After a few minutes, divers brought the lifeless body of five-year-old Edward Romero to the shore, where the boy's distraught family was gathered. By this time, television crews had arrived on the scene. As the family members, in public view at the edge of the lake, began to grieve, all of the photojournalists and videographers had to decide whether and how they would shoot the story. The television crews opted out; they decided not to film the moment. Harte edged around the sheriff and, using a 24 mm lens and a motor drive, shot eight frames.

Managing editor Robert Bentley was called into the offices of the *Bakersfield Californian* that Sunday evening to decide whether one of Harte's gripping photos should run. He was persuaded that the photo would serve as a potential warning and help stem the high number of drownings in the county.

The publication of the photo, which was also distributed by the Associated Press, generated more than five hundred protest letters and calls from throughout the nation but primarily from Bakersfield residents. The paper also lost about forty subscribers over its decision, most of whom returned (Stein 1986).

A week later, Bentley explained his decision in an editorial column. "Some claimed the *Californian* showed callous disrespect of the victim. Others felt the photograph had forced their visual intrusion on what should have been a family's private time of shock and grief. Most combined the dual protests" (Bentley 1986).

Bentley eventually decided that the photo should never have been published. He has said that by publishing the photo, he learned that journalists are seriously out of touch with their readers' sensibilities. "The reaction was too intense and widespread to just shrug it off and say we're just doing our job" (Stein 1986).

The picture was nominated for, but did not win, the Pulitzer prize.

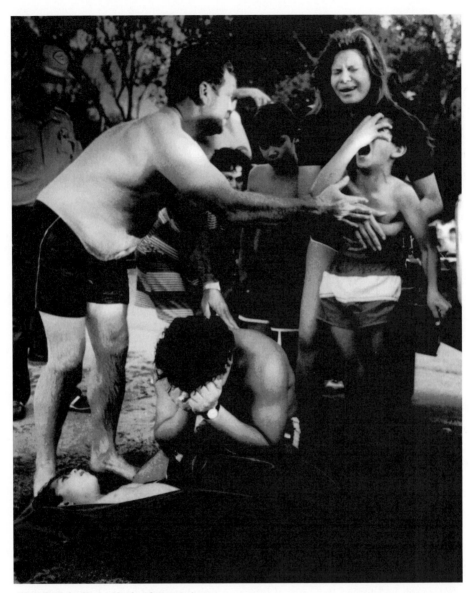

*Photo by John Harte. Used with permission.*

Editorial judgments about photographs ordinarily hinge on two kinds of standards, moral standards and standards of taste.

The most commonly recognized moral standards are those concerning privacy and those about inflicting additional harm on victims. These were the moral basis of response to Harte's picture.

Standards of taste are more difficult to identify and describe. No photographer or photo editor to my knowledge has identified what exactly we mean by "in bad taste." The closest they come is to note that people do not want bloody pictures (mangled bodies, or the uncovered dead, for example) at the breakfast table. Some find such pictures offensive at any time of day.

So what can we say about the *ethics* of taking and publishing *aesthetically* offensive photos?

First, we are more likely to agree on what is good (ethics) than on what is beautiful (aesthetics). The philosophers have long known that. Philosophers, whose function is inquiry into the good (ethics), the true (epistemology), and the beautiful (aesthetics), have been far more successful and helpful in uncovering standards for the true and the good than for the beautiful. Matters of taste seem far more subjective and idiosyncratic than do matters of morality and truth. Some of us admire Wagner and eschew Elvis.

Second, ethical judgments and aesthetic judgments are often closely related. The mushroom cloud from the atomic bomb, for example, has always appeared beautiful to me ever since I saw pictures of the cloud over Hiroshima. Those pictures led to moral rejoicing that the war was about over and that my father would soon be coming home from the Navy. For others the cloud is symbolic of human evil, power, and inhumanity. We tend to like aesthetic symbols of moral good, and we dislike symbols of moral evil.

Third, the decision to take news photos (and the decision to publish them) is ultimately moral and not aesthetic. Harte clearly intruded upon the family in Bakersfield, and that was a moral choice based on his pursuit of somebody's good. Bentley's decision to publish was a moral one: he hoped to prevent others from drowning by running the picture as a warning. He was willing to risk aesthetic harm for moral gain.

Fourth, photo editors sometimes have a moral duty to readers to publish pictures many would regard as in bad taste. Few would object to a warning that saved a life even if the warning was aesthetically objectionable.

The occasional moral duty to be aesthetically offensive rests upon the duty of accuracy, the duty not to deceive. The logic is this: in order to function in the world readers need an accurate image of that world, not one sanitized by well-meaning but misguided journalists. Where the world is bloody it is dishonest and deceptive to hide blood from readers. Aesthetically alarming pictures of starving children in Somalia brought action precisely because they showed ugly reality.

Fifth, photo editors have a moral duty *not* to publish aesthetically offensive pictures except when a significant moral purpose demands publication. The reason is that pictures can plant images in our minds that genuinely harm us. They can be haunting images that we cannot escape.

Morals and taste interrelate in interesting ways. The moral standard for photojournalism also seems clear: we have a moral obligation to others not to publish aesthetically offensive pictures except when publication is reasonably likely to advance some greater public good. Perhaps you can refine and improve that standard through your own critical analysis.

## Micro Issues:

1. Who made the correct ethical decision at the scene, the television crews or Harte?
2. Does the truly exceptional nature of the photo change your reasoning?
3. Would an interview without a photo have been any less intrusive? Should the print journalists present have decided not to write a story?
4. Where would you run the photo? How big?
5. Should the funeral be covered? Is the funeral newsworthy?

## Middle-range Issues:

1. Is the rationale that the picture would serve as a warning a compelling one?
2. Should newspapers outside the Bakersfield area have published the photo?
3. Could the photo have been cropped in such a way as to avoid some of the problems?
4. In cases like this, is there a distinction between a single newspaper photograph and thirty seconds of videotape?

## Macro Issues:

1. Do the potential prosocial benefits resulting from publishing the photo justify taking it? Running it?
2. Should the profession stop rewarding photos of tragedy?
3. Have the newspapers' actions made the family newsworthy figures? Does the existence of a dramatic photo change the newsworthy elements of the story? Should it?
4. What is the relationship of aesthetics to ethics in this particular instance of photojournalism?

## CASE II-D
## Reporters and Confidential Sources
STEVE WEINBERG
*University of Missouri—Columbia*

Bob Woodward became a living legend among journalists the day Richard Nixon re-signed from the presidency in 1974. Woodward was thirty-one, and his book about investigating Nixon—written with fellow *Washington Post* reporter Carl Bernstein—had already reached the best-seller list. *All the President's Men,* the movie of the same name, cast Robert Redford as Woodward, making him an even greater hero.

Nixon's resignation led to a second book, *The Final Days.* It topped best-seller lists, too, and became a made-for-television movie. Woodward next tackled perhaps the most secretive bureaucracy of all—the hallowed Supreme Court. *The Brethren,* written with Scott Armstrong, became another best-seller. Woodward followed with revelatory books about the Central Intelligence Agency, the Pentagon, Vice President Dan Quayle and the drug-related death of actor John Belushi.

As a result of his unparalleled successes, Woodward has come to represent "investigative reporting" more than any other journalist. Woodward's colleagues have said, only half-jokingly, that the only controversial subject left for him to investigate is God.

Woodward, like all real-life heroes, has his imperfections. He failed to detect that *Washington Post* reporter Janet Cooke made up a story until after it won a Pulitzer prize the newspaper had to return. He supervised an article that a jury decided libeled an oil company executive, a case the *Post* won on appeal at great cost. Both debacles—as well as Woodward's earlier successes—were tied to Woodward's use of anonymous sources, a regular practice of his that allows powerful people to speak to journalists with the confidence that their identities will not be revealed. Woodward's most famous such source "Deep Throat" is still unnamed, years after Watergate. Woodward's willingness to let sources go "off-the-record" is well known in Washington D.C.; sources he consults on a regular basis know that, when Woodward is doing the interview, they will not be named in the resulting stories.

Woodward's reliance on anonymous sources is compounded by his writing style. He writes almost entirely omnisciently, without attribution. His narrative is unbroken by "she saids" or "according to's." The technique is novelistic, and, like novels, almost all of Woodward's work lacks source notes.

Questions about Woodward's heavy reliance on anonymous sources, widely emulated by other journalists since Watergate, have been raised occasionally, including an otherwise admiring profile by Steven Brill's in *Esquire.*

Brill's initial questions pinpoint Woodward's legacy for investigative reporting. While he has broken stories of historic import, high-level sources, even those paid with tax dollars, think, "If Bob Woodward will let me say anything I want without attaching my name to it, why should I go on the record with any journalist?" The journalists play along, thinking, "If relying on anonymous sources has made Woodward rich and famous, who am I to do otherwise?"

As a result, reporters have allowed calculating sources to defame competitors, settle scores with enemies, float trial balloons as if they were under serious consideration—knowing they can practice deniability.

Woodward seems unfazed by questioning of his methods. He trusts readers to distinguish between valid and invalid information. He recites how well his reporting has withstood challenges over the decades. He names scholars whose books are filled with on-the-record sources and endnotes but fail to unearth the hidden information that produces what Woodward calls "the best obtainable version of the truth."

Though Woodward has influenced the professional practice of investigative reporting more than any journalist working today, it does not have to be done Woodward's way. On the national level, Seymour Hersh—probably the only investigative journalist as feared and respected as Woodward—has written about controversial, contemporary topics while naming many of his sources, citing documents and providing endnotes.

Hersh relied on a controversial source for portions of his most recent book, *The Samson Option: Israel's Nuclear Arsenal and American Foreign Policy.* He chose to name the source—Ari Ben-Menashe—even though he knew disclosure would lead to questioning of the book's credibility. As a result, there is an element of self-correction in Hersh's work that is lacking in Woodward's. My own work reflects Hersh's rather than Woodward's approach.

I have no quibble with Woodward's ends. But his means will never be the best path for me, nor for many readers. Like Woodward, I will continue to listen to sources who speak off-the-record, on background, not for attribution. Unlike Woodward, I will usually decline to pour their unattributed words into my books and articles. I will try to find other sources just as knowledgeable who will speak for attribution. I will search the paper trail for confirming documents. If I fail, I will probably never publish the information.

In conversations with him, Woodward has told me that I am naive or idealistic or both for trying to work by this standard. He says much attributed journalism is further away from the truth than his reporting. I wish he thought differently.

## Micro Issues:

1. Some newspapers have a policy of refusing to quote off-the-record sources who say something negative about a particular person or institution. Evaluate this policy based on the foregoing discussion.
2. Is there a difference in the kind or quantity of information that a reporter who refuses to go off-the-record in print can obtain?
3. As an editor, what guidance could you provide a young reporter who came to you wanting to know how to handle a local source who wanted to go off-the-record for a routine story? For an investigative piece?

## Middle-range Issues:

1. Are there some institutions, such as the Supreme Court or the Pentagon, whose work is so secret that good reporting can be done only if sources are allowed to go off-the-record?
2. Examine the Brock Adams case in chapter 6. Would you allow anonymous sources under these conditions? If you would, what is different about
   (*a*) this type of story;
   (*b*) the way the paper explained the identity of its sources.

## Macro Issues:

1. Using Aristotle's notion of a person of practical wisdom, evaluate Woodward's impact on professional reporting practice? Is Woodward worthy of emulation? Is Hersh?
2. Using Ross's taxonomy of duties, which do you believe guide the reporting of Woodward and which guide the reporting of Hersh?

## CASE II-E
## Rodent Wars and Cultural Battles: Reporting Hantavirus
JOANN M. VALENTI
*Brigham Young University*

Media coverage of an outbreak of hantavirus in 1993 in the Four Corners region of the western United States and the resulting negative portrayal of Navajo culture reminds us that our relationship with indigenous peoples needs attention. The hantavirus case may suggest that reporting about environmental and health risks involving diverse cultures requires more than traditional journalism training provides.

Although hantaviruses are distributed worldwide, when the emergence of a new strain of hantavirus in the United States reached the mass media agenda in 1993, charges of media stereotyping and environmental racism came in tandem. The initial storytelling was laden with negative images of a Native-American culture and erroneous generalities associating the disease with a particular people and their culture. Within weeks of the discovery of yet another strain of hantavirus, a National Public Radio (NPR) report (June 9, 1993) broadcast interviews with Navajo spokespersons, who already resented the insensitivity of journalists covering the story and linking the disease to the tribe. From the onset, Navajo spokespersons attempted to respond to what they saw as a crisis in the public sphere and correct misperceptions, as well as defend themselves in the face of ethnocentricism from both the media and health communities.

Within one year, 40 people had died in 17 states. The disease was tagged as "an Indian ailment" only because the new viral strain had been first discovered on a Navajo reservation covering parts of Utah, Arizona, Colorado and New Mexico. *USA Today* may have been first to use the tag "the Navajo flu," although a representative from the National Center for Infectious Diseases (CID), a physician who authored the original formal notices announcing the new viral strain, claims a headline in the *Albuquerque Tribune* first used the label "Navajo Flu." *Albuquerque Tribune* science reporter Lawrence Spohn equated that to calling AIDS "the gay disease." The *Arizona Republic* used the label "the Navajo epidemic," and the NBC News made reference to "the Navajo disease." Dewayne Beyal, public information director for the Navajo nation, told one writer that while the spread of the disease might end, "the false image of Navajo life as impoverished and unsanitary may persist in the minds of many Americans." The Navajo people were left to confront a host of hostile publics.

Shortly after the outbreak, the University of Colorado and New Mexico State announced that Indian students would need a medical screening. Marshall Plummer, then vice president of the Navajo nation, responded, "Be assured that this illness is not Navajo-specific. The illness has struck non-Indians and people who live far away from Navajo lands. This is not a racial illness, but a regional one. I believe it behooves you as an educational institution to learn the known facts about this illness before resorting to actions that discriminate against our students."

The Centers for Disease Control and Prevention (CDC) based in Atlanta, Georgia, became a key government source for the story, although CDC made an effort to refer media to state and local health departments. CDC press officer Bob Howard labeled the problem a "data dump," referring to the estimated 25,000 annual media calls he receives. In hindsight, CDC spokespersons describe the case of the hantavirus outbreak as an example of "dueling amateurs," a CDC investigator trained in epidemiology and a non-specialist reporter, rather than a case of cultural insensitivity.

Even the scientific naming of the new hantavirus strain exacerbated the cultural problem. The first name proposed for the strain of hantavirus, Muerto Canyon virus (MCV), in use in the scientific literature, was derived from Canyon del Muerte (canyon of death), a site on the Navajo reservation. Traditionally, new viruses are named after where they are discovered. "The hantavirus was all over the United States," Navajo National Council member Genevieve Jackson told an Associated Press reporter. "We resent the fact that it is named after a canyon here . . . CDC should have a little more respect and consideration for the Navajo people." In response, CDC changed the name to Pulmonary Syndrome Hantavirus. The name finally accepted for the new strain, "Sin Nombre," means "without a name." Ongoing studies by state, federal and Indian groups indicate rodents throughout a number of states including much of the west, the northeast and the south carry the hantavirus disease.

Continuing stories reported new cases of the disease. Follow-up coverage of the Four Corners story analyzed long-term economic woes created as fearful tourists cancelled plans to visit the area, and, in a related turn of events, the CDC announced a "war" on diseases, comparing "virulent cholera ravaging India" to "hantavirus killing Americans."

As would be expected in most major news stories, the majority of sources used were government representatives, although most journalists also sought out Navajo spokespersons. The president of the Navajo nation said at a press conference: "Navajos are finding themselves shunned in public places and business establishments. Navajos have been made to feel like plague bearers or lepers whose touch is to be feared." Most national media editors and news directors relied heavily on wire services to report the story, recreating a fearful image of an entire region of the country and a culture.

## Micro Issues:

1. As the PR representative for the Tribal Council, what strategies or advice do you offer to council members? To the media?
2. As information official for the universities, how would you respond to this statement by Plummer and by media questions about your university's actions?
3. A CNN report includes this statement: "An army of health care workers has descended on the U.S. Southwest. Its mission, to identify a mysterious illness

that has killed 13 people, mostly Navajo Indians. The professionals have all the tools of modern medical investigation, but tribal traditions and taboos are complicating their probe." Develop an effective communication strategy for (a) the Tribal Council, or (b) the State Health Department.

## Middle-range Issues:

1. A recent survey from the American Society of Newspaper Editors found minorities account for just over 10 percent of the total population of newsroom professionals. Native-Americans are the least represented at less than one half of 1 percent. Until these figures are more representative of the population, what training in cultural sensitivity could be built into our media processes to offer more promise of accurate and fair coverage to minorities?
2. When reporting on risk, media generally offer little or no information about the likelihood of its occurrence, often leaving an inaccurate public perception and unnecessary anxiety. Describe the ethics of communicating risk in a story such as the hantavirus outbreak. How could the risk of contracting the hantavirus have been placed in context?
3. ABC reported that Navajo children from Arizona were sent home after being told they could not visit with their pen pals at a Los Angeles school. The principal of the California school and her students were worried they might catch the disease from the Navajo children. Analyze the resulting PR crisis from the viewpoint of the Los Angeles school system that sent the children home.

## Macro Issues:

1. According to census data the Navajo have the highest proportion (48.8%) of members living in poverty of any Native-American tribe. What stereotypes of Native-Americans might have contributed to the reporting in the hantavirus story?
2. To help media accurately report on Indian issues and write articles involving tribal lifestyles, the Bureau of Indian Affairs encourages reporters to call for correct terminology or phrasing, and handbooks have been developed (see for example *The American Indian and the Media*). What role do the media play in perpetuating persistent racial bias? What role can media play in correcting persistent racial bias?
3. A Navajo reporter who spoke the Navajo language filed numerous stories on the virus. She said, "I have to put my Navajo-ness in the back seat and go on." Discuss the pros and cons inherent in her position as a native Navajo and a reporter.

## CASE II-F
## Too Many Bodies, Too Much Blood: A Case Study
## of the Family Sensitive Newscast Movement
BILL SILCOCK
*University of Missouri*

Thirty minutes before deadline the KIVI-TV reporter took a phone call in the video editing booth. "This is the Idaho Fish and Game department. The radio says your TV station's helicopter discovered the body of our officer, Conley Elms, floating naked, upside down in the Owyhee River. Will we see that on the 6 P.M. news? If so, we want to warn his wife."

Twenty-four hours before, in a remote part of Idaho's wilderness, Elms, and fellow officer Bill Pogue, sustained gunshots to the chest and back of the head. Claude Dallas, a fur trapper who portrayed himself as a self-styled mountain man, enraged over the game wardens' inspection of his camp, ambushed them. Dallas dumped Elms' body in the river and buried Pogue's 40 miles away in the desert sand.

"Well," the reporter replied to the phone inquiry, "yes, we did shoot Mr. Elms' body from the air. Some of it will be shown." A news staff debate broke out in the crowded editing booth. The reporter, his photographer/editor, chief photographer, news director, and even the newscast anchor, all offered opinions on the ethical dilemma of how much video of Elms' body to air during dinnertime.

Any amount was too much for Elms' wife, Sheri. Writer Jack Olsen would describe her reaction to that January 1981 newscast in his true crime book, *Give a Boy a Gun.*

> Sheri Elms' friends had stayed with her all day. She refused to accept that Conley was dead. Missing, yes. In trouble, maybe. But dead? Dead was impossible. The evening newscast showed a naked body swinging in the current. Just like Conley, the man had thick upper torso and spirals of fine black hair down his back. She rushed out the door and banged her head against the side of the house. Then she ran down the street. She didn't want to be home. (Olsen 1985, 139)

The story would generate two books, a *Rolling Stone* article and a made-for-television movie. This author experienced the above case in 1981 as a fresh-from-college KIVI reporter. Later that year, the Idaho Press Club would award a First Place in Television Spot News Award for our coverage. While launching one new reporter's career, the broadcast embedded forever a jagged, painful image for at least one member of the audience, Sheri Elms, the victim's wife. The impact of that image on one individual played a minor influence in decision making by the news team that night. More prominently debated was the exclusivity of their station's video. The story not only led the newscast but was slotted additional time beyond the typical 1:30 television news package story length.

Fourteen years later, a trend labeled "family sensitive" news was born. The January 1994 brainchild belonged to John Lansing, news director of WCCO-TV in Minneapolis. Encouraging it was Lansing's news consultant, Ed Bewely, of Audience Research and Development in Dallas. Lansing's news staff conducted 100 focus groups and round tables and then decided to promote WCCO's 5 P.M. newscast as "family sensitive." The movement's intent was to clean up the depiction of crime coverage for newscasts aired during the dinner hour. This time period, 4 P.M. to 7 P.M., is when young children and family viewership rates high, hence the movement's label as "family sensitive."

## Micro Issues: (The News Workers)

1. Should a new reporter have been assigned to such a high-profile case? Would a more experienced reporter and photographer argued for airing more or less of the graphic video?
2. Should the editorial gatekeepers (news director, chief photographer) have anticipated the potential for controversial video earlier and raised the issue of how to handle the graphic but truthful video much earlier in the news cycle?

## Middle-range Issues: (The Community Standard)

1. What responsibility do television newsmakers have for the innocent victims, friends and especially family caught up in a sensational case of violence?
2. What bearing does an outside phone call from an interested party have on how a story with sensitive video is treated?
3. Should the station edit the video in a different way, allowing for more detailed footage for the late evening 10 P.M. newscast?
4. What impact should ratings and competitive pressure have on the decision of how much to air since only KIVI-TV's helicopter had the video of Elms' body?
5. Did radio news reports of the body's "discovery" by the KIVI chopper, aired at 5 P.M., bring pressure of performance by their journalism peers in the decision making of how much exclusive video to air at 6 P.M.?

## Macro Issues: (Industry Standard)

1. Does any uniform code of ethics (RTNDA or SPJ) provide guidelines on handling such video?
2. Television newsrooms are nomadic cultures where staff members move frequently. How much does "other market experience" verses "what is the correct choice for this community" bear on the decision? Does the acceptable amount of graphic video vary from Boise to Boston?
3. What role does the "thirst for awards" play in a reporter and a news department's decision in how to handle coverage of sensational video?

## The Family Sensitive Newscast Movement

Lansing's news staff conducted 100 focus groups and public round table meetings. The move prompted nationwide media attention. The *New York Times* (Meisler 1994, 20) reported Lansing's finding that "a distinct majority responded that the news was too violent" and the *Los Angeles Times* (Braun 1994, 1) quoted Lansing as saying that "people are just tired of being afraid and tired of what we've been selling them." As many as 15 stations across the country, many of them clients of Audience Research and Development, copied Lansing's concept. AR&D's Ed Bewely became a spokesman for the movement defending it on "Nightline."

　Within two months critics were accusing Lansing's movement of "sanitizing the news." One outspoken critic, Terry Heaton, News Director of WRIC-TV in Richmond, called the concept a "marketing ploy." In an editorial for *Electronic Media* Heaton wrote:

> The media is under scrutiny from a lot of different places in this day and age and we don't need to be shooting ourselves in the foot by criticizing each other. . . . In stating publicly that we are part of the problem of violence in our culture, we are opening the door to a journalist's most dreaded nightmare, legal government limitations on press freedom. (Heaton, 1994)

Others raised additional concerns over the movement, including RTNDA President David Barlett who observed if "we're not going to cover the crime story—five people got murdered in the ghetto—because we're family sensitive, we're not going to report reality."

　The family sensitive news movement did not catch on. Eleven months and three ratings books after its conception, eight out of ten stations adopting it sustained drops in their family sensitive newscast ratings (Lafayette 1995, 3)

## Micro Issues: (The News Workers)

1. What policies and coverage patterns can a news staff follow to insure a sensitivity to viewers concerned with too much violence?
2. Under what conditions, if any, should the guidelines be broken?
3. Should the news team be concerned their news crime coverage airs in a television environment, often right before or after programs labeled "reality based" fiction, such as "Cops" or "Rescue 911"?

## Middle-range Issues: (The Community Standard)

1. Who decides what constitutes a family?
2. How should a station serve a diverse audience comprised of those wishing to foster traditional family values and new definitions of a family emerging in society today?

3. Does "family sensitive" as a label automatically recall the same definitions of the political term "family values."

## Macro Issues: (Industry Standard)

1. Should RTNDA or the NAB encourage an industry standard?
2. Charles Kuralt calls local television news a "notoriously copycat business where what works in one market is immediately tried in another." How can legitimate change occur in a medium's coverage patterns noting such criticism?
3. Should Congressional panels of inquiry encourage and the FCC adopt more strict regulation on the amount of video violence depicted in local newscasts? Could this be an issue during a station's licensing renewal process? Should regulators encourage sensitive coverage, especially during hours when children might watch? Does this conflict with First Amendment freedom of news workers?
4. Should newscasts be rated like the motion picture industry and television entertainment programming?

## CASE II-G
## Nine Days in Union: The Susan Smith Case
SONYA FORTE DUHÉ
*University of South Carolina*

On October 25, 1994, a nationwide manhunt began in Union, South Carolina, for two young boys after their mother claimed a man stole her car with her children inside. Susan Smith, 23, said the man got into her car when she stopped at a red light, forced her out, and drove off with Michael, 3, and Alex, 14 months.

Sheriff Howard Wells called in state law enforcement, the FBI, and the media to the 200-year-old mill town to help search for the two young boys and the alleged carjacker. Soon, the media and the nation would become transfixed by the case.

The story began with an emergency call to 911. "There's a lady who came to our door," the caller told the operator. "Some guy jumped into her car with her two kids in it and he took off."

"And he's got the kids?"

"Yes Ma'am, and her car. She's real hysterical, and I just thought I need to call the law and get 'em down here."

Susan was the only eyewitness.

She described the carjacker as a black man in his twenties, wearing a dark-colored cap, a plaid jacket and jeans and armed with a handgun. Smith told police the subject told her to drive northeast on Highway 49, just below the John D. Long Lake. Then, the man told her to stop and ordered her to get out of the car. When asked about getting her children out, the man said, "I don't have time, I won't hurt them," and then he proceeded northeast on Highway 49.

Tearfully, Susan told the media, "When he made me get out of the car, you know I tried to get my children, I begged him please let me take them. He said, no, he didn't have time because they were in car seats and it was going to take time to get them out." He had a gun, and my big thing is they were screaming, crying, and hollering, and I'm just scared he lost his patience or something."

Within hours of the first report of the missing children, Union became besieged by the growing press corps, including the tabloid television shows. Television live trucks and cable lined the street in front of Union's courthouse—all waiting to hear something about the missing boys.

But after day one, Susan went into seclusion.

Still, the media reported on the search for the African-American suspect and the missing boys. With no new information about the search, the media's attention began to focus on Susan and her troubled life.

Stories about Susan's relationships began to surface. Her marriage to David Smith, an assistant manager at the Winn-Dixie, had fallen apart in August. The two had met while working at the local supermarket. They married in 1991 and had Michael seven months later. Just one year after the birth of their second child, Susan and David's marriage was virtually over. Divorce papers had been filed in September.

Susan had been working as a secretary at Conso Products, a textile plant. She had been having an affair with the boss' handsome 27-year-old-son, Tom Findlay. A week before the boys disappeared, he wrote Susan a letter on his computer. He wanted to be with her, he said, but he was not ready for the responsibilities of a ready-made family. After news spread of the crime, Findlay printed out a copy of the letter and gave it to police. "At no time," he said in a statement, "did I suggest to Ms. Smith that her children were the only obstacle in any potential relationship with her."

Although neither the media nor the public were aware, by day three of the search, an investigator asked Susan why she had murdered her children. Susan strongly denied the allegations.

On day four of the search, Susan was asked to take a lie detector test. Sheriff Wells publicly called the results "inconclusive."

The manhunt continued. Day five, day six and day seven passed. Still, there were no signs of the boys or calls for ransom, but evidence began to point toward Susan. NBC news had even captured video of agents wearing gloves going into Susan's home.

By day eight, Susan's image in the media was deteriorating. Reporters knew of two failed lie detector tests and a troubled marriage and also had learned that a portion of her original story was untrue.

Under increasing scrutiny, by day nine, Susan came out of seclusion. She appeared on all three network's morning news programs. With her husband David at her side, Susan made sorrowful pleas as the television cameras rolled. "I can't even describe what I'm going through. It just aches so bad. I can't sleep. I can't eat. I can't do anything but think about them." Susan pleaded that the kidnapper feed and care for young Michael and Alex. An artist's sketch of the black man she described as the carjacker was also broadcast nationwide.

That same afternoon, Susan broke.

Sheriff Wells told Susan there was surveillance at the intersection where she said the carjacking occurred and that he knew she wasn't telling the truth. Susan asked the sheriff if he would pray with her. Finally, Susan confessed to murdering her two sons. She had driven her car into Union's John D. Long Lake and left Michael and Alex inside—strapped to their car seats.

Outside the courthouse, gasps could be heard as Sheriff Wells announced the news. "Susan Smith has been arrested and will be charged with two counts of murder in connection with the deaths of her children, Michael, 3 and Alexander, 14 months. The vehicle, a 1990 Mazda driven by Smith, was located late Thursday afternoon in Lake John D. Long near Union." The car was exactly as Susan said. Both children were strapped in the back seat—Michael on the driver's side and Alex in his car seat on the passenger side.

"In her confession, Susan wrote, "I felt I couldn't be a good Mom anymore, but I didn't want my children to grow up without a Mom. I felt I had to end our lives to protect us all from any grief or harm. I've never felt so lonely and sad throughout my life." ". . . I dropped to the lowest point when I allowed my children to go down that ramp into the water without me." ". . . I broke down on Thursday, November 3, and told Sheriff Howard Wells the truth."

On July 22, 1995, a jury convicted Susan of murdering her two sons. Although cameras were barred from the courtroom, coverage of the trial drew as much attention as the search itself. For many, the trial brought back the horror of those nine days in Union. A broadcast reenactment of the drownings used by the prosecution made the memories even more vivid.

Days later, that same jury took only two and one-half hours to decide against imposing the death penalty. Susan is serving a life sentence in the Women's Correctional Institution in Columbia, South Carolina.

## Micro Issues:

1. Should the media have converged upon Union, South Carolina, to cover the disappearance of Michael and Alex Smith?
2. Should the local, regional and national media have televised Susan's plea to get her children back?
3. Should the media have aired the artist's sketch of the alleged carjacker?
4. Should the media have been allowed to air the prosecution's drowning reenactment?

## Middle-range Issues:

1. Should the media have print and broadcast information about Susan Smith's troubled relationships?
2. When should the media use artist's sketches of alleged criminals?
3. Should the television media be allowed to air the reenactment of an incident where a death has occurred?

## Macro Issues:

1. To what extent should the media play a role in the search for missing persons?
2. What responsibilities do news people have regarding a news source's personal life?
3. What guidelines should the media follow when showing artists' renderings of alleged criminals?

## CASE II-H
## Handling the Media in Times of Crisis: Lessons from the Oklahoma City Bombing
JON HANSEN
*Oklahoma City, Oklahoma*

*Author's note: On April 19, 1995, Oklahoma City Assistant Fire Chief Jon Hansen was on the phone to a local reporter when Hansen interrupted the conversation by saying a bomb had gone off downtown. He couldn't know then that he would spend the next two weeks talking to reporters and to millions of viewers worldwide about one of the greatest acts of terrorism in U.S. history. Here are his thoughts on that experience excerpted from* Oklahoma Rescue, *authored by Hansen.*

As you could tell from the dramatic pictures that were seen on television and in newspapers across the country, the local media arrived on the scene within minutes of the blast.

Local police and highway patrol officials gave the initial media news briefings as both Chief Marrs and I were working feverishly to set up the command center and initiate rescue operations. Since the fire department was in charge of all rescue and recovery efforts, it wasn't long until the media began requesting time to talk with someone from our department.

Accordingly, I went to the building to get an updated and accurate status report and to check on the progress of our special operations team, which I was responsible for. Once I returned to the media area and did my first interview, it became clear to me that our department would be the one with the information the media would be most interested in over the coming days.

It was critical that all journalists be given equal access to information at precisely the same time. So the creation of a media center was something we had paid attention to early on, settling in an area two blocks northwest of the Federal Building. As the area was slightly elevated, it provided a reasonably good view. Most cameras could capture images of the building from the fourth floor up, with the lower floors and the pancake area pretty much blocked from view by other buildings in the foreground.

We were sensitive to the media's need for a "good shot," so the public could relate to what was happening. We also had to be considerate of the rescue workers, victims and the victims' families.

The first time I realized that anyone outside Oklahoma City was watching the rescue effort was when a local reporter told me that their coverage was being fed to the national network as well as to CNN. This situation was news being telecast worldwide.

One of our local TV stations was the first to video the disaster from the air, providing extraordinary footage for the world to see. Based on what he saw on television from the helicopter shots, Governor Keating immediately issued a "declaration of disaster."

Within one hour of the incident, all our local stations had live trucks or satellite uplinks in place. At the time, they didn't remotely suspect that they were setting up for coverage that would extend over the next sixteen days. Because it took the out-of-state journalists a few hours to begin arriving, the local media secured and maintained prime placement throughout the incident.

Anytime we asked, reporters were also eager to help broadcast updates for needed supplies. Before we had time to set up systems to obtain supplies from local relief agencies, this support was invaluable. Ironically, the only drawback was the public's overwhelming generosity. Whenever we requested something, we always got far more than we needed of each and every item.

Our covenant with the media was that we would always provide them with factual and up-to-date information. Providing periodic updates from the site and meeting any specific requests from the media became my responsibility. I did everything humanly possible to honor every commitment we made.

By the second day, we had nicknamed the media area "satellite city," as there was almost a two-square block area of nothing but satellite trucks and live trucks lined up side by side. Several prestigious network television journalists told me that in their long careers they had never seen that many media trucks covering any single incident, including the O.J. Simpson trial. A number of reporters commented

© THE DAILY OKLAHOMAN. *Reprinted with permission.*

that there hadn't been this much media attention focused on one event since the assassination of President Kennedy back in 1963.

Soon, regular coverage was not providing enough information to satisfy the public's appetite for news from the scene. Invitations began pouring in from "Nightline," NBC's "Dateline" and other special news magazine shows. CNN was asking for more frequent updates as they, along with our local affiliates, were providing round-the-clock coverage. There was no precedent for the extensive coverage we received from our local television stations. It was the following week before they returned to any significant amount of regular programming.

As more and more reporters arrived from all across the country, I admit that I was in awe. On the other side of the microphones and tape recorders were the voices and faces we all know from "Nightline," "20/20," "Dateline," "48 Hours" and other shows.

The national publications and large metropolitan newspapers were here in full force as well. The major news magazines had large crews covering the story. It was certainly a different experience to have print journalists approach me for an interview, saying they were from the *New York Times* or the *Dallas Morning News* or the *Washington Post.* Just as unusual was talking to reporters from *Newsweek, Time, U.S. News & World Report* and *People.*

Many of the cities that had sent FEMA/USAR teams also sent reporters. We paid particular attention to their needs because we wanted citizens from those communities to know how deeply grateful we were that they sent their firefighters to assist us. We invited members of the individual search and rescue teams to the media area to talk with their local reporters so some of the messages sent back to cities came directly from their own rescue personnel.

Media restrictions existed in the covering of this situation that have not been imposed in other large-scale disasters such as areas hit by hurricanes, earthquakes, floods, or tornadoes. The reason, of course, was because this was also a crime scene of gigantic proportions with massive amounts of evidence and leads that had to be protected by federal investigators. Within the first hour after the bombing, a secured perimeter had been set up around the mass murder scene. Although members of the media respected it, the limitation was also frustrating to them.

It was difficult for reporters to capture the sights and sounds of the incident—to feel what rescue workers were going through, to get a close-up view of the destruction caused by the bomb. For people charged with creating pictures and verbal images for the public, I know it was sometimes hard for them to rely on us for descriptions, especially since we often had a difficult time putting into words what we were experiencing.

By day three there were so many media crews here, people began calling the camera staging area "media row." It was difficult to stand in one place where everyone could have access, so when we did an update, I would move down the rows of reporters so everyone could receive the same information.

One of the most interesting reporters was Boris Notkin, the Russian journalist. The questions he asked were different from everyone else's. He asked about the political system and why the two political parties weren't blaming each other for what happened. I asked him if he found the building as staggering as we all did. I'll never forget what he said. "If you see the capital of Grozny with six hundred thousand people and half of it looks exactly like this, you wouldn't be much impressed by one single building. But the response of the people really makes me admire the Americans."

Being accurate, telling the truth and honoring our commitments to fulfill their requests—those were the three objectives in our media strategy. There were times when something happened in the building that caused us to miss interviews, but even then the media were amicable. None of us ever lost sight of what the priority was: search, rescue, and recovery operations.

What was a good time to ensure that a deadline could be met for one person was often a terrible time for someone else. We set up structured briefing times:

| | |
|---|---|
| 4:30 A.M. | National news |
| 5:00 A.M. | Local affiliates |
| 10:00 A.M. | Formal briefing by the fire chief, FBI, police chief, public works director, FEMA director, etc. |
| 11:00 A.M. | Status of the rescue operation |
| 3:00 P.M. | Status of the rescue operation |
| 4:00 P.M. | Status of the rescue operation |

Those were the times for standard reports, but we talked with the media a great deal more than that. Anytime we had a change in the operations, or we had a structural problem, or the fatality count went up, we would do our best to bring the news media up to speed in a timely fashion.

We also made the decision to take pool cameras inside the building. The pool concept, of course, required us to secure permission from the FBI and all the other law enforcement agencies since the building was classified as a mass murder crime scene.

We did what it took to get the media inside, however, because we believed that the rescue workers needed the public to understand why the operation was moving so slowly. We wanted America to see how tough each step of the way was for rescuers. We wanted people to see workers removing debris by hand and to observe the tremendous amount of shoring that was required to keep rescuers out of harm's way. Those who went inside were deeply moved and somewhat afraid for their own safety—and rightly so.

I guess it would be impossible to get that many reporters together for anything without running the risk of rumors and inaccurate stories. There were rumors that Geraldo Rivera had dressed up in a uniform so that he could get into the area. I'm not certain what clothes he wore when, but I can tell you that he never made it into the restricted area.

It is true that the rescue effort came to a halt when a TV tabloid reporter made his way into the restricted area. That person was quickly caught and arrested.

The media story everyone wants to hear about is the interview with Connie Chung for the "CBS Evening News." Connie had just arrived in town and was driven in her limousine to the site for the national news update. Just a short time later, she was interviewing me live when she turned and asked point-blank, "Can you [the Oklahoma City Fire Department] handle this?"

My initial reaction was certainly surprise, because that's exactly what we'd been doing, and doing well, since 9:02 A.M. I had done dozens of interviews by that time and no other member of the press had questioned our ability to deal with the crisis. At the time, I didn't really take offense. I simply answered what seemed to be a silly question as politely as possible.

I had no idea at the time that her doubts about our department would so deeply offend many of my fellow Oklahomans and even the rest of the nation. By the time she was interviewing me, cities and states all over the country were feeling great empathy with Oklahoma City, and the public rushed to our defense. They had watched our hard work for hours and knew that our rescue workers were doing an incredible job.

Did I think at the time the question was a little inappropriate? Yes, I did. Emotions were running high, and the question was certainly insensitive to the moment. Citizens here have always felt a pride of ownership in the fire department, and after watching the rescuers at work all day on April 19, they interpreted her remark as degrading and frankly ridiculous. It hurt our citizens in ways that even I didn't realize at the time.

It wasn't until the next day that I realized the problem that Ms. Chung had created for herself. People began saying they were offended by the way she had treated me in the interview. To tell you the truth, I had to think back about what she said. I was doing so many interviews that they were all running together in my mind. The anti-Connie Chung T-shirts that showed up on the streets downtown sent a message to CBS that the problem wasn't going to go away easily.

The news director from our local CBS affiliate contacted me two days after my first on-air conversation with Ms. Chung, saying that Connie wanted the opportunity to try to set things right in a live TV interview with me. I agreed to do the interview later that day, though it was very awkward for several reasons. Obviously, the last thing I needed at the time was to be in conflict with a major network news anchor. On top of that, my wife works for the CBS affiliate that was requesting the satellite rematch. Fortunately the interview would be refereed by another anchor.

Before I talked with Ms. Chung again, I talked with our fire rescue personnel and asked their opinion about how they wanted me to respond to her remark. Almost to the individual they were saying, "Chief, you know we have to stay focused on what we're doing. Let bygones by bygones. Just let it go." So that's what I did.

Ms. Chung was very apologetic when the cameras rolled this time, and she told the people of Oklahoma that she hadn't meant to slight them in any way.

I realize that coming from New York, Ms. Chung probably looked at the situation and wondered if the job was too big for the Oklahoma City Fire Department.

The thought never even occurred to me. Apparently she felt it was her responsibility to ask me what she believed were tough questions. I saw the public get tough as they responded to her question with a huge outpouring of support and respect for the firefighters searching for survivors.

Was her question insensitive? That is a question the American public answered for us all, and I was deeply touched by their answer.

# CHAPTER III

## Persuasion Ethics: What's Fair in Advertising and Public Relations

**At the end of the chapter, the student should be familiar with:**

- The balance and cognitive dissonance persuasion theories and their role in advertising.
- The prosocial and antisocial aspects of advertising.
- Why the relationship between the media and public relations is both symbiotic and strained.

## Introduction

Since the days of ancient Greece, a major function of communication has been to persuade. Greek citizens used the art of rhetoric to their advantage in the Greek city-states where democracy was practiced through an elaborate court system. Eventually, the courts of Athens became crowded with those who sought to use their persuasive powers for gain. Today's airwaves and printing presses are likewise filled with messages designed to increase the influence and wealth of their sponsors.

But advertising is not the only persuasion that you find in the media. Thousands work in professions designed to "spin" or otherwise manipulate the news in favor of their clients. Just as one motive for learning rhetoric in ancient Greece was to persuade for financial gain, wealth is still a major motivation in professional practice today. An ad that gets attention or a news story with just the right slant are now the goals of those who make a living at persuasion.

However, one crucial difference exists between Athens and Madison Avenue. While the Greeks *overtly* attempted to persuade, modern persuasion is more *covert.* Indeed, theory from the past forty years has evolved in an attempt to explain how means of persuasion that are not readily recognizable as attempts to persuade fail or succeed.

Twentieth-century persuasive messages abound. With only 6 percent of the world's population, Americans consume 57 percent of the world's advertising and a similarly disproportionate amount of its public relations output. Any study of the ethics of advertising and public relations must examine how the professions impact both the individual consumer and the U.S. media system. At the individual level, the goal of the professions is information acquisition, opinion change, and sometimes behavioral change. At the system level, advertising provides needed financial support for the media while public relations provides necessary, if controversial, assistance in the newsgathering process.

Both levels raise distinct although related ethical issues. We will begin this chapter with a focus on advertising and the individual and then examine the larger role of both professions on the U.S. media system.

## Persuasion Theory

Psychologists first began to try to understand persuasion working from a *stimulus-response model.* This early behavioristic approach led many to believe that the media could act as a "hypodermic needle" or a "magic bullet," sending a stimulus/message to an unresisting audience. These researchers, called powerful effects theorists, found examples to support their theory in the public panic after Orson Welles's "War of the Worlds" broadcast on October 30, 1938, and in the success of propaganda during both world wars.

But the stimulus-response model proved a poor predictor of much human behavior. By the 1940s, most researchers were concluding that media effects were limited or nonexistent. However, by studying only behavior change (i.e., changing my vote) the researchers overlooked the true power of the media in the cognitive (knowledge) and affective (emotional) realms.

Later, communication theorists focused on cognitive psychology. Rather than viewing persuasion as a simple behavioral reaction to a sufficient stimulus, these scholars theorized that how people think helped to explain persuasion. According to these theories, people strain toward cognitive balance. Simply put, we are most comfortable when all of our beliefs, actions, attitudes, and relationships are in harmony, a state theorists called *symmetry.*

Such theories have become known as *balance theories,* since they stress the tendency of people to strive for cognitive balance in their lives. A person achieves balance only when his or her attitudes, information, and actions are in harmony. Leon Festinger coined the term *cognitive dissonance* to describe the state where a message and an action give conflicting and uncomfortable signals. The desire to eliminate that dissonance is a strong one, strong enough to influence purchasing behavior, voting behavior, habits, or opinions.

Advertisers employ this psychological construct. A frequent scenario in advertising copy is to knock a consumer off balance early and then restore that balance through the purchase of a product. For instance, the headline of an ad might suggest that your dandruff is making you a social outcast, and the subsequent copy promises you social approval if you use the correct shampoo. A television ad might suggest that the wrong choice of tires means you don't care about your family's safety, while the correct choice of tires restores peace of mind by providing the needed protection.

While use of stimulus-response theory in advertising has raised few ethical questions—the sight of a mouth-watering pizza to stimulate the buying of pizzas is a well-accepted way of marketing—the use of cognitive dissonance in advertising opens a wide range of ethical questions. Is it ethical, for instance, to lower the self-esteem of a consumer only to raise it again if the proper product purchase is made? Or to create mental anxiety that is resolved only with a purchasing behavior?

## Advertising as Advocacy

American consumers think of advertising as a form of selling or persuasion. However, some research on advertising indicates that people can seldom be persuaded to purchase something that is either truly bad for them or that they truly do not need. For example, advertising is not a process of persuading people to buy toothpaste, as if their only choices were buying toothpaste or buying no toothpaste at all. Instead, advertising helps consumers select from among competing alternatives, in this case, particular brands of toothpaste.

In this light, much advertising within American culture can be viewed as advocacy for a particular brand. This concept of advertising as advocacy gives advertising practitioners a great deal in common with other professions where the role of advocate is important. Much of the American legal system, for example, is based on the concept of advocacy, and other professions, such as teaching, include an element of advocacy. In addition, viewing advertising as a form of advocacy blunts the criticism that advertising itself violates Kant's command to treat individuals as an end rather than a means.

When advertising is viewed as a form of advocacy, it takes on important ethical dimensions. Most scholars who have written about the concept agree that advocates should be evaluated on both *motive* and *method.* An advocate should be genuinely motivated by and be willing to offer good reasons for taking a particular point of view.

Philosopher Robert Audi links the principle of sincerity with advocacy. This link is particularly appropriate to advertising and provides advertising practitioners with a two-part ethical test. First, is there a sincere need for this particular product within the range of products and services available? Second, are the reasons given the consumer for purchasing the product presented in a way that would also motivate the person who developed and wrote the ad? We'll see how the test can be applied in the example of the proliferation of prescription medicine ads that began running in the late 1990s.

Today, you see the ads for prescription medications in virtually every magazine, often running several pages. You see the commercials during the nightly network news, when the audience is older. The typical format shows an average sufferer of an ailment such as high cholesterol, asthma, enlargement of the prostate or allergy symptoms living a happier and healthier life thanks to a drug.

A few years ago, the makers of these products could advertise only to physicians, according to Federal Drug Administration rules. Today, the ban is lifted and the race is on for drug manufacturers to convince consumers that their brand of medication is superior to their competitor's, both prescription and over-the-counter. At stake is a chance to influence a share of the more than 2 billion prescriptions written annually by convincing consumers to ask their physicians whether they should be using an advertised medication.

It's difficult to assert that there is not a sincere need for most of these advertised medications. And, in this day of active patient involvement, it's also difficult to assert that advertising prescription medications directly to the consumer is detrimental to patient care. So, the ads pass the first part of the test—there is a sincere need for some prescription medications.

But, the ads also suggest that a particular medication is the best (and possibly only) way to achieve this result. Missing is any mention of over-the-counter medications that might give many consumers equal relief at less cost or risk. Also missing is any discussion of the impact of a good diet, proper lifestyle, sufficient rest and even genetics in the prevention of certain diseases. In addition, potential side effects of the medication, adverse reaction to other drugs and the like, is relegated to small print, usually on another page from the stylish ads. Yet these are exactly the sort of issues a well-trained physician will examine before writing a prescription.

By emphasizing only the positives of the prescription drugs, glossing over the negatives and omitting any references to non-prescriptive remedies, the pharmaceutical companies fail the second part of the sincerity test. No one would want to be persuaded to take expensive drugs, some of which are riskier than other options, without weighing all the issues.

## Accuracy without Honesty

Based on the analysis of the ads above, we can modify the sincerity test as follows. Sincerity in advertising means that claims are made within a context clearly understood by both the advertising copywriter and the consumer. If the ad's claims fall outside the contextual capabilities of the audience, or if the context is incomplete or misleading, then the ad is suspect. Sincerity works precisely because consumers are savvy enough to know when it's being faked.

Thus modification of the sincerity test does not mean that advertisers are required to present evidence counter to their own claims in advertisements. It merely means they use motivations they would wish others to use when trying to persuade them. This leaves room for advertisers to employ what Eric Eisenberg (1984) has called "strategic ambiguity." Strategic ambiguity is the use of abstractions without interpretation. Strategic ambiguity allows advertisers room for creativity, but it can also muddle the message for the receiver.

Ads play on strategic ambiguity by employing "built-in vagueness," words used when the writer or speaker does not want to be pinned down (Oran 1975). For instance, only the perceptive viewer of the Duracell battery ads featuring motorized figures powered by the famous "coppertop" battery will recognize that they claim only to be better than their previous batteries, *not* better than any other battery on the market. This built-in vagueness sells because it demands an alert consumer, not passive viewers.

Postman (1986), using an argument from Bertrand Russell, criticizes advertisers who use the "seduction of eloquence" in their ads rather than making direct product claims. There are no rebuttals, he says, to jingles such as "You deserve a break today at McDonalds" since no product claim is made. Johannesen (1990) asserts that in order for a persuasive message to be considered ethical, it must make a claim that the reader or viewer can check. The absence of a verifiable claim, for example ads employing ridicule or commercials promoting "image," should alert the consumer to a potentially unethical approach to persuasion.

Stripping a claim of its context so that an autonomous moral actor can evaluate its truthfulness is an important ethical issue in advertising. Consumers need information in a context they can understand to reach a rational decision. The enormously enjoyable Budweiser commercials that feature the frog's quest for beer is an example of a commercial with sufficient entertainment value and production quality to make the viewer ignore the fact that the commercial not only lacks information but also could be construed as an appeal to underage drinkers. This approach cannot be heavily faulted when used to sell beer. But when used to "sell" presidents, as Reagan's "Morning in America" ads did in 1988, information without context raises ethical questions.

## Criticisms and Defenses of Advertising

Americans are wary of advertising, and rightfully so. In a Gallup survey, respondents ranked advertising twenty-fourth out of twenty-five occupations in ethical standards and honesty, one notch below politicians and one notch above car dealers. Another poll found that 81 percent of the American public believe most advertising claims are exaggerated, and 52 percent find them "seriously misleading."

Advertising is a more than fifty-billion-dollar-a-year industry in the United States alone. With these stakes, some abuses occur, and some criticisms are appropriate.

First, it is said that advertising is an intrusive, ubiquitous process, interrupting reading, viewing, driving, etc. to register a message. It has been called "the ultimate invasion of privacy." A second complaint asserts advertising heightens expectations and glorifies acquisition (what commercials have called "the good life") at the expense of the environment, the economy, and civilization itself (Lasch 1979). Third, critics allege advertising is a manipulative process that treats people "as a means to an end" (Mander 1979).

Advertising's defenders, however, note advertising fulfills several important functions. First, and most importantly for our purposes, advertising *provides financial support* to the media, keeping the media free from government ownership or direct subsidies and the controls that go with them. The price of this "free" information—news and entertainment—is embedded in the price of advertised goods we purchase, a fact George Gerbner (1987) points out in his saying, "You pay when you wash, not when you watch."

Second, advertising *fuels the economy* (see fig. 3.1). Since mass production requires mass consumption, advertising provides the news of product availability to the mass markets. Third, advertising *provides needed information.* Whether shopping for designer jeans or for off-road vehicles, the consumer is better served when information is readily available. If you know something about the relationship between fiber in the diet and lower cholesterol and cancer rates, where did you get the information? Chances are it was from some advertiser with a high-fiber product to sell. One study (Patterson and McClure 1972) even found that in one presidential election, more issues information was available through commercials than in all television news coverage of the campaign. Other studies have shown that readers of print media, when offered copies without advertisements, preferred the copies with ads, since they regarded the ads as part of the informational content of the medium.

These three arguments in favor of advertising are those most often found in advertising texts. However, the portrait they paint is an old-fashioned one. Fewer than one-third of the jobs in the United States are the result of manufacturing; we have become a service economy, where jobs are not as directly related to advertising and marketing forces. Furthermore, the U.S. government already subsidizes the mass media in many ways—from placing of legal ads in newspapers to lower postal rates. Other democracies, for example, the United Kingdom, have aggressive media heavily supported by the government. These facts have altered the arguments about the role of advertising in a free press.

**Figure 3.1**
*The economic cycle*

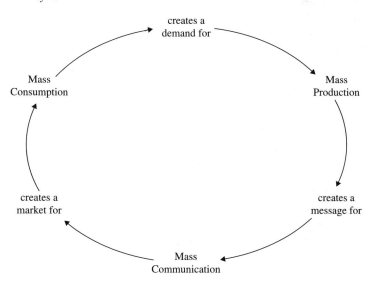

At the root of most of the ethical issues in advertising is this question: Is caveat emptor (let the buyer beware) a morally justifiable position? This philosophy of dealing places a responsibility on the buyer to separate claims and performance, appearances and reality. Because of caveat emptor, one of the major ethical considerations in advertising is deciding whether a line exists between allowable persuasion and dishonest trickery. The government is ambiguous on the matter. This ambiguity has led Michael Schudson (1984) to call advertising "the art form of bad faith." In the following section, we will examine two problems that are illustrative of the ethical issues in advertising. First, we will look at the blurred lines between the editorial and advertising content in the media. Then we will examine the recent trend toward singling out particular groups for targeted messages.

## How Close Is Too Close?

"Advertorials"—ads that look like news—have become controversial for both broadcasters and print journalists. Advertisers took advantage of the explosion of video-needy cable channels in the 1970s to find a home for "infomercials," thirty-minute ads that resemble programming. Magazines, too, published feature-like articles on everything from cars to countries that were, in fact, paid advertising. These practices heightened the controversy over not only *where* to draw the line between advertising and editorial content, but also how recognizable it should be. Critics see the blurring of the walls between advertising and editorial content as a media disease with two overt symptoms.

First, advertisers may directly or indirectly cause staffs to eliminate controversial topics from editorial content. For example, studies show that news stories about the dangers of smoking are less frequent in print outlets that rely heavily on cigarette advertising (Kessler 1989).

Daniel Okrent, former editor of the *New England Monthly,* claims that such overt censorship of editorial content is on the rise.

> A publisher will say, "I hear you are doing a story on, say, John Deere. Don't let this affect you, but John Deere is buying forty-eight pages of advertising." At one time it was unthinkable that a publisher would ever say that to an editor. Now it happens all the time. (Hoyt 1990, 39)

The second visible sign is the intentional creation of a favorable media environment for certain advertisers. This type of alliance has been around at least as long as the *Good Housekeeping* Seal of Approval, awarded for decades to those products deemed worthy of the magazine's pages. But where a near church/state separation once existed between advertising and editorial, recent pressures have encouraged editorial departments to be more supportive of advertisers. In a Magazine Publishers of America (MPA) poll in *Folio,* 40 percent of the 250 magazine editors responding said that they had been told by management to do something they felt "seriously compromised" the editorial function of the magazine (Hoyt 1990). *People* magazine's editor called the pressure "huge" and often successful, a feeling echoed by *Ms* magazine's publisher who subsequently banned all ads from her magazine.

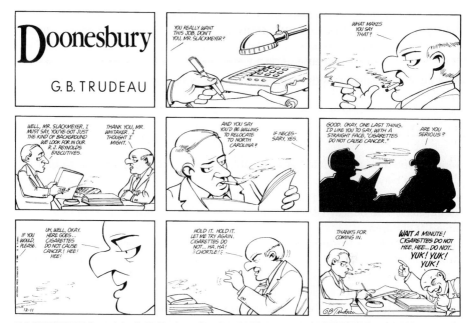

*DOONESBURY Copyright G. B. Trudeau. Reprinted with permission of UNIVERSAL PRESS SYNDICATE. All rights reserved.*

Stuart Ewen, author of *All Consuming Images,* attributes the pressure to a change in the way advertisers view the media properties in which they advertise.

> At one time marketers viewed magazines as a place they could rent space for advertising. Today they view them as real estate holdings. Once you own real estate, you begin to think about the neighborhood, the surroundings, changing the shrubbery and so forth. (Hoyt 1990, 37)

In the late 1980s, roughly five hundred magazine titles were added each year to compete for relatively static ad budgets. Advertisers used the resulting clout of their position to brighten up the neighborhood considerably, extracting many favors for their dollars. Controversial practices included:

- Allowing ads or commercials to look like editorial copy, often without the Magazine Publishers Association's suggested markings at the top of every other page.
- Favorable mentions of products and advertisers in articles.
- Sending stories to advertisers for approval before publication.
- Using staff members to create "advertorial" sections and flagging the sections on the cover of the magazine, in violation of MPA guidelines.
- Contests linking the medium and one of its sponsors, such as the essay contest in *Esquire* in which Absolut vodka had to be mentioned twice in the essay. All of this activity has put additional pressure on other magazines to go along. (Hoyt 1990, 38)

Hollywood too, exploits "the big blur." With a plurality of movies in the 1980s failing to break even (Medved 1992) Hollywood sought other income sources to offset production costs. One place they found ready money: advertisers willing to pay large sums for prominent placement of their product on the screen. For instance, Lark cigarettes paid a reported $200,000 for use of its cigarettes in the James Bond film *License to Kill.*

## The Ethics of Target Advertising

Target marketing, ads pointed at a specific demographic group, appear to blur the connection between means and ends. The strategy itself is simple: target advertising aims advertising dollars at segments of the population most likely and able to buy the product. The ethical issues of target advertising include stereotyping and ads aimed at children.

Exactly when advertisers began to actively court ethnic consumers is uncertain. Brooks (1992) quotes a 1940 *Business Week* article that reported an organization was established in Los Angeles to help guide advertisers who wished to garner the patronage of African-American consumers. The businesses were cautioned against using words like "boss," "boy" and "darkey" in their advertisements. Instead, the stores were urged to refer to African-American consumers as "Negroes" who want the same things as other shoppers.

But, the real attempt to court ethnic audiences began when those audiences acquired buying power. Dates (1990) says that during the 1980s the advertising community took real notice of the African-American consumer, whose collective income virtually doubled in that decade and stands at more than $200 billion today. The tremendous numerical growth in the Hispanic market during that same decade made Hispanic audiences impossible to ignore. It is projected that Hispanics will be the largest minority in the United States by the year 2001. The Asian market, though still relatively small, increased substantially during the 1980s yet few advertisers have incorporated Asians into their campaigns. And Native-Americans, because of their small numbers and low incomes, have been virtually ignored—with the exception of using Native-American images for major marketing campaigns and as mascots for athletic teams.

Despite the growth in ethnic minority markets, some advertisers have been slow to understand the needs, desires, and sensitivities of these particular groups. Some blunders are humorous, such as General Motors discovering that Nova meant "no go" in Spanish only after the car did poorly in Mexico. Other examples are not so humorous—the "Frito Bandito" illustrates the use of offensive and stereotypical ethnic images in persuasive communications.

More recently a telephone company translated one of its major market campaigns for the Hispanic market without considering culture. The commercial, in which an adult child had to be reminded by the phone company to call his elderly mother, was considered insulting by some in the target audience. According to Hispanic advertising executive Marta Miyares, "We never need to be reminded to call our mothers. It is just something we do."

African-Americans were offended by a cigarette company developing a brand exclusively for African-Americans. It is estimated that 46 percent of all illnesses and deaths in the African-American community are the result of cigarette smoking. Yet, the R. J. Reynolds Tobacco Company spent untold dollars in its planned launch of the Uptown cigarette with target ads aimed directly at the African-American market. Consumer outrage was so strong the company was forced to pull the brand before it was distributed.

Camel cigarette advertisements have been heavily criticized and even lampooned by Doonesbury for their "Joe Camel" figure. Critics claim the ads target children. R. J. Reynolds, manufacturer of Camel cigarettes, denies the ads are targeted at children. However, sales figures show that Camel cigarettes are the number one choice of underage smokers and that their popularity with underage smokers has skyrocketed during the tenure of the Joe Camel campaign.

Sometimes it's clear to see how advertising insults and stereotypes ethnic audiences. Other times, the offense is more subtle. Because the lines are unclear and because of the potential for bad publicity in response to a perceived racial slur, some advertisers opt to ignore ethnic consumers altogether. Others hire ethnic advertising agencies and consultants to help them develop campaigns. Others venture into unknown territory, only to find themselves surrounded by controversy and consumer backlash.

## Journalism and Public Relations: The Quintessential Struggle

Advertising's occasional shortcomings are best viewed in light of potential alternatives—higher costs to the consumer or government subsidy and possible control of the media. Similarly, any controversy surrounding public relations as a profession must be viewed in light of the alternative. If the more than 200,000 public relations professionals in the U.S. did not exist, many stories would go unreported. Indeed, public relations began as a profession early in the twentieth century when many newsmakers found it difficult to get past journalism's gatekeepers to get their stories told. PR practitioners offered a way to unlock the gate and get stories into the newspapers for their clients. At the same time they offered "free" news to publishers.

Despite the occasional animosity between journalists and public relations practitioners, the relationship is truly symbiotic—they simply could not live without each other. No news organization is large enough to gather all the day's news without several public relations sources. Business pages are full of press releases on earnings, new product lines and personnel changes all supplied by writers not paid by the media. Travel, entertainment and food sections of newspapers would be virtually nonexistent if not for press releases. On the other hand, the media provide the all-important audience for an institution that wants the publicity.

With this common need, why are the two professions sometimes at odds? Editors point their fingers at public relations practitioners who perceive their job in terms of the quantity (much) and the quality (favorable) of exposure they can get for their clients or causes. These practitioners, in turn, point to editors and reporters who come to each story with an agenda (a polite word for bias) that influences the outcome of the final story, usually in a manner unfavorable to the public relations professional's client.

Much of the problem stems from how each of the two professions define news. To the public relations professional, the lack of breaking news is newsworthy. Plants that operate safely and are not laying off any employees, nonprofit organizations that operate within budget and provide needed services, companies that pay a dividend for the fiftieth consecutive quarter are all signs that things are operating smoothly and make for a story that the public should hear.

However, to the journalist, news is a change in the status quo—a plant that pollutes, employees who embezzle, firms that go bankrupt are all worthwhile news stories. Caught in the middle, the news consumer probably prefers a choice of both stories. However, shrinking newsholes and static amounts of airtime won't allow both, and the editorial bias is toward disruption more often than efficiency.

As the journalistic gap has grown between the two professions, public relations professionals have found it necessary to resort to staging events to get their good news on air or in the newspaper. Such events—ribbon cuttings, press conferences, open houses, and the like—are a phenomenon Daniel Boorstin (1962) calls the "pseudo-event." The timing, the staging, and the location of a pseudo-event are set with the cameras in mind. Media owners, sensing a cost-efficient story with good visuals that foster community goodwill, have historically been willing to attend (Epstein 1974).

A story from Minneapolis illustrates the quintessential pseudo-event. The story announced that former University of Oklahoma law professor Anita Hill, who in 1991 publicly charged Supreme Court Justice Clarence Thomas with sexual harassment, would *not* be coming to Minneapolis. Advance publicity of her visit had generated so many donations for an endowed professorship in her name that Hill did not need to appear in person, said the promoters. In short, the publicity had made the event moot. While pseudo-events are normally "news" staged solely for the benefit of the media, in this Alice-in-Wonderland-type case, the media actually kept the news event from occurring by giving coverage to the announcement of the upcoming event.

Boorstin claims that as much as one-fourth of all news fits this scenario—events that would not have occurred or would have occurred differently if not for the presence of a camera, including such examples as bill and treaty signings, official send-offs, most press conferences, photo opportunities, and most demonstrations, sit-ins and strikes. Reporters and photographers don't always share their publisher's enthusiasm for these events for two reasons. First, they feel used. Second, reporters prefer stories that they research themselves to stories handed to them.

While the Minneapolis case is an extreme example, many nonjournalists attempt to trade on the credibility of the news to advance their cause. A news story carries more clout with readers or viewers than an advertisement. Although readers and viewers may not know the terminology, they have a sense that a media gatekeeper is at work screening stories of dubious reliability. When the public relations professional successfully places a story in the media, it has the credibility of having passed through the gate, a benefit of the doubt paid advertising does not receive.

Add to that the serendipity that the story is free and an ad is not, and the motivation is great for the public relations professional to attempt to influence the editorial content. This is done either by hyping a nonimportant story or by putting the company's "spin" on a legitimate story, making sure that only the company line gets heard. With the stakes high—promotions, for instance, hang in the balance for those who continuously get favorable coverage for their institution—the chance for abuse is high as well.

Public relations professionals place a strain on news desks with their constant flow of news releases to the print and electronic media. As many as 90 percent of all press releases received are dumped by editors after a quick glance (Honaker 1978). Yet the flow of news releases continues virtually unchecked, since many organizations measure the effectiveness of a PR office by output, not publication. This system creates resentment on the part of the public relations professional whose articles never seem to be printed, and resentment by the editor who must sift through the mass of releases against the possibility of overlooking a usable one.

## When Seeing Isn't Believing: News Releases on Video

In the 1990s, the press release has gone high tech, produced on video and distributed via satellites to television stations. For instance, when television news showed "smart bombs" hitting their targets during the Persian Gulf War, the footage was produced by the military and the public relations firm of Hill and Knowlton, not by news organizations (Safer 1992). Much of the video coverage of the Gulf War came courtesy of these military video news releases, commonly referred to as VNRs.

Video news releases are a relatively new phenomena. In one well-used public relations text updated in the mid-1990s, the term "VNR" does not appear in the book's 25-page glossary. In the text the authors devote only two paragraphs to video news releases, noting that VNRs initially "met with some resistance from news directors who felt they had less control over packaging news stories that come in this form from an outside source." But, they assure public relations students that now, "It's so easy to edit videotape cassettes that few news directors balk any longer at accepting a video release" (Newsom 1993, 443). There's no mention of ethical considerations.

Medialink, a firm involved in the distribution of VNRs, says that health and medical subjects are "the most useful" (read: most aired) VNRs. Business, political and lifestyle/fashion, or sports followed as good VNR topics, in that order. The 106 news directors responding to the survey preferred a 90-second, timely story to an "evergreen" release ("news" that could be aired at any time). They were likely to use a VNR in whole or in part when it could be incorporated into a local interest story. Nearly 75 percent of the news directors also indicated they would consider airing "issue-oriented" VNRs. More than half said VNRs should be clearly identified as public relations releases, including naming the source; 25 percent said they identify a company only if it is clearly relevant to the story. Some 18 percent said they do not identify the sponsor behind an aired release at all.

The general public probably didn't notice the growing VNR industry until a mid-1990s *TV Guide* cover story headlined: "Fake News." The article warned viewers they were being tricked into assuming that sponsored messages were real news. In response, the public relations industry retrenched and surfaced with a code for good VNR practice and a "seal of approval" to be affixed to VNRs that meet the guidelines. The Public Relations Service Council (PRSC) code recommends that an opening slate—seen by the folks in the newsroom, not by the viewers at home—include clear identification of a VNR as such, the name of the sponsoring company or organization, a contact person and full information about anyone seen on the video. This provides the "stuff of information" should anyone in the television newsroom choose to follow up on the release. The code requires that all information contained in a VNR be accurate and verifiable "to the extent possible." Yet except for the seal, the code calls for no signal to the viewer that the material comes from an outside source.

## Conclusion

While the proliferation of news releases is a source of mild irritation between the professions of journalism and public relations, it is a minor nuisance compared to the differences in how the two sides approach "hard" news stories. Unfortunately, some public relations practitioners see their jobs as not only to tell the good news about their company, but also to keep the bad news from being told. This standoff results in the perpetuation of a vicious cycle. Business executives perceive that the press is out to "get" them, so they refuse to speak, while the press perceives that the corporation has something to hide by its silence.

Public relations began as a profession when certain newsmakers wanted more media coverage. Today because of what business perceives as a negative bias, many public relations professionals are used as dissemblers of legitimate stories. Some businesses have found it expedient to refuse to cooperate with the media, and some have extended the policy to all employees. For instance, one major retailer does not even allow its managers to grant interviews about the expected best-selling toys for the upcoming Christmas season. Though this policy seems a bit extreme in a Christmas feature story, it is based on the assumption that most of the time the media want information that will harm a business.

The average consumer of news rarely observes this constant struggle for control over the content of the news, yet he or she is affected by it. How should we evaluate a profession with the goal of persuading in a manner that does not look like traditional persuasion or preventing the dissemination of information that might harm the illusion that has been created?

Practitioners in the field justify their profession with the following arguments. First, the stories they attempt to tell are the unreported or the underreported stories of products that work, employees who are honest, and corporations that are good community citizens. Second, the rules are set by the other players in the game—the media. Finally, if the media would ever agree that good news *is* news, the animosity and duplicity might diminish.

## Suggested Readings

Boorstin, Daniel. 1962. *The image.* New York: Atheneum.

Leiss, William, Stephen Kline, and Sut Jhally. 1986. *Social communication in advertising: Person, products and images of well being.* New York: Methuen Publications.

O'Toole, John. 1985. *The trouble with advertising.* New York: Times Books.

Patterson, Thomas E., and Robert D. McClure. 1972. *The unseeing eye.* New York: G. P. Putnam's Sons.

Schudson, Michael. 1984. *Advertising: The uneasy persuasion.* New York: Basic Books.

## CHAPTER III CASES

## CASE III-A
## The Plagiarism Factory
JOHN P. FERRÉ
*University of Louisville*

Terry had not long been advertising manager for the *Louisville Cardinal* when she received camera-ready copy of an advertisement for ready-made research papers. "RESEARCH PAPERS," it announced. "16,278 to choose from—all subjects. Custom research also available—all levels. COD or Visa/MasterCard." The ad urged students to send two dollars or to call a toll-free hotline for a catalog. With the camera-ready advertisement, the company enclosed a check for a year's space in the weekly university newspaper.

Because the *Cardinal* is an independent student paper, Terry was not compelled to run questionable advertisements by university administrators. Furthermore, the newspaper had run the advertisement weekly for years. Tradition was on the side of publishing the ad, yet Terry felt uneasy about it. She voiced her uneasiness at the next staff meeting, and the staff agreed to reject the ad. Terry mailed the following letter:

> I am sorry to inform you that we cannot run your advertisement for research
> assistance. The staff of the *Louisville Cardinal* reserves the right to refuse any
> advertisement it feels could be harmful or insulting to the students of this university.
> Therefore, out of respect for the integrity of the student body and for the protection of
> the ethical policies of the University of Louisville, I am returning your check for
> $111.36. I apologize for any budgeting inconveniences this may have caused you.

Although Terry lost a commission and the newspaper lost some revenue, the staff of the *Cardinal* felt confident that they had made the right decision. The mail-order research paper firm contacted the newspaper a couple of years later to no avail.

At least one of the newspaper's advisers was highly critical of the staff's decision. "Newspapers should print ads, not reject them," he argued, "especially since the *Cardinal* is the only newspaper on campus. It should not act as a censor. Its advertising columns should be open to anyone who is willing to pay for the space, whatever the product or service. Editorial judgments should be made only in regards to news and feature stories."

Despite the adviser's fear that the student newspaper was beginning a campaign of advertising censorship, the *Cardinal* has refused space to no other national advertiser. It prints advertisements for alcoholic beverages, for instance, even though alcoholism and drunk driving are arguably more dangerous for students than academic dishonesty. Apparently, the *Cardinal*'s primary moral criterion for the acceptance of advertisements is honesty. All ads that neither deceive nor encourage others to deceive are acceptable in the pages of the *Cardinal*.

## Micro Issues:

1. If the research paper company queries the newspaper once again, should the newspaper reconsider its decision, or should it stand firm?
2. Is the financial health of the paper an ethically relevant factor? If the paper's budget was in the red, could an argument be made that it is better for the student body to have a newspaper with offensive ads than it is to let the paper die?
3. At some time in the future, the paper receives an ad for *Cliffs Notes.* The staff knows that some students are tempted to rely on plot summaries rather than read whole novels that are assigned in various courses in the humanities. Furthermore, the campus bookstore stocks a wide variety of *Cliffs Notes.* What should the newspaper do? If your answer differs from your decision on the research-paper ad, distinguish between the two products.

## Middle-range Issues:

1. What types of advertisements should student newspapers reject? Community newspapers?
2. Should papers decide advertising policy in advance, or should they make these decisions on a case-by-case basis?
3. Suppose your campus newspaper receives an advertisement from a local nightclub for a "Drink or Drown" promotion. The campus radio station has refused air time to the advertiser. Is the newspaper under any obligation to reject it in light of the radio station's decision?

## Macro Issues:

1. Are a newspaper's advertising columns a common carrier—selling space without discrimination—or should they operate with the same editorial freedom that applies to news and feature stories?
2. Is a newspaper morally responsible for everything it prints, whether or not the content originated at the newspaper?
3. Is it right to impose one's standards on information others receive?

## CASE III-B
## Public Relations' Role in the Alar Scare
PHILIP PATTERSON
*Oklahoma Christian University*

David Fenton was given a difficult task in October of 1988: to get the public interested in yet another study by an activist group with a small budget. The group was the 100,000-member Natural Resources Defense Council (NRDC) and the study was entitled "Intolerable Risk: Pesticides in Our Children's Food." At issue was the effect of the pesticide Alar on cancer rates in young children. For a fee of $25,000 (Anthan 1990), Fenton attacked the challenge with vigor, and met with huge, but controversial success.

Fenton's work began in October, 1988 when he agreed to promote the group's announcement that children were being exposed to the pesticide Alar beyond recommended levels, according to NRDC calculations. Alar, the trade name of the chemical daminozide, acts as a growth retardant to keep apples on the tree longer and preserve them on the way to market, producing redder fruit with a longer shelf life (Bad Apple 1989).

However, exposure to an excess amount of Alar is linked with cancer, and the EPA has established strict levels acceptable for human consumption. Unlike pesticides, Alar is absorbed into the fruit, making it impossible to wash off. NRDC contended that children were at risk of receiving too much Alar for two reasons: the disproportionate number of apples they eat and their smaller body size.

Fenton's goal was to create a story "to achieve a life of its own" (How a PR Firm 1989, 9). Obtaining this goal required deal making not unlike a Hollywood press agent. An agreement was made with "60 Minutes" to allow them to break the story February 26, 1989. Interviews with monthly magazines, which operate on the industry's longest lead times, were booked months in advance to assure publication at the peak of the talk show appearances by recruited celebrities.

Media exposure of the Alar announcement included the covers of *Time* (Toufex 1989), *Newsweek* (Beck 1989 and Begley and Hagar 1989) and *Consumer Reports* (Bad Apple 1989). Fenton also claimed credit for placing the story on "Good Morning America," "Today," "CBS This Morning," "Donahue," and the network newscasts. Additional coverage came in newspapers, *U.S. News & World Report* (Siberner 1989), *People, Redbook, Family Circle, Woman's Day* and *New Woman* magazines and a cover of *USA Today*.

Other methods were used to spread the message. A 900 phone number was installed to give consumers up-to-the-minute information on the Alar situation. Meryl Streep and cast members from the television shows "thirtysomething" and "L.A. Law" joined news conferences. Streep conducted 16 interviews by satellite with local anchors in major television markets and testified before a Senate subcommittee on Alar's use.

Controversy over the message came almost immediately, while controversy over the method soon followed. The initial "60 Minutes" report opened with Ed

Bradley making an assertion called a "flat out lie" by the Washington Apple Commission. He began:

> "The most potent cancer-causing agent in our food supply is a substance sprayed on apples to keep them on trees longer and make them look better. That's the conclusion of a number of scientific experts. And who is most at risk? Children who may someday develop cancer from this one chemical called daminozide." (Warren 1989, 1).

The "60 Minutes" segment was viewed by approximately 30 million viewers. This report and the resulting intense coverage led to a scare in the marketplace. Actions taken included the banning of apples by several school systems, including New York City, Chicago and Los Angeles, and the opening of pesticide-free produce sections in grocery stores, actions which Fenton claims occurred as a result of his publicity.

"Our goal was to create so many repetitions of NRDC's message that average American consumers (not just the policy elite in Washington) could not avoid hearing it—from many different outlets within a short period of time. The idea was for the story to achieve a life of its own, and continue for weeks and months to affect policy and consumer habits." (How a PR Firm 1989, 9)

Evidently the strategy succeeded in that respect. The spokesperson for the Chicago Board of Education, Bob Saigh, blamed a "media stampede" on the Chicago school system's decision to ban apples in its cafeterias.

Why the intense media publicity and the massive public reaction surrounding the findings? The effect of Alar was not a recent discovery. In fact, in 1973 tests on animals showed its carcinogenic qualities, and the EPA had earlier tried to ban it.

Theories of the media's fascination with the Alar announcement abound. *Newsweek's* environmental reporter suggested that perhaps the attraction to the media was what Hitchcock played out in his movie *The Birds:* one of our deepest seated fears is that the benign will suddenly turn menacing (Carlson 1989). Forensic psychiatrist Park Dietz suggested: that "part of what happened here is something characteristic of all mass hysteria incidents, a perceived threat to children or childbearing. Then there is the element of invisible hazards. Here you have the issues of children and invisibility. They were very powerful" (Warren 1989, 1).

Peter Sandman, former director of the Environmental Communication Research Program at Rutgers University, thinks it was the made-for-media symbolism of the apple. "Apples are a symbol of innocence and innocence betrayed. Kids eat them. There's the Adam and Eve story and Snow White" (Haddix 1990, 44).

When a well-orchestrated media campaign threatened to challenge the ages-old assumption that "An apple a day keeps the doctor away," the media appeal was irresistible.

The media rarely, if ever, revealed that the information they were airing came from the NRDC's point of view. Chemical industry spokesperson Elizabeth Whelan was, by her own count, quoted in or interviewed by the two U.S. wire services, several newspapers including the *Chicago Tribune,* the *Washington Post,* two news services and talk shows such as "Larry King Live" on the Alar issue without the media once mentioning that she was funded by industry sources, including Uniroyal

Chemical Company, the manufacturer of Alar (Kurtz 1990). In an interview for *Columbia Journalism Review,* Whelan said that to worry about such matters is "chilling the discussion," adding that "Everyone is funded by someone" (Kurtz 1990, 44).

Eventually, however, the strategy backfired. In October, 1989, the *Wall Street Journal* (How a PR Firm 1989) used a leaked memorandum between Fenton and the NRDC in an editorial that ran under the headline "How a PR Firm Executed the Alar Scare." The confidential memo obtained by the *Wall Street Journal* outlined the strategies used by Fenton, but taken out of context it looked less like strategy than manipulation. Media watchdog groups, such as Accuracy in Media, jumped on the issue, spending thousands of dollars getting the "real" Alar story out to their constituencies, and trying to force CBS chairman Laurence Tisch to retract the original "60 Minutes" story.

The result was an unwanted type of publicity for the NRDC. Its executive director, John Adams, later told a reporter for the *Washington Post,* "We wanted to get a maximum amount of coverage. What we did instead was that we blew it. We got everybody angry at us. I'll never let myself get in this situation again" (Haddix 1990, 45).

Predictably, the apple industry struck back with a $2 million campaign launched by the apple growers. Full-page ads appeared on Friday, March 10 in the *New York Times, Washington Post, USA Today* and *Los Angeles Times,* asserting that a person would have to eat 28,000 pounds of Alar-treated apples a day for 70 years to obtain a dose of the chemical comparable to that given the laboratory mice in the NRDC study. By March 14, the ad had run in several dozen other newspapers (Warren 1989).

Other counter-measures were tried as well. The public relations firm of Hill and Knowlton was hired to counter the negative publicity. Both the EPA and the FDA publicly disputed the report. But even while working with a bigger budget, the apple grower's effort lacked the media impact of the campaign designed by Fenton. "We got rolled," explains Hill and Knowlton's Frank Mankiewicz. "When you're dealing with a nutritionist named Meryl Streep, you haven't got a chance."

Many consumers were not convinced by the rebuttals. By the fall of 1989, the effect of the first apple crop without Alar was being felt, particularly in the Northeast, where the McIntosh apple, a variety particularly susceptible to early dropping, was down more than a million bushels, forcing some growers out of the apple business. Two years later, one Colorado legislator would introduce a bill in the Colorado House of Representatives that would make it a crime to disseminate "false information . . . which casts doubts on the safety of any perishable agricultural food product" (Goodman 1991). Years later in the fall 1996 issues of *Columbia Journalism Review,* the controversy still brewed with claims that the scare was for real and a long letter to the editor in the following issue from Whelan stating the industry's position once again.

When questioned in 1989 about his tactics, Fenton says that the methods differed only slightly from the marketing campaigns of the corporations that are polluting the environment with their products. "These corporations spend millions on their campaigns and when a small group attempts to use the same methods, they get criticized" (Fenton 1989). Clayton Yeutter, agriculture secretary at the time of the incident, is among those who disagree, calling Fenton's methods "environmental terrorism" (Anthan 1990).

As for the leaked document, Fenton says that the biases of the *Wall Street Journal* are well known and that "they do this type of thing all the time" (Fenton 1989). He refused to share any of the rest of the information in the memo, saying that it was proprietary information belonging to the NRDC. Lorraine Voles, national coordinator of Mothers and Others for Pesticide Limits, the group that secured the services of Streep, echoed the sentiments of Fenton. "I think those tactics (used by Fenton) have to be used. It's like handicapping yourself if you don't do it" (Haddix 1990, 45).

## Micro Issues:

1. Did the techniques used by Fenton appear to be overly aggressive? If so, in what way? From what you know, were the tactics justified by the evidence?
2. Is there an alternate approach that would go beyond the frequently ignored press release yet stop short of creating the widespread consumer concern caused by this campaign?
3. Was the *Wall Street Journal* justified in exposing the confidential memo?
4. Is a representative such as Whelan obligated to inform interviewers of the funding for her organization even if she is not asked?

## Middle-range Issues:

1. The headline of the *Wall Street Journal* op-ed piece claimed that Fenton's organization executed the scare. From what you have read in this case study, is that correct or is that an overstatement? What statements, if any, in the story above lead you to believe that the scare was executed by Fenton?
2. Fenton's organization managed the Alar story, including timing the breaking of the story, making spokespersons available for interviews, staging press conferences, and the like. Does that amount of management affect the truthfulness of the story?
3. You are a journalist seeking to write a story about Alar. Of what use are celebrities like Streep and the casts of "L.A. Law" and "thirtysomething" to the story? Do you interview them? Do you accept their expertise on the issue? Is the fact that celebrities are being used to spread the message a story in itself?
4. Of the media that ran the story, is there a difference in the amount of fact checking that should be done by the staff of "60 Minutes" and the staff of "Oprah" before airing a story about the apples? Are the editorial expectations in a story such as this different for *Redbook* than for *Newsweek?*
5. Were the media guilty of hyping the Alar story since it contained the pathos and good visuals required for airing or publication?

## Macro Issues:

1. If you were in the position of helping to publicize an issue like the Alar issue, how important would it be to you to be on the side you perceive to be correct? Could you, for instance, take the apple grower's money in this case? Could you take the NRDC's money? If the issue were abortion, could you help either side? Gun control? Toxic-waste disposal?
2. Before issuing a news release, should the public relations practitioner weigh the consequences, such as the farmers' going bankrupt? In light of the government's assurances that the apples were safe, was the action of Fenton Communications morally justifiable?
3. What should be the relationship between public relations and the news? Should public relations press releases be identified as such? Should they always be rewritten if they are used? Should the facts be checked by the media?
4. Should news be labeled as originating from a point of view? Could the average reader or viewer have known the individual biases of the NRDC? Of Whelan? Of Streep?

## CASE III-C
## A Case of Need
DENI ELLIOTT
*University of Montana*

The call came to Portland, Maine, newsrooms on a snowy, quiet day in early February. Norma Lynn Peterson, a seven-year-old from the neighboring town of Windham, had end-stage liver disease. A candidate for a liver transplant at the well-respected Pittsburgh transplant center, Norma, her family, and supporters had little to do but wait and hope that a suitable donor organ would become available in the year that doctors said Norma otherwise had to live.

It soon became obvious that while they waited and hoped, the family would also need to raise money: the associated costs of Norma's illness were a tremendously hard burden for the working-class Peterson family, even with health insurance that would cover 80 percent of the $200,000 surgery. That's what the phone call was all about. A Valentine's Day potluck dinner had been planned to raise money for Norma Lynn. The volunteer fund-raiser who contacted news media did so because he thought that the community's willingness to help Norma Lynn might make a good news story.

Fund-raising activities on behalf of Norma Lynn continued throughout the spring. In mid-July, the long-anticipated call from Pittsburgh came. A liver had been found. Norma and her parents flew from Portland to Pittsburgh in a private ambulance airplane, paid for by donations.

By this time, thanks to local news coverage, almost everybody in the state knew about Norma Lynn. The Petersons' willingness to cooperate with news media allowed readers and viewers an inside look at the medical crisis and how one family coped. Norma Lynn's dark eyes, long hair, delicate ivory skin, and sweet, shy nature quickly won the hearts of reporters and opened the pocketbooks of those who got to know of her plight.

More than $100,000 in cash donations had been placed in the Norma Lynn Fund. Local merchants had donated items to the Peterson family, including a video camera and a puppy. Well-wishers showered the little girl with cards, gifts, and testimonies to her bravery.

Norma Lynn's transplant surgery was successful. Two serious complications arose in the first few weeks after surgery: she required a second operation to repair a leaking bile duct and then developed a liver virus from which she recovered.

It was a surprise to the Petersons when the doctors announced a month after the transplant that Norma was ready to return home. The air-ambulance company that had transported Norma to Pittsburgh for her surgery was caught by surprise. The costs of the trip home had not yet been covered. A local business had donated a private jet and pilot. The wages of a nurse to accompany Norma on the flight had been donated as well. But the jet's fuel costs would run about nine hundred dollars.

The manager of the air-ambulance company had an idea. Local television news had certainly been getting a lot out of the Norma Lynn story; they should be willing to give something back. He called the first of the three network affiliates, picking the one that he thought had done the best job on Norma Lynn, and asked for three hundred dollars, one-third of the amount he needed. The news director was willing to make the donation, but only if the station could send a reporter and photographer on the plane in exchange. It turned out that there were two empty seats on the plane. The station could have them, the manager decided, but only if they donated the full nine hundred dollars.

## Micro Issues:

1. Was this story newsworthy?
2. Without media coverage, the Petersons would not have raised more than a few thousand dollars. Is there a problem with the Petersons' using local news coverage as a fund-raising tool?
3. How much and what kind of news coverage was appropriate?
   (*a*) Pre-surgery?
   (*b*) During her hospitalization?
   (*c*) Afterwards?
4. Was it acceptable for the address of the Norma Lynn Fund to appear in nightly news stories?
5. Should the news stories have made clear that 80 percent of Norma Lynn's medical costs were covered by insurance? Was it deceptive not to tell the audience how much money her family actually needed to complement insurance coverage?

## Middle-range Issues:

1. How should the news organizations have responded to the air-ambulance company's request for donation? Did the local media owe something to Norma Lynn?
2. The news organization that came up with the nine hundred dollars effectively shut out its competition from riding home from Pittsburgh with Norma Lynn. The competitors complained that the station had bought exclusive news coverage. Did their action constitute buying the news?

## Macro Issues:

1. What criteria should news organizations use in determining whether an individual with medical or financial need is newsworthy?
2. Some doctors complain that media coverage of one individual's wait for an organ donation can result in that individual's getting an organ more quickly than other, sicker patients. Should medical need influence coverage decisions?

3. Should news organizations be concerned about issues of fairness to other families in financial need? Should they provide equal coverage for the next child? And what about the next?
4. When news organizations publicize an individual's financial need, do they owe the audience any reassurances about the worth of the cause or about how the donations will be used?
5. Should news organizations give an accounting of how much money is actually used for the medical crisis and what happens to the remainder?
6. Does it matter if excess funds raised:
   (*a*) Go into a trust fund to offset future expenses?
   (*b*) Go to help other sick children in financial need?
   (*c*) Go toward other non-related expenses, like the purchase of a new car or house?
7. Do news organizations incur a responsibility to tell the audience where their donations are going?
8. Is there a story in the fact that some children die because their families cannot raise the money for catastrophic health care?

## CASE III-D
## Exxon's Whipping Cream on a Pile of Manure
JOANN M. VALENTI
*Brigham Young University*

In March 1989 over 10 million gallons of Alaskan crude oil spilled into Prince William Sound when the Exxon tanker *Valdez* hit a reef. Ultimately, miles of coastline were fouled, thousands of birds, fish and marine mammals died and a legacy to exploiting natural resources was born. It took ten days for the company to run a full page ad, called "An open letter to the public," in 165 daily newspapers plus a handful of major magazines. According to Exxon's New York media relations manager Sara Johnson, the ads, which cost the company $1.8 million, were intended to offer an apology for the environmental disaster. Johnson explained to *St. Petersburg Times* reporter Ken Otterbourg that Exxon wanted the public to know that "we're concerned" and that "we'll be there for the duration."

Few "bought" the apology. Exxon brought media specialists in to field phone calls and sent top executives on the television talk show rounds. The media blitz failed to satisfactorily explain what had happened and what was being done. Buddy Davis' editorial for the *New York Times* Regional Newspaper group in late April typified media and public response:

> "Standard Oil of New Jersey was the granddaddy and is known today as Exxon. Aside from stealing consumers blind as a monopoly in the early years, the company played it awfully cozy with the German Nazis in the 1930s and spent $55 million in attempts to buy the Italian government in the 1960s and 1970s. Otherwise, Exxon seems to have been a fairly decent low-profile citizen until the Exxon *Valdez* crunched into Alaskan shoals last month."

During the height of the crisis, the company released twelve video news releases (VNRs) with stunning aerials of Alaskan scenery and shots of majestic ships. The voice-over exclaims, "It's cruise time in Alaska, and business is booming . . . none of the cruise lines are skipping (the port called Valdez)." The spots offered testimony from tourists not at all unhappy about their Valdez vacations and shots of whales and seals without crude oil on them with the "news" that concerns about the spill "seem to (have) abated."

Exxon public affairs manager Jim Morakis reported to *Technology Review* writer Susan E. Davis that between 27 to 30 million viewers saw at least one of the dozen VNRs with the embedded Exxon messages. Even though sending reporters to Alaska to cover the story ate into tight news budgets, some networks refused to air the Exxon VNRs, among them CNN news producer Eric Scholl.

## Micro Issues:

1. Was the Exxon VNR series intended to inform the public or was it an attempt to deflect attention away from controversy?

2. An estimated 81 million viewers learned how to buy dolphin-safe tuna from a VNR produced by StarKist. What difference does it make when public relations releases environmental or medical news as opposed to military or corporate information?
3. As part of an estimated $11 million PR campaign, citizens for a Free Kuwait spent over $600,000 to produce pro-Kuwait videos for American television networks during the Iraqi occupation and war. Is the amount of money spent to produce a VNR a story? A factor in its use?

## Middle-range Issues:

1. Newspapers have relied on press releases from PR for decades. Has this practice of inter-reliance between print media and PR resulted in reduced credibility for the press? What are the ethical considerations in news media use of public relations releases?
2. PR professionals worry their clients will object to a visible logo or VNR-sponsored ID because viewers will confuse the news release with infomercials. What *is* the difference between a VNR and an infomercial? Who should be responsible for making sure the audience understands different media formats?
3. During presidential elections, television audiences are exposed to VNRs from virtually all of the major candidates. Try to recall what you saw during the 1992 and 1996 campaigns. What effect does it have on the voting process when campaign staffers produce what you see about election contenders?

## Macro Issues:

1. What is the relationship between credibility and ethical behavior?
2. Where is the line between news and propaganda? Does creating a story in-house assure that it is objective? Does accepting a VNR from an interested source assure that it is propaganda?
3. What are the ethics of advocacy in communication?

## CASE III-E
## If You Let Nike Play . . .
RENITA COLEMAN
*University of Missouri—Columbia*

It takes you by surprise. A television commercial without a product. Just a half-dozen or so pre-teen girls of various ethnic backgrounds in a working class playground. With the rhythm and cadence of a song they voice the refrain: "If you let me play; if you let me play sports." The verse goes like this:

*I will like myself more;*
*I will have more self confidence;*
*I will be 60 percent less likely to get breast cancer;*
*I will suffer less depression;*
*I will be more likely to leave a man who beats me;*
*I will be less likely to get pregnant before I want to;*
*I will learn what it means to be strong.*

At the end of 30 seconds, the screen goes black and the familiar Nike logo appears with the slogan: "Just Do It."

Unusual, certainly. Only a few advertisements have departed so radically from standard practice. Benetton with its AIDS patients, comes to mind. Is this advertising designed to sell a product or a company's image? Is this commercial socially responsible or ethically questionable? Is its audience children or their parents? This 30-second commercial is startlingly effective precisely because of its ambiguity. It grabs your attention with its rapid-fire visuals; it makes you sit up and pay attention with its hard-hitting issues; and, it makes you curious to know what this unusual ad is all about. The net effect is that this subtle pitch of a sportswear company becomes all the more memorable.

The Nike "If you let me play" ad makes unique use of the time-honored advertising technique of cognitive dissonance. It knocks the viewer off balance with the incongruous image of pre-teen girls discussing such adult subjects as spouse abuse, breast cancer and depression. It is emotionally and cognitively unsettling to hear children discussing such things because we assume youth equals innocence. We would rather not have to face the fact that many children today are intimately acquainted with such topics. Perhaps a mother or other family member has battled depression or even lost a fight with breast cancer. Or, more unsettling yet, perhaps children have seen daddy hitting mommy.

Even absent first-hand knowledge, children today are subjected to such situations via the news and entertainment media. Who really thinks children have been shielded from the facts of O.J. Simpson's battering of his ex-wife Nicole? And the trend is for family secrets to be less concealed than they once were. Children today are not the innocents of the past or the innocents we would still like to believe they are. This ad is an in-your-face testimonial to that. And true to the formula of ads that use cognitive dissonance as a tool, Nike proposes a solution to restore the viewer to balance: let me play, and inferentially, let me do so in Nike apparel.

"Our goal wasn't to be alarmist, just direct," said Andrea Bonner, who helped create the "If you let me play" commercial. "We just wanted to be real." She acknowledges that this issue-oriented commercial is "a different kind of animal for Nike." In fact, she says, it "borders on being a *pro bono* message."

Nike has been questioned on ethical grounds in the past. In 1994, a commercial featuring basketball's bad boy, Dennis Rodman, was criticized for reinforcing an ends-justifies-the-means mentality when Santa Claus grants Rodman his Christmas wish of expensive new shoes despite his unsportsmanlike conduct. African-Americans criticized the company for using Rodman as a role model when other, more positive African-American role models were available. Nike has similarly been criticized for advertising its shoes on billboards located in poor, inner-city neighborhoods where parents can ill-afford $100 shoes.

The company was even accused of helping to cause thefts and violence in ghettos where the apparent reason for the assault was the victim's expensive sports shoes. The children in the "If you let me play" ad appear to be from working-class families. While it is rather ambiguous, the appearance of the playground and the children's clothes provide visual cues to suggest this. Perhaps Nike tried to avoid being accused of marketing expensive products to socio-economic groups who either cannot afford them, or who would do without necessities in order to purchase them.

The subject of target markets also brings up the issue of advertising to children. The poor and elderly as well as the young have often been singled out as audiences deserving special sensitivity and responsibility from advertisers. Because they are potentially more vulnerable, less experienced and adept at sorting out product claims, and more subject to peer pressures and advertising's influence, children's advertising must assume a greater sensitivity than advertising to the general population, an audience considered to be active and autonomous. Research by Carol Gilligan and others has shown that adolescence is a particularly formative time for a girl's self-esteem. Adolescence is a time for issues of attachment for girls, and identity formation takes place within relationships. There is special vulnerability for girls in finding a way of caring for themselves while maintaining connections to others. The topics in this commercial are all of a connective nature—pregnancy involves a male and a child; domestic violence involves a relationship with a male, at least; strength, self-confidence, depression and even breast cancer, with its strong ties to feminine issues, are all issues of self-caring and identity formation.

Another controversy centers on the source of the statistics in the ad. In "If you let me play," Nike claims it got its statistical information from the Women's Sports Foundation (WSF), a non-profit organization that collects studies regarding athletics and women and girls. However, a representative of the WSF said the Foundation would never knowingly provide its research to Nike because it is sponsored by Reebok, Nike's chief competitor. The advertising agency that created the commercial also claims that the information was obtained from WSF.

## Micro Issues:

1. Is Nike guilty of using "scare tactics" to sell its clothing line?
2. Nike claims the message borders on being a *pro bono* message, in other words a free public service ad for a worthy cause. Critique that claim.

## Middle-range Issues:

1. Would the same commercial have been any less arresting had it featured adult women? Would it be less effective?
2. Nike never produced a similar ad for boys although there are documented health and social benefits for males who play sports. Why do you think there was not an "If you let me play" ad made featuring young boys?

## Macro Issues:

1. The Women's Sports Foundation gets its research data from a variety of academic and not-for-profit sources. Given its goals of promoting fitness through sports for women, why would it consider the statistics in the Nike ad to be proprietary information? Shouldn't they be pleased at the larger audience generated by the Nike ad?
2. Obviously many girls who do not play sports do not suffer any of the maladies mentioned in the ad later in life either. Is Nike guilty of portraying women as more vulnerable than they are in order to sell clothing?

## CASE III-F
## A Sobering Dilemma
BEVERLY HORVIT
*University of Missouri—Columbia*

The music of "Pomp and Circumstance" plays as puppies cross the stage at their graduation from obedience school. One dog, the class valedictorian, carries a bottle of Canadian Crown Royal whiskey. The images are part of a Seagram's television commercial that first aired June 9, 1996, on a television station in Corpus Christi, Texas. The airings continued for a month. By running the ad, Seagram's ended an almost 50-year-old, self-imposed ban on the television advertising of distilled spirits. Although beer and wine commercials are routinely seen on television, ads for "hard" liquor had not been visible since 1948.

Why break the ban in the summer of 1996? For one thing, there is the opportunity to enlarge Seagram's stake in the $98 billion per year alcoholic beverage market. But more specifically, Seagram's spokeswoman Bevin Gove points to the changing times and the changing media landscape. She said the distinctions between types of media are not as clear-cut as in the past, making old policies that allow print but not broadcast ads outdated. "The industry code is outdated," Gove told *USA Today*.

Not mentioned by Gove is the fact that sales of distilled spirits are down. While beer consumption has been flat for years, liquor sales have fallen 32 percent since 1979. Seagram's chose Texas as a test because the Crown Royal brand has been selling well there, with sales doubling since 1980.

Seagram's actions were almost immediately decried by consumer groups, the president of the United States and a bipartisan group of lawmakers. The same week the commercial first appeared, U.S. Representative Joe Kennedy introduced legislation to ban television and radio advertising of hard liquor.

For the television station and Seagram's, the decision to run the ad was largely fueled by the profit motive and justified with free speech concerns. T. Frank Smith, owner of KRIS-TV, the independent NBC affiliate in Corpus Christi, was eager to line up advertising for hard liquor and discussed the ad with Seagram's for months. For her part, Gove said the company believes the distiller has the same right to "responsibly access electronic advertising" as do beer and wine manufacturers. She claims Seagram's products are at a competitive disadvantage compared to beer and wine when they are not advertised on television.

From the perspective of Seagram's and the Distilled Spirits Council of the United States (DISCUS), there is not a legitimate reason why beer and wine makers should enjoy free speech protection, while the manufacturers of distilled spirits do not. Twelve ounces of beer, five ounces of table wine and one and one-half ounces of distilled spirits (the council's preferred term) in a mixed drink contain the same amount of alcohol. "There is no beverage of moderation, only a practice of moderation. It's not what you drink that's important, but how much you drink that counts," the council says. Similarly, DISCUS and other groups say the notion of "hard" liquor is a misnomer, pointing out that beer and wine can lead to drunkenness just as easily as distilled spirits.

Walter Wurfel, a spokesperson for the National Association of Broadcasters (NAB), argues that because "alcoholic beverages are a legal product, there should be a legal right under the First Amendment to advertise them." However, Wurfel adds the NAB has cautioned individual broadcast stations that they should consider the impact of such advertising within their own communities.

The problem with the advertising, Rep. Kennedy says, is that it comes "at a time when our society is trying to curb the impact of alcohol abuse." According to Mothers Against Drunk Driving, an estimated 17,461 people were killed in alcohol-related crashes in 1993 and those deaths accounted for 43.5 percent of all the traffic fatalities that year. In addition, about 24 percent of the 15- to 20-year-old drivers killed in traffic accidents had a blood alcohol content of .10 or higher, above the legal minimum for driving in every state. Alcohol abuse takes other tolls as well. According to the National Council on Alcoholism and Drug Dependence, alcohol contributes to 100,000 deaths annually, making it the third leading cause of preventable mortality in the United States after tobacco and diet/activity patterns.

Seagram's and KRIS-TV's Smith counter that they are acting responsibly. Seagram's, Gove said, has a 60-year history of promoting the responsible use of alcohol, including a slogan advising moderation in drinking and programs to encourage parents to talk to their children about alcohol. Smith said his station airs frequent public service announcements, including one featuring the station's news anchor, that warn viewers against drunken driving. Smith estimates the station runs the spots about 40 times a month.

DISCUS reports that the number of teenage drunken drivers involved in fatal accidents is down 62 percent since 1982; alcohol-related traffic fatalities in 1993 were 21 percent below the 1990 level; and drunken driving fatalities for all age groups have declined 31 percent since 1982.

Those most critical of the Seagram's ad say it targets the young. The commercial, said George Hacker of the Center for Science in the Public Interest, "features the gracious and familiar strains of music that millions of teenagers will hear during the high school graduation ceremonies." Hacker argues that teens "already get an overdose of ads on television teaching them that drinking beer is fun, that it's cool, that it will help them score with girls. The last thing they need is another avalanche of powerful electronic messages assuring them that liquor will make them successful—even valedictorians—and that drinking should be a part of their lives." KRIS-TV owner Smith said he was not worried about children seeing the ad, because "a kid can't buy liquor. A kid can't even go into a liquor store."

Despite the national publicity, Smith reports receiving only about 75 letters, more than half from a local church, and fewer than 20 phone calls. In addition, the station conducted an unscientific poll asking viewers to call in to say whether they opposed or approved of the ad. More than 6,000 people called in, 70 percent of whom said they had no problem with the commercial and 30 percent of whom were opposed to it, Smith said. While the poll was not scientific, Smith believes it's a pretty accurate reflection of the community's feelings.

By the fall of 1996, the FCC announced that it was going to look into the Seagram's ads. FCC Chairman Reed Hundt told *USA Today* that his own "informal poll" had produced a "100 percent opinion" that the public did not want to see liquor ads on television. "If they (Seagram's) won't play by the unwritten rule, do we need a written rule?" Hundt asked in an interview with the Associated Press.

On the same day Hundt was conducting his interviews, in a move sure to heat up the regulatory rhetoric, Seagram's was announcing its upcoming holiday-themed radio and television ads for the 1996 Christmas season.

## Micro Issues:

1. Should the makers of distilled spirits be subject to different standards for broadcast advertising than the makers of wine and beer? If so, on what basis?
2. Does the ad described seem to target children, as Hacker claims? Does the ad imply that drinking Seagram's will make one more academically successful?
3. Gove claims that Seagram's started to advertise now because the distinction between print and electronic ad policies no longer makes sense. Do you agree or disagree with that?
4. Does Gove's justification lose any of its validity in light of the shrinking sales of "hard" liquor?

## Middle-range Issues:

1. If the community survey had revealed that 70 percent of those responding wanted the commercial off the air, what should Smith do?
2. Would it make any difference in the controversy if the ads had been moved to the late evening hours where presumably fewer children could see them?
3. What should be the role of the FCC in policing or prohibiting liquor ads on television?
4. You are the copywriter at the agency that is developing a similar campaign. Do you agree to work on the campaign? What can the agency demand of you as an employee?

## Macro Issues:

1. Should station policy be dictated or even backed up by non-scientific polls?
2. The makers of distilled spirits have a strong case for free speech. However, the opponents of advertising of alcohol claim that it contributes as greatly to our society's problems. Does a product lose First Amendment rights because it has a potential to harm. What other products can you draw a parallel to besides alcohol?

# CHAPTER IV

## *Loyalty: Choosing between Competing Allegiances*

**By the end of the chapter, the student should:**

- **Understand why the articulation of loyalties is important in professional ethics.**
- **Know Royce's definition of loyalty and at least one of the major problems with that conceptualization.**
- **Understand how journalists' role in society provides them with an additional set of loyalties to consider.**
- **Be familiar with and able to use the Potter Box as a justification model for ethical decision making.**

### Loyalty as Part of the Social Contract

Decisions involving loyalty occur routinely for media professionals. When journalists make a decision to air or not to air a story, they have decided to whom they will be loyal. When recording executives cancel the contract of a controversial artist to avoid a boycott, they have chosen a loyalty. Most ethical decisions come down to the question "To whom (or what) will I be loyal?"

The original discussion of loyalty in Western culture was written by Plato in *The Trial and Death of Socrates* (see Russell 1967). In Plato's *Apology,* Socrates bases his defense against the charges brought against him on his unwavering adherence, or loyalty, to divinely inspired truth. When asked by his accusers if he will stop teaching philosophy, Socrates responds:

> Men of Athens, I honor and love you: but I shall obey God rather than you, and while I have life and strength I shall never cease from the practice and teaching of philosophy, exhorting any one whom I meet. . . . For know that this is the command of God; and I believe that no greater good has ever happened in the State than my service to the God.

While the word *loyalty* is not present in English translations of the *Phaedo,* the overall tone of the work is a tribute to loyalty, in this case a willingness to die for a cause. This willingness to make one of the ultimate sacrifices has troubled those who wrote about loyalty in subsequent centuries.

Social-contract theorist Thomas Hobbes was the first major Western philosopher to assert that God did not have to be the focus of loyalty and that people could have competing loyalties. In his historic work on the theory of the state, *The Leviathan,* Hobbes asserted loyalty is a social act, that it is the core of the agreement that allows people to form the social contract that is the basis of political society. However, Hobbes, unlike Socrates, admitted loyalty has its limits. Loyalty to the ruler stops when continued loyalty would result in a subject's death. One has a higher loyalty to self-preservation in this instance than to the ruler. The turmoil surrounding U.S. involvement in the Vietnam War is a classic example of this type of conflict of loyalties.

Hobbes made two central alterations in the Socratic notion of loyalty. First, he emphasized its social nature. Second, he acknowledged that people could have more than one loyalty and might, at certain times, be forced to choose among them. These two elements, in addition to the original insights of Socrates and Plato, provide the basis of contemporary philosophical discussion of the concept.

## The Contributions of Josiah Royce

American theologian Josiah Royce, who taught at Harvard in the early 1900s, wrote more about loyalty than any other modern ethicist. Royce believed that loyalty could become the single guiding ethical principle. In *The Philosophy of Loyalty* (Royce 1908), he wrote, "My theory is that the whole moral law is implicitly bound up in one precept: 'Be loyal.' " Royce defined loyalty as a social act: "The willing and practical and thoroughgoing devotion of a person to a cause." Royce would be critical, therefore, of the stereotypical journalist found in Ben Hecht's "The Front Page"—a cynic of everything and everyone, a professional who gets a story at all costs and whose only loyalty is to himself. In Royce's view, loyalty is an act of choice. A loyal person, Royce asserted, does not have "Hamlet's option"—or the leisure not to decide. For in the act of not deciding, that person had essentially cast his loyalty.

Loyalty also promotes self-realization. Royce spent much of his academic career fascinated with what were then the new insights of Freudian psychology, and he viewed loyalty in a psychological and developmental light. As a person continued to exercise loyalty, Royce believed, he or she would develop habits of character that would result in systematic ethical action. Like other aspects of moral development, loyalty can be learned and honed, Royce believed.

Loyalty—and the ability to be loyal—was a virtue, one that could be exercised and strengthened by continuing devotion to a cause. Yet loyalty as an ethical guide has problems. First, loyalty, incompletely conceived, can be bias or prejudice cloaked in misleading language. Second, few people maintain merely a single loyalty, and if loyalty is to become a guiding ethical principle, then we need to develop a way to help distinguish among competing loyalties. Third, with the advent of a mass society, the entire concept of face-to-face loyalty has lost much of its power to compel ethical action. Finally, one of the most troubling questions arising from the concept of loyalty is whether an ethical person can be loyal to an unethical cause, for example racism or genocide.

However, Royce suggested a way to determine whether a specific cause was worthy of loyalty. A worthy cause should harmonize with the loyalties of others within the community, which can be defined a number of ways. For instance, the loyalty of the journalist should be in harmony with the loyalty of the reader. The loyalty of the advertising agency should not conflict either with the loyalty of its client or the consumer. Surely, loyalty to concept of free and unfettered political discussion—the basis of modern democracy and journalism—would meet Royce's test of loyalty.

A true understanding of loyalty allows people to reject unethical causes, Royce believed. The true problem was not a poor choice of loyalties but failure to adhere to chosen loyalties. "The ills of mankind are largely the consequence of disloyalty rather than wrong-headed loyalty" (Royce 1908). The cause that is capable of sustaining loyalty, Royce noted, has a "super-individual" quality, one that is apparent when people become part of a community. A spirit of democratic cooperation is needed for Royce's view of loyalty to result in ethical action. For instance, advertising agencies are demonstrating an ethical loyalty when they view their role as providing needed information for intelligent consumer choice, but more often they opt for loyalty to the bottom line.

Royce's thought has been criticized on a number of grounds. First, some philosophers assert that Royce's concept of loyalty is simplistic and that the adoption of loyalty as a moral principle may lead to allegiance to troubling causes. For instance, the advertising copywriter who scripts distorted television spots about an opponent in the belief that she must get her candidate elected is demonstrating a troubling allegiance to a politician over the democratic process. Similarly, a reporter who must get the story first, regardless of its completeness or accuracy, would be demonstrating a misplaced loyalty to the professional ideal of the scoop.

Second, others have noted that Royce provides no way to balance among conflicting loyalties other than his assertion that loyalty to a particular cause should evoke a similar response in others. Who the others are, in this case, becomes an important question. The executive producer who relegates all but the most important foreign news to the end of the broadcast because Americans aren't interested in hearing about activities in other nations may have an excessively narrow definition of who the others are the viewers are concerned about.

Third, it is unclear how Royce's ethical thinking would balance majority notions against minority views. Royce's notion of loyalty could inspire adherence to the status quo or strict majority rule. For instance, advertisements that stereotype groups of people despite evidence to the contrary help perpetuate incorrect images. The ads work because they appeal to the majority, but by stereotyping they have crowded out more accurate impressions.

Yet despite these criticisms, Royce's thought has much to recommend it. First, Royce speaks to the development of ethical habits, something most modern ethical theorists believe is necessary for continuing ethical behavior. Second, Royce reminds us that the basis of loyalty is social, and loyalty requires we put others on an equal footing with ourselves. In this sense, his view of ethics is not a purely rational one, but one that is founded in a concept of relationships. Most important, however, is the overriding message of Royce's work: *when making ethical choices, it is important to consider what your loyalties are and how you arrived at those loyalties.* We believe this is particularly pertinent when people are acting in a professional role in a society which has given that profession both rights and responsibilities.

## Journalism as a Profession

Loyalty is not a fixed point but a range within a continuum. In *Loyalty: An Essay on the Morality of Relationships,* George Fletcher identifies two types of loyalty. The first is minimal loyalty: "do not betray me." The second is maximum loyalty: "be one with me." Between these two poles is a range of possibilities for allegiance and for corresponding media behavior. The location on the continuum for *Spy* magazine will differ from that of the *Nation* magazine.

One of the problems that the modern news media face is that a large percentage of the American public subscribes to the notion that if the media are not maximally loyal—i.e., be one with government, the military, etc.—then they are traitorous. The public believes this mainly because big institutions assert it is true. The media have been called disloyal by more than one politician on the election trail, often for no greater sin than fulfilling the watchdog role.

Loyalty can be linked to one's role. A role is a capacity in which we act toward others. It provides others with information about how we will act in a structured situation. Some roles are occupationally defined—account executive, screenwriter, editor. Others are not: mother, spouse, daughter. We all play multiple roles, and they help us sort out situations and know what to expect from others.

When the role you assume is a professional one, you add ethical responsibilities. Philosophers claim that "To belong to a profession is traditionally to be held to certain standards of conduct that go beyond the norm for others" (Lebacqz 1985, 32), and journalism qualifies as one of those professions with a higher expected norm of conduct.

However, not all journalists agree in practice. Hodges (1986) makes the distinction in this manner. When asked what she does for a living, one journalist says, "I am a journalist" while another says, "I work for the *Gazette.*" Hodges claims that the first speaker is a journalist who recognizes her responsibility as a professional while the latter merely acknowledges her loyalty to a paycheck. The first would be expected to be loyal to societal expectations of a journalist, the second may or may not.

Journalists and their employers have debated whether journalism should be considered a profession. For some, the concept of professionalism itself is not inherently positive. Advocates of professionalism assert that professionalism among journalists will provide them with greater autonomy, prestige, and financial rewards. Critics see the process of professionalization as one that distances readers and viewers from the institutions that journalists often represent.

Despite these debates, we intuitively sense that journalists have two central responsibilities that are distinct because of the role journalists play in modern society. First, they have a greater responsibility to tell the truth than most professions. Second, journalists also seem to carry a somewhat greater obligation to foster political activity than the average person.

Philosophers note that while specific ethical dilemmas are transitory, roles endure. Role expectations carry over from one situation to another. Most of the time, loyalty to the profession means loyalty to the *ideals* of the profession. To Aristotle, loyalty to a profession also would mean being loyal to and maintaining high professional standards. The Aristotelian notion of virtue means being the best television producer or advertising executive you can be in the belief that you are being loyal to the profession and its abstract ideals.

## Conflicting Loyalties

As the foregoing discussion indicates, we are no longer merely talking about a single loyalty. We live in an age of layers of loyalties, creating added problems and complications.

Sorting through competing personal and professional loyalties can be difficult, particularly when loyalties in one role appear to conflict with the loyalties of another. However, those concerned with professional roles and the loyalties they generate have done some thinking about this issue. We have adapted one such frame-

*Ed Stein. Reprinted courtesy of the Rocky Mountain News.*

work from William F. May who outlined these layers of loyalties for college professors. We suggest a similar approach for those who work in the media.

1. Loyalties arising from shared humanity:
   —demonstrate respect for each person as an individual;
   —communicate honestly and truthfully with all persons;
   —build a fair and compassionate social and cultural environment that promotes the common good;
2. Loyalties arising from professional practice:
   —fulfill the informational and entertainment mission of the media;
   —understand your audience's needs;
   —strive to enhance professional development of self and others;
   —avoid the abuse of power and position;
   —conduct professional activities in ways that uphold or surpass the ideals of virtue and competence;
3. Loyalties arising from employment:
   —keep agreements and promises, operate within the framework of the law, extend due process to all persons;
   —do not squander your organization's resources or your public trust;
   —promote compassionate and humane professional relationships;
   —foster policies that build a community of ethnic, gender and socioeconomic diversity;
   —promote the right of all to be heard;
4. Loyalties arising from the media's role in public life:
   —serve as examples of open institutions where truth is required;
   —foster open discussion and debate;
   —interpret your professional actions to readers and viewers;
   —serve as a voice for the voiceless;
   —serve as a mirror of society.

The problem of conflicting loyalties is evident in the media employment reality of the late twentieth century. Most media practitioners work for a corporation. They owe at least some loyalty to their corporate employers. However, such loyalty is tenuous because it seldom involves a face-to-face relationship. Modern corporations often demand employee loyalty but are much less willing to tell employees their corporate loyalties or responsibilities. These mutually understood promises are essential to corporate loyalty, where the fear is that one's allegiance to the organization will advance the interest of the organization without reciprocal loyalty to the employee.

In the final analysis, most ethical decisions are not about loyalties to corporations or abstract concepts such as freedom of the press. They are about how you treat the subject of your interview or the consumer of your advertising. An element that is essential in such ethical decisions is the notion of *reciprocity*. Simply articulated, reciprocity requires that loyalty should not work against the interest of either party.

Even in an era of sometimes shifting loyalties, there are some loyalties that should only be most reluctantly abandoned. We recommend you give further consideration to two of them: loyalty to humanity and loyalty to truth. *Virtually no situation in media ethics calls for inhumane treatment or withholding the truth.* Maybe you can think of other loyalties which you would rarely, if ever, break. Even if you can't devise a list of every conceivable conflict of loyalties, knowing where your ultimate loyalties lie isn't a bad place to start.

## The Potter Box

In the first chapter, we introduced you to an ethical decision-making model developed by Sissela Bok, one that could help you make an ethical choice. In this chapter, we would like to introduce you to a second decision-making model, one that incorporates articulation of loyalties into the reasoning process.

The model was developed by Harvard theologian Ralph Potter and is called the Potter Box. Its initial use requires that you go through four steps to arrive at an ethical judgment. The case below will be used to help familiarize you with the model.

> You are the assistant city editor for a newspaper of about thirty thousand circulation in a western city of about eighty thousand. Your police reporter regularly reports on sexual assaults in the community.
>
> While the newspaper has a policy of not revealing the names of rape victims, it does routinely report where such assaults occurred, the circumstances surrounding the attack, and a description of the assailant, if police can provide it.
>
> Tonight the police reporter is preparing to write a story about a rape that occurred in the early morning hours yesterday on the roof of the downtown bus station.
>
> Police report that the young woman who was raped went willingly to the roof of the bus station with her attacker. Although she is twenty-five, she lives in a group home for the educable mentally handicapped in the city. She is one of seven women living in the facility.
>
> She could not describe her assailant, and police have no suspects.
>
> Your reporter asks you for advice about how much detail, and what detail, he should include in the story.

The Potter Box has four steps (see fig. 4.1) that should be taken in order. They are (1) understanding the facts, (2) outlining the values inherent in the decision, (3) applying relevant philosophical principles, and (4) articulating a loyalty.

---

**Figure 4.1**
*The four steps of the Potter Box.*

| Facts | Loyalties |
|:---:|:---:|
| Values | Principles |

Printed on the previous page is a graphic of the Potter Box. You proceed through it in a counterclockwise fashion, beginning with the factual situation. We will examine each step individually.

**Step One:** Understanding the facts of the case. In the scenario, the facts are straightforward. You, the newspaper editor, have the information. Your ethical choice rests with how much of it you are going to print.

**Step Two:** Outlining values. *Values* is a much abused word in modern English. People can value everything from their loved ones to making fashion statements. In ethics, however, the word *values* takes on a more precise meaning. In this sense, when you value something—an idea or a principle—it means you are willing to give up other things for it. If, as a journalist, you value truth above all things, then you must sometimes be willing to give up privacy in favor of it. In the foregoing case, such a value system would mean that you would print every detail, because you value truth, and would risk invading the privacy of a person who is in some important ways unable to defend herself. If, as a journalist, you value both truth and privacy, then you may be willing to give up some truth, the printing of every detail, to attempt to preserve the victim's privacy.

Truth and privacy are lofty ideals, and an important element of using the Potter Box is to be honest about what you really do value. Most of us value keeping our jobs; journalists often value getting the story first. A forthright articulation of *all* of the values wrapped up in any particular ethical situation will help you see more clearly the choices that you face and the potential compromises you may or may not have to make.

**Step Three:** Application of philosophical principles. Once you have decided what you value, you need then to apply the philosophical principles outlined in the first chapter. For example, in the above scenario, a utilitarian might argue that the greatest good is served by printing a story that alerts the community to the fact that some creep who rapes women who cannot defend themselves mentally or physically is still out there. Ross would argue that a journalist has duties both to the readers and to the victim and they must be weighed before making a decision.

Aristotle's golden mean would counsel a middle ground that balances printing every detail against printing no story at all. Kant would suggest that the maxim of protecting someone who cannot protect herself is a maxim that could be universalized, making a decision to omit some information justifiable.

In this case, application of several ethical principles leads to the same general conclusion: the newspaper should print some story, but not one that inadvertently reveals the victim's identity or that makes her out to be hopelessly naive in her trust of strangers.

However, you should be alert that while application of different ethical principles in this scenario leads to the same conclusion, other ethical dilemmas may not produce such a happy result. This is precisely why use of the Potter Box demands the application of more than one ethical principle, for if ultimate judgments may vary, you need to be able to explain why.

**Step Four:** Articulation of loyalties. Potter, too, viewed loyalty as a social commitment, and use of the Potter Box will reflect that sort of ethic. In the fourth step, you need to articulate your loyalties—and to decide whether any of them conflict. In the foregoing case, you may have a loyalty to telling the truth, to alerting the community to a potential danger, to protecting of individual privacy, or to doing your job well. Again, in this case, your loyalties are not in severe conflict with one another unless you adopt an absolutist view of the truth the community needs to know. It is possible to counsel your reporter to write a story that tells the truth but omits some facts (for example, the woman's residence in a group home and her mental retardation), alerts the community to a danger (there's a creep out there who police haven't caught), protects the victim's privacy (you won't print her name or where she lives), and allows you to take pride in the job you've done (you've told the truth and not harmed anyone).

However, use of the Potter Box often highlights a conflict between loyalties. In these instances, we refer you to Royce's conception of loyalty itself. What you choose to be loyal to should be capable of inspiring a similar loyalty in others who are both like and unlike you. Journalists are often accused of being "out of touch" with their viewers or readers, and it is at precisely this point of idiosyncratic loyalties that the profession is most highly criticized. Nowhere was that more evident than in the Persian Gulf War when the majority of the press chafed at military restrictions out of a loyalty to freedom of the press, yet the majority of the public didn't care about the sanctions—demonstrating a loyalty to patriotism instead. However, you should be warned that loyalties are not subject to popular opinion, and that you might often hold unpopular loyalties in your particular professional role in society.

Our experience with the Potter Box has been that the vast majority of ethical decisions will allow you to sustain a variety of loyalties. Those decisions that are truly most troubling are ones in which loyalty to one particular cause or principle becomes so dominant in your reasoning process that you are forced to abandon a variety of other loyalties that once seemed quite essential to you.

While you may initially find the stepwise process of the Potter Box somewhat cumbersome, as you learn to use it you will become fluent in its application. You may also discover that you can go through the Potter Box on different levels of abstraction.

The following case study, "The Pimp, the Prostitute, and the Preacher," illustrates how you might use the Potter Box when making an ethical decision.

**The Pimp, the Prostitute, and the Preacher**    You are the court reporter for a daily newspaper in a city of about 150,000 in the Pacific Northwest. About a year ago, the local police force began to crack down on prostitutes working the downtown mall. However, the stated goal of the department's activities was to limit prostitution by arresting pimps—men who make money from prostitutes—rather than by arresting either the prostitutes or their customers. The first of those arrests has now come to trial, and your paper has assigned you to cover the story on a daily basis.

In his opening statement, the local assistant district attorney tells the jury that in order to convict a person of pimping under state law, the state must prove first that money was exchanged for sexual favors, and second, that the money was then given to a third party, the pimp, in return for protection, continued work, etc. During the first two days of the trial, he calls as witnesses four young women, ages fourteen to sixteen, who admit they have worked as prostitutes in the city but are a great deal less clear on the disposal of their earnings. Your story after the first day of the trial capsulizes the police activities, the prosecutor's goals in the case, and the public testimony of two of the young women without disclosing their names.

Near the end of the second day in the trial, the prosecuting attorney begins to call as witnesses men who say they paid one or more of the four young women to have sex with them. Among those who testifies is a middle-aged man who in an almost inaudible response to a question lists his occupation as a minister at one of the more conservative Protestant churches in the city. He admits to having paid one of the young women for sex, and that day's portion of the trial ends soon after his testimony is complete.

About forty-five minutes later you are back in the office to write the story of that day's testimony when the newsroom secretary asks you if you have a few minutes to speak with "Rev. Jones." The name itself doesn't register, but you look up and realize you are facing the minister who testified earlier in the day. In the open newsroom he begs you, often in tears and at one point on his knees, not to print his name in your story. He even holds out a copy of the story you wrote, which appeared on page one of this morning's paper, outlining why the names of the prostitutes had not been used. He asserts that, should a story with his name appear, his marriage will crumble, his children will no longer respect him, and he will lose his job.

After a few minutes and a whispered conversation with the newsroom secretary, the paper's managing editor realizes what is happening and calls you, the minister, and the news editor into his office for a conference. What do you say?

Using the Potter Box, determine how you would report the story above. Your decision will reflect a set of loyalties as well as the values and principles you have chosen. Others may choose differently. A justification model such as Potter's or Bok's, which we introduced in the first chapter, does not eliminate differences. What it will do, ideally, is assure that your choices are grounded in sound ethical reasoning.

The final casting of loyalties will inevitably create another fact for the first quadrant of the box. For instance, in this case, if the decision is to run the name, anything that might subsequently happen to the minister as a result—firing, divorce, even possible suicide—is now an additional "fact" for the first quadrant of the Potter Box. If you decide not to run the minister's name and his parishioners discover his indiscretion anyway, the loss of credibility the newspaper suffers from those who find out the name was withheld is a "fact" to be entered into the first quadrant of the Potter Box also. Considering these additional "facts," (even though they are at present hypothetical) you may want to go through the process again to see if your decision will remain the same.

Now that you've made a concrete decision about revealing the name of the minister based on the facts, we'd like to introduce you to additional facts. After you read them, go through the Potter Box again focusing less on the minister and more on larger issues that affect how the story is written and how it is run in the newspaper. This time, think about the notions of stereotyping, how members of minority communities are portrayed in news reports, and the idea of what exactly we mean by the journalistic watchwords, "objectivity" and "truth."

As the trial continues, it becomes increasingly clear to you that there are other factors at work. In your largely Caucasian community, the only people arrested for pimping have been African-American. All the young women who work as prostitutes are Caucasian, as are the customers who testify. As far as prostitution goes, your Pacific Northwest version is relatively mild. There are no reports of drug use among the prostitutes and their customers, and none of the prostitutes has complained of physical violence. Further, the prosecuting attorney cannot make any of the young women admit under oath that they ever gave the pimps any money. The jury verdict in this case is not guilty.

We recommend that you try using both the Bok and Potter justification models at various times in your ethical decision making. Becoming a competent practitioner of both methods will provide you with greater flexibility and explanatory power. But we also recommend that, regardless of the approach you use, an unvarnished and critical discussion of loyalty becomes part of your ethical dialogue. We believe it will enable you to anticipate situations as well as react to them.

## Suggested Readings

Fletcher, George P. 1993. *Loyalty: An essay on the morality of relationships.* New York: Oxford University Press.

Fuss, Peter. 1965. *The moral philosophy of Josiah Royce.* Cambridge, MA: Harvard University Press.

Hanson, Karen. 1986. "The demands of loyalty." *Idealistic Studies, 16,* pp. 195–204.

Hobbes, Thomas. 1958. *Leviathan.* New York: Bobbs-Merrill.

Oldenquist, Andrew. 1982. Loyalties. *Journal of Philosophy, 79,* pp. 173–193.

Powell, Thomas F. 1967. *Josiah Royce.* New York: Washington Square Press, Inc.

# CHAPTER IV CASES

## CASE IV-A
## The Anchor as Activist
FRED BALES
*University of New Mexico*

Frank Larue, fifty-five, is the leading television anchor in your city, one of the top seventy-five markets in the nation. He has been a prominent journalist in the city for more than twenty-five years and has anchored the 6:00 P.M. and 10:00 P.M. news at each of the three local network affiliates at various times. He is an active Roman Catholic, known for supporting charitable organizations in the community. On the air he promotes good causes, including a segment featuring children awaiting adoption. As a result, most of the children shown find homes, and some are shown again in follow-up reports.

Recently the local chapter of Forces Against Abortion staged a protest outside a downtown clinic where abortions are performed. About fifty of the protestors blocked the entrance to the clinic and were arrested after being asked to move by police. The protestors did not attempt to resist arrest by city police. Larue joined another group of protestors, about thirty-five in number, who maintained a prayer vigil outside the clinic but did not block the building's entrance.

Larue stayed and watched the arrests but took no other action. The event was covered by local newspapers and television stations, and Larue's presence was noted in at least one news account. One newspaper reported incorrectly that Larue left before the arrests.

Larue did not inform his news director or other station officials of his plans to protest, saying that he made his decision to appear outside the clinic at the last minute.

Larue's station receives more than forty calls after the incident. The callers split about evenly over the propriety of Larue's taking part in the protest. Many callers wondered whether the anchorman was there as a reporter or a participant.

At the beginning of the 6:00 and 10:00 P.M. news that evening, Larue's co-anchor reports on the protest, but immediately afterward Larue informs the viewers that he was at the protest "as a matter of personal conscience." He assures viewers that his position on the abortion issue does not affect his coverage of the news and that he has not been involved with the coverage of those events.

In a follow-up newspaper account of the incident, the station's general manager expresses disappointment that his anchor took part in the event. The general manager adds that news personnel should be observers and not participants at events which may become the object of news coverage. He promises to talk with Larue in the next few days about the anchorman's action.

Larue says in the same article that he is unhappy about having to learn about his general manager's comments from a newspaper reporter. Larue maintains that what he did was right and that he did not attend the protest as a journalist. "I don't see how anyone can tell me when and where I can pray, and about what I should pray," he says.

Larue says he has made no decisions about future participation in anti-abortion protests, adding, "I'm a big boy, and I know what the consequences are."

# Micro Issues:

1. Is Larue's presence at the protest newsworthy? Should he have commented on the story at all on his own news show?
2. How does Larue's act affect the station's credibility?
3. Should Larue have warned his news director about plans to be part of the protest?
4. What decision should management make about Larue and his future anti-abortion activities?

# Middle-range Issues:

1. Does Larue's action cause credibility problems for journalists in general, giving ammunition to those who say that journalists have extreme biases that influence their reports?
2. If a journalist unknown to the public—a newspaper copy editor or a production assistant at a television station, for example—took the same action as Larue, should that journalist be admonished in the same manner that Larue was admonished? Why?
3. What differences lie in allowing Larue to vote in elections—where by definition he clearly expresses a political bias and is seen by fellow voters— but not allowing him to spend a few minutes in a silent vigil at the anti-abortion event?
4. As Larue's boss, would you object more strenuously to his belonging to the board of directors of Forces Against Abortion than to his participation in the protest?

# Macro Issues:

1. Do journalists have to give up all community activity and any outward representation of personal views because of their position? If not, then cite some cases where community activity is allowable.
2. What obligations of stewardship does a journalist in Larue's position have that might prompt him or her to lay aside personal inclinations for the good of journalism as a whole?

## CASE IV-B
## The Wonderful World of Junkets
RALPH D. BARNEY
*Brigham Young University*

***Author's note:*** *While the events described below happened in the fall of 1986, similar events have been held since both at the Disney parks and other entertainment attractions, and the appropriate media response to such offers is an on-going issue.*

Tourist attractions located in relative isolation outside major media areas seek effective ways of attracting national media attention that will, in turn, catch the attention of vacationers and conventioneers making their travel plans. It is a public relations/promotional challenge.

Disney World of Orlando, Florida, with a voracious appetite requiring tens of thousands of paid admissions daily, drawing from most of the United States and the rest of the world, assembled a complex package of events and enticements to assure worldwide media attention for its 15th anniversary celebration in October 1986.

The entire Florida tourist industry contributed to create what was believed to be a $7.5 million pot to bring some 10,000 journalists and other media people to Orlando and Disney World. The assumption is that Disney World hoped these 10,000 would report in their media on the three-day event. Such reporting would stir consciousness of Disney World and Florida in the minds of potential customers throughout the United States.

Those invited were offered fully expense-paid trips to Florida to give them access to the event.

Elements on the schedule, beyond the tourist attraction itself, were a "kickoff" of the U.S. Bicentennial, with former Chief Justice of the Supreme Court Warren Burger. Another special guest was a U.S. journalist, Charles Daniloff, who had just been released by the Soviet Union after a detention.

Disney offered three options: Guests could pay all expenses, which many did (mostly from the larger media outlets); they could pay $150 per day to defray some of the total costs; or Disney and participating hotels and airlines would cover all travel, lodging and food costs.

Disney said its offer did not require guests to write anything about the event, but the offers drew media criticism from the beginning. In 1973 the Associated Press Managing Editors association (APME) had adopted a code of ethics calling on journalists to refrain from taking junkets or accepting more than token gifts.

Disney spokesmen also pointed out that fewer than half the media guests were from newsrooms. Most came from other media jobs, such as disc jockeys, promotion departments, advertising and management.

Some tensions surfaced among some reporters who felt a need to distinguish themselves from those who accepted the junket. One said an entrepreneur could have prospered with an "I'm paying my own way" button.

Florida newspapers were critical, most notably the *Orlando Sentinel, Tampa*

*Tribune* and the *St. Petersburg Times*. "Can the reader trust an account by someone who has not paid his own way?" one newspaper asked.

## Micro Issues:

1. What ethic justifies Disney offering the paid trips?
2. Does the Constitution Bicentennial observance and the special guest justify the event as legitimate news? Why were they a part of the event?
3. If your newspaper or broadcast station would not pay for the trip, should you accept the invitation?
4. How does it benefit my audience for me to accept a free trip to a popular tourist destination, and later write about it?
5. Would a Disney World story written with my specific audience in mind be significantly different than a similar story from a generic source (syndicate, wire service, etc.)? How?

## Middle-range Issues:

1. Does whether the audience expects (or cares) that such junkets are paid for by the industry matter?
2. Will the following considerations consciously or subconsciously affect your writing or decision making?
   (a) An obligation to Florida and Disney World.
   (b) A hope that other travel destinations would invite me on similar junkets.
   (c) The fact that so many resources had been spent on the junket (i.e., two or three workdays, other staff filling in my absence, etc.).
   (d) The fact that Florida is a popular vacation destination for my readers, listeners or viewers.
5. What are the virtues of prominently disclosing to my readers that I was the guest (in all respects) of Disney World in the stories I write about the trip? Am I inclined to do that?

## Macro Issues:

1. Does the benefit to your audience from coverage of an event (when the budget would not otherwise permit it) overcome the question of credibility if the sources pay a significant amount?
2. Would acceptance of the junket confirm in my audience's minds a suspicion that "money will buy everything," including time (space) on my television station (newspaper)?
3. Is it more important to have credibility with my audience or to bring information to my audience it would otherwise not have?

## CASE IV-C
## One Person's Tragedy, Another Person's Prize
PHILIP PATTERSON
*Oklahoma Christian University*

July 22, 1975, was a busy day for the *Boston Herald* photographer Stanley Forman. Early in the day he climbed towers and rode elevators all over Boston to get pictures of the city's skyline for a Sunday magazine feature. During that time, he remained on call for other daily assignments.

After returning his film to the newspaper, he was hoping to leave for the day when a call came about a fire in one of the city's older sections of Victorian row houses. The dispatcher mentioned that some people might be trapped in the burning structure. Forman followed the fire engine to the scene and heard an SOS on his scanner ordering a ladder truck to the scene. When he arrived, he followed a hunch and ran down the alley to the back of the row of houses.

There he saw firefighter Bob O'Neil and two people, a two-year-old girl and her nineteen-year-old godmother, on the fifth-floor fire escape. The fireman was calling for help from a fire truck below. The truck raised its aerial ladder to the trio. Forman climbed aboard the bed of the truck to get a better angle of what he anticipated would be a routine rescue.

Meanwhile the WBZ radio traffic helicopter had landed on the next roof, and the pilot was offering to take the child. Though he is visible in most of the photos, he never got a chance to help.

As Fireman O'Neil reached for the ladder of the fire truck below, there was a loud noise—either the sound of a scream or the shriek of metal bending. The fire escape gave way, sending the two victims falling and leaving O'Neil clinging for his life to the ladder. Forman saw it all through his 135 mm lens and took four frames of pictures as the two were falling, before turning away to avoid seeing them hit the ground. The woman, Diana Bryant, broke the fall of the girl, Tiare Jones, who survived. Bryant sustained multiple head and body injuries and died hours later.

O'Neil was rescued shaken by the experience. "Just two more seconds. I would have had them," he said repeatedly. Though Forman took a few more pictures, he was shaking too much to hold the camera still.

Returning to the newspaper, he waited anxiously to see if he had the photos that he thought he had. When it was obvious he did, he stayed to help with some of the prints and went home, exhausted. At 8:00 P.M. he learned that Diana had died. He wondered if the newspaper would still run the photos.

He saw the first morning edition of the paper shortly after 2:00 A.M. and was surprised to see that the key photo in the sequence (the one reprinted here) was printed on page one and measured 11 1/2 inches by 16 1/2 inches—virtually the entire tabloid page. A full sequence of the four photos ran on page three.

By 4:00 A.M., Forman had made a set of prints for the Associated Press, which gave the pictures worldwide distribution that same day. Tearsheets on the photos came from 128 U.S. papers and several foreign countries.

*Stanley J. Forman. Used by permission.*

Within twenty-four hours, action was taken in Boston to improve the inspection and maintenance of all existing fire escapes in the city. Fire-safety groups around the country used the photos to promote similar efforts in other cities.

Numerous awards came as well. The Pulitzer prize committee gave Forman its 1976 news photo prize. The National Press Photographers Association named the photo Picture of the Year. Several other groups, including the Society of Professional Journalists, honored the photo as well. Forman would go on to win the Pulitzer prize again the following year, making him the only photographer to win consecutive Pulitzer prizes for news photography. His awards earned him a Nieman Fellowship at Harvard and lecture engagements around the world.

## Micro Issues:

1. What are the rights of victims of a tragedy such as this one? Should they have protection from being photographed? Being interviewed?
2. Forman's instincts and resourcefulness enabled him to capture photos that no other photographer got. Is the exclusive nature of the photos a factor in whether to run them?
3. Forman said that when he heard that Diana had died, he assumed that the photos would not run. Should the death of one of the girls have affected the treatment of the photos?
4. Did the newspaper sensationalize the photo shown in this case?
5. Do the rights of the other people pictured—O'Neil and the helicopter pilot—enter into the decision of whether to use the photos?

## Middle-range Issues:

1. Is the repair of aging fire escapes a morally justifiable reason for running the photos?
2. Many newspapers outside of Boston ran the photos as well. When the local news peg (the fire) is absent, what is the ethical reasoning for running the photos?

## Macro Issues:

1. Photos such as Forman's are often singled out for awards within the industry. In fact, more than half of all photos that have won the two major prizes in photojournalism have involved tragedy. Should one person's calamity be a photojournalist's good fortune?
2. Are prizes too important to the profession of journalism?

## CASE IV-D
## Keeping Secrets: A Public Relations Dilemma
JAY BLACK
*University of South Florida*

Nancy B. is public affairs officer in Jonesville for the city's largest employer, the National Steel Corporation (NSC). In her middle-management position she has access to her firm's immediate and long-range plans. She has attended a meeting of top management and the company's board of directors at which it was decided that economic conditions have made it absolutely necessary to close down permanently the NSC's Jonesville plant. Factors include a glut of inexpensive, imported steel, which is diminishing the market for NSC's products, plus the government's insistence that the Jonesville plant's forty-year-old blast furnaces and scrubbers are environmental hazards that will cost ten million dollars to remedy.

Jonesville is in a sensitive economic position. It is a town of twenty thousand, located eighty miles south of the state's capital and economic center. There are few job possibilities for Jonesville's unemployed, who would probably have to sell their houses and move. Until a generation ago, the region was primarily agricultural, with only a moderate amount of manufacturing. After World War II, the NSC plant's growth changed the economic balance. The sons of farmers became ironworkers or developed skills in fields allied to the steel mill, and the numerous family farms were consolidated into several larger farms, with far fewer employment possibilities. Today, three thousand people work at the NSC plant. The plant has paid decent wages, and most of its workers own their own homes in or around Jonesville.

Nancy B. is a single parent of two high school children. She owns her own home and has been saving money to send her children to a moderately expensive out-of-state college. She has a sister, Elizabeth, who is the mother of three children and works part time as a real estate salesperson. Elizabeth is very excited about having five "hot" prospects for house sales in town; the deals should go through in about three weeks. Elizabeth's husband, Frank, has been employed by NSC for fifteen years and now has a good-paying job as a shift foreman. Elizabeth and Frank have been very close to Nancy, especially since ten years ago when Nancy's husband died in an industrial accident at the NSC plant.

At the board meeting where the decision was reached to close down the plant, arguments were made that a great deal of harm would come to the company—its reputation, its inability to fill a final set of orders for one last major contract, and the response of the stock market—if word about the impending closure got out. All persons attending the meeting were asked to promise not to say anything to anyone about the closure, nor to act in any way that would set off either rumors or a panic.

Nancy B. was among those who were told by top management that NSC would make every effort to secure equivalent employment for them at another division of the corporation. In her case, her immediate supervisor reminded her of how well the firm had treated her upon her husband's death a decade earlier: she had gone from secretary to executive secretary to public relations assistant to public relations officer in quick succession.

## Micro Issues:

1. Should Nancy protect herself by searching for a job and putting her home on the market?
2. Should she help Frank and Elizabeth by giving them the information?
3. Are her duties or responsibilities in this matter changed in any way by the fact that she is a single parent?

## Middle-range Issues:

1. If Nancy acts out of loyalty to family and tells Elizabeth the news, can Elizabeth then claim the same loyalty to her clients who might need to sell their homes quickly? Do you see any difference in the situations?
2. What should Nancy do if she gets a call from the press attempting to confirm a rumor that the company is closing the plant and leaving?
3. Nancy will be offered a chance at another job and probably will get her relocation costs paid. Frank and Elizabeth, however, will not. Nancy has information that they need, but she badly needs to keep her job. Is she protecting her own comfort at their expense?

## Macro Issues:

1. The request to remain quiet about the move was unilateral—Nancy listened to the request but did not make a promise to abide by it. Does this silence free her to do as she pleases, or is it implied that she understood the request and agreed to abide by it? Can a duty be assumed by failure to object to it?
2. Is it ever justifiable to lie to the media? If so, under what circumstances?
3. If you were in Nancy B.'s position, can you think of arguments that would persuade management to be more forthright with employees? How would the concept of proactive public relations help or hurt in this regard?
4. Are Nancy B.'s loyalty conflicts any more or less severe than those of a newspaper reporter who might "get wind" of the story?

## CASE IV-E
## Standing Behind a Reporter: The CBS/*News Journal* Controversy
JOHN SWEENEY, PUBLIC EDITOR
*Wilmington* News Journal

To most people, Wilmington, Delaware, is a blurred traffic sign on Interstate 95—a non-destination between Baltimore and Philadelphia. Major sporting events are rare. For Delawareans, the annual McDonald's Classic is more than just another stop on the Ladies Professional Golf Association's tour; it's a major spring social event. People wrangle to get tickets. It's a place to meet friends and make a day of it. It's also a place to see and be seen. The golfers are treated like celebrities. The natives proudly enjoy the attention as television broadcasts Wilmington live to the world.

The local newspaper, the *News Journal,* treats the week-long event as more than just another sports show. In addition to actual golf coverage, the paper covers the fashions, the economic ripples, and the show-biz aura of a nationally televised event.

In May 1995, when the tournament was underway, the *News Journal* sent reporter Valerie Helmbreck for a color story, just like other feature writers did every other day of the tournament.

Helmbreck, a former television writer for the paper, decided to talk with the CBS television staff. She knocked on the door of the CBS trailer, explained who she was and climbed inside. The interview started with staff members and then Ben Wright, the CBS golf commentator, joined. The others soon left and Helmbreck and Wright continued their talk.

The interview became international news. Wright was quoted as saying, "Let's face facts here. Lesbians in the sport hurt women's golf." Among his comments: "They're going to a butch game and that furthers the bad image of the game. " He also said, "Women are handicapped by having boobs. It's not easy for them to keep their left arm straight, and that's one of the tenets of the game. Their boobs get in the way."

Before the article ran, the *News Journal*'s editors grilled Helmbreck. When they became convinced of what she had, they assigned other reporters to get reactions from the golfers and the network.

CBS officials were interested in knowing one thing: Did Helmbreck have the comments on tape? When they were told no, they issued a denial. Wright didn't say these things. The reporter made it up.

Wright was summoned to New York for a CBS interrogation and sent back to Wilmington where he issued his own denials, calling the article a pack of lies. Wright was in the broadcast booth for the final day of the tournament. His on-air colleagues expressed their sympathy for the shabby treatment he got. The athletes at first voiced their dismay at the comments but soon backed down. He didn't say it, they said in unison. It was all made up.

Many Delawareans attacked Helmbreck for embarrassing the state. The tour won't come back, was a typical response. Meanwhile, the *News Journal* was deluged with interview requests. The reporter was ordered by her editors not to respond to questions from other reporters. Camera operators from tabloid television shows roamed the paper's parking lot and peered in the cafeteria window, hoping for a sight of Helmbreck. The editor of the story was besieged by radio talk-show hosts from around the country.

Soon, reporters at other newspapers and radio and television stations said they were beginning to hear from New York people that Helmbreck was a lesbian, the paper's primary writer on gay topics, a well-known male hater, and that she had written extensively about lesbians.

None of this was true. But the tenor of the questions changed. It was no longer "What did he say?" It was now, "What's her lifestyle?"

One golf writer told the *News Journal*'s sports editor he had heard Wright say similar things. But Helmbreck was outside the club. Her article was bad for golf, the writer said. CBS continued to issue its denials. She has no proof, its officials said.

Essentially, the issue became: Who do you believe? CBS or a reporter from a nowhere paper.

Eventually, the controversy subsided. Ben Wright went on broadcasting. Valerie Helmbreck went on reporting in Wilmington. Wright's contract was renewed. But Helmbreck still had to answer questions and accusations. She never had the chance to defend herself.

Then in December of the same year, *Sports Illustrated* printed an article claiming that Wright had changed his story. He told friends he had made the remarks, but they were supposed to be off the record. *Sports Illustrated* also produced a witness to the original interview, a tour caddie who had overheard the conversation. He told *Sports Illustrated* that Helmbreck was accurate. She wrote what Wright said, the witness told the magazine.

In his defense, Wright told *Sports Illustrated* that at the time of the interview Helmbreck was going through a divorce and had lost custody of her children. He characterized her as a lesbian. None of the charges were true.

The fire storm erupted again. This time CBS fired Wright.

## Micro Issues:

1. Should the original story have been published?
2. Why is it news?
3. If you were the editor, would you automatically believe the reporter if an interview subject cries foul?
4. Should newspapers answer critics?
5. Was the newspaper right to let the attacks go unanswered?

## Middle-range Issues:

1. Was this story news outside Wilmington?
2. Should reporters always use a tape recorder?
3. In a one-on-one interview, who is believable? How do you know?

## Macro Issues:

1. Would the newspaper's response have differed if it affected circulation or advertising?
2. Big money was at stake here. Advertisers would have been scared off. What was CBS's responsibility?
3. How many stories go unreported because only reporters "inside the club" witness them? Should a reporter remain "outside the club?" If so, what steps can a reporter take to make sure he or she stays outside the club?
4. If a media barrage like this could happen to a reporter, what must it feel like to someone unfamiliar with the ways of the press?
5. Should reporters rethink their behavior in media feeding frenzies?

## CASE IV-F
## She Chose Before Losing the Choice
TOM LYONS
*Sarasota Herald-Tribune*

**Authors' note:** *Columnist Tom Lyons had talked with Lorraine Orr previously for a column on the Hemlock Society, an organization that advocates the right to end one's life. While Florida law allows for persons to enact living wills and "do not resuscitate" orders, Orr wanted the law to go a step further to decriminalize voluntary euthanasia. The 79-year-old Orr called Lyons shortly after suffering a mild stroke—her second—that left her temporarily incapacitated earlier in the week. At that point, she had decided to end her life before she was no longer able to make such choices for herself. What follows is the column he wrote about their conversation.*

"It's time for me to go," Lorraine Orr told me by phone Tuesday morning.

During the 10-minute conversation, she sounded completely rational, as well as crystal clear and calmly committed to her plan.

That plan would have sounded drastic and even crazy to many people and was terribly sinful by the teachings of some religious.

But suicide simply made good sense to Orr.

Given her assessment of her medical condition, Orr's intention was in perfect harmony with her beliefs about life and death. It fit with the right-to-die philosophy that she had been promoting for years, most recently as a Sarasota member of the Hemlock Society.

Her views had been shaped years ago, as she watched her husband die slowly of a cancer that led to removal of both sides of his jaw in multiple surgeries, only to have doctors insist on other operations as death approached—long after he had lost the power to refuse.

Because I had talked to her in 1994, I already knew Orr believed strongly that our laws should be changed. They should allow people to arrange for doctor's help in ending their lives, she had said, when advanced age, medical problems and failing mental abilities made existence on Earth a painful and pointless horror.

But I never expected the phone call I got Tuesday morning.

Orr and her minister called to say that Orr had made preparations to end her life. She planned to start in just a few hours and to be dead that afternoon.

She sounded mentally competent. She even seemed cheerful. She still had a sense of humor, a ready laugh.

I asked her how old she was and she told me "I'll be 80 next month." The irony of her words struck me, and I remarked in all seriousness: "No, it doesn't look like you will."

She just laughed, quietly, and agreed with me.

Orr had already told me that she had gathered drugs that would do the job.

"I've been collecting them one way and another for quite a while," she said. She would not give details for fear of getting other people into trouble.

That was just about the only concern she had about her decision, it seemed. She said she was not afraid of death. If the information she had gotten from the Hemlock Society was correct, she should be able to end her life painlessly, she said.

"This is her morning to self-deliver," said George Exoo, the Unitarian-Universalist minister there with her. He is a Hemlock Society chaplain, and an old friend of Orr's. He had flown down from Pennsylvania to be with her in her last hours.

He said he planned to read poetry to her and pray with her as she died.

Was Orr depressed, hopeless, feeling lost in an uncaring world?

No, not at all, judging by her words and her tone of voice.

"I'm fine," she assured me. She had led a colorful life, and she had friends, though her only close relative was a sister living in Canada. Orr didn't say whether she had called her sister, but did say she certainly didn't want to be a burden to that woman.

Orr said she had been feeling pretty good, actually. She said she would actually prefer to wait on this suicide plan.

If Florida's laws were more tolerant of her wishes, she explained, she wouldn't be taking her life just now.

"I could have had more nice times," she said. "I'm not desperately sick. But I can't take that chance."

She needed to act while she was still mentally and physically able to, she said.

That is what she wanted everyone, especially Florida's legislators, to understand. It shouldn't have to be this way, she said.

In February, while already coping with emphysema, she had had a stroke. It had left her in fairly good shape, considering, despite some memory problems. But she believed that more strokes were probable. She thought it all too likely that sooner or later, she would be paralyzed, seriously brain damaged, maybe unable to talk.

Then, she thought, she might face years of existence in a nursing home bed with no control over her life, and no way out.

No matter what she wrote in her living will, Florida law would not allow a doctor to end her life when that time came. A simple injection can be used to put a beloved pet to death, but people are forced to suffer, she said.

That had to change, she said.

On Monday, she had what she thought was a second stroke. It left her unable to talk for a while. When she could talk again a few hours later, she still couldn't think of some words and names she knew well.

That had passed by Tuesday morning. But she saw the episode as a clear warning. She believed it was time to act, while she still could.

"I couldn't take the chance of being paralyzed and stupid in the head," Orr said.

She made one point very clear: Her minister was there at her request, and he shared her belief in the right to die. But he would not be administering the drugs or doing anything of the sort. Assisting her, they both knew, could mean a manslaughter charge.

"He won't be helping," she emphasized. "He's just sitting with me."

Then she summed it all up in understated words that seemed full of her love for life, as well as optimism about whatever lies ahead.

"It's time for me to go," she said. "I've had a nice time."

Lorraine Orr's minister friend called late Tuesday afternoon and told me it had gone as planned.

Talking through tears at times, Exoo said Orr had eaten a bitter mix of applesauce and drugs, and washed it down with a gulp of whiskey. She died peacefully sometime after a long discussion of her life, and after he had read her Emerson's essay on self-reliance and the 23rd Psalm.

It wasn't the first suicide he had witnessed, but it was the hardest for him, he said. He said he kept reading to her long after she stopped breathing.

Eventually, he left to join mutual friends at their home.

That evening, they all went back to Orr's house and then called 911 to report Orr's suicide.

Sarasota County sheriffs investigators questioned Exoo and the friends at length.

The death, though still under investigation, is listed as a suicide.

Exoo hopes that people will realize that this suicide wasn't the act of someone who was depressed and miserable. He said it was the act of an optimistic, courageous woman who wanted to keep control of her life, and hoped that her final act might help her right-to-death cause.

Lorraine Orr would still be alive, he said, if the law had allowed her to make her own choice about her own death.

## Micro Issues:

1. What were Lyons' options after he received the call?
2. Should the newspaper have run the column? Justify your answer.
3. Are there other stories that should also have been run, such as stories about where to go for help, etc.?
4. Would your answer be different if the caller had been a teenaged girl who advocated the right to end her life? Justify your answer.

## Middle-Range Issues:

1. How would you answer the charge that Lyons was "used" by a reader who wanted her death to generate publicity for her cause?
2. Would you run the column if the caller were committing suicide to protest a cause like abortion?
3. What is the difference, if any, in publicizing this suicide and publicizing a hunger strike? Publicizing a physician-assisted suicide?

## Macro Issues:

1. In a situation like this, where should a reporter's loyalties lie?
2. Can you anticipate other situations similar to this where a reporter might be brought into an ongoing story?
3. Is the ideal reporter a detached observer and recorder of events or a participant? Do the rules change for columnists or commentators?

# CHAPTER V

## Privacy: Looking for Solitude in the Global Village

**By the end of the chapter, the student should:**

- Appreciate the difference between the right to privacy and a need for privacy.
- Be able to distinguish between the law and ethics of privacy.
- Understand the concepts of discretion, right to know, need to know, want to know, and circles of intimacy.
- Understand and be able to apply Rawls's veil of ignorance as a tool for ethical decision making.

## Why Privacy in the New Millenium?

We see it every day on television and read it in the newspaper. Princess Diana and Prince Charles both admit marital infidelity to a worldwide audience. Russian President Boris Yeltsin's medical history becomes a matter of international public discussion. Family members of Nicole Brown Simpson listen as her private life is made a part of the public record in the civil trial of O. J. Simpson. Investigative reporters routinely search data bases for individual driving records, financial records and some medical information using only a readily available social security number as a starting point. Magic Johnson goes on television to announce that he has tested HIV-positive.

A *Newsweek* cover story has proclaimed that voyeurism is the "safe sex" of the 1990s. But it wasn't so safe for a male guest on an episode of the "Jenny Jones" talk show which was never aired. On that show a male guest learned during the taping that he was the subject of adoration from another man. Three days later that same man—who had a history of mental problems—murdered his would-be admirer. Although he was convicted of second degree murder in November of 1996, jurors told news organizations that they held the talk show partially responsible for the crime. In fact, it was a factor in why they returned a verdict on the lesser charge of second degree murder. The unwanted publicity had been a mitigating factor in the killing.

We watch people starve to death in Somalia and Rwanda or emerge distraught from the rubble of Hurricane Andrew or the tragedy of the Oklahoma City bombing. Through it all, we are part voyeur, part normally curious human being and almost certainly confused about where we ought to draw the line of privacy, not only as working journalists but also as readers and viewers.

## The Need for Privacy

Much has been written on the "right to privacy," a right made problematic by the fact that the term never appears in the Constitution. Relatively little, however, has been written about the "need for privacy." Philosopher Louis Hodges has attempted to focus attention on the need for privacy. He says that "without some degree of privacy, civilized life would be impossible" (Hodges 1983). Both a personal and societal need for privacy exists, Hodges claims.

First, we personally need privacy to develop a sense of self. Constance T. Fischer (1980) states that people need privacy to "try out" new poses, future selves, etc. without fear of ridicule by outsiders. If we are to become the person we wish to be, a certain degree of privacy is needed to develop that person apart from observation. Religious cults that seek cognitive control over their members do so in part by depriving the members of any real degree of privacy, restricting both growth and reflection.

Second, society needs privacy as a shield against the power of the state. As the state gains more information about its citizens, it is increasingly easy to influence, manipulate, or control each one.

Precisely because the state is seen as the agency of the citizen's own authority, its independent power is feared, and limitations on the power of the state, such as the Bill of Rights, were established in order to protect private life (Neville 1980). Throughout history, totalitarian regimes have used extensive government surveillance—the near absence of privacy—as a major component of any attempt to create a uniformly subservient citizenry. George Orwell's *1984* is an example of one author's image of government in the absence of privacy.

Therefore, while much of the debate focuses on the *right* to privacy, an equally compelling argument must be made for the *need* for privacy. Privacy is not to be viewed as a luxury or as an option, it is a necessary component of a democracy upon which many of its values such as freedom, individual dignity, and autonomy rest.

Perhaps no issue in contemporary journalistic ethics has been as troubling as invasions of privacy. That trouble exists for at least two specific reasons. First, community and national standards are changing. What was once strictly private, for instance the mention of breast surgery in the newspaper or on television, is not only common but also is credited with saving lives. Second, privacy is both a legal concept in the domain of the courts and an ethical concept debated by philosophers. A confusion over which analysis is appropriate confounds our thinking.

The result is that journalists have been caught between what the law allows and what their consciences will permit. This confusion has led to ethical bungling on a scale that has probably undermined the entire profession's credibility and fed two stereotypical notions: One, that journalists will do anything to get a story, and two, that audiences will willingly consume anything the journalist delivers. These images are not only at odds with reality, but they also make getting and understanding legitimate stories even more difficult.

In this chapter, we will provide you with an overview of the concept of privacy from both the legal and ethical perspective and explain why we believe that ethical reasoning is the more appropriate way to make decisions about privacy. We also will outline two of the continuing tensions inherent in the concept of privacy and explain why journalists are likely to remain caught in them. Finally, we will introduce you to some philosophical concepts of privacy we believe will help you in your ethical reasoning about this evolving issue.

## Legal and Ethical Definitions

The legal notion of privacy began in 1890 with a *Harvard Law Review* article written by lawyers Samuel Warren and Louis D. Brandeis (who eventually became a U.S. Supreme Court justice) calling for a constitutional right to privacy. Today privacy is guarded legally in four distinct ways:

1. Intrusion upon a person's seclusion or solitude, or into private affairs, such as invading one's home or personal papers to get a story;
2. Public disclosure of embarrassing private facts, such as revealing someone's notorious past when it has no bearing on that person's present status;
3. Publicity that places a person in a false light, such as enhancing a subject's biography to sell additional books;
4. Misappropriation of a person's name or likeness for personal advantage, such as using Michael Jackson's likeness to sell Pepsi without his permission.

While the four-part list is straightforward, the court's interpretation of it is not, placing privacy among the least satisfactory areas of Constitutional law. Not only are decisions themselves contradictory, but also some of the concepts themselves are open to question or change. What once might have been an embarrassing, private fact—for example, that an unmarried woman is pregnant—is now commonplace knowledge and, some would argue, fashionable. Information once available for the asking, such as a student's telephone number, is now, closed by a maze of privacy legislation enacted in the 1970s and 1980s.

To further cloud the issue, the claim to privacy is different for different categories of people. Public figures, for example, are subject to a different standard than are others as are "limited" public figures and even "accidental" public figures thrown into the spotlight by chance. Just exactly who the courts will consider a public figure fluctuates. As the newspaper attorney in the film *Absence of Malice* tells the reporter when she asks if the subject of her story could be considered a public figure, "I don't know, madame, they never tell us till it's too late."

When the media invade privacy, the legal remedies occur after the fact. A huge monetary award can make a plaintiff rich, but it cannot return that sense of control the initial invasion takes away. For this reason alone, the law provides an unsatisfactory solution. Ethical thinking prior to broadcast or publication is preferable to a court battle.

The ethical basis for privacy is much older than the legal one and appears throughout literature. The bulk of this work asserts that privacy is something we all possess by being human. Modern philosophical interpretations make the assumption that privacy is considered a right, a way of protecting oneself against the actions of other people and institutions. Privacy carries with it the connotation of control and limited access. The individual should be allowed to control who may have certain sorts of information and sometimes the context within which that information is presented.

## The Continuing Conflicts

Most would agree with Grcic (1986) that while privacy is a prima facie right, it sometimes can be negated by other, more compelling rights. In simpler times, the right to invade privacy belonged almost exclusively to the government. The government can demand, for example, that an individual relinquish control of a substantial amount of private information to complete federal and state income tax forms. Further, failure to provide such information is legally culpable. For the survival of the entire political community, the government demands that its citizens provide it with certain information that is otherwise private. However, specific rules govern such disclosure. The government cannot legally give your tax return information to other interested parties. Such a check on government power theoretically allows the maintenance of some level of individual privacy.

However, the government is not the only institution today that can demand and receive private information. Banks, credit companies, doctors, attorneys, all can request and usually receive a variety of highly private information, the bulk of it willingly disclosed. Inevitably, such disclosure is one-directional. While you are required to provide your physician with your medical history to ensure proper treatment, your physician might be surprised if you inquired about his success rate with a particular surgical procedure, and she certainly is not required to give it to you. Doctors in Massachusetts were uncomfortable and protested when the state passed a law requiring such information be made available to patients.

Computers and data bases have become a tool for gathering and a repository for storing private information. Huge industries have cropped up selling a single commodity: private information. When you buy a house or apply for a job, you will watch as the information industry disgorges huge amounts of legal and financial information about you with a 40 percent chance of some error, according to industry figures. The tensions over what should or should not remain private are not resolved; they are merely accounted for and debated in today's complex society.

But Warren and Brandeis had the press, not the government or financial institutions, in mind when they wrote their precedent-inspiring article. The pair developed their novel legal argument after one of Mrs. Warren's parties for Boston's social elite was covered in personal and embarrassing detail during the era of yellow journalism. Warren and Brandeis could not have anticipated trash television, "kiss-and-tell" books, computerized data bases, or the myriad of other ways the mass media disseminate private information about people who are more or less willing to disclose it. The issue is not more complex today than it was during the country's formative years, but the ways privacy is violated are substantially different, and perhaps more threatening (Hixson 1987).

The combination of a voracious media and a curious public means that journalists need to become adept at ethical reasoning when applied to privacy issues. Understanding the concepts that follow—the distinction between secrecy and privacy, the concept of circles of intimacy, the meaning of discretion, and the ethical distinctions among right to know, need to know, and want to know—will provide you with a vocabulary to help in thinking about privacy questions. Finally, Rawls's concept of the veil of ignorance will provide you with a framework in which to use that vocabulary, balance competing claims, and arrive at an ethical choice.

But despite all of this philosophical equipment, decisions about privacy will continue to be difficult. They are very much worth reexamining as you develop professionally.

## Distinguishing between Secrecy and Privacy

People tend to think of private information as something they would like to keep secret, but such thinking confounds these two related but separable concepts.

Secrecy can be defined as blocking information intentionally to prevent others from learning, possessing, using, or revealing it (Bok 1983). While secrecy ensures that information is kept from *any* public view, privacy, however, is concerned with determining who will obtain access to the information. Privacy does not imply that information will never reach public view, but rather that an individual has control over what information becomes public and to whom.

Secrecy often carries a negative connotation. However, we agree with Bok in asserting that secrecy itself is neither morally good nor bad. Privacy and secrecy can overlap but are not identical. "Privacy need not hide; and secrecy hides far more than what is private. A private garden need not be a secret garden, a private life is rarely a secret life," (Bok 1983, 11). Privacy can and should be balanced against other considerations; secrets are something an individual decides to keep.

In his opinion in *Dietemann* v. *Time,* jurist Alan F. Westin viewed privacy as the ability to control one's own circles of intimacy. In the case, two reporters lied to Dietemann to enter his home and later expose him as a medical quack practicing medicine without a license, at home. While the courts saw some social utility in exposing such behavior, Dietemann, they ruled, had a reasonable expectation of privacy in his own home. Philosopher Louis D. Hodges has used the concept of "circles of intimacy" to develop a working concept of privacy for journalists and other professionals.

If you conceive of privacy as a series of concentric circles, as figure 5.1 illustrates, in the innermost circle you are alone with your secrets, fantasies, hopes, reconstructed memories, and all of the rest of the unique psychological "furniture" we bring to our lives. The second circle you probably occupy with one other person,

**Figure 5.1**
*The concept of circles of intimacy*

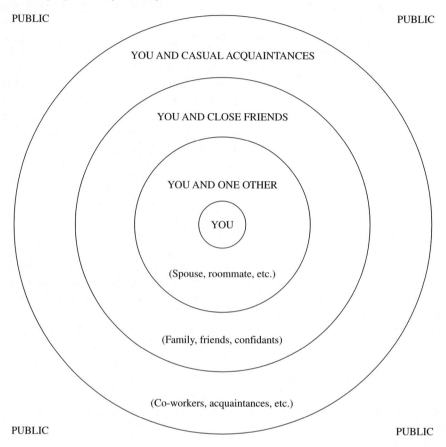

PUBLIC

PUBLIC

YOU AND CASUAL ACQUAINTANCES

YOU AND CLOSE FRIENDS

YOU AND ONE OTHER

YOU

(Spouse, roommate, etc.)

(Family, friends, confidants)

(Co-workers, acquaintances, etc.)

PUBLIC

PUBLIC

perhaps a spouse, a parent, roommate, or loved one. In that circle, you share private information. In order for that relationship to work well, it needs to be reciprocal, and it should be based primarily on trust. The third circle contains others to whom you are very close—probably family or friends, perhaps a lawyer or clergy member. Here, the basis of the relationships is still one of trust, but some communications can be primarily one way—and you do not expect to have complete control over them. As the ripples in the pond of intimacy continue to spread, what you reveal about yourself becomes progressively more public and less intimate, and you lose progressively more control over information about you.

Using this model of expanding circles, privacy can be considered individual control over who has access to your various circles of intimacy. Invasion of privacy occurs when your control over your own circles of intimacy is wrestled from you by people or institutions. Rape victims who unwillingly see their names in print or their pictures broadcast frequently speak of the loss of control they felt during the experience as being similar to the loss of control during the rape itself.

Journalists both as individuals and as representatives of powerful institutions can and sometimes do invade circles of intimacy. Awareness of the concept will allow you to consider the rights of others as well as balance the needs of society in critical ways, particularly when the issue is newsworthy. Under at least some circumstances, invasion can be justified, but under other circumstances invading privacy constitutes usurping an individual's control and stripping them of individuality and human dignity.

## Discretion: Whether to Reveal Private Information

With the distinction between privacy and secrecy in mind, the next problem confronting the ethical journalist is discretion—a word not usually associated with journalism. Bok (1983, 41) defines discretion as "the intuitive ability to discern what is and is not intrusive and injurious."

We all decide to reveal private information, and doing so wisely is a mark of moral growth. Discretion demands moral reasoning where the interests of more than one party are balanced. For instance, once a source decides to reveal private information, a reporter's discretion remains the sole gatekeeper between that information and a public that might need the information or might merely want the information. The journalist is forced to rely on moral reasoning to decide if he is feeding the voyeur or the citizen in each of us.

What is a journalist to do with information resulting from another's indiscretion? Kantian theory would suggest that the journalist treat even the indiscreet source as the journalist herself would wish to be treated, making publication of the indiscretion less likely. Yet, many journalists claim that, in practice, everything is "on-the-record" unless otherwise specified.

In situations like these, a return to Ross's list of prima facie duties could be helpful. What is my duty to an often vulnerable and sometimes unwitting source? To a curious readership or viewership? To a media owner who wants (and pays for) my story? Which duties emerge as foremost to the journalist should make such decisions more consistent.

Perhaps no new medium is more "on-the-record" than the Internet. We speak of information as "being posted" without examining the assumptions or the motives of those doing the posting. As of 1997, the courts have not yet determined whether posting on the Internet constitutes actual publication.

However, it is not merely sources who can be indiscreet. Computers and their data bases are ready storehouses of information that only add to the problem of multiplying the amount of private data available to the probing journalist. While journalists can never entirely prevent such situations, they can work to develop their own sense of discretion and to refuse to allow a lapse in judgment by others to cloud their own thinking.

# When Right to Know Is Not Enough

Just as the distinction between secrecy and privacy is easily confused, there is also a misconception both on the part of journalists and the public among the concepts of "right to know," "need to know" and "want to know." However, the three concepts are distinct and not interchangeable.

Right to know is a legal term often associated with open-meeting statutes and based on the philosophy that government runs more honestly in the open. Right to know is a form of counterbalancing government power. In recent years both federal and state governments have passed right-to-know laws. These laws are a legal, not ethical, construct. Journalists have a legal right to the same information that other members of the public may obtain, for instance, the transportation of hazardous materials through their communities.

At least two ethical problems can emerge from right to know information. First, is it ethical to print everything a journalist has a legal right to know? For instance, police reports routinely carry the names of suspects, victims and witnesses to a variety of crimes. Does the journalist publish such information, even though it has been legally obtained? Clearly, even right to know carries with it ethical considerations.

Need to know originates in the realm of philosophy. Media ethicists such as Deni Elliott (1986) have argued that one of the functions of the mass media is to provide information to citizens that will allow them to go about their daily lives in society, regardless of political outlook. Citizens may have a legal right to much of this information, but perhaps not all of it. In this view, providing information the public needs to know includes within it the concept of journalistic tenacity and responsibility.

Too often, when journalists assert that the public has the "right to know" a fact, what they mean is that citizens "need" such information to get along in their daily lives. For example, the average citizen cannot examine bank records. That duty is left to auditors and the government. But, with the recent wave of savings and loan and bank failures, journalists could reasonably argue that at least some information about the health of financial institutions and the character of those who run them is needed by the public to make informed economic decisions. Need to know often requires a tenacious journalist, as the law is not a tool to access information for such stories.

Need to know is the most ethically compelling argument of the three. Need to know demands that an ethical case be constructed for making known information that others wish to keep private. Need to know also demands that journalists present the information in a manner that will make its importance evident to a sometimes lazy citizenry.

When an argument is framed in terms of right to know, it reduces the journalist to ethical legalism: I will do precisely what the law allows. When an argument is framed in terms of need to know, however, it means that counterbalancing forces have been weighed and that bringing the information to light is still the most ethical act. Asserting your right to know may be the best way to get the facts regarding a crime, but only by weighing the public's need to know will you be satisfied with the decisions you make in airing the story.

Finally, there is the issue of want to know, which speaks to the curious human being in all of us. Want to know is the least ethically compelling rationale for acquiring information and disseminating it. We all want to know a lot of things—what our neighbors do in the evening hours, how much money other people earn, and who in Hollywood is sleeping with whom. But, while we may want that information, we don't really need it. It serves the function of gossip, providing us with small talk or a smile.

By nature of their occupation, journalists often become repositories for much "want to know" information. A number of media outlets have been founded on the public's desire to know about celebrities, criminals, and even common folk. More than half a century ago, *Police Gazette* titillated its readers with information they wanted to know that no other media outlet provided. Today *People* magazine is a perfect example of want to know transformed into huge profits. Tabloid television, such as "Hard Copy" and many syndicated talk shows have successfully transformed news into a "want to know" style. "COPS" and "Rescue 911" have garnered significant ratings by exploiting the public's curiosity about others' misery. And, shows such as "America's Funniest Home Videos" even provide us with some insight into what our neighbors do in the evening hours.

Want to know speaks to normal curiosity, and fulfilling that curiosity can be profitable. But, it is not a good basis for ethical decisions particularly when another's privacy is the issue.

## John Rawls and the Veil of Ignorance

Preserving human dignity in times of crisis is a difficult task. Political philosopher John Rawls, considered this century's most articulate proponent of the social contract theory of government, has provided a helpful exercise to help make decisions about particularly thorny privacy issues.

Rawls's theory of "distributive justice" is designed to take the best from utilitarian theory while avoiding some of its more fundamental problems. It begins with the premise that justice should be equated with fairness. In order to achieve "justice as fairness," Rawls suggests an exercise that we recommend which he calls the "veil of ignorance." In the exercise, before any member of a social or political community makes an ethical decision affecting others, he or she must take an "original position" behind a veil of ignorance.

Behind the "veil," everyone starts out in the original position as equals who do not know whether they will be powerful or powerless when they emerge into the community from behind the veil. Rawls suggests that rational people would be willing to make and to follow those decisions when individual distinctions made on the basis of gender or socio-economic status are cast aside.

For example, if the issue was whether to photograph or interview survivors at the scene of an airline crash, one could gather many people with diverse views behind the veil. Among them could be a reporter, a photographer, a survivor, a victim's family, an average reader or viewer, the management or owner of the media outlet, the owner of the airline, paramedics at the scene, the flying public, and others. Behind the veil, in the original position, none of the participants would know what their status would be when they emerged. Their arguments would then be free of bias that comes from points of view. The participants would argue the pros and cons of the public's need to know and the victim's right to privacy without knowing whether they would emerge as a reporter, a reader, or a victim.

Rawls's veil of ignorance provides journalists with an important tool to use when they begin an ethical dialogue much like the one Bok recommends in chapter 1. Behind the veil of ignorance it is possible to walk in the shoes of the stakeholders, to air various views, and then to make a reasoned choice.

When people begin their deliberations behind such a veil, Rawls suggests that two values emerge: *we will act so that individual liberty is maximized and weaker parties are protected.* We will look at each concept separately.

First, Rawls suggests the liberty of all will be valued equally. Behind the veil, freedom of the press (a liberty journalists cherish) becomes equal to freedom from unwarranted intrusion into private life (a liberty readers cherish). How one retains both becomes a debate to be argued from all points of view without the bias of status since each participant is in the original position.

Second, under the framework the weaker party is usually protected. Few participants would make an ethical decision that might not be in the interest of the weaker party unless the evidence was overwhelming that it would better the lot of the entire group. Behind the veil participants would be forced to weigh the actual and potential harm that journalists, as powerful people representing powerful institutions, could inflict on people who are less powerful.

*It is important to note that consensus is not required, and maybe even not expected, behind the veil.* The veil of ignorance is designed to facilitate ethical discussions, not stymie them from lack of unanimity. By going behind the veil, the ethical decision maker arrives at what Rawls calls *reflective equilibrium.* In the state of reflective equilibrium some inequalities are allowed. However, they will be the inequalities that contribute in some significant way to the betterment of most individuals in the social situation. For instance, some might run a photo of a victim of tragedy if it might prevent a similar tragedy from occurring.

Reflective equilibrium summons what Rawls calls our "considered moral judgment." Decisions would be based on the principles we would be most unwilling to give up because we believe doing so would result in a grave wrongdoing for all. Balancing the liberties of various stakeholders, while protecting the weaker party, allows for a thorough exploration of all of the issues involved, which utilitarianism sometimes fails to address.

Using the concepts of right to know, need to know, discretion and circles of intimacy, along with Rawls's concept of distributive justice, will provide you with the ethical tools to begin the work of balancing conflicting claims. These tools will enable you to better justify your choices, to make decisions systematically and to understand what went wrong when mistakes occur.

## Selected Readings

Alderman, Ellen, and Caroline Kennedy. 1995. *The right to privacy.* New York: Alfred A. Knopf, Inc.

Bok, Sissela. 1983. *Secrets: On the ethics of concealment and revelation.* New York: Vintage.

Grcic, Joseph M. 1986. "The right to privacy: Behavior as property." *Journal of Values Inquiry 20,* pp. 137–144.

Hixson, Richard F. 1987. *Privacy in a public society.* New York: Oxford University Press.

Hodges, Louis W. 1983. "The journalist and privacy." *Social Responsibility: Journalism, Law, Medicine 9,* pp. 5–19.

Rawls, John. 1971. *A theory of justice.* Cambridge, MA: Harvard University Press.

Schoeman, Ferdinand D., ed. 1984. *Philosophical dimensions of privacy: An anthology.* New York: Cambridge University Press.

Westin, Alan F. 1967. *Privacy and freedom.* New York: Atheneum.

# CHAPTER V CASES

## CASE V-A
## Naming Names: Privacy and the Public's Right to Know
JOHN B. WEBSTER
*Purdue University*

A fifteen-year-old boy living in an affluent Hitesville neighborhood, considered normal and bright by his teachers, is arrested for sexually abusing his half sister and ten neighborhood children. Through questioning him, police learn that the molestations occurred over a period of four years and that the youth himself had been molested nearly all his life, first by his natural parents and later by his foster father—a well-respected citizen. The foster father is also arrested.

The daily newspaper (circulation 48,000) chooses not to print the names of offenders or to identify the neighborhood where the crimes occurred. As a result, numerous readers express concern, some by letter but most by phone.

> **Says one reader:** "For the past couple of years, the public has read on nearly a weekly basis the names of countless molestation arrests, convictions, and sentences in the *Gazette.* And if one reads details, he or she would have noticed that the addresses of the molesters were not in the affluent sections. So along comes a big case with a rich molester and rich victims involved, and all of a sudden the *Gazette* is protecting these young victims."
>
> **A caller says:** "Give me his (the foster father's) name. What are you protecting him for? I've heard he works for the *Gazette.*" Another caller says: "You didn't use the man's name because he is one of your best advertisers." Still another adds: "I just want to protect my children. You're not doing your job by not printing his [the fifteen-year-old offender's] name in the paper."

The newspaper's editor responds by publishing an editor's note denying the charges. He adds, "The *Gazette* has an ethics policy—and a good one, we believe—that protects innocent victims in the reporting of rapes and cases of incest and child molesting. The policy reads:

> We will NOT use the name of a rape or incest victim. We will NOT use the names of any person charged with or convicted of incest—man or woman. We will NOT run names in morals cases (such as rape, child molesting, indecent exposure) until official charges have been filed in court."

The editor concludes his column with the following remark:

> "Why did we use the details about the affluence of the neighborhood and the fact that the foster father holds a management position with a local company? The answer is simply that it was important to point out the fact that child-molesting and incest cases can happen in all neighborhoods and to all manner of people: It just doesn't happen on the wrong side of the tracks; it knows no financial or educational bounds."

In another published commentary by the city editor, he admits that the rationale behind not printing the specific name of the neighborhood was a hard question and adds that "a lot of soul-searching was involved." While it is the job of the newspaper to print the names of criminals so they can be identified and watched by society, he says, readers should not forget that there are other victims—the children and the families in the neighborhood.

Eventually, the father receives a sentence of five years' supervised probation for molesting his teenage son after a judicial hearing that includes testimony from the man's wife, letters from counselors, and attorney's pleas. In crafting the sentence, the judge requires that the offender submit to random lie-detector tests during the five years to determine whether he repeats his offense while on probation.

The article does not name the offender even after the court hearing, even though it is pointed out that he plans to remain in the community, continue in his same job, and to be active in his local church as well as to attend a sexual-abuse family program. A policy note follows the article, stating once again that the newspaper policy is not to print the names of child molesters in incest cases in order to protect the identity of the victims.

## Micro Issues:

1. Most newspapers have policies that would not allow revelation of the victimized children's names. Is that a justifiable policy in this case?
2. Should the newspaper have identified the neighborhood where the molestations took place?
3. Should the teenager have been identified upon arrest?
4. Should the foster father have been identified upon arrest?
5. When the decision of the court had been made final, should the name of the molester have been printed then?

## Middle-range Issues:

1. Do any of the following circumstances enter into your decision to publish or not to publish the name of the father after the trial?
   (*a*) The fact that the man now wishes to live in the community;
   (*b*) The fact that the trial is a matter of public record;
   (*c*) The fact that the man pled guilty.
2. If one of the following were true, would you feel compelled to tell what you know to the parties involved? If so, why?
   (*a*) Your neighbor's son has been invited to spend the night with the boy who was the victim/perpetrator in the case;
   (*b*) You have friends who attend church with the molester;
   (*c*) You have friends who live on the same block as the molester.
3. If the answer to any of the questions above was yes, how do you justify your newspaper's decision not to tell the entire community at once?

## Macro Issues:

1. Did the paper open itself to accusations of protection of the affluent establishment and rumors of economic ties to the newspaper when it refused to reveal the specific neighborhood? Did it handle the resulting controversy well? How could the concept of right to know, need to know, want to know have helped the paper explain its decision?
2. List the pros and cons of a policy naming child molesters when incest is involved.

## CASE V-B
## Public Grief and the Right to Be Left Alone
PHILIP PATTERSON
*Oklahoma Christian University*

In March 1983, *Riverside Press-Enterprise* photographer Fred Bauman rushed to the scene of an accident. A twenty-two-month-old boy had been hit by a car in front of his home. The driver of the vehicle was entering the driveway to drop off another child with the babysitter.

The mother of the boy, Dawna Read, rushed to the site and sank to her knees in prayer, covered by the blood of her son, as paramedics attempted to save him. It was at this moment that Bauman shot the photo.

According to Bauman, who was also the photo editor at the time the photograph ran, a lengthy discussion was held in the newsroom before the decision to publish was made. Bauman said the determining factor in the decision was the possibility that the stark reality of the picture might prevent future accidents through safer drivers or more watchful parents.

"We decided that even if one life was saved, it was worth it," Bauman said.

In the days to follow, reader response poured in largely against running the picture. Bauman said that no other picture in his three decades with the *Press-Enterprise* created the outpouring of emotion that this one did. Among the callers were some who threatened Bauman.

## Micro Issues:

1. If you had been dispatched to the scene of the accident, would you have photographed the grieving mother? With a telephoto lens?
2. If other media (e.g., a competing newspaper, the television stations) were shooting the woman, would that fact enter into your decision?
3. Could the drama of the moment have been told equally well in some other manner?

## Middle-range Issues:

1. Is the decision to take the photo a different ethical decision than the decision to run the photo? In other words, what do you think about a shoot first, decide later policy?
2. If a local television station obtained videotape of the incident, would you run it? Is there a distinction between a still photograph and a video? Would a color photograph be more objectionable?

*Photo by Fred Bauman. Riverside Press-Enterprise. Used by permission.*

## Macro Issues:

1. The rationale used by the editors of the *Press-Enterprise* to run the controversial photo in hopes of preventing future accidents is a utilitarian one. In this case do you think the greatest good to society outweighs the emotional damage done to the woman by running the photo?
2. Is utilitarian ethics a good rationale to apply to these situations? If yes, defend it; if no, what moral philosophy would you put in its place?
3. How might the concept of discretion have helped the photographer and his editors explain their choices?

## CASE V-C
## A Reporter's Question: Propriety and Punishment
STANLEY CUNNINGHAM
*University of Windsor, Ontario, Canada*

The following Canadian case is based on fact. A television reporter (call him Hector) and camera crew were assigned to interview a prominent politician who was announcing his retirement from politics. The recorded conference was followed by a *scrum*—an informal, more relaxed question period in which interviewees make themselves available to reporters for questions on other and related matters.

During this scrum, Hector asked the following: "There was some talk a while ago about (federal politician) Svend Robinson declaring himself as being gay some time ago. Are you, sir, gay?" The politician did not answer the question and walked away from the scrum. This exchange was witnessed by others, notably the cameraman and another radio reporter; it was recorded on video and audio tapes.

Hector's question was not really a wild and unpremeditated shot. Rumors had been circulating in political circles about the politician's sexual orientation. Hector had learned about these rumors, and his suspicions had been reinforced by other stories and interviews he had done. Just prior to this interview, he had discussed this issue with his assignment editor, but she told him to drop it. When Hector posed the question at the scrum, he clearly disobeyed the order (or advice) of his assignment editor.

Later that day, the tapes were reviewed by the assignment editor, the senior news producer, and the news director. The scrum tapes were never broadcast. Instead, that same afternoon, Hector was suspended with pay.

The next day, after discussions between the news director and top management, Hector was fired. Management's reasons were that (a) the reporter had been insubordinate, and (b) that Hector's question violated journalistic ethics in such a way that he could no longer be trusted not to damage the station's reputation.

## Micro Issues:

1. Was Hector's question ethically defensible?
2. Was the question in poor taste? Was it badly motivated? Do either of these matter?
3. Did management have the right to reprimand or fire him?

## Middle-range Issues:

1. Does the difference between taped interviews (which can be reviewed and edited) and live interviews have any bearing on the ethics of a reporter's questions?
2. Should reporters probe into the personal and sexual lives of public officials and politicians? Sports luminaries? Entertainment stars?

## Macro Issues:

1. Does management's action against Hector amount to an assault on the democratic ideal of free speech?
2. If this kind of case had taken place in the United States, would Hector's firing be an abridgment of his First Amendment rights?
3. Was Hector's question an important one? Does the public need such information about its elected officials? Do they have a right to know this information?

## CASE V-D
## Arthur Ashe and the Right to Privacy
CAROL OUKROP
*Kansas State University*

**Authors' note:** *Arthur Ashe died from AIDS-related complications in February 1993.*

"Tennis great Arthur Ashe has AIDS, . . ." began the dispatch fed by *USA Today* to its overseas edition and the Gannett News Service April 8, 1992.

Ashe, a disciplined athlete who overcame racial barriers, was 48. He was the first African-American to win the U.S. Open and Wimbledon tennis championships. He was reluctant to go public with his disease, but was given little choice.

On April 7 he was contacted by a *USA Today* reporter Doug Smith about a rumor telephoned in to the newspaper that Ashe had AIDS. After speaking with Smith, Ashe talked with *USA Today*'s executive editor/sports, Gene Policinski. Policinski asked Ashe if he was HIV-positive, and the response was "could be." Ashe asked Policinski to delay the story for 36 hours. Policinski would not promise Ashe the delay. Ashe called a press conference for April 8.

The call from *USA Today,* Ashe said at the press conference, put him in the unenviable position of having to lie if he wanted to protect his family's privacy.

"I am sorry that I have been forced to make this revelation at this time. After all, I am not running for some office of public trust, nor do I have stockholders to account to. It is only that I fall in the dubious umbrella of, quote, public figure, end of quote."

Later Ashe wrote in the *Washington Post* that going public with a disease such as AIDS was "akin to telling the world in 1900 that you had leprosy."

Ashe was married and was the father of a 5-year-old daughter, Camera, thought to have been protected from knowledge of his disease prior to the call from *USA Today.* Ashe had known since 1988 that he had AIDS, apparently contracted from a blood transfusion required during heart surgery in 1983. Blood was not routinely checked for the virus before 1985.

It is clear in articles appearing since Ashe's press conference that a number of journalists knew about Ashe's disease, but chose to protect "Arthur Ashe's Secret" (Frank Deford, *Newsweek,* April 20, 1992).

"Keeping my AIDS status private," Ashe wrote in the *Washington Post,* "enabled me to control my life."

Was *USA Today* right or wrong? An editorial in *The Christian Century* (April 22, 1992) called this a "tale of media irresponsibility and corporate greed," an example of "entertainment posing as information."

Is Peter Prichard, editor of *USA Today,* correct in saying "When the press has kept secrets . . . that conspiracy of silence has not served the public. . . ."? "Journalists serve the public by reporting news, not hiding it. By sharing his story, Arthur Ashe and his family are free of a great weight. In the days ahead, they will help us better understand AIDS and how to defeat it."

© 1992 Gary Markstein. Used by permission.

Public figure/privacy decisions are often difficult, this one perhaps particularly so. Ashe had, over the years, earned much respect. In addition to his accomplishments in tennis, he participated in human rights struggles in the United States and was a leading critic of apartheid in South Africa. He was the author of a lauded history of African-American athletes in the United States.

Fred Bruning writes, however, that "Cruel as it may seem, the wishes of a stricken man cannot substitute for editorial judgment. The process is imperfect, and its justice notoriously rough, but the objective is clear. Personal concerns are secondary to the principles of a free press."

## Micro Issues:

1. Should Policinski have promised Ashe the requested 36 hours during which to prepare a statement?
2. Were Deford, Roy Johnson and others who knew about Ashe's disease months before the press conference right to keep Ashe's secret?

## Middle-range Issues:

1. What if the news of Magic Johnson's HIV status had not been yet made public? Did that story have an effect on the Ashe story?

2. What if Ashe's ailment were an inoperable lung cancer or Lou Gehrig's disease?

## Macro Issues:

1. Does the Ashe case really differ significantly from, say, the rape of a celebrity? Both are public figures, but according to the policy of many news media only the rape victim would be afforded anonymity.
2. What is the public's stake in knowing Ashe had AIDS?

## CASE V-E
## Computers and the News: A Complicated Challenge
KARON REINBOTH SPECKMAN
*Truman State University*

Reporter Paula Baldwin has a ten-year-old son who regularly rides the school bus. One day her son tells her he doesn't want to ride the bus anymore because he thinks the bus driver "isn't safe." He tells Paula he has smelled alcohol on the driver's breath and that the bus has almost been involved in an accident several times.

Baldwin regularly covers the education beat, but she is aware that several newspapers have won awards for matching the names of school bus drivers with a variety of computerized law enforcement data bases, all of which are public records.

Baldwin approaches the paper's crime reporter, Marty Tharp, and pitches the story: Baldwin will obtain a list of the district's bus drivers, the paper will purchase the state's list of motor vehicle traffic violations and the National Crime Information Center data base. The two reporters will then load the data bases into the paper's computer system.

The computer will match the names of the bus drivers with driver's license records. Then, using the driver's license numbers, they will match individual records with the state violations and the national crime center data base.

The two reporters estimate that acquiring the data bases would cost the paper about $2,000 and that it would take a month to analyze the information and write the story. However, they tell their city editor that using such methods, other reporters have found school bus drivers with suspended licenses, a history of bad driving and even records of criminal activity, including child sexual abuse. They tell the editor that they believe the financial investment is worth the gamble, particularly where the safety of children is involved.

The editor reluctantly authorizes the purchase and allows the reporters to begin work on the story, although he will not free them completely from their daily duties.

The acquisition and downloading of the information goes well. However, Baldwin and Tharp discover that the national crime data base lists only the arrest and charge, not the final disposition of the case. Further, the state records are updated only every six months, and some of the names of bus drivers Baldwin has acquired cannot be matched with certainty with driver's license records.

However, of those records that can be matched, the team has learned that at least six of the district's drivers are driving on suspended licenses and that several others have moving violations, including driving under the influence, on their records. The national data base indicates that two of the drivers had been arrested on felony charges.

They are convinced they have a story, but that all the details aren't yet nailed down.

The reporters ask their editor for advice on how to proceed.

The editor, meanwhile, has developed a dilemma of his own. His tennis partner is the paper's circulation manager, and in the process of informally discussing the story, both realize that the state's driver's license data base could provide them with information about potential subscribers.

Using the data base, they can determine current addresses, ages and the social security numbers of many living in the paper's circulation area. Then, using the social security numbers from the driver's license records, they can perform credit checks on potential subscribers, learn what magazines and other services many of them receive, discover what property they own, and then conduct a target marketing circulation campaign geared to different demographic groups with different needs.

The circulation manager adds she believes the paper's advertising director would love to have some of the same information. She wants to know when the news side will be done with the data base so circulation can have it.

## Micro Issues:

1. What steps should the reporters take to check out the facts in the data bases?
2. At what point, if ever, should the paper notify the individual drivers of its investigation? Its findings? Should the school district be notified? When?
3. Whose interests are more important—the children or the bus drivers?

## Middle-range Issues:

1. Are there any differences, in terms of ethical decision making, between this data base story and the data base story (referred to in chapter 7) about the federal budget that won two Philadelphia reporters the Pulitzer prize?
2. How much reliance should the paper place on the overall accuracy of the data bases? Does it have a responsibility to report inaccuracies to the agencies in charge of the data bases? To its readers?

## Macro Issues:

1. Design a policy for your news organization outlining what it will and will not do with data bases it acquires after the "news side" has used them.
2. Do computer data bases raise new privacy issues? Does the use of computer data bases reframe existing privacy concerns? Which ones?

## CASE V-F
## Honor to Die For: *Newsweek* and the Admiral Boorda Case
PHILIP PATTERSON
*Oklahoma Christian University*

In May of 1996, Adm. Jeremy M. (Mike) Boorda, the Navy's chief of operations, committed suicide hours before he was about to be interviewed by *Newsweek* magazine regarding allegations that he had previously worn commendations he had not earned.

The suicide began yet another round of media introspection into how news is put together, and whether journalism organizations are responsible for the fallout from their stories. The harshest of *Newsweek*'s critics claim that the reporters caused his death. The magazine's defenders claim that Boorda had a lapse of honor in a closed community where honor matters most and that, as the public official who headed the Navy, his actions were appropriately the subject of public scrutiny.

The *Newsweek* inquiry began with a tip that the admiral had been seen and photographed wearing two "V-for-valor" clips over two of his medals. The tip came from the National Security News Service, a known critic of the military establishment that supplies news leads about the military to mainstream media outlets.

The "V-clips" are traditionally awarded for valor under fire. Nothing in Boorda's military record directly indicated he had served under fire; however, during the Vietnam War he had served on ships off Vietnam in the South China Sea. He had quit wearing the clips about a year before *Newsweek* was tipped to the story. Navy Secretary John Dalton, in an interview given after the suicide, said that Boorda's service off the coast of Vietnam would have given him "every right to believe" that he was qualified to wear the "V-for-valor" insignia. Dalton's statements do reflect historical fact. Former President Lyndon B. Johnson justified intensifying American involvement in Southeast Asia by noting that American ships had been fired on by the North Vietnamese—statements which prompted Congress to pass the Gulf of Tonkin Resolution in 1964.

Evan Thomas is *Newsweek*'s Washington bureau chief and was one of two reporters scheduled to interview Boorda before he committed suicide. In an interview for *American Journalism Review,* Thomas said that the controversies surrounding the Navy in 1996 (sexual harassment charges, cheating scandals at Annapolis, etc.) were among the contextual factors that prompted *Newsweek* to pursue the story.

"The Navy's under the gun right now. Here's a guy whose job it is to restore the integrity of the Navy. If he is possibly fudging on his own medals, that's something you look into. There wasn't a moment's hesitation" (Rieder 1996, 6).

However, the interview never occurred. While Thomas was en route to the Pentagon for the scheduled interview, Boorda went to his home and shot himself in the chest. He left behind two notes calling the wearing of the V-for-valor clips an "honest mistake."

*Newsweek* ran an article after the suicide that indicated that at least one *Newsweek* writer, Retired Army Col. David Hackworth, who writes on military affairs for the magazine, commented that Boorda "might just put a gun to his head" if the story was pursued. However, his comment was made to an office assistant in Montana and did not reach *Newsweek* editors until after the suicide.

Hackworth, when questioned about the statement by *Newsweek*'s managing editor, characterized his earlier comment as "the remotest thought" and said that he would have called Thomas had he thought Boorda would kill himself. In the magazine's coverage of the suicide, Hackworth in a side bar wrote that he personally believed wearing unearned medals was the most egregious ethical violation any military officer could commit.

Reader reaction to *Newsweek*'s pursuit of the story was overwhelmingly negative. One writer to the magazine wrote: "I hold you directly responsible for the death of Adm. Boorda." Press reports of the flap stated that *Newsweek* lost hundreds of subscribers in protest of its handling of the story. Politicians and military figures took the opportunity to once again lambast the media.

However, Thomas sees it differently.

"I'm not insensitive to the fact that people are angry at the press. . . We've got to do our job. Part of that job is checking on the truthfulness of people in positions of power. Like the admiral" (Rieder, 6).

## Micro Issues:

1. Was the Boorda story newsworthy? Why?
2. Should the fact that Boorda apparently stopped wearing the decorations influence your decision?
3. Should Hackworth have voiced his concerns, no matter how minor?

## Mid-range Issues:

1. If Boorda had continued to wear the medals, would your decision change?
2. Should *Newsweek* have interviewed other military officials about the medals and when they should be worn?
3. Did *Newsweek* rely too much on its own insider knowledge which clearly had a point of view?
4. Should the magazine have been concerned about the point of view of the original source of the story?

## Macro Issues:

1. How can a reporter who had not served in the military evaluate the role of medals in the service?
2. Was this story about the Navy worthy of *Newsweek*'s time and resources? What other stories might the magazine have explored?
3. In this era of "gotcha" journalism, should reporters and editors consider that story subjects will believe journalists will portray them in the worst possible light? Should that fear of "gotcha" journalism influence journalistic behavior?

## CASE V-G
## Competition, Deadlines and the Mistreatment of Richard Jewell
GREG LISBY
*Georgia State University*

**Authors' note:** The Atlanta Journal *and* The Atlanta Constitution *as well as WSB-TV are all owned by Cox Enterprises, Inc., headquartered in Atlanta.*

On July 27, 1996, around 12:45 A.M., Richard Jewell, a security guard employed to protect AT&T's interests and property in Atlanta's Centennial Olympic Park during the Summer Olympic Games, showed an agent with the Georgia Bureau of Investigation an unattended green knapsack lying beneath a bench outside a sound and light tower that was being used for a performance at the AT&T Global Olympic Village stage. Federal agents called to the scene determined that the knapsack contained a bomb, and Jewell and other law enforcement officers quietly began evacuating the area.

At 12:58 A.M., a bomb threat was called in to law enforcement officials from a pay phone three blocks from the scene. The tower and most of the immediate area surrounding the bomb had been cleared by the time it exploded at approximately 1:20 A.M., killing one visitor, leading to a fatal heart attack for a foreign journalist on the scene, and injuring 111 others.

For the next two days, the 33-year-old Jewell was hailed as a "hero." He was interviewed by several major newspapers and television networks, including NBC's "Today" show, about his role in spotting the knapsack, alerting authorities, evacuating the area, and helping the injured.

On Tuesday, July 30, however, FBI agents interviewed Jewell about the bombing while telling him he was participating in a training film on how to investigate suspicious packages. When agents asked Jewell to "pretend" to waive his right to an attorney, he called his lawyer and ended the meeting.

That same day, *The Atlanta Journal* learned of police suspicions and revamped the front page of its special afternoon Olympics "Extra" supplement to spotlight Richard Jewell as "the focus of the federal investigation." Although the story was not attributed to any source, the paper has since said that three of its employees independently confirmed the investigation. The newspaper was distributed around 4:30 that afternoon, and a CNN anchor read the story verbatim on the air shortly afterwards.

That night each of the three major networks' newscasts picked up the story, and the next day virtually every one of the country's major newspapers gave the story front-page billing. An exception was the *New York Times,* which ran a piece inside the "B" section, focusing more on the media than on Richard Jewell.

Many news organizations later cited not wanting to "appear foolish" by not running a story or the suspect's name when so many other organizations were. Many were also careful to point out that Jewell had not been charged, or even officially named as a suspect. Investigators had been discovered staking out Jewell's apartment, and by late afternoon the media, led by CNN and local Atlanta television sta-

tions, joined them. By mid-day Wednesday, an estimated 200 national and international journalists were on the scene as federal investigators, including agents from the FBI and the Bureau of Alcohol, Tobacco & Firearms, searched the apartment Jewell shared with his mother, and took away boxes of belongings and Jewell's pickup truck. In one of the few statements he made to the media at the time, Jewell "categorically" denied being the Centennial Olympic Park bomber in response to a reporter's question, an exchange that was also shown on CNN and NBC.

NBC also reported on July 31 that agents that day had searched the shed near a cabin Jewell had rented in northeast Georgia before he had moved to Atlanta in May. ABC and CBS, however, reported that the FBI's suspicions of Jewell might be diminishing, with ABC citing the lack of evidence—of fingerprints at the phone from which the 911 call originated, of a voice match, and of the short time span between the 911 call and the explosion.

On Thursday, August 1, the front page of *The Atlanta Constitution* detailed the search in an article that included the name and location of Richard Jewell's apartment complex. The apartment number, its address, and a map detailing its location were included in an inside story.

According to the *Constitution,* Jewell became a suspect after the president of Piedmont College, a small campus in north Georgia, contacted authorities after seeing Jewell interviewed on television. He said that Jewell, who had once worked as a security guard for the college, had been "overzealous" in the pursuit of his duties there, harassing students and asking to work undercover.

Prior to his job at the college, Jewell had been a deputy for the Habersham County Sheriff's Department until he wrecked his patrol car, was demoted to jailer, and subsequently resigned. His 1990 arrest for impersonating a police officer in Dekalb County in metropolitan Atlanta was also widely reported. Media organizations stated that the FBI was looking at whether Jewell fit the "profile" of a loner who might have planted the bomb in order to draw attention to his heroism; indeed, some said he had sought out interviews after the bombing. (It was later revealed that an AT&T spokesperson, not Jewell, had solicited interviews on his behalf.)

On Friday, August 2, two of the bombing victims filed suit against Richard Jewell. They alleged that he failed to clear the area around the bomb before it exploded.

On August 3, the FBI returned to Jewell's apartment with a subpoena for hair samples and fingerprints. Jewell and his lawyer, G. Watson Bryant, Jr., refused to allow more voice samples or a polygraph test. About two weeks later, Jewell passed a lie detector test administered by an expert his legal team hired because they "didn't trust" the FBI to conduct the exam. In an article detailing the results, *The Atlanta Journal-Constitution* quoted several people extolling the expert's integrity, but the next day reported that the expert had also "cleared" two other men subsequently convicted as felons.

Richard Jewell left his apartment for the first time in five days on Sunday, August 4, when Bryant spirited him past law enforcement officers and the media still keeping vigil in the parking lot. He met with criminal lawyer Jack Martin, who with Bryant on Monday tried without success to unseal the affidavits filed by the FBI to obtain its search warrants.

During the next week the *Journal-Constitution* reported Bryant's assertion that a piece of bomb shrapnel recovered by the FBI from the apartment was a "souvenir" given Jewell by other guards at the park, and Martin's demonstration by walking the route involved with a reporter that Jewell didn't have the time to make the 911 call.

The role and behavior of the media during the investigation were examined on ABC's "Viewpoint" on August 22. Discussing "The Bizarre Case of Richard Jewell" were Martin and Bryant along with representatives from CNN, ABC, CBS, NBC, and NBC's Atlanta affiliate. The FBI, GBI, and *Journal-Constitution* declined to attend.

Four days later, at a news conference called by Jewell's lawyers, Richard Jewell's mother made an emotional appeal to President Bill Clinton, asking him to direct the Justice Department and the FBI to state whether or not they intended to charge her son. She also asked the media to leave them alone, stating that their life was a "nightmare." The White House did not comment, but a few days later Attorney General Janet Reno declined to exonerate Jewell, saying that she understood the Jewells' feelings but that the investigation had to be pursued. *The Atlanta Journal-Constitution* commented that the exchange was part of a public relations campaign mounted by Jewell's lawyers—by then four in number—to get the FBI and the Justice Department to clear and apologize to their client.

A federal magistrate ruled on September 14 that the lawyers would be permitted to see portions of the FBI affidavits submitted to justify the search warrants. On September 22, Richard Jewell gave his first public interview since coming under investigation, by appearing on CBS's "60 Minutes." The discussion, with correspondent Mike Wallace, focused on whom he would sue if he were not charged.

By the end of September, the FBI agreed to "less obtrusive" surveillance of the Jewell apartment, and on Saturday, October 5, returned most of the property it had seized from the apartment and the north Georgia sites, including Mrs. Jewell's collection of Tupperware. The following day, in lieu of taking an FBI polygraph, Jewell submitted to a six-hour interview in what the *New York Times* called a deal approved by the Justice Department in which Jewell would receive a letter clearing him within six weeks of the interview if no damaging information was revealed during the questioning. Attorney Lin Wood later told *The Atlanta Journal-Constitution* there was no guarantee of such a letter.

In a court hearing on October 8, U.S. District Judge J. Owen Forrester rebuked the media for "the worst example of media coverage I've ever seen since watching *La Dolce Vita*" (Federico Fellini's 1960 film depicting journalists as vultures). Forrester cited published reports of material in the sealed affidavits for search warrants as evidence of a probable leak by law enforcement officials, and was assured by U.S. Attorney Kent Alexander that a Justice Department and FBI investigation into the leaks was underway.

Fourteen guns were returned to Richard Jewell that day. Two days later, *The Atlanta Constitution* published a "letter to the editor" from Alexander that defended the FBI's conduct in the investigation.

On Saturday, October 12, the *Journal-Constitution* reported "little progress" in the bombing investigation "as the FBI turns its attention away from Richard Jewell."

The next day, it reprinted an *American Journalism Review* article critical of the media coverage the Jewell story had received.

Less than two weeks later, on October 24, Judge Forrester ordered public disclosure of the affidavits in response to a motion filed by the *Journal-Constitution* and the Atlanta ABC affiliate, WSB-TV, saying he believed Jewell was no longer the focus of the investigation.

Although the affidavits had already been released to Jewell's legal team, and the disclosure of such documents during a criminal investigation was unusual; Forrester called the situation "unique."

On Saturday, October 26, Alexander issued a letter to Richard Jewell's lawyers notifying them that Jewell was no longer considered by the Justice Department to be a target of the investigation. The letter expressed regret that "the Jewells have . . . endured highly unusual and intense publicity that was neither designed nor desired by the FBI." The absolution received front-page treatment in the *Journal-Constitution* and the *New York Times* the next day.

Richard Jewell held a news conference on Monday, October 28, which was carried live by CNN and all three network affiliates in Atlanta. Introduced by his lawyer as the "114th victim" of the Olympic bombing, Jewell characterized press coverage of him as "all lies," said he had never asked for media attention before that day, and declared the day the start of "the other part of my nightmare—trying to restore my reputation and good name."

## Micro Issues:

1. In the days following Jewell's press conference, media organizations defended the manner in which they had reported the story, saying they were following "common procedures." Identify the "common procedures" of reporting a news story such as the one described here. Discuss the ethics of each procedure.

2. Richard Jewell's attorneys indicated that he was planning to sue several news organizations, including the *Journal-Constitution,* NBC News and its anchorman, Tom Brokaw. However, many people don't sue to win, instead they win by suing. What are the ethical issues involved in Richard Jewell's attempt to restore his reputation by threatening a lawsuit for libel, when—as a public figure—he would have an extremely difficult time establishing the necessary legal standard of fault required to collect monetary damages?

## Middle-range Issues:

1. The results of an ABC News poll conducted at the time of Jewell's exoneration revealed that 69 percent of Americans thought Jewell had been unfairly treated by the media; 82 percent said it was not acceptable for the media to identify a suspect before he or she was charged. Under what circumstances, if any, is it ethically permissible for the media to identify a suspect before he or she is charged with a criminal offense?

2. Justify your answer to the previous question using ethical reasoning and principles.
3. In late 1996, NBC agreed to pay Jewell more than $500,000 to avert a lawsuit over comments made by Tom Brokaw. In your opinion will the threat of lawsuits "chill" the media from reporting on suspects in the future?

## Macro Issues:

1. Deadline pressure, the competition for news, and "pack journalism"—the individual assignments of a number of reporters to follow a single person or issue for weeks or months at a time "like a pack of hounds sicked on a fox" (Crouse 1974, 7) all contributed to the media's coverage of Richard Jewell's heroics at the Olympics. How might deadline pressure have been handled differently yet within an ethical framework? How might the journalists have competed for news differently in this situation?
2. How is the journalistic standard of objectivity twisted by "pack journalism"?
3. How did the concept of authority as an accepted source of information affect the media's attitude toward Richard Jewell? Under what circumstances, if any, is it ethically permissible for the media to allow themselves to be used as either an investigative or surveillance arm of the police? Do they have any different ethical obligations than do ordinary citizens witnessing a similar situation?

# CHAPTER VI

# *The Mass Media in a Democratic Society: Keeping a Promise*

**By the end of the chapter, the student should:**

- **Appreciate how a society's media are shaped by the form of its government.**
- **Be familiar with many of the criticisms leveled at the way the U.S. media cover government and elections.**
- **Be familiar with why the media should be concerned with social justice for the powerful and the powerless alike.**

## Introduction

Americans view the written word as essential to political society. The First Amendment to the U.S. Constitution states

> Congress shall make no law respecting an establishment of religion, or prohibiting the free exercise thereof; or abridging the freedom of speech, or of the press; or the right of the people peaceably to assemble, and to petition the government for a redress of grievances.

In academe, scholars such as John C. Merrill (1974) assert that the First Amendment should be interpreted purely as a restriction on government. This view emphasizes the role of freedom of expression and downplays assertions of journalistic responsibility.

Some journalists concur. *Washington Post* managing editor Leonard Downie, speaking to a 1989 meeting of journalism educators, said he expects his reporters to act as if they live on an island," he said. "I know that makes me unpopular . . . but my interpretation of the First Amendment is that it means strictly that government should not interfere with the press."

We prefer a different view. Madison, Hamilton and Jay, in *The Federalist Papers,* asserted that communication among the citizens serves an important political purpose. The founders expected citizens to be informed and then to participate in politics. They expected that political debate, including what was printed in the press of the day, would be partisan and biased rather than objective and truthful. But they also believed that from this cacophony of information, the rational being would be able to discern the truth.

As the authors made clear by circulating those documents as a series of newspaper articles, one way to enhance political learning was publication in the media of the time. Citizens had an obligation to read such information; the press had an obligation to provide it.

Tucked within all of this, we believe, is a promise; that the mass media, both in 1791 and two hundred years later, will provide citizens with what they need to know to get along in political society. Scholars have labeled this analysis of the media's role in a democratic society the *social responsibility theory* of the press. However, assuming such a responsibility is becoming progressively more difficult. Some of the difficulties emanate from the structure of the contemporary American political system and, hence, are appropriately the subject for political reform. Others reflect the ethical choices contemporary journalists are making. After providing some historic context, it is to those issues we will turn.

## A Democracy without Mass Communication

In ancient Greece, the highest form of human existence was the *polis*—literally "community." But the polis was special, for as Aristotle noted, it was "an association of free men." The polis governed itself; the ruled were the rulers.

In the ancient myth, the art of politics was a gift from the gods, who provided men with *adios,* a sense of concern for the good opinion of others, and *dike,* a sense of justice, or that which makes civic peace possible through the adjudication of disputes. In the ancient myth, these gifts were bestowed on everyone, not only on some ruling economic or social elite. All men were able to exercise the art of politics through rhetoric and argument in the assembly, a form of direct democracy that survived for only a few years in Athens. Certain Native-American tribes exercised a similar form of democratic decision making, but in Europe, ancient Greece was the first—and last—place it was seriously attempted.

Socratic teaching took issue with the myth. Not everyone, according to Plato and Socrates, was capable of knowing adios and dike. Democracy was the refuge of the herd; it took a philosopher king to rule. Indeed, I. F. Stone in his book *The Trial of Socrates* maintains that the Athenians condemned Socrates to death not because he insisted on teaching philosophy but because the philosophy he taught was profoundly anti-democratic.

The Greeks, of course, had no media system; their political interaction was face to face, at least among the men who ruled. But their democracy, founded as it was on conceptions of knowing and rhetoric, never assumed an uninformed or lackadaisical citizenry. The Greeks didn't need newspapers or television to govern themselves, but they did demand political and cultural literacy. Without fully knowing it, their highly debated vision of democratic theory anticipated the core of modern problems in late-twentieth century democracies.

## Modern Mediated Problems: Learning about Leaders

Athens was small enough that "pure" democracy was possible. By the late 1700s when the framers were crafting the U.S. Constitution—on which almost all other modern democracies have been modeled—the architects of government knew it was not possible for each citizen to be involved in every political decision. They established a representative democracy where certain members would be elected by their fellows to speak for them—to represent their views—in the legislature. (In ancient Athens, leaders were named by drawing lots.) This concept of representative government drew heavily from the ancient Greek tradition of adios, a concern for the good opinion of others.

In the twentieth century, the issue has been reframed: Can people become well enough acquainted with any candidate to acquire an opinion? Except for a small group of government and corporate insiders, the mass media have become the primary mode of receiving political discourse. In addition to providing voters with facts, something that is generally assumed to be the role of news, the media also provide citizens with a framework to understand those facts, the realm of culture and myth that is the role not only of news but also of entertainment and advertising.

Study of media coverage of political campaigns has uncovered some disturbing trends. Journalists function as a pack; there is seldom any really distinctive political reporting during elections (Crouse 1974; Sabato 1992). However, campaign assignments remain sought after by members of the national press corps for reasons of personal prestige. The person who covers the winning candidate for the network will almost assuredly become the White House correspondent for the next four years, a guarantee of celebrity status, increased income, and, many would argue, real political power. The journalists covering a national election have almost as much at stake as the candidates they cover.

Further, journalists treat front-runners differently than they do the remainder of the candidate pack (Robinson and Sheehan 1984). Front-runners are the subject of closer scrutiny. But those examinations are seldom about issues, even though it is issue-oriented reporting that tends to provoke political interest and public participation (Patterson 1980). Instead, electoral reporting focuses on personality, a key component of political leadership but certainly not the only one.

Candidates and their paid consultants seem to have intuitively understood what academic research has shown. They've developed strategies that will allow them either to capitalize on front-runner status and image or to compensate for a lack of it. Free media—synonymous with a positive story on the 5:00 P.M. news—has become the watchword of most state and national political campaigns. The candidates have created the "photo opportunity" and the "Rose Garden strategy." Both seem designed to thwart anything but the most carefully scripted candidate contact with the voting public.

At the same time, the media has the right, and some would say even the responsibility, to get "behind the curtain" (Molotch and Lester 1974) to the real candidate. What happens then often makes news in ways the candidates could not have foreseen, as the following three illustrations show.

In 1972, Senator Edwin Muskie of Maine was considered the Democratic front-runner going into the New Hampshire primary. Just days before the primary, Muskie, reacting to media criticism of his wife, broke down in tears according to reports in the *Washington Post* that were disputed even by some on the scene, including Muskie. But the damage was done. Muskie was finished as a political contender.

During the 1980 primary season, CBS correspondent Roger Mudd concluded an interview with Democratic challenger Edward Kennedy with this question, "Mr. Senator, why do you want to be president?" The rambling answer that resulted clearly revealed that Kennedy had no scripted answer for why he was challenging incumbent Jimmy Carter and led many of his critics to continue to claim he was running only on the family name.

During the 1984 primary season, the media staked out the Georgetown townhouse of Colorado Senator Gary Hart while he was the front-runner in the campaign. He subsequently left the presidential race amid allegations of an extramarital affair.

But journalists face a number of questions in cases such as these. Just because the information is available and even accurate does not automatically mean that it is relevant. While political character is definitely a bonafide issue in an election of national importance, where is the threshold for what counts as a mark of character or the lack thereof?

Did the reporting on Hart, reporting that focused on his personality rather than his stands on the issues, preempt voters from making a rational political choice? Did the decision to run the inarticulate answer of Edward Kennedy accurately portray his abilities if he were elected? Was Senator Muskie's reaction to the criticism of his wife really an indicator of what type of president he would have become?

Voters must winnow the field of candidates in some way. The question is whether this sort of journalism is adequate for making that political decision.

These changes in the electoral process take place in a cultural backdrop where the word *politician* has become synonymous with *crook* and *liar.* Instead of being perceived as the honorable calling it was in ancient Greece, politics for many Americans is viewed as an unsavory activity. Such images come to us not only through the news but also through entertainment. Frank Capra's film *Mr. Smith Goes to Washington* paints the exceptional politician as common man and hero—against a backdrop of crooked politics as usual. A similar vision is manifest in the 1993 film *Dave.* Our current views are equally skewed. Whether it's *The Candidate, Rambo,* or *Top Gun,* the entertainment media portray politicians at best as absent or weak, at worst as downright sleazy.

## Modern Mediated Problems: Getting Elected

Political scientists agree that the mass-mediated election has redefined electoral politics. How should an ethical journalist function under this changed view?

The connection between money and politics is well recognized and reported on in American politics—with one exception. The news and advertising industries seem locked in a battle over whether politicians should be "sold" like soap. Advertising's packaging of senators, U.S. representatives, or would-be presidents became one of the "hot buttons" in both the 1992 and 1996 elections.

Political ads, even of the negative variety, are literally as old as the republic. One early patriot, Yale President Rev. Timothy Dwight, claimed that if Jefferson were elected, the Bible would be burned, the French national anthem sung in Christian churches, and women dishonored in the most biblical of senses. Andrew Jackson and Abraham Lincoln were the targets of scurrilous attacks circulated via anonymously published handbills, the precursors to paid print advertisements. Contemporary political society, as the 1992 and 1996 candidacy of Texas billionaire and super salesman Ross Perot demonstrated, is flooded with political ads of enormous variety.

Everyone seems to agree on a single starting point: political advertising is unique. More is at stake than a single sale or corporate profits. Political advertising is advertising that matters. As such, it is open to ethical inquiry about both content and tactics which might not be applied to other persuasive messages.

Contemporary research supports this assertion. Voters sometimes learn more about candidates' stands on issues from advertising than they do from news (Patterson 1980). Factual accuracy, therefore, must be the starting point for ethical political advertising. As philosopher Hannah Arendt has noted, "freedom of information

*Ed Stein. Reprinted courtesy of the* Rocky Mountain News.

is a farce unless factual information is guaranteed and the facts themselves are not in dispute" (Arendt 1970).

While some have argued that it is ethical for advertisers to fail to disclose certain sorts of information or to engage in "strategic ambiguity" (see chapter 3 for a more detailed discussion), this ethical standard fails to be persuasive when what is at issue is leadership or public policies. Ethical analysis of political advertising should question instead whether the missing information is necessary for the electorate to make an informed decision and whether the information was intentionally withheld to make a false and misleading impression (Kaid 1992).

Further, many philosophers link facts with rationality, particularly in the area of political debate. The use of emotional arguments designed to stir listeners or viewers "to set aside reason" has been characterized as a "violation of democratic ethics" (Haiman 1958, 388). There may, however, be times when valid issues have strong emotional content, such as the ongoing debate over abortion. At those times, the melding of emotion with issue content in such cases is not *prima facia* unethical.

Televised political advertising can invite the visual and the visceral to replace a reasoned response.

> "Because it is multimodal, television is more easily comprehended than print. We don't think we need to be taught to read television. Additionally, because visuals reinforce and contextualize what we hear, making sense of televised news is easier than deciphering the meaning of a newspaper article. By speaking to us in our native language, television eliminates the decoding required to turn C A T into a furry, purring beast. . . .
>
> "The evocative power of television's visual grammar couples with its use of music to invite strong emotional reactions to what is seen in ads. Because our judgment of information is influenced by the emotional reactions we experience as we process it, these cues can shade and shape our response to a candidate, issues, or both."
> (Jamieson 1992, 50–51)

Ethically questionable political ads could include visual or verbal references to: contrasts between "us" and "them," loyalty vs. treason, the God-fearing vs. the worshippers of a false god, superior vs. inferior race, natural vs. the unnatural, or the normal vs. the abnormal. Attack ads or those that include negative associations divorced from the creator and source of the message also are problematic.

Students of history will realize that many totalitarian regimes have used such appeals to either gain or retain power. However, such ads usually lack any public revelation of evidence to support the claims. Making the evidence behind political assertions public—what Kant called the transcendental principle of publicness—has historically been the role of the news media. However, rather than acting as an arbiter of the veracity of the claims made in political ads, news reporters have relegated their role to reporting on the campaign strategy that hard-hitting ads represent.

Perhaps the best example of an ad itself being treated as news is the infamous Willie Horton ad of the 1988 election. Created by a committee supporting the Bush campaign, the ads claimed that Horton, an African-American inmate of the Massachusetts prison system who was sentenced to life in prison, murdered a Caucasian woman while on a weekend prison furlough. The furlough program was initiated by Michael Dukakis, Bush's opponent.

The ads relied on incomplete and inaccurate information and visual images that established an "us vs. them" racial stereotype. News journalists who should have checked out the facts before they wrote about the ads instead assumed the ads were factually correct. In reality, Horton had never used the name "Willie" on any document—it was given to him by the advertising campaign. More significantly, the ad distorted the number of prison inmates who had "escaped" from the Massachusetts furlough program.

When the ads became news—and the Horton ad was the subject of more news accounts than any other ad in 1988—the distortions and innuendo persisted (Jamieson 1992). The result had been foreseen by Lippmann. "In the absence of debate, restricted utterance leads to the degradation of opinion. By a kind of Gresham's law the more rational is overcome by the less rational, and the opinions that will prevail will be those which are held most ardently by those with the most passionate will" (Lippmann 1982, 196).

If political advertising is indeed a special case, then journalists and their audiences should demand higher standards, more regulations, or both. While some of the solutions to the current problems have First Amendment ramifications, they are worthy of discussion. They include:

- Allot limited amounts of free time to qualified candidates for major office to level the playing field for candidates without destroying the bottom line at already strapped broadcast outlets.
- Strengthen state regulations against corrupt campaign practices and find ways to enforce those regulations.
- Establish a federal campaign commission to hear complaints about ethical abuses in campaign communication, particularly in advertising.
- Encourage journalists to stop covering the "horse race" aspect of campaigns and focus on problem and policy solutions.
- Hold candidates accountable for their ads, not only in verbal terms but in visual and audio terms as well.
- Teach journalists to read and report on the visual imagery of a campaign, and to ask candidates questions about it.
- Allow attack ads only if they include the image of the candidate directing the attack.
- Reject unfair or inaccurate ads created by political action committees.
- Conduct ad watches as part of media coverage of a campaign analyzing the ads for omissions, inconsistencies and inaccuracies.

Finally, the audience of voters has a responsibility as well. Citizens need to demand that the candidates speak to each other about the issues. When they do demand such engagement, they get surprisingly good information—from journalistic accounts and from the candidates themselves. Political advertising represents an important area of shared political responsibility in contemporary democracies.

## Modern Mediated Problems: Getting Connected with the Community

Beginning in the early 1990s, the buzzwords "public journalism" or "civic journalism" began to invade the newsroom. To some, it was a direct surrender of the editorial process in a blatant attempt to regain dwindling readership. To others it was a praiseworthy response by newspapers to be less conflict driven and more responsive to reader interests in determining what is news.

What is the public journalism movement? Some say it isn't even defined. However, Jay Rosen, one of public journalism's leading proponents suggests "what public journalism is fundamentally about is using the power of the press to re-engage people in public life, in the belief that disengaged, complacent or cynical people cannot make use of what journalists have to offer" (Rosen 1995, 6).

The notion of public journalism as a link to re-connect the disenfranchised is echoed by Davis Merritt (1995) in *Public Journalism and Public Life.* Merritt sees the aim of public journalism as ensuring that "Americans understand the true choices they have about issues so they can see themselves, their hopes and their values again reflected in politics."

Just how to operationalize this goal is problematic. One starting place for some news operations has been to make the newsroom culture more open, more democratic and more deliberative, often engaging the public in a decision-making process that was formerly tightly held by a few editors. For instance, in 1990, Merritt led the *Wichita* (Kansas) *Eagle* in "Your Vote Counts." The project identified twelve issues of importance to Kansans and gave intense coverage of them in the final two months of the campaign rather than the usual "horse race" coverage of most elections. That effort was followed in 1992 by "The People Project," a comprehensive review of four major Wichita community issues: education, crime, government gridlock and stress on the family.

Perhaps the most documented instance of community journalism was the *Charlotte Observer* project. The project began with a poll in late 1991 to determine the "Citizens' Agenda," the issues most important to the residents of Charlotte. The *Observer* responded by focusing its coverage in the 1992 elections on those issues determined by the public to be of consequence to them. Furthermore, the newspaper held the candidates accountable to that agenda by focusing on where they stood on those issues and downplaying polls, tactics and the usual pseudo-events of a political campaign.

In the end more people registered and voted in Charlotte than ever before. Edward Miller (1994, 3) of the Poynter Institute for Media Studies assisted in the project and reported the following findings:

- Readers can be partners as well as customers
- Exploring solutions is as important to readers as exposing problems
- Journalism's allegiance to "objectivity" often comes at a price of community understanding and engagement

- Political coverage should be about what's important to citizens, not just what's important to politicians or the press
- News organizations can change; so, too, can the forms of journalism;
- Erosion of citizenship and news readership are linked; to revive one you need to revive both.

However, not every journalist agrees with Miller. "Newspapers are not to take sides—even for Mom and apple pie and the flag. . . . That stuff should be saved for the editorial pages" according to Michael Gartner, publisher of the *Des Moines Register* and a former president of NBC News (Fitzgerald, 1995, p. 20). William Henry III, former media critic for *Time,* lambasted the "shameless panderers who 'edit' by readership survey" in his posthumously published book *In Defense of Elitism.* "They sample audience opinion and use that as their primary guide. . . as though readers already know news before they see it (Henry 1994, 6).

Can public journalism stray too far from the journalistic norm of objectivity and detachment? Some see the end result of public journalism as an abandonment of objectivity in the name of a greater good.

Merritt disagrees. "It doesn't have anything to do with objectivity. There's a difference between objectivity and detachment. Journalists don't give up their ability to evaluate the facts when they care about the issue." Merritt compares the journalist's ability to be passionate and objective at the same time to that of a scientific researcher.

What is public journalism? "Public journalism is (and virtually has to be) an invention of each newspaper that uses it," says Arthur Charity in *Doing Public Journalism.* This lack of a precise definition of what constitutes public journalism probably fuels the debate.

When it is broadly defined, probably many of the critics of public journalism actually practice it. More narrowly defined, public journalism is still in the experimental stages.

Will public journalism last? The Charlotte experiment, easily the most publicized public journalism project of the 1990s, might not work at another location or even at another time. But what must be found is a way for the media to reclaim its role in preparing a citizenry to participate in a democracy.

## Modern Mediated Problems: Covering Political Character

Conceptualizations of character have changed significantly since the founding of the republic, when character was defined in Aristotelian terms—an observable collection of habits, virtues and vices. Freudian psychology has altered that definition to include motivation, the subconscious, and relationships that help to form all of us as people. What journalists cover is *political character:* the intersection of personality and public performance within a cultural and a historical context. Character is dynamic; it represents a synergistic interaction of a person within an environment (Davies 1963).

Journalists who explore character often do so for an ethical reason, despite apparent invasions of privacy. Privacy in Western culture is regarded as a right that can be negated by other more compelling rights (Grcic 1986, 141). Political figures are powerful people. Ethicist Sissela Bok (1978) has noted that when an unequal power relationship is involved, it is possible to justify what would otherwise be considered an unethical act. To paraphrase Bok, at the core of any serious investigation of the private character of public people is the notion that if the person one wishes to investigate is also in the position to do one harm, then invading privacy in an attempt to counter that threat is justified.

However, that invasion also needs to meet some tests:

- The invasion must be placed in a larger context of facts and history. Since one of the definitions of invasion of privacy is the subject's loss of control over the context of information (Westin 1967), an effort to study character must include enough context to provide meaning.
- The revelation of private facts about political figures should meet the traditional tests of journalistic publicity and evidence. Further, these private facts need to be linked to public, political behaviors before publication or broadcast becomes ethically justifiable.
- The invasion of privacy must further the larger political discourse. Investigation of the character of political figures must meet the most demanding ethical test: the need to know (Schoeman 1984).

Careful reporting on character can pass these tests. However, journalists must also be willing to weigh the harm done to others, particularly those who have not sought the public limelight. While public officials do have the capacity to do harm, that argument is much less compelling when applied to parents, spouses, children, friends and other family members. Journalistic investigation of character may often involve others, but publication or broadcast of what is learned should be considered only if public awareness of such facts furthers the political discourse.

Even reporting that passes these three tests must be filtered through discretion. Merely publishing private information without this tie to a more public role is a form of "tabloid journalism" that casts doubt on journalistic motives and credibility. More seriously, such publication denigrates politicians in such a way that every official becomes a "crook," "liar," or "philanderer" without some larger understanding of why those character traits may or may not be important in doing the public's business.

Reporters covering political character should be aware of some or all of the following building blocks of character:

- The politician's development of a sense of trust;
- A politician's own sense of self-worth and self-esteem;
- The development of a politician's relationship to power and authority;
- Early influences on adult policy outlook;
- How a politician establishes contact with people;
- The flexibility, adaptability, and purposefulness of mature adulthood;
- The historical moment.

The media's current emphasis on covering political character provides the best illustration of the need to balance the demands of governing with privacy considerations. No culture has ever expected its leaders to be saints; in fact, some cultures have prized leadership that is decidedly unsaintly. By emphasizing an almost inhuman standard of public behavior, the mass media may be setting a standard of public behavior that may be impossible to meet as well as politically inadvisable.

However, an in-depth and nonjudgmental explanation of character can spur and expand the political debate, particularly if journalists treat character as one political story among many and if they are willing to imbed character in a history and political context Americans share. A deep exploration of character may help Americans think deeply about what we as a political system mean by and need from leadership.

## Modern Mediated Problems: Governing

One of the ironies of democratic politics is that, in order to accomplish something, you first have to get elected. But accomplishing something—not getting elected—is the major work of politics. Many inches of newspaper space are devoted to the process on the local level. Local television news provides much less attention to policy-making. Regulatory agencies, the courts, and even the Congress are not considered glamour beats by the national press corps.

But the national press corps particularly has changed how the policy process operates. No one is quite certain when the "media leak" originated, certainly back in the last century. Not only has a leak to a reporter become a fact of political life; it appears to alter how policymakers work, sometimes policy itself.

Political scientist Martin Linsky (1986) describes how leaks have become part of the Washington policy-making process. Government officials, both elected and appointed, use the mass media to help make policy in a variety of ways, he says. Sometimes they leak a story to find out how others will react to an idea, a practice known as floating a "trial balloon" in the press. Other times, policymakers will leak a story because they wish to mount either public or bureaucratic support for or opposition to a set of options.

Sometimes leaks take the form of whistle-blowing when a government employee honestly believes the public good is not being served by working through the system. Watergate's famed and unnamed source "Deep Throat" apparently was motivated by such a belief when he leaked parts of the government investigation into the break-in to *Washington Post* reporters Bob Woodward and Carl Bernstein. Anti-Vietnam War activist Daniel Ellsberg admits a desire to fuel opposition to national policy was much of his motivation in leaking the Pentagon Papers to the *New York Times.*

Still other times, government officials leak a story to put a particular reporter or publication on notice about who really holds the power in a particular situation. Network news correspondent Bill Moyers was taught that lesson by Lyndon Johnson, who told him that he planned to fire J. Edgar Hoover, a scoop Moyers reported. Johnson appointed Hoover director of the FBI for life the very next day. Moyers was stuck with a story that was accurate but not true. Worse, he had become the subject of Johnson's well-known propensity for power plays. It was a lesson in trust and political power Moyers never forgot.

Linsky's work about the role of the media in the policy-making process raises at least two important points regarding ethical journalistic practice.

First, leaks are becoming a more acceptable way of doing government business and policymakers are using them skillfully. In the summer of 1989, when terrorist groups in the Middle East threatened to kill one or more of the Americans they held hostage, then-President George Bush allowed a staff member to leak a story to a trusted *New York Times* reporter that the United States would retaliate militarily if hostages were killed. Bush's message was sent to the terrorists not through diplomatic back channels but on the front page of the *New York Times.*

Second, leaks can alter the outcome of the policy process itself. President Bill Clinton's 1993 trial balloon about the potential of freezing the Social Security cost of living allowance provoked immediate congressional opposition yet enlarged the range of politically acceptable options—including taxing a larger percentage of some Social Security benefits—to reduce the nation's deficit.

Of fundamental importance for journalists is the question of whether reporters, editors and their news organizations should become consciously involved in the process of governing, and in what manner? Such willing involvement runs counter to established notions of objectivity but not to the history of the media themselves. Leaks are so common that journalists can no longer plead ignorance of either their existence or of their impact. Instead they must decide if, and how, they are willing to be used—and for what political purposes. These are difficult questions, particularly when big stories, professional prestige, and the chance to influence world events hinges on the outcome of ethical decision making.

## Modern Mediated Problems: Arrogance without Authority

Although the evolving role of the mass media in a democratic society has been widely analyzed, most ethicists agree that the media's primary function is to provide citizens with information that will allow them to make informed political choices (Hodges 1986; Elliott 1986). As part of performing that job, the media are expected to act as a watchdog on government. This watchdog role arises from the founder's original skepticism of concentrated political power. The watchdog media enable citizens to learn about and then check inappropriate government activity.

While the founders built many checks and balances into the original American system, those checks and balances were designed to enable government to continue to function. The founders tried to guard against any single check fundamentally undermining the American experiment. The watchdog media—examined from this perspective—also have a "guide dog" function. Their goal is to help citizens make their way through the political process, not to immobilize them with a series of false trails or a sense that all political activity is futile.

However, many contemporary media critics argue that a particular style of covering politics, one emphasizing conflict and wrongdoing, has soured both journalists and citizens on American democracy. Political reporter E. J. Dionne in *Why Americans Hate Politics* (1991) argues that definitions of news that emphasize conflict inevitably help to degenerate political debate into a shouting match between diametrically opposed factions that have no reason to compromise. He notes that contemporary debate both over abortion and race has taken on this "us vs. them" quality, one that fails to acknowledge an important series of majority agreements on both issues—namely that abortion is not a particularly good method of birth control and that a sizable majority of Americans accept that human beings are of equal value and that learning to get along with one another is crucial in daily, political life.

Dionne adds that politics without government, a concept that seems to have rhetorical support across the political continuum, is an oxymoron. And, while he does not blame the mass media for creating these sorts of false rhetorical divisions, he does hold his own profession accountable for failing to point out what they mean in the context of a democratic form of government. In this, Dionne agrees with Plato, who said that democratic politics, while a "degenerative" form of government, was probably the best available system considering that human beings were its primary components.

Media critic James Fallows goes one step further. He holds a journalism permeated by a cynical and conflict-laden view of politics directly responsible for voter apathy, Congressional gridlock and government via opinion polls rather than political leadership.

> The harm actually goes much further than that, to threaten the long-term health of our political system. Step by step, mainstream journalism has fallen into the habit of portraying public life in America as a race to the bottom, in which one group of conniving, insincere politicians ceaselessly tries to outmaneuver another. The great problem for American democracy in the 1990s is that people barely trust elected leaders or the entire legislative system to accomplish anything of value . . . Deep forces in America's political, social and economic structures account for most of the frustration of today's politics, but the media's attitudes have played a surprisingly important and destructive role." (Fallows 1996, 7)

In fact, media critic Katherine Hall Jamieson has suggested that, when it comes to politics, journalists should get themselves a new definition of news. Instead of emphasizing events and conflict, Jamieson believes news stories could equally revolve around issues and multiple policy perspectives. This suggestion even has some support in academic research; readers are more interested in coverage that emphasizes policy issues as opposed to fights and horse races (Sheehan and Robinson 1984).

Implicit in this and other criticism is a concept not only of journalistic rights but also of responsibilities. Fallows and others insist that journalists have a right to report on government. But implicit in that right in the sense that successful governing is a political outcome that matters and that the media themselves are a powerful institution within the democratic system and hence partially responsible for its continued well-being. The cynical assumption that government can never act for the public good, and the arrogant stance that journalists and the media organizations they represent are somehow outside the political system, are almost nihilistic in this view. We, like many journalists and scholars, believe there is real meat behind this critique of "mad dog" journalism. Conscientious ethical practice will allow journalists and media consumers alike to begin the work of carving out new understandings of our *responsibilities and rights* when the mass media become involved in the American democratic political system.

## Mediated Modern Problems: Social Justice

Just as there are members of a power elite, there are also those who feel excluded from political society. While some scholars have argued that one interpretation of American history has been the gradual extension of the franchise to ever more diverse publics, that extension of basic rights has been uneven and contentious. All of these minority groups seek access to the political process and, since the mass media have become major institutional forces in that process, they seek access to media as well.

Media ethicists suggest these political and social out-groups provide the mass media with a further set of responsibilities. They assert that the mass media, and individual journalists, need to become advocates for the politically homeless. Media ethicist Clifford Christians suggests that "justice for the powerless stands at the centerpiece of a socially responsible press. Or, in other terms, the litmus test of whether or not the news profession fulfills its mission over the long term is its advocacy for those outside the socioeconomic establishment" (Christians 1986, 110).

This socially responsible view of the media suggests that journalists have a duty both to promote community and to promote the individuals within it. Those who are in significant ways outside the community—economically, socially, or culturally different—need a voice.

By advocacy, Christians does not mean reporting that espouses only one sort of political or social agenda. Rather, he insists,

> Press portrayals feed into public discourse and play a portentous role in the shape our culture and the sociopolitical realm ultimately take. In its loftiest sense, the press ought to amplify public debate and reconstitute the argument so that it becomes an important public forum where significant issues of social justice are fruitfully raised and resolved. (Christians 1986, 123)

Christians's argument can be amplified beyond democracy's racial, ethnic and economic out-groups. Clearly in contemporary democratic society, some "things" also are without political voice. The environment, racial equality, and events beyond American shores all have difficulty finding a powerful domestic spokesperson. These issues cross traditional political boundaries. Those who will be affected by them also seem to be without a voice.

What makes many journalists uneasy about a socially responsible media is that it smacks of a kind of benevolent paternalism. If individual human beings carry moral stature, then assigning one institution—in this case the mass media—the role of social and political arbiter diminishes the moral worth of the individual citizen. The mass media become a kind parent and the citizen a sort of wayward child in need of guidance. Such a relationship does not promote political maturity.

While the weight of recent scholarly opinion sides with Christians, such a view is not without risk. If accepted, it means a thoroughgoing change for the mass media in the American political system. That change would bring about other changes—some of them not easy to anticipate. But whether change is what's needed, or merely a return to the strict libertarian view, both call for some sophisticated ethical reasoning. As Thomas Jefferson said, being a citizen of a democracy is not easy. To which journalists might well add, neither is covering one.

## Suggested Readings

Dionne, E. J., Jr. 1992. *Why Americans hate politics.* New York: Touchtone.

Fallows, James. 1996. *Breaking the news: How the media undermine American democracy.* New York: Pantheon.

Fry, Don, ed. 1983. *The adversary press.* St. Petersburg, FL: The Modern Media Institute.

Jamieson, Kathleen Hall, and Karlyn Kohrs Campbell. 1983. *The interplay of influence.* Belmont, CA: Wadsworth Press.

Linsky, Martin. 1986. *Impact: How the press affects federal policymaking.* New York: W. W. Norton.

Madison, James S., Alexander Hamilton, and John Jay. *The Federalist papers.*

Merritt, Davis. 1995. *Public journalism and public life,* Hillsdale, NJ: Lawrence Erlbaum Associates.

# CHAPTER VI CASES

## CASE VI-A
## Victims and the Press
ROBERT LOGAN
*University of Missouri*

Alice Waters's daughter, Julie, seven, has leukemia. Her illness was diagnosed in its early stages in March 1990. Julie's physicians believe her condition can be successfully treated.

Ms. Waters, thirty-seven, lives in a mobile home in an unincorporated area a few miles from Metroplex, a city of 1.5 million. Ms. Waters's street is the only residential section in the area. At the north end of the street—which has twelve mobile homes on each side facing one another—are four large service stations, which catch traffic off the interstate that runs a quarter-mile away to the west. At the south end of the street (about a quarter-mile away) are two large tanks that are a relatively small storage facility for Big Oil Inc. Next to this—starting almost in her backyard—is the boundary of a successful, seven-hundred-acre grapefruit orchard, which borders on a municipal landfill. About a quarter-mile away are large well fields that are the principal source of drinking water for Metroplex.

In July 1989, a six-year-old boy in the household two doors down from Ms. Waters was diagnosed as having leukemia. He was not as lucky as Julie; his diagnosis was late in the progression of his disease, and he died in December 1990. In 1991, an infant girl became the second baby born with birth defects in the neighborhood within seven years. Both families moved before Ms. Waters came to the neighborhood in 1989.

Internal specialists Dr. Earnest and Dr. Sincere met Julie soon after she was admitted to the hospital in October 1990. They were instrumental in getting funding for Julie's care when her mother was unable to pay. They are members of Worried M.D.'s for Social Responsibility, a self-proclaimed liberal, national public-interest group that gets actively involved in national political issues.

The physicians told Ms. Waters that they were suspicious about the causes of Julie's illness. Two cancer and birth-defect incidents on the same street, the physicians said, were not a coincidence.

In November 1991, they began to collect water samples from the well head at Ms. Waters's house. They sent the samples to a well-regarded testing lab in another city. Since then, they have tested the water at a professional lab every four months. Every test revealed traces of more than 10 human-made and natural chemicals often associated with oil storage tanks, pesticides, and grapefruit orchards, gas-station leaks, lead from automobile emissions, and a large landfill.

But each chemical occurs consistently at six to fifteen parts per billion, which is considered safe for drinking water via standards set by the EPA. At higher levels these chemicals are associated with carcinogenic risks or increases in birth defects, but the levels found at Ms. Waters's well head are within safety thresholds set by the

EPA. There is no evidence the chemicals are associated directly with the health problems found in Ms. Waters's neighborhood.

At a fund-raising party last night for mayoral candidate Sam Clean, Drs. Earnest and Sincere privately tell Clean what they have found. Clean is a well-known public figure, has a reputation as an environmentalist, owns a successful health-food restaurant chain, is media wise, and looks good on television. He is a long shot to become mayor and needs fresh issues to draw attention to his candidacy.

At 11:00 A.M. today, KAOS news radio begins running as the top story in its twenty-minute news rotation "Clean Attacks City Lack of Cleanup." In the story, Clean gives a sound bite attacking city officials for "ignoring cancer-causing agents in water in a neighborhood where children have died, which is next door to the city's water supply." He describes the neighborhood's medical problems and describes (without naming) Julie and Alice Waters. The news report explains that water from the neighborhood has several "toxic agents believed to cause cancer at higher levels" and points out that the city's water wells are within a quarter-mile of oil tanks, gas stations, a grapefruit orchard, a landfill, and septic tanks. County officials are said to be unavailable for comment. The report runs throughout the day at twenty-minute intervals.

By 2:30 P.M., calls to the switchboard have jammed the newsroom. The callers who get through are frightened about their drinking water. City Hall's switchboards are jammed. The callers sound upset and ask whether their water is safe to drink.

By 4:00 P.M., reporters from the local ABC affiliate are already knocking on doors in the trailer park and sending live reports from the scene. Neighbors tell them where Alice and Julie Waters live.

At 4:15 P.M., your managing editor gives you the story. You are an ambitious reporter for *Metroplex Today,* the only morning newspaper in Metroplex. Both of you realize this is clearly page one potential, but you have only a few hours before deadline for the next morning's edition. After a few phone calls, you discover that the mayor, the city council, and most city and county officials are all out of town at a retreat and are unavailable for comment. The regional EPA office is not answering the phone.

A trusted spokesperson for Regional Hospital tells you that Sincere and Earnest are furious at Clean for releasing the story and have no comment. She fills you in with all of the above information.

The same Regional Hospital spokesperson says Ms. Waters does not want to be interviewed. She suddenly realizes that her husband, whom she walked out on several years before, might see the story and return to town.

Sam Clean is more than happy to talk to you.

## Micro Issues:

1. Is Clean a reliable enough source on whom KAOS radio could base its reports?

2. Should KAOS have broadcast the story?
3. Should you respect Ms. Waters's wishes and leave her and her daughter out of the story?
4. Are Dr. Earnest and Dr. Sincere reliable sources?
5. What do you tell the public about whether the water supply is safe?

## Middle-range Issues:

1. Would you be working on the story if KAOS and ABC had ignored it?
2. Would you be working on the story if there was little public reaction after KAOS broadcast?
3. If Ms. Waters decides to do an interview on ABC later today, do you then include her in your story?
4. If city and county officials remain unavailable, how do you handle their side of the story? Does that delay publication until you can get more information, or do you go with what is available?
5. Are there unbiased sources you can contact about risk assessment? Who?

## Macro Issues:

1. How do you handle the discrepancy between the information from the EPA and the skeptical scientists-environmentalists?
2. What is the public's probable reaction to reporting this story? Should your newspaper take any precautions to prevent public panic, and if so, what should they be?
3. How risky is the water compared to risks we take for granted, such as traveling by car? Can you think of a relevant comparison for your article comparing the relative risk of the water to a well-known risk?
4. Is it the media's role to speak for a society that is averse to many risks? How might the media accomplish this function?

## CASE VI-B
## The David Duke Candidacy: Fairness and the Klansman
KEITH WOODS
*The Poynter Institute for Media Studies*

In the fall of 1991 David Duke, the former Ku Klux Klan Grand Wizard, made a run for the Louisiana governor's mansion.

He had sat for the past year in the state Legislature, an ineffective representative from a small Republican district in the New Orleans suburbs. He had not passed a single piece of legislation, was routinely heckled when he took the House floor, and found that many of his colleagues would avoid even standing close to him, lest they get captured in the same photograph or the same video frame.

The media had alternately ignored him and held him up to public scrutiny and criticism. Though he had repeatedly disavowed any recent connection to the Klan, Duke was discovered selling white supremacist materials from his Legislative office.

The evidence was compelling that the only difference between the old Duke and the new Duke was minor cosmetic surgery, a haircut and the stamp of approval from voters in Metairie's District 81.

Then he ran for governor. His primary opponents were formidable: Incumbent Gov. Buddy Roemer, a Democrat-turned-Republican held in generally high regard by the media because of his reformist ideals; former Gov. Edwin Edwards, a populist Democrat with enough charisma to withstand two federal indictments in his previous 12 years in office; and Republican Congressman Clyde Holloway, a conservative whose legitimacy with voters would surely siphon votes from Duke.

For most of the campaign, Duke was given very little chance of even making a runoff. When the votes were counted on Oct. 19, he had come within three percentage points of finishing first in the primary.

He would face primary leader Edwards in the runoff, and Louisiana voters would face the unpleasant task of choosing between a former Klansman and a proven scoundrel.

The *New Orleans Times-Picayune* had underestimated Duke twice before: when he ran an impressive, though losing, campaign for the U.S. Senate against powerful incumbent J. Bennett Johnston and when he shocked the newspaper and many voters by capturing District 81. Having witnessed Duke's statewide popularity yet again, the newspaper took decisive and controversial steps to help defeat him.

Two days after the election, the newspaper's top editors and editorial writers gathered around a newsroom conference table for a meeting that would greatly influence everything from the paper's editorial direction to the focus of its daily coverage.

The unusual meeting, fruit of an election-night brainstorming session between Editor Jim Amoss and then-metro editor Peter Kovacs, produced this plan: The newspaper would employ its best editors to research and write a series of five editorials—twice as long as the standard editorial—that would make a fact-based,

AP/WORLDWIDE PHOTOS

methodical argument against Duke's candidacy. Each editorial would be promoted on the front page.

The decision to use key newsroom editors to write the editorials, including the capitol bureau chief in charge of state government coverage, pushed the *Picayune* newsroom across the line of objectivity at the outset of its runoff coverage. Amoss characterized the four weeks that followed as no less than a battle for the soul of the electorate.

In those four weeks, the newspaper focused the attention of more than 40 staffers on the election, with much of the focus falling upon the flaws and fallacies of Duke's candidacy. As themes developed in the campaign and in the newsroom— Duke's recent racist and anti-Semitic musings, his dubious religious conversion, his ties to bigots, his political immaturity—the newspaper hammered away on the front page and editorial page. Sometimes the editorials were on the front page.

Many readers howled with displeasure. Most were Duke supporters who blasted the newspaper's obvious bias. Some were Edwards supporters worried that the *Picayune* would provoke a ground swell of sympathy support for Duke. The newspaper began running full pages of letters to the editor, most opposing Duke, some praising the newspaper. It was a break from the *Picayune*'s tradition of refusing letters that support political candidates; a break the newspaper explained to its readers in an editorial page blurb.

When the unprecedented editorial series, "the Choice of Our Lives," had run its course, the *Picayune* mailed out reprints of the series to newspapers across the state, encouraging them to quote the editorials at will.

Several staffers wrote op-ed pieces before the election, giving readers a glimpse into an angst-torn newsroom where the prospect of Duke becoming governor brought some to tears and kept emotions on edge.

The angst found its most profound expression in an internal debate about the fate of a story dubbed "The Duke Voters." Aware that Duke's supporters were regarded as racist extremists, particularly by those in the newsroom, the newspaper sought to show the faces and hear the voices of the ordinary voters who supported such a controversial politician.

Once written, the story became the center of unusual attention. Several editors visited Amoss in his office in the days before the story was to run, pleading with him not to print it. Some said that by showing the Duke supporters in all their simple humanity so close to the election, the newspaper was giving comfort to racists and encouraging their votes. Amoss listened, but the story ran as written on the front page of the Sunday newspaper one week before the election.

Though Duke received 671,009 votes, he was soundly beaten in the runoff, with Edwards taking 60 percent of the vote. Duke blamed his defeat on a lot of negative press, the *Picayune* and its sources.

## Micro Issues:

1. What is the reporter's responsibility to objectivity when covering a person so widely believed to be a social pariah?
2. Is it possible for the reporters to be fair to Duke without being objective?
3. Did the *Times-Picayune* owe equal loyalty to readers who supported Duke as to those who opposed him?

## Middle-range Issues:

1. Should newsroom editors, who assign and help shape the bulk of the day's news stories, ever be allowed to write editorials related to those stories? If yes, under what circumstances?
2. What effect, if any, do you think the publication of staff op-ed pieces critical of Duke might have had on the newspaper's image and credibility in the community?
3. Is it possible for a newspaper in such a situation to be as aggressive with its editorial push—including publication and dissemination of the editorial series—without unduly influencing the news coverage?

4. What are the challenges to a reporter trying to reflect the views and wishes of a community so polarized, particularly when politics and prejudice are so enmeshed?

## Macro Issues:

1. Are there circumstances under which a news organization can so clearly identify a harmful political choice that it is justified in campaigning against a candidate? If so, when?
2. Where would such a line be drawn in this case? At membership in the Klan? At associations with Klan members? What if the candidate held racist views but never disclosed them publicly?
3. How does a news organization fairly cover a candidate whose notoriety becomes such a huge part of the story?
4. Editor Jim Amoss said that if the paper had taken a less aggressive tack and Duke had won, he knew the paper would be held culpable to some extent. Is that a legitimate concern for a newspaper or its editor?

## CASE VI-C
## Whose Abuse of Power: The *Seattle Times* and Brock Adams
LEE WILKINS
*University of Missouri—Columbia*

On March 1, 1992, Brock Adams, Washington state's liberal Democratic senator, abandoned his U.S. Senate re-election campaign. Adams quit, he said, because he had been destroyed by "hypothetical comments by hypothetical people."

The "hypothetical people" involved were actually eight women who had been quoted in the Sunday, March 1 edition of the *Seattle Times*. In that page-one story, the women claimed to have been the victims of Adams' sexual harassment for most of his twenty-year career that included a term in President Carter's cabinet. The *Times* had published their accounts after three years of digging. The revelations came weeks into a re-election campaign that Adams was likely to win.

While the story itself was controversial, the *Times*' reporting methods were equally unorthodox: the paper had allowed the women to remain anonymous in its accounts. The editors reached this decision only after serious and protracted discussions.

Political reporter David Boardman began work on the story in 1988 when rumors of Adams' behavior surfaced. At that time, one of the women, Kari Tupper, former Congressional aide and Adams' family friend, claimed Adams had first drugged and then molested her. The Washington D.C. police, where the complaint was filed, exonerated Adams. Boardman wrote a single story about the allegations.

During the next three years, Boardman says, he and other reporters at the *Times* began receiving calls and tips that other women had encountered similar experiences with Adams. Slowly, the *Times* began to build a file on Adams, often checking with the women, their friends and acquaintances, for any possible way to verify situations that had always occurred in private. No reporter worked full time on the story, and the paper was unable to convince anyone other than Tupper to go on the record.

By mid-1990, the list of Adams' accusers had grown to eight. Even though the women themselves remained anonymous, the *Times* had checked their stories in every way it could. Most of the women did not know each other; those who were acquainted were unaware that others were making similar charges. All were respected members of the community, and most were active in state and city politics. Furthermore, their accounts revealed a pattern. Boardman believed them.

However, the paper and its staff were reluctant to publish the charges without sources willing to go on the record. Beginning in mid-1990, when the actual reporting on the case began to consume more staff time, the paper tried to convince the women to go on the record. Eventually, seven of the eight women signed a statement swearing that what they were saying was true and acknowledging that they would be asked to testify openly in court if Adams sued the newspaper.

The *Times* published its story on March 1. While only Tupper was named in the story, the *Times* provided thumbnail sketches of the others, including their job titles, employment histories, or work relationships to Adams. Boardman has stated that, based on what the newspaper printed, it was impossible for Adams not to have known the specific identities of his accusers even without the names.

In a front-page column explaining why the paper had printed the story, Executive Editor Michael R. Fancher said the women were credible people with no reason to lie about Adams. The editorial continued: "The alleged incidents described were not consensual love affairs or 'womanizing,' but abuses of power and of women. As such, they raise questions about Adams' character, both personal and political, that we believe voters should have an opportunity to evaluate."

The *Times'* use of anonymous sources in the Adams story has been widely discussed. Some have suggested that the paper should have held the story until it had sources willing to go on the record, regardless of the impending election. Others saw the publication as the inevitable outcome of so much expenditure of the *Times* resources. Thomas L. Shaffer, a visiting professor of law at Boston College of Law, represented this view when he wrote:

> A news organization's sitting on three years of diligent investigation, by four creative news people, is like the leaders of a fully equipped army of millions wondering if the army should go to war. A clear-eyed placer of bets will give you odds on publication in the one case, war in the other. This is not to accuse the *Times* people of cynicism but only to notice that the real decision in the Adams case was made in 1988, when the *Times* decided to significantly invest in the story.

## Micro Issues:

1. At what point should the *Times* have considered running a story about the allegations?
   (*a*)  When one other victim had a similar story to Tupper's?
   (*b*)  When multiple victims had a similar story to Tupper's?
   (*c*)  Not at all?
2. Adams was informed of the story before it went to press. He refused to comment. Do you include that in your report?

## Middle-range Issues:

1. In the neighboring state of Oregon, Senator Bob Packwood was accused of a pattern of sexual harassment over his career, a story that broke late in 1992. Yet the Portland *Oregonian* did not run the story until after the November 1992 election. Did the *Oregonian* show too much restraint? Did the *Times* show too little?
2. Also in Seattle, a judge committed suicide on the eve before a story ran in the rival *Seattle Post-Intelligencer* accusing him of sexual misconduct with several boys who came before his court. As the rumors circulated during the months-long investigation by the paper, he had announced that he was not seeking re-election and was moving out of town. The newspaper ran the story

anyway. When the issue is abuse of power, is the story moot when the accused is no longer powerful? If Adams had decided to retire *before* the stories ran, does that kill the story or do you run it anyway?

3. Critique the quote by Shaffer that the real decision occurred when the newspaper decided to pursue the story in 1988.
4. What should a news organization's policy be about using
   (*a*) anonymous sources?
   (*b*) leaks?
   (*c*) off-the-record information?

## Macro Issues:

1. The *Times* worked on the story for three years. During that time did it have a responsibility to Adams' associates to tell what was suspected? What is the role of the newspaper in informing its readership about alleged but not convicted sexual offenders?
2. What rights does the accused have in cases such as this?
3. Fancher claims in his front-page editorial that the allegations about Adams went beyond "womanizing" and spoke to the issues of his personal and political character. Do you agree or disagree? Why?
4. Is the media a proper institution to judge character?
5. On issues such as sexual harassment, can the media afford to be objective?

## CASE VI-D
## The Gym Shoe Phenomenon: Social Values vs. Marketability
GAIL BAKER WOODS
*University of Florida*

Sprinkled between the abandoned burned-out buildings and the glass-covered vacant lots of Chicago's South Side are bigger-than-life billboards featuring famous athletes wearing expensive Nike gym shoes. Basketball superstar Michael Jordan claims he can jump higher while wearing the shoes; former football great Bo Jackson boasts he can run faster in Nike athletic shoes. Controversial movie director Spike Lee says people of different backgrounds would get along better wearing good athletic shoes.

The company is excited about the "Air Jordan" and "Bo Knows" athletic shoe campaigns it developed for the African-American market. And to ensure that the campaigns are sensitive to African-American consumers, Nike hired legendary Georgetown University basketball coach John Thompson as a $200,000-a-year consultant.

In addition, Nike is careful to select only athletes with "squeaky clean" reputations. Neither Jordan nor Jackson has ever been involved in drugs. Both are family men who are active in their communities. The company believes they can clearly be considered role models for the African-American youths who see, hear and read the advertisements. It is thought that these celebrities add credibility to the product and enhance the image of the expensive shoes, which cost between $50 to $125 a pair.

Back in the Chicago ghetto, a 16-year-old black youth is shot and killed on his way to school. Police surmise that he is murdered for his $125 gym shoes. They are the only pieces of clothing missing from his bloody body when the authorities arrive. Unfortunately, this is not the first case of assault or murder provoked by a pair of expensive shoes. Because they have become so fashionable and because they are so expensive, inner city children are robbing and killing each other to look more like the athletic celebrities they wish to emulate.

Some gangs name themselves after the shoes and shave the name into their haircuts. Parents sometimes sacrifice necessities to purchase the shoes for their children.

The popularity of the shoes and the violence that is sometimes associated with them is noticed by leaders in the African-American community. Nike is criticized in the media for selecting black athletes as spokespersons.

Eric Perkins of the Educational Testing Service, calls the use of black athletes, "exploitative, because advertisers are playing into the subliminal fascination with black superiority in the white collective psyche." Others criticize Nike for what they believe to be a lack of minority hiring and black community support. Nike is also accused of promoting athletics over academics. Only one in 10,000 high school athletes ever becomes a professional, and only 20 percent of all black college athletes ever finish college.

Jesse Jackson and other religious and civil rights leaders call for a national boycott of Nike to protest the company's business practices. Rev. Jackson is particularly critical of the African-Americans who endorse athletic shoes, saying "They are exploiting an ethos of mindless materialism."

Operation PUSH (People United to Save Humanity), a civil rights organization founded by Rev. Jackson, joins the boycott effort. PUSH officials complain that sales of Nike shoes to blacks total $200 million annually, while the company has no high-ranking black executives and does not do business with black-owned advertising agencies. The company responds by saying that sales to non-whites account for only 14 percent of its sales. Nike also states that 7.5 percent of its 4,200 U.S. employees are black.

Fourteen weeks into the boycott, the Rev. Tyrone Crider, executive director of Operation PUSH, says the boycott would continue "until Nike decides to put money in black-owned banks, advertise with black-owned media, do business with black-owned businesses and put a black on its board of directors."

On the other side of the issue, Nike spokespersons say it was just good marketing to use Bo Jackson and Michael Jordan in their advertisements. "He (Jackson) is a person kids can look up to. He's crazy about his kids and his wife and family. He's somebody who has applied himself and came from a really humble background," said Melinda Gable, public relations executive for Nike.

Jordan, Lee and Thompson meet with Jackson in an effort to stop the boycott. The meeting is unsuccessful and the boycott continues.

Nike announces during the boycott that it would hire a minority vice president and named a minority to its board of directors by 1992. The company also hires a minority advertising agency, Muse Codero and Chen, out of Los Angeles, to handle a portion of its account.

Nike shoe sales, unaffected by the boycott, increase 58 percent over the same period the previous year. After several months and a number of news articles and television stories, the Nike boycott fades from the national headlines and Nike continues its use of black athletes in its advertising campaigns. Inner city crime continues, but few news reports link the violence to clothing or shoes.

Following the boycott, the company develops a "Bo Knows School" campaign, featuring Jackson, and distributes thousands of book jackets to inner city schools. On it Jackson appears in a graduation cap and gown, a band uniform, a scientist's white lab coat and a Greek philosopher's toga. The book jacket read "Bo knows all this stuff because he stayed in school."

Although the company now receives applause for its interest in education, critics still question the tie-in with African-American athletes.

## Micro Issues:

1. Is Nike advertising responsible for the inner city violence that occurred after its campaign?
2. Did Nike's decision to hire an ethnic advertising agency relieve the company of its social responsibility or was it just a public relations ploy?

## Middle-range Issues:

1. Is Nike guilty of stereotyping African-Americans by using athletes in their ads?
2. If Nike didn't use athletes to promote athletic shoes, whom should it select?
3. Should athletes be used as role models in advertising aimed at black youths since such a small percentage of African-Americans ever play professional sports?
4. Do product manufacturers need to be sensitive to the social and economic conditions of their potential clients or should they be able to market any product that sells, as long as it's legal?

## Macro Issues:

1. Should advertisers respond to pressure placed upon them by community activists?
2. Can advertising be held accountable for social problems that stem from poverty and lack of opportunity?

## CASE VI-E
## Denver's Rocky Flats: The Role of the Alternative Press
LEE WILKINS
*University of Missouri—Columbia*

*Westword* is one of the Denver metropolitan area's two alternative weekly newspapers. It specializes in stories that the two metropolitan dailies and four television stations won't touch. It often winds up being criticized for reporting that is on the edge of both advocacy and ethics.

Early in 1992 *Westword* Editor Pat Calhoun and one of her staff reporters received a tip that a federal grand jury was ready to issue indictments over the management of the Rocky Flats nuclear facility, the only plant in the U.S. making plutonium triggers for nuclear bombs. Further, the tipster indicated that the grand jury's conclusions were meeting resistance from U.S. Attorney Mike Norton, who had been assigned to the case.

Calhoun knew the tip represented a potentially big and important story. Rocky Flats had been the subject of suspicion and protest in the Denver area for thirty years. Its most recent history included an FBI investigation, charges of improper storage of highly dangerous radioactive waste, questions about employee safety and security, and possible cost overruns. As the Cold War came to a close, Denver-area debate over Rocky Flats intensified. The facility employed about 6,000 people, but, it also was a focus for anti-war, anti-military, and environmental concern. The plant was located only eight miles from Denver, in an area that was becoming ever more densely populated. Further, the plant produced potentially deadly waste and several local municipalities had sued the plant and its various owners for contamination of local water supplies.

The twenty-three-person grand jury was empaneled after the FBI conducted a surprise raid on the plant in August of 1989, carrying away boxloads of documents as evidence. When Denver Judge Sherman Finesilver empaneled the grand jury, he swore them to secrecy but added that the grand jurors were free to tell him their own conclusions about any potential criminal wrongdoing. A local mainstream newspaper, the *Boulder Daily Camera,* published the names and the professions of the grand jurors at that time. The group met for an afternoon a week for the next two and one-half years, issuing a report about the case in January of 1992. Finesilver dismissed the twenty-two jurors (one had died during the investigation) in March and sealed the grand jury's report without making it public.

Soon after the grand jury was dismissed, U.S. Attorney Norton struck a plea bargain with the plant's now-former operators, Rockwell International. Rockwell agreed to plead guilty to ten environmental law violations and pay a fine of $18.5 million. Charges never were brought against any individual associated with the corporation. The fine was levied on activities that occurred during a year in which Rockwell had reported profits in excess of $100 million.

When Calhoun and her reporter first received the tip, they decided to pursue the grand jurors, based on the previously published list, to see if they could get any of them to talk about the grand jury's findings. They agreed that they should publish only if they could get a majority of the grand jurors to speak.

Working part-time over the next 12 months, Calhoun and her staff gradually convinced 11 of the grand jurors to talk. Their work became much easier after the plea bargain, when several of the grand jurors—including the grand jury foreman—began to assert that the grand jury had wanted much more serious charges brought not only against Rockwell but also against individuals in the corporation. They even gave copies of documents presented to the grand jury to Calhoun.

Calhoun and her staff had a series of decisions to make, knowing that the grand jurors and the paper potentially risked contempt of court proceedings.

## Micro Issues:

1. What should Calhoun print and how should she source her story?
2. Should the paper try to contact the judge, the U.S. Attorney, and other interested parties about its findings before publication?

Calhoun and her staff did print the story, along with some of the leaked documents, in the paper's September 30, 1992 edition without naming the individual grand jurors they quoted. "I knew we had to print this," Calhoun said. "The public has a right to know . . . and there was a government coverup involved."

Five days before the story was to appear, the paper contacted both Finesilver and Norton for comment. Neither responded. Four days before the story appeared, Finesilver issued a ruling in which he explained why he had sealed the grand jury findings. In that ruling, he stated that the grand jury had exceeded its authority and that some of the jury's conclusions were based on speculation.

The *Westword* story was picked up by the *New York Times,* where it ran on page one, and by all the mainstream Denver media. Former Denver Democratic Congresswoman Pat Schroeder asked for an investigation of the U.S. Attorneys office's handling of the case. Several of the grand jurors ultimately went public, including the foreman, a Colorado rancher who held a press conference on the steps of the state capitol building in Denver. The grand jurors appealed to President-elect Bill Clinton to investigate the case, and a Washington D.C. attorney tried to strike a deal with Congress whereby some of the grand jurors could testify before a congressional subcommittee without risking contempt charges. All of this was extensively covered by the mainstream media.

## Middle-range Issues:

1. Does *Westword's* standing as an alternative newspaper make it easier for it to print and pursue such stories?
2. Should the grand jurors have been allowed to remain anonymous in the original report? Why?

3. What responsibility do the mainstream media have to credit the story and the reporting to *Westword?*
4. How do you evaluate Calhoun's justification for printing the story?

## Macro Issues:

1. When the criminal justice system and media clash, how can journalists determine which institution should dominate?
2. Are there issues—or kinds of questions—that journalists should not be allowed to cover for fear of undermining another democratic institution?
3. If the congressional investigation determines that the judge and the U.S. Attorney acted properly, what should be the response of the mainstream media? Of *Westword?*

## CASE VI-F
## Terrorist Use of the News Media; News Media Use of Terrorists
JACK LULE
*Lehigh University*

Americans die abroad every day; they die of illness, auto accidents, murder, drowning, and other reasons. But when death occurs by an act of political violence, commonly called terrorism, news reporting intensifies and occasionally approaches saturation coverage.

Terrorism existed long before the news media. And to this day, most terrorism—by states, groups, and individuals—receives no media attention. So what qualifies a very few terrorist incidents for saturation coverage? Journalists must consider not only how terrorists use the news media—but, conversely, how the news media use terrorists.

Many journalists and media critics argue that the news media "legitimize" and thus encourage terrorists by giving them coverage. Some have called for voluntary or even mandatory guidelines for terrorism coverage. Yet others have argued that more coverage of terrorism is desirable, suggesting that the media can provide an important outlet for the expression of public concern and thus reduce political violence.

These issues were raised dramatically in one memorable case—the 1985 hijacking of TWA 847. On June 14, 1985, two members of the Shiite Moslem group the Islamic Holy War commandeered the jetliner with more than 150 people aboard. The gunmen forced the plane to make repeated flights between Athens, Beirut, and Algiers, settling finally in Beirut. Then, a passenger, U.S. Navy diver Robert Dean Stethem, was severely beaten and killed, and shot in the head. His body was then pushed from the plane onto the runway. Holding American passengers as hostages, the hijackers demanded the release of seven hundred Shiite Moslems jailed or detained by Israel.

Immediately, the incident commanded intense news coverage. The story dominated newspaper front pages and magazine covers. More than half of each evening newscast was devoted to the hijacking. Regular programming was repeatedly interrupted by special reports, a service the media were happy to provide since terrorism plays well in America.

From the beginning, reporters were forced to confront a number of ethical questions. For example, on the first day, as the plane sat in Algiers, networks and newspapers decided to report that an elite U.S. commando squad had been dispatched to the Mideast for a possible rescue mission. Within hours, the hijackers arranged for the jet to be flown back to the relatively more secure site of Beirut. There, hostages were taken off the plane and held captive in the city, making a rescue mission much more difficult.

By the second day, the original hijackers had been joined by members of the Shiite Amal movement. As negotiations stalled, reporters seemed to become arbiters between the Amal movement and U.S. officials. Nabih Berri, a leader of the Amal, especially was given much media time and space. Often, Berri was permitted to give live, unedited statements about the negotiations.

Reporters also agreed to "interview" the hostages in custody of the Amal. Gathered around the jetliner, reporters questioned the jet pilot Captain John Testrake—who spoke with a gun at his head. Not surprisingly, the pilot echoed the hijackers' statements and advised authorities not to attempt a rescue mission. Similarly, the next day, five of the hostages gave a "news conference" at the airport. Surrounded by Shiite gunmen, they talked with sympathy of the hijackers and their cause.

At home in the States, reporters were faced with a more common ethical decision—whether to interview the hostages' families. Reporters for many news outlets contacted the families of hostages. Posing with photographs of a hostage, family members wept and prayed on camera that loved ones be returned. Extensive national coverage was given to the family of Robert Dean Stethem, the slain Navy diver.

As the hijacking drew to a close, reporters in Beirut continued to interview hostages in custody. On June 28, the hostages were taken to a luxury hotel for what was seen as a farewell banquet before their eventual release. As at some Hollywood premiere, hostages were interviewed upon their arrival, and microphones were thrust in their faces as they were driven away.

After seventeen days in captivity, the hostages were freed. They were flown from Lebanon and then to Syria, where they were convinced to give a press conference for the hordes of reporters. Some in the news media arranged to get more detailed accounts; NBC flew the families of four hostages overseas and paid hotel accommodations in exchange for exclusive interviews on its news shows.

## Micro Issues:

1. Did U.S. news media, especially network television, use proper news judgment in the extended, special coverage given to TWA 847? Were stories hyped by such coverage? Did the media help create a crisis to attract an audience to the drama?
2. Should reporters have interviewed the terrorists and their hostages while the situation was still unfolding? What should have been the proper relationship between the networks and the terrorists?
3. Were stories about the hostage families exploitive? What was the news value of repeated stories on hostage families? Was it acceptable to pay the families?

## Middle-range Issues:

1. What is the distinction, in terms of manipulation, between White House photo opportunities/press conferences and terrorist press conferences?
2. Do the news media legitimize and thus encourage terrorists by giving them international status, airing their demands and explaining their motives?
3. Should there be voluntary media guidelines? How would they read?

4. Should the media be prevented from making public certain information, such as military movements or policy options, that might be useful to terrorists?

## Macro Issues:

1. Is the kidnapping or killing of an American on foreign soil worthy of national news coverage? What are the distinctions between the killing of an American during a robbery in Paris and the killing of an American by terrorists in Beirut?
2. What are the benefits for the U.S. news media of ongoing terrorist incidents? To what extent do those benefits influence news coverage?
3. Does the technology of instant picture transmission of terrorist events alter ethical decision making? Does compelling video dominate news coverage of the terrorist events over the issues that give rise to them?

# CHAPTER VII
## *Media Economics: The Deadline Meets the Bottom Line*

**In this chapter, the student should learn:**

- How advertisers gain influence in the media economic equation and the ramification of that additional influence.
- The economic realities of the social responsibility theory of the press.
- The effect of the economy and deregulation on the industry in the 1990s.
- That economic and legislative initiatives have combined to place control of information in the hands of fewer and larger corporate entities.
- The problems of programming for diversity in a numbers-driven media.

## Introduction

In the movie *Absence of Malice,* Paul Newman is asked if he has taken his complaint concerning an inaccurate article about him to the newspaper. He replies, "Have you ever tried to talk to a newspaper?" For most Americans, the point is well taken. A faceless, nameless, non-locally-owned media is becoming a reality in all but a few communities. Today the media are predominantly corporate owned and publicly traded, with media conglomerates such as Time Warner among the largest of the world's corporations. The corporate owners of the average news operation are more insulated from contact with the consumer of their product than virtually any other business owner in America.

The pace and size of the mergers that created these media conglomerates in the 1990s is staggering. General Electric bought NBC, Westinghouse bought CBS and the Walt Disney Co. purchased ABC in rapid succession, with each deal in the billions of dollars. Westinghouse/CBS then merged with Infinity Broadcasting to create the nation's largest radio chain. Time Warner, created by a $14.3 billion merger earlier in the decade, acquired the Turner Broadcasting System including such properties as WTBS, TNT, CNN and Headline News. MCI paid Rupert Murdoch $2 billion to gain a 13.5 percent interest in News Corp., the parent company of Fox Television, while Microsoft and NBC combined to create MSNBC, a multimedia venture. Microsoft owner Bill Gates also has acquired the rights to the largest library of still images in existence for future multimedia use. Even the telephone companies, broken up by anti-trust legislation in the 1980s, are getting back together as evidenced by a $17 billion merger of Southwestern Bell's and Pacific Bell's parent companies.

As they get bigger, the media must increasingly satisfy competing publics to survive. The desires of stockholders must be balanced with the mandate to keep the audience happy in programming and content decisions. At the same time, advertisers, who demand large numbers of readers and viewers for their messages, make claims on the media as well. The inherent tension created in trying to satisfy these competing publics creates many of the ethical problems of the media.

## The Penny Press Revolution

Financing the American media through advertising is so deeply ingrained in the system that it is hard to imagine any other way. Yet newspapers thrived in America for more than a century supported solely by their readers. And as recently as 1920, then-Secretary of State Herbert Hoover argued in vain for a commercial-free broadcast industry to be funded by the sellers of the receivers. While the airways eventually became filled with commercials, Hoover and the Federal Radio Commission (now FCC) won one important battle: the public is the owner of the airwaves and the station is merely the "trustee" of that commodity.

Today each medium has found its own formula to economic security, from "free" network television on one end of the continuum to books, movies, and a handful of magazines such as *Ms.* and *Consumer Reports* on the other, that pass virtually all of the cost of production on to the consumer. Most media organizations lie somewhere in between.

On September 3, 1883, Benjamin Day, publisher of the *New York Sun,* started a revolution when he lowered the price of his newspaper to a penny, at a time when his competition was selling newspapers for a nickel. He gambled that he could overcome the losses with additional advertising revenue—if circulation increased. When his gamble paid off, virtually every publisher in town followed his lead. Soon after, Frank Munsey lowered the cost of *Munsey's Magazine* from a quarter to a dime and watched as his circulation increased eightfold in two years to half a million readers.

What Day and Munsey did was farsighted. By pricing their products below the cost of printing, they cast their economic future with their advertisers. What was not foreseen, however, was the diminished role the consumer would play in the process.

Under the old pricing structure, subscribers were an end in themselves. Each represented a percentage of the profit, no matter how minuscule. Under this system, readers purchased news, entertainment and opinion content. Under the new system, advertisers purchased readers. The individual subscriber became a means to an end. Content is now relegated to the status of "bait" to catch readers and viewers to be sold to advertisers, as Bill Moyers points out in an interview for PBS's "The Promise of Television":

> Every manager or owner I know in commercial television now simply accepts
> television as a by-product of the merchandising process. That changes how you regard
> the people for whom you are producing or creating television. They are there to be

seduced, to be sold something that somebody wants to sell. You are simply a transmission belt between someone trying to sell a product and the person who has the money to buy it, and it changes altogether your sense of your mission, your purpose, or your obligations to that viewer.

## Casualties from the Revolution

Three problems emerged from the penny press revolution that shifted the profit center from consumers to advertisers. *First,* in an attempt to attract the largest audience possible, media outlets "homogenized" their content, dealing in topics guaranteed to offend few individuals while hoping to garner large audiences. The result is journalism that takes no risks unless research shows that the audience will follow. In fact, Gannett's *USA Today* was developed from a marketing plan—not as a news concept.

Network news presidents "know," for instance, that the public has an interest in only one foreign story at a time. So while the "pack" went first to the Persian Gulf and then Somalia in the early 1990s, the horrors of Bosnia or the continued killing fields of El Salvador went unreported or at best underreported. Similarly, events are reported more than processes. Stories written for the masses focus on quick-onset disasters such as Hurricane Andrew but not on the slow-onset disaster of global warming that may be spawning ever larger hurricanes.

*Second,* the penny press revolution made it more difficult for diverse voices to find a mainstream forum. The late Randy Shilts of the *San Francisco Chronicle,* the first reporter in the U.S. assigned to the AIDS beat, claims that AIDS coverage was stymied in its early stages as it was perceived to be a "gay plague" of interest only to the homosexual community (Shilts 1987). Only when celebrities such as Rock Hudson and "innocents" such as Ryan White contracted the disease did it get widespread mainstream media coverage (Rogers and Chang 1991).

*Third,* the penny press revolution hastened the inevitable conflicts between the interests of the now powerful advertisers and the interests of the less powerful consumer over controversial content. Advertisers exert both obvious and subtle influence over a media content, a topic also discussed in chapter 3. For instance, scholars (Kessler 1989; Miller 1992) found that magazines which received a great deal of revenue from the tobacco industry were significantly less likely to print articles about the health impact of tobacco. This omission was even more startling because many magazines, particularly women's magazines, claimed to focus on women's health issues. Kessler credits the indirect influence of the tobacco industry on these publications as a factor in the rise of tobacco-related cancers in women during the latter half of the twentieth century. And, with three tobacco companies consistently ranking in the top ten spenders among all U.S. advertisers, the influence of that money on editorial content continues to be felt, a fact the *Seattle Times* acknowledged in June 1993 when it stopped accepting tobacco ads worth about $100,000 annually to the paper.

However, advertiser influence needn't hamper good reporting. *MacWorld,* which bills itself as "The Macintosh Magazine," ran an in-depth cover story in July of 1990 on the potential health hazards of computers, focusing on evidence that low-frequency electromagnetic emissions from computers could damage the user's health. The magazine gets virtually all of its advertising revenue from the computer industry.

Just what role profit ought to play in the media depends in part on the view one takes of the media's role in society. In the section below, we will examine two important descriptive theories of the press that have dominated American thought and look at the role profit and economics play in each.

## The Libertarian and Social Responsibility Theories Revisited

Mass communication research has several descriptive theories. An underlying assumption of descriptive theories is that any media system "takes on the form and coloration of the social and political structures within which it operates" (Siebert, Peterson, and Schramm 1956, 3). Eventually, theorists predict, the media will reflect the political and economic structure of a society. For instance, a capitalist society will eventually create a media system funded by the hope for economic gain, i.e., advertising.

Two of the best known descriptive theories of the press are the libertarian and social responsibility theories. Together they describe more than 200 years of thinking on the role of information in a society and how it should be delivered.

The *libertarian theory* of the press grew from the changes that swept Europe from the Reformation to the Renaissance. In keeping with the basic tenets of the Enlightenment, libertarian theory assumes that people are rational and that truth is discoverable in a secular, empirical way. Under libertarian theory, political authority rests with the individual. Government's role is to ensure the domestic and foreign peace, but the individual is supreme in politics—a belief spelled out in the Preamble to the U.S. Constitution. Because the individual is rational, government should do the individual's bidding. People are viewed as having both the time and the inclination to become literate and involved in public affairs.

With these assumptions, the libertarian theory of the press reflects Milton's concept of the "marketplace of ideas." Anyone could operate a printing press, particularly anyone aligned with a political group. Those who ran the presses of the day, because they were partisan, would provide partisan versions of reality. The rational citizen would select the truth from among the partisan versions available.

Under this theory, the press's most potent antagonist would be government, which libertarians viewed as locked in a perpetual power struggle for political supremacy with the individual. The duty of the press was to support the individual in that fight. The result was a media system that supported a well-informed individual in a quest for well-being and happiness.

The ensuing five hundred years have done much to change our view of humanity and of society. Three intellectual changes were instrumental in this shift. First, Freud and modern psychology have changed our view of rational humanity. We now believe that people are often illogical, sometimes irrational, and motivated by a variety of needs and drives (Davies 1963). People are not uniformly energetic or educated. For this reason, they will not always seek out and sometimes will not understand information to which they have access.

Second, knowledge, indeed reality itself, has been transformed. Societies have begun to realize that what we think of as a "fact" is subject both to perception and change, a philosophical view known as pragmatism. The "fact" that matter cannot become energy was successfully challenged by Einstein. Truth has become ephemeral.

Third, society has become more cosmopolitan. As people moved to cities and as waves of immigrants reached American shores, people discovered they were as different from one another in culture and language as they were alike in their quest for a better life. What was truth for one group was not truth for another. Literacy, at least literacy in English, was a cherished ideal, not a reality. Mass markets of many sorts emerged.

These shifts transformed the press of the 1800s into the mass media of the late twentieth century. Gone were the homogenous, politically-interested audiences. Replacing them were diverse, often self-interested subgroups. In short, a new media system was required. Today, the mass media are no longer the written word, but also television, public relations, advertising, entertainment and every conceivable hybrid including the Internet. Few people, even in the age of the personal computer, can own a media outlet. Existing outlets are largely corporate owned and eschew partisanship in favor of objectivity. The marketplace of ideas became a monopoly supermarket, and the goods it carried were uniformly vanilla.

With these changes came a new descriptive theory of the press. The theory was developed in the 1940s by a panel of scholars, the Hutchins Commission, with funding from Henry Luce, the conservative founder of *Time* magazine. No journalist sat on the commission. Despite this, the *social responsibility theory* of the press continues to fascinate both academics and practitioners because it attempts to compensate for changes in modern political, social, and cultural life.

Social responsibility theory acknowledged what was already a reality by the 1940s: the number of media outlets is limited; people are often self-interested and sometimes lazy. Because of these changes, the media have certain responsibilities in the political system. According to the Hutchins Commission, the media have the following five functions in society:

1. To provide a truthful, comprehensive, and intelligent account of the day's events in a context that gives them meaning;
2. To serve as a forum for exchange of comment and criticism;
3. To provide a representative picture of constituent groups in society;
4. To present and clarify the goals and values of society;
5. To provide citizens with full access to the day's intelligence.

The goals of social responsibility theory are troubling to journalists. While the theory acknowledges the world is intellectually and socially a different place than that of the libertarian view, it provides no clear guidelines for journalistic behavior in this new era.

Indeed, some of the guidelines the theory does provide are ambiguous. How should the forums operate? Whose values should be presented and clarified? Others appear to be mutually exclusive. For example, the media's role as mirror and critic may conflict with some interpretations of media objectivity. Other guidelines might simply be impossible to achieve, i.e., providing intelligent discourse about the day's events in a nightly newscast of less than twenty-three minutes.

An even more fundamental problem hobbles social responsibility theory: it gives little attention to modern media economics. This omission occurred in part because the multinational corporations and chain ownership were still on the horizon when the Hutchins Commission codified the theory. And, because the theory was developed early in the McCarthy period, there was an unwillingness to link economic and political power for fear of being labeled Marxist. This central omission means that *the social responsibility theory, like libertarianism, does not deal with the realities of concentrated economic power,* particularly in an era when information has become an increasingly valuable commodity. Today some of the most troubling problems in media ethics stem from journalism's dual responsibilities to citizens and to stockholders. But the social responsibility and the libertarian views of the press provide little guidance on these issues.

## Media Economics in the Modern Era: Cutbacks and Consolidations

If the founders envisioned a marketplace of ideas where all views would be aired and the truth would emerge, by the late twentieth century the dream had died. Information in the U.S. had fallen into the hands of a very few, well-financed corporations. In every key media format—radio, television, newspapers, magazines, cable television and motion pictures—more than half of the gross revenues were concentrated in the hands of fewer than five corporations. The result is what media economics researcher Ben Bagdikian has called "a defacto ministry of information within a democracy" (Bagdikian 1990, 5).

The history of newspapers is indicative of the consolidation trend in all media. At the turn of the century, William Randolph Hearst, Joseph Pulitzer and the Scripps family sought to widen their influence and enlarge their bank accounts by building the first newspaper chains. For the first time, profits made by selling information and advertising within a community left that community destined for corporate accounts in distant banks. And gradually, the concept of what a newspaper owed a community changed as well. Newspapers were no longer a public trust, but a public utility akin to the power company. Newspapers were delivering a necessary product to a community—information—without any of the regulations of those companies that deliver electricity and gas, and most often without competition. Consequently, the profits of newspapers are three to five times higher than most corporations.

Today, corporate chains own more than 80 percent of the nation's daily newspapers, compared to 20 percent at the end of World War II. Chains account for 90 percent of all newspapers sold. One chain, Gannett, owns nearly one hundred newspapers in addition to the nationally-circulated *USA Today.* Fewer than thirty cities are currently served by competing dailies. Recently, Dallas, Minneapolis, Cleveland and Los Angeles have joined the growing list of cities served by a single newspaper.

To many, the rise in corporate ownership marked a decline in the quality of journalism. In *The Media Monopoly,* Bagdikian quotes media acquisitions expert Christopher Shaw, telling clients that profits from a newspaper can be tripled in two years through a combination of staff reductions and increases in advertising and subscription rates. "No one will buy a 15 percent margin newspaper without a plan to create a 25 percent to 45 percent margin," Shaw said (Bagdikian 1987, 7). Former Gannett chairman Allen H. Neuharth told Bagdikian, "Wall Street didn't give a damn if we put out a good paper in Niagara Falls. They just wanted to know if the profits would be in the 15 to 20 percent range" (Bagdikian 1987, xxi).

Corporate cost-cutting has not been confined to newspapers. In the mid-1980s, when all three major television networks changed ownership (not to be confused with an identical situation a decade later as all three sold yet again), each newsroom operation was downsized. ABC cut a total of two hundred employees from its news operation; CBS axed 215. NBC virtually cut the "Nightly News" writing and producing staff in half, in part because parent company GE saw nothing wrong with the on-air product during a seventeen-week writers' strike that caused the newsroom to operate shorthanded (Schoenbrun 1989).

The current media system has allowed the players in the media game to get bigger. Even prior to the new looser ownership regulations in the Telecommunications Act of 1996, the merger of Time and Warner Communications created a $13.4 billion media conglomerate that required approval by the U.S. Justice Department. Becoming a player in the media game today is a far cry from the days of the single editor beginning a partisan newspaper envisioned by Milton. When Gannett wanted to launch the idea of a national newspaper, the corporation spent more than $800 million before *USA Today* turned a profit. When media mogul Rupert Murdoch wanted to create a fourth television network, he lost nearly $100 million in the first two prime-time seasons of his now-healthy Fox network. At the same time that technology is making more media outlets available than ever before, these staggering start-up costs have closed the door to all but a few and changed the complexion of the media industry to an exclusive club where only the rich and powerful need apply for membership.

The net effect of the Telecommunications Act of 1996 is to assure that the media ownership will get increasingly concentrated thanks to more relaxed multiple and cross-ownership rules. Here are a few of the changes brought by the 1996 legislation:

• Companies may now own as many radio and television stations as they wish, up from 14 radio stations and seven television stations as recently as the early 1980s. The only restriction on ownership of broadcast stations is that the total reach of the stations can only be 35 percent of the nation's households.

- Waivers of the rule barring owners from owning a television and radio station in the same market were extended to certain parties by the law. More lenient rules in this area and a reconsideration of the ban on newspapers owning broadcast outlets in their communities are possible in the near future.
- A single owner can own up to eight radio stations in the nation's largest markets and up to half of the stations in the nation's smaller markets. This is a radical change from long-time policies that prohibited any media "duopolies" in a single market.
- Television networks can now own and operate cable television systems and telephone companies can now be cable television providers in their local service areas, a cross-ownership previously denied by the FCC.
- It is now legal for the phone company to provide programming content in addition to phone services. Conversely, it is now legal for cable television companies to compete for your phone business.

One effect of the changes was seen almost immediately as major radio chains such as Infinity and Clear Channel Communications went on cross-country buying sprees of radio stations, driving the prices up as they went. Less than six months after the signing of the Telecommunications Act, both chains were approaching 100 stations. In some cases, a single chain would own all of the talk radio stations—a major source of news and information—in a single market. In some cases, acquired stations were re-formatted with automated programming meaning fewer jobs and higher profits for the new owners.

As the mass media have themselves become enormous, economically powerful institutions, they have joined what political scientist C. Wright Mills (1956) called the power elite, a ruling class within a democratic society. Power is found not only in the halls of government but also on Wall Street. And power is found not only in money or armies, *power is found in information.* Media organizations, precisely because they have become multinational corporations engaged in the information business, are deeply involved in this power shift.

This emergence of media as economic and political power brokers leads to a question of how a powerful institution such as the mass media, which traditionally has had the political role of checking other powerful institutions, can be checked. Can the watchdog be trusted when it is inexorably entwined with the institutions it is watching? As media corporations expand exponentially in the pursuit of profit, who will watch the watchdogs?

Government is probably the only institution capable of providing a counter to the massive economic power of the media. Yet, government provides a variety of subsidies to the industry. In addition, government functions as a regulator of the broadcast and advertising industries, assuring profits to both these groups by limiting access to the airwaves and legislating fair play in advertising. So, more often than not, government supports big media rather than acting as a counterweight.

# Economics and News

As media ownership becomes the privilege of the rich, an elite few control an important ingredient of democracy: news. And when the few who own the media view it only as a business, the problem gets worse. Dan Rather, CBS's "Evening News" anchor, expressed the concern of many journalists in an op-ed column he wrote in the *New York Times:*

> News is a business. It has always been. Journalists understand and accept that. But journalism is something else, too. Something more. It is a light on the horizon. A beacon that helps the citizens of a democracy find their way. News is an essential component of a free society. News is a business, but it is also a public trust. (Rather, 10 March 1987, sec. I, 27)

Rather's comments were made in response to the wave of cuts at his network after its sale in the late 1980s. But the worst times were yet to come. In 1990, the recession clobbered the industry. Even media conglomerates reported huge profit declines. Dow Jones was down 66 percent, NBC 21 percent, Knight-Ridder 40 percent, and the *New York Times* company was down 75 percent, prompting massive layoffs and hiring freezes (Rothmeyer 1991). Three years later, with a new administration elected largely on the mandate to boost the economy, media profits were only beginning to rise slowly.

The lean years focused attention on the fact that good journalism is often expensive. And in an era of static subscriptions and smaller ad revenues, few newsrooms enjoy budgets as large as those of a decade ago. The three television networks closed entire bureaus, and many newspapers pulled back on overseas correspondents, leaving coverage of foreign news to the wires and CNN.

The effect of these cutbacks is lost news for the consumer. One photojournalist, Brad Clift, told the authors that he went to Somalia months before American troops were dispatched, using his own money because he felt the starvation there was an underreported story. Only an occasional network crew and a handful of newspapers pursued the Somalia story until then-President Bush committed American troops to the region in December of 1992. Most news organizations, like the photojournalist's employer, declined to cover the emerging story, pleading that they had spent depleted international budgets covering Desert Storm.

In *Doing Ethics in Journalism,* a handbook published by the Society of Professional Journalists (SPJ) in 1992, two of the "guiding principles" of journalism speak directly to the ethics of media economics: (1) seek truth and report it as fully as possible; and (2) act independently.

Seeking truth can be financially and personally expensive. Several media outlets that have been honored in the "Darts and Laurels" column written by *Columbia Journalism Review* managing editor Gloria Cooper demonstrate that many media organizations and professionals do seek truth at great personal and corporate cost.

*Indianapolis Star* reporter Larry MacIntyre spent three months investigating a story on gubernatorial candidate Pat Rooney, who ran on a promise that he would "treat taxpayers like customers" of his Golden Rule Insurance Company. After three months of research, including studying a hundred court files and interviewing more than 50 people, MacIntyre's three-part series in October of 1995 showed that Rooney's health insurance customers were not well treated at all. MacIntyre found customers left hanging with cancelled policies, unpaid claims and rate increases that had made Golden Rule a billion-dollar company and President Rooney a multi-millionaire at the expense of ill and debt-ridden customers. Rooney quit the governor's race before the series ran, partially because of his knowledge of the investigation, according to his former campaign chair.

*New Orleans Times-Picayune* staff writer Chris Adams ran a computer-assisted examination of more than 60 million records and conducted 400 interviews to prove that public funding of private psychiatric care for Louisiana's poor had jumped 9,000 percent in five years. Among his findings were profit margins of 40 to 50 percent on services rendered, doctor salaries of more than $1 million annually and former state politicians and their family members drawing $50,000 salaries to sit on hospital boards. The 1995 series prompted five state investigations and a promise from all seven candidates for governor that each would, if elected, work on solutions to the problem.

*Atlanta Business Chronicle* and staff writer Carey Gilliam dared to take on one of the most revered corporations worldwide and one headquartered in Atlanta in an August 1995 series investigating the death of a UPS worker crushed by a truck backing up to a loading dock. Gilliam looked at federal inspection records, interviewed UPS workers and safety regulators and combed scores of Occupational Safety and Health Administration (OSHA) penalty and settlement documents and found thousands of stories of injured and killed workers. His findings documented a corporation obsessed with efficiency, often at the expense of safety and a company that is far different in reality than in its advertising and public relations campaigns.

Two reporters for the *Philadelphia Inquirer,* Donald L. Barlett and James B. Steele, read the entire 1991 federal budget act which ran more than 1,000 pages, then compared it to the equally lengthy Tax Reform Act of 1986. They discovered that the law would raise taxes for the middle class and lower them for the rich in the long run, the opposite effect of what was announced by Congress and then-President Reagan. They also discovered that the deficit reduction package wouldn't come close to generating the $10.8 billion in revenues that supporters claimed. They won a Pulitzer prize for their work.

Acting independently, another of the SPJ's guidelines, can also be expensive. For many media outlets, independence is as simple as buying tickets to the movies reviewed and sports events covered. However, it goes far beyond that for others, such as the journalists and photographers who were captured and held by Iraq soldiers when they ventured away from U.S. military pools to see the Persian Gulf War firsthand.

Both the *Lexington Herald-Leader* and the *Syracuse Post-Standard* faced reader boycotts and threats against individual reporters when they opened investigations of local, successful college basketball programs. Reporters for the *New York Daily News* exposed the numerous allegations of incompetence by a medical doctor who was spending more than $150,000 a year in advertising in the *News.*

Unfortunately, these uplifting stories of personal corporate enterprise are far too rare in an industry that demands more than 20 percent pretax profit from its holdings. This demand for profits generates subsidiary problems as well. Entry-level salaries for journalists in both print and broadcast are among the lowest starting salaries of any jobs requiring a college degree—under $20,000 in the mid-1990s. The all-consuming focus on ratings in the broadcast entertainment industries is often blamed for a variety of ills, among them programming more concerned with attracting masses than creating quality.

## Finding Profit through Service

Advertising revenue declines in the late 1980s and early 1990s hit virtually every medium. The economy forced American media owners to rethink the methods that were once so profitable. What many found was that a return to treating the consumer as an end rather than a means was not only the right thing to do, it was profitable as well.

McKinsey and Company made "excellence" a buzzword in business circles with their studies that formed the basis of the best-selling *In Search of Excellence.* In 1985, the firm was hired by the National Association of Broadcasters to study eleven of the nation's great radio stations, such as WGN in Chicago, and report to the group's annual convention about what made an excellent radio station. Their findings were (1) the great radio stations were audience-oriented in their programming, often breaking down the traditional walls that defined formats and (2) the great radio stations were community-oriented in their promotions, becoming synonymous in their communities with charitable events and community festivities.

The attitude is summed up by WMMS general manager Bill Smith (NAB 1985):

> If you want a car to last forever, you've got to throw some money back into that car and make sure that it's serviced properly on a continual basis. Otherwise, it's going to break down and fall apart. We know that we're constantly rebuilding the station one way or another. We throw the profit to the listening audience . . . to charities, to several nonprofit organizations, to free concerts or anything to affect the listeners of Cleveland as a whole. If we can donate the money to light up Terminal Tower, if that's what it's going to take and nobody else is going to do it, we'll do it . . . and we get and hold our listeners, year-in and year-out, because they identify us as being community-minded.

## Conclusion: Social Responsibility in the New Millennium

When the social responsibility theory was framed in the 1940s, the primary informational concern was scarcity: people might not get the information they needed for citizenship. Today, however, the primary informational concern is an overabundance of raw data: people might not filter out what they need through all the clutter. Media and their distribution systems changed, but the theory remained silent, especially about the role of profit in the development of systems for gathering and disseminating information. This meant that until recently, government agencies such as the FCC were still basing policy decisions on the scarcity argument when any consumer with cable or a satellite dish knew otherwise.

The Newspaper Preservation Act in the 1970s, the AT&T anti-trust suits of the 1980s, the Telecommunications Act in the 1990s and other battles finally focused the attention of the government on the fact that delivery of entertainment and information is indeed big business and is currently in the hands of a very few—something the libertarian framers of the Constitution sought to avoid.

The clash of large, well-financed institutions for control of information is a modern phenomenon. Classical ethical theory, which speaks to individual acts, is of little help in sorting out the duties and responsibilities of corporations larger than most nations that control the currency of the day: information. Political theory, particularly Marxist theory, is of some help identifying the problem, but communism has been rejected as a potential solution throughout most of the world.

Americans are equally unwilling to accept government as the solution to counter the concentrated economic power of the media, and government has been loathe to break up the large media conglomerates. During the lifetime of the readers of this book, the power and role of "big media" such as AT&T and Time Warner should emerge as *the* most important issue in media ethics. Can an institution that began as a lone printer with a press "flourish" as a multinational with billions in assets without a change in vision?

History says no. Adaptability is the key to survival. The largest of the dinosaurs, scientists say, possibly died when they outgrew their inability to "feel" in their extremities. Similarly, the Roman Catholic Church lost much of its intellectual and political hold on Western Europe when devotion to dogma overruled commitment to parishioners. The Reformation resulted. Likewise, the Mandarin class lost political control in ancient China because it could not change with a country that was moving into the twentieth century. Neither biology nor social and political history has been kind to big entities.

An example of how huge corporations are inept at knowing what all parts of their operations are doing is seen from a controversy in the early days of Time Warner—a conglomerate including magazines, movie production companies, book companies, record labels and cable television systems. In 1992 the media giant made the news when one of its smallest subsidiaries pressed a CD by rap artist Ice-T. The CD included a song entitled "Cop Killer" which included the following lyrics according to an article by Time Warner shareholder Charlton Heston in *National Review:* "I got my 12 gauge sawed off; I'm 'bout to bust some shots off; I'm 'bout to dust some cops off." Later in the song, Ice-T goes on: "I got my brain on hype—tonight will be your night. Die, die, die, pig die" (Heston 1992, 53). Boycotts by members of the Fraternal Order of Police eventually alerted Time Warner's executives, who pulled the CD from distribution. Time Warner eventually sold the record label. However, the issue of how socially responsible a huge conglomerate could be for the actions of each of its subsidiaries went largely unresolved.

Media conglomerates will thrive only to the extent that they can adapt to serve the diverse communities into which their far-flung empires take them and react quickly when they fail. The ones that do it well will survive.

## Suggested Readings

Auletta, Ken. 1991. *Three blind mice: How the TV networks lost their way.* New York: Random House.
Bagdikian, Ben H. 1983. *The media monopoly.* Boston: Beacon Press.
Mills, C. Wright. 1956. *The power elite.* New York: Oxford University Press.

## CHAPTER VII CASES

### CASE VII-A
### Union Activism and the Broadcast Personality
STANLEY CUNNINGHAM
*University of Windsor, Ontario, Canada*

Dale Goldhawk was the host of a national phone-in show, "Cross-Country Checkup," produced and broadcast weekly by the Canadian Broadcasting Corporation. CBC is a public broadcasting organization that operates with arm's-length independence from the government that funds it. The open-line show deals with current issues, usually of a controversial nature. As moderator, Goldhawk was expected to act with impartiality. Goldhawk also served as president of the Alliance of Canadian Cinema, Television, and Radio Artists, a powerful, 9,200-member union. He was elected to this position prior to signing on with "Cross-Country Checkup."

The matter of U.S.-Canada free trade became the major issue in the national elections. The Conservative ruling party in Canada strongly supported the Free Trade Agreement, while ACTRA opposed it. Goldhawk authored a column in the union magazine suggesting that free trade posed a threat to Canada's cultural industries and urged his members to fight against free trade. There is no evidence, however, that he aired his opinion as radio show moderator.

A disgruntled freelancer, Charles Lynch, publicized Goldhawk's dual role in his syndicated column in the last weeks of the election campaign. Lynch's motives were complex. In his column he wrote that he resented having to belong to ACTRA in order to work on television. Because he supported free trade, he resented having to pay dues to a union that resisted it.

Lynch argued that Goldhawk's dual role, as union spokesperson and as moderator on a show where free trade was a recurrent theme, constituted a serious conflict of interest.

In a compromise move, Goldhawk voluntarily withdrew from "Cross-Country Checkup" until the end of the campaign. After the election, CBC management presented him with a "choice" (others called it an ultimatum): resign as president of the union or as moderator of the radio show. CBC management insisted that its demand was motivated by its own policies of fairness and balance and by its desire to maintain credibility.

Goldhawk resigned his presidency and chose to stay with "Cross-Country Checkup."

## Micro Issues:

1. Goldhawk's antigovernment opinions were never broadcast to the wider radio public; they were targeted at the union membership only. Does that reduce or eliminate the element of conflict?

2. Goldhawk might have been removed from the show. Did he do the right thing in voluntarily resigning from the moderator's post?
3. How would you evaluate Charles Lynch's performance as a journalist in blowing the whistle?
4. Keeping in mind CBC's official commitment to balance and objectivity in its news service, how would you assess its demand? Did it have adequate grounds to demand what it did of Goldhawk?

## Middle-range Issues:

1. Should apparent or potential conflict be sufficient grounds to dismiss or reassign a journalist?
2. If Goldhawk had been employed by a privately owned network, such as those in the U.S., would the issues be any different?
3. What were the CBC's obligations to Goldhawk when he was first named anchor?

## Macro Issues:

1. Given the increasingly influential role that the mass media play in a nation's political life, should journalists avoid:
   (*a*) Membership or leadership in unions?
   (*b*) Working with charities such as United Way or Habitat for Humanity?
   (*c*) Membership in political parties?
   (*d*) Running for political office?
   (*e*) Participation in special-interest groups?
2. Do owners and corporations have the right to require as much? Should corporation managers reveal their political preferences?
3. Should the private opinions and involvements of journalists be as newsworthy and publicized as those of politicians?

## CASE VII-B
## *Ms.* Magazine—No More Ads!
PHILIP PATTERSON
*Oklahoma Christian University*

*Ms.* magazine printed its last commercial issue in October 1989, and returned in June of 1990 as one of the few mass circulation magazines in history to eschew advertising and rely entirely on its readers for support.

While vowing to continue in the tradition begun by the group of women activists who founded the magazine in 1972, one thing was now different: the price. Readers would be asked to pay $35 for six issues, a price that has since increased.

The new publisher, David Lang, who bought *Ms.* when it was struggling to make ends meet, at the prompting of the magazine's editors, decided to fund the magazine entirely on reader's subscriptions.

Gloria Steinem, a co-founder of *Ms.* and currently a contributing editor, said the magazine has always walked the line between unvarnished advocacy and the demands of the people who pay the bills. She authored an exposé for the premier issue entitled "Sex, Lies and Advertising." In it, Steinem revealed the stories of advertisers who "didn't want to be placed near articles dealing with abortion, gun control, illness, large-size fashion, anything depressing" she told a *Chicago Tribune* reporter.

The new editor-in-chief, Robin Morgan, told the *Denver Post,* "Now we can say all the things we never got to say for 18 years. We have to keep reminding ourselves of that" (*Denver Post,* March 8, 1990).

Andrea Kaplan, spokesperson for Lang Communications, said *Ms.* would need 50,000 to 100,000 subscribers to show a profit, a standard achieved by its third issue. At the time of its suspension in 1989, *Ms.* had 550,000 subscribers, but was losing money.

*Ms.* is not the only magazine to take action against the constraints of advertisers. Some magazines, for example *Consumer Reports,* refuse advertising altogether. Other publications such as *Modern Maturity, The New Yorker,* and *Mother Jones* have implemented strict advertising policies. *Modern Maturity* refuses all ads that depict aging in a negative light. Robert E. Wood, publishing director of the magazine told the *Los Angeles Times,* "We know that advertising is just as important as editorial in shaping the overall feel and cadence of the magazine."

At *The New Yorker* all proposed advertisements are sent to a committee that evaluates each ad's motives and relevance to the magazine's targeted audience. Only if the committee approves the ad will it be published. Similarly, the staff of *Mother Jones* magazine refuses to publish ads that are sexist, racist, or exploitive.

*Ms.* magazine's decision to eliminate advertising drew attention to the difficulties publishers face regarding ethics and advertising today. It raised questions about the role of the media as an information outlet and questioned the motives of advertisers and publishers alike.

## Micro Issues:

1. Is *Ms.* infringing on the advertiser's right to freedom of speech?
2. Is *Ms.* courting financial ruin by shunning the advertising that supports it?
3. Is *Ms.* depriving its readers of an informative medium through its elimination of ads?
4. If a magazine edits an article to satisfy an important advertiser, does it have any obligation to inform the reader of the decisions?

## Middle-range Issues:

1. Are consumers able to distinguish between editorial content and advertisements? Does it matter?
2. How could *Ms.* magazine responsibly satisfy the desires of its advertisers and its readers simultaneously?
3. How would the particular advertiser problems of a liberal feminist magazine such as *Ms.* compare to another periodical such as *Newsweek?*

## Macro Issues:

1. Is it the media's job to censor advertisements for the public?
2. By running an ad, is a publication endorsing the product being advertised? Should publications be held responsible for the claims of their advertisers?
3. Is a magazine ethically required to be an open forum for all advertisers who have the ability to pay? On what standards?

# CASE VII-C
## A Salesperson's Dilemma: Whose Interests Come First?
CHARLES H. WARNER
*University of Missouri—Columbia*

Janet Holcombe loved calling on Harry Hill. In spite of the difference in their ages and background, and the fact that Janet was a salesperson for WCZZ/FM and Harry was an advertiser, they had become good friends.

Her job at WCZZ/FM is Janet's second one in sales. She had started at a radio station in a small Ohio town and then moved to nearby WCZZ/FM in a much larger market—one just below the top 25. WCZZ/FM featured an oldies-based, personalities-laden, well-promoted adult-contemporary format that was consistently number-one in the market in the 12+ audience, and an even stronger number-one in the desirable 25–54 demographic.

Hill owns the city's largest jewelry store. He had been in the same downtown location for 30 years, and prospered there. He sells a variety of jewelry lines and has earned a reputation for customer satisfaction and community service. When Janet Holcombe first called on Hill, he was placing small schedules totaling several thousand dollars per year on one of WCZZ/FM's competitors.

At first, Janet was intimidated, but Hill sensed her nervousness and put her at ease. Janet conducted a thorough needs-assessment and problem-identification and returned two days later to make an intelligent, problem-solving presentation. Over the four years that Janet had called on Hill, he increased his advertising investment on WCZZ/FM until he was spending 100 percent of his $10,000 yearly radio budget with Janet. And, he was a terrific customer. He paid his bills on time, he paid unreasonably high rates, he never negotiated, and almost always bought the packages, including special programming, she offered.

One afternoon, Janet gets a call from Bill Tanton, the young manager of the new Hess jewelry store opening soon at the city's largest mall. On her way out the door to keep the appointment, her boss tells her, "Be careful, Janet, when you put a claim in for the Hess Jewelers account. I did some background checks. They pay their bills so we'll approve their credit, but they always pay after 90 days. Also, they are fierce negotiators. I was also told there are several unsubstantiated complaints about them at a couple of Better Business Bureaus—standard stuff like the karats on their gold chains aren't what they claim or that they bait-and-switch. Remember, we need the account."

When the interview begins, Bill says, "Janet, I'm here to win. My career and future depend on me winning, and that means beating that slob of a dinosaur at Hill Jewelry. I want to put him out of business. He's small; we're a chain and buy in volume. We can offer lower prices. We promote our sales, which means we spend a ton in radio advertising."

Janet gets uncomfortable. A new order would mean improved commissions. However, she does not want to do anything to hurt Hill.

"Here's what I'll do: One, I'll spend three times what Hill spends, but to do this I must know exactly what he spends and precisely what he is going to spend for his

Christmas promotion. I want to know his schedule, his rates, and his expenditures. If I don't get this information, I won't buy you.

"Two, because I want to dominate your station, I want guaranteed commercial positions on the break before and break after any commercial break in which a Hill spot appears.

"Three, I will give your station an equal amount of business in all four quarters of the year if you will give me a 33 percent discount off the rate Hill is paying. My business is better: more volume and better spread throughout the year.

"Furthermore, if you make this deal with me, I'll give you 75 percent of my radio advertising dollars *and* a top-of-the-line Rolex ladies watch. If you don't meet my demands I will put all of my money on your competitors.

"Do we have a deal?"

## Micro Issues:

1. If you were Janet, would you take the deal Bill Tanton offered? Explain the thinking behind your reasons either for taking it or not taking it.
2. If you take the deal, what would you tell Hill when he hears the Hess commercials on your station?
3. If you do not take the deal, what reasons would you give to your general sales manager?

## Middle-range Issues:

1. Are there any counterproposals you can think of? If so, please give examples.
2. Is your station responsible for promoting competition among its advertisers? Financial health of its advertisers?
3. How should Janet respond if a request of Tanton included:
   (*a*) Favorable comments in a newscast from the consumer reporter?
   (*b*) On-air mentions by radio personalities?

## Macro Issues:

1. To what extent should a radio station's advertising policies foster community?
2. What word or phrase best describes the advertiser-media relationship? Is it antagonistic? Symbiotic? Are they partners? Adversaries?

## CASE VII-D
## "Bonding" Announcements in the News
JOANN BYRD
*Seattle Post Intelligencer*

The "Wedding Book" in the Sunday NW Life section of *The Herald* in Everett, Washington, includes weddings, engagements, and 25th and 50th wedding anniversaries. Each event submitted is reported with a one-column picture and about two inches of copy. People who want a more detailed announcement or their own language can buy a reduced-rate display ad, for which they write the copy.

In the fall of 1990, a lesbian couple filled out the form used to collect information and submitted it for the "Wedding Book" page. The women wanted to announce they had made a lifetime commitment to each other, in a bonding ceremony attended by family and friends in a local park.

*The Herald* serves an area combining the suburbs of Seattle and surrounding rural communities. Many in the core communities had made it clear over the years that they expected the paper to reflect and reinforce conservative family values. The county had grown 36 percent in the previous decade and showed an increasing diversity of races, cultures, and lifestyles. Other institutions, including the state's biggest bank, had adopted policies recognizing unmarried relationships and the city of Seattle had recently been involved in a visible campaign to have domestic partners of city employees declared eligible for medical insurance.

The decision to accept the announcement was made almost instantly. Simultaneously, Stan Strick, the paper's then-managing editor, suggested expanding the page to include, as the in-paper announcement put it, "significant personal milestones in people's lives, everything from adoptions to retirements."

Readers were notified of the change Sunday morning, November 25, 1990, in a story alongside the jumps of section-front pieces about gay couples who had exchanged vows and ministers discussing church positions on gay commitment ceremonies. The paper, with its page renamed "Celebrations," would be "one of the first in the nation to accept bonding ceremonies other than weddings," said the announcement.

The decision was condemned from pulpits in the county that morning, and people in the community began to protest. The women's announcement ran on the revamped page December 2, under a standing head, "Bondings," that matched the labels for "Weddings," "Engagements," "Anniversaries," and "Birthdays."

The community reaction became intense. Hundreds of angry subscribers canceled their subscriptions (as did some people who didn't have subscriptions). Letters and phone calls flooded the newsroom; a local businessman organized a protest group and visited *The Herald* advertisers, urging, although unsuccessfully, a boycott of the paper. Delegations from the conservative Christian community came to the paper to demand that the policy be rescinded.

Seattle television covered the debate and national media interviewed Strick. The storm continued for months. Letters to the editor and organized letter-writing and telephoning campaigns followed national news stories. As other newspapers across the country were approached to publish gay bonding ceremonies, editors phoned for details of *The Herald*'s experience.

Most of the complaints centered on Biblical interpretations condemning homosexuality. Those callers and letter-writers felt *The Herald* was endorsing sin, and giving to homosexual relationships the sanction that should be reserved for heterosexual marriages, engagements, and wedding anniversaries.

*The Herald*'s position was that sexual orientation was not a morally relevant basis for refusing to accept the announcements, that a page of reader-generated "significant personal milestones," simply had to give people equal access.

Two years later, the policy has not been changed. But no other gay couple in the county has submitted an announcement. One advertiser quit advertising for several weeks. Many of those who canceled subscriptions have not returned.

## Micro Issues:

1. Should the paper have accepted the announcement?
2. What options could you imagine? (Should the paper, for instance, have treated it as a news story rather than institutionalizing gay commitments in its announcement page?)
3. Some critics thought *The Herald* was bragging about being "one of the first" to accept gay bonding announcements. Would it have been better to skip the advance notice and simply publish the bonding ceremony and the new publication procedures for the page?
4. Some defenders likened the paper's decision to publishing mixed-race marriages before such notions were thought "socially acceptable." Is that a legitimate parallel? Are there others?

## Middle-range Issues:

1. Gay commitments are not recognized by most state laws. Should the paper publish any arrangements that do not have legal status?
2. This case arose on a page where "news" is defined by people who want to make the announcements, not by reporters working a beat. Does that raise different ethical questions in the newsroom?
3. How far should the newspaper go in giving people equal access to its pages? Is anything anybody wants to announce OK?

## Macro Issues:

1. Offending people and their most deeply held beliefs is not morally justified unless there is an overriding moral obligation. How much should the paper weigh the probability of offending a large portion of its audience by doing what it considers morally correct in this case?

2. Chances are that there would have been less dispute if the change had occurred at a paper in a big city. Are the values at stake here different from community to community, and should all newspapers' decisions recognize that?
3. How much should a secular entity like a newspaper reflect religious beliefs?
4. The women involved in this case were harassed by conservative groups for months afterwards. Does a newspaper have an obligation to censor news that may harm those submitting it? If so, what are the criteria?

## CASE VII-E
## Turning Off the *Light:* The San Antonio Newspaper War
FRED BLEVENS
*Southwest Texas State University*

On October 6, 1992, the Hearst Corp. announced it was putting its *San Antonio Light* up for sale, purchasing Rupert Murdoch's competing *San Antonio Express-News* and, if it could find no buyer for the *Light,* closing it. Hearst and Murdoch went to the Justice Department, the anti-trust regulator in such arrangements. The bureaucratic machinery moved slowly enough to let the case pass between presidents and, under stipulation of law, give interested parties time to make offers for the *Light.* Two months later, as President-elect Bill Clinton prepared to take office, employees were hoping a new and more populist White House would quash the deal and keep *La Luz,* as the *Light* was known in the Hispanic community, on the street. To soothe their anxieties, staffers built a newsroom altar of wilted flowers, photos, scraps of paper, trinkets and blinking Christmas lights. There were several pieces of bread, molded in the shape of butterflies, symbolizing *pan de muertos,* which Mexican families offer to deceased relatives on November 2, the Day of the Dead.

But six days after Clinton's inauguration and without a sitting attorney general, the Justice Department chose not to challenge the acquisition. Murdoch took his newfound wealth, $185 million, to retire debt in his collapsing American newspaper division. Industry analysts agreed that this quick sale at an inflated price suited his needs much more than the "marginal" *Express-News* profit. Hearst kept its promise to protect the jobs of those working under Murdoch, laying off 650 of its own people and shuttering the *Light* on January 27, 1993.

The *Light* had lost about $10 million in each of the past five years, the principle culprit was an oil-based economy that bottomed out in 1987. Both newspapers had lost one-third of their advertising revenues to a shrinking market and intense, competitive pricing that made the city one of the cheapest places in America to subscribe or advertise. At the same time, the publishers were spending millions on campaigns to generate the circulation to satisfy claims to advertisers.

The peculiarities of the San Antonio deal set it apart from previous monopoly episodes in large cities. This one involved the purchase of the winning newspaper by the losing newspaper and the closing of the newspaper traditionally favored by the Hispanic plurality. The 1990 Census showed the metropolitan area was 49 percent Hispanic, 42 percent Anglo, 7 percent African-American and 2 percent "other." In addition, the Hispanic community between 1980 and 1990 grew by nearly 28 percent, compared with nearly 20 percent for African-Americans and 11 percent for Anglos.

The *Light* generally served the Hispanic community well, excelling editorially over its competition and gaining a modicum of respect in national media circles. During the previous 10 years, *Light* reporters won more than 75 percent of all local writing awards in annual independent judging by out-of-state news organizations for the Society of Professional Journalists. That dominance in the only head-to-head contest between the two papers was confirmed in statewide contests in which the *Light* without exception performed better than the *Express-News*. In 1984, it began an intense minority recruiting program that resulted in the highest percentage of Hispanic staff representation of any paper in the nation. Nationally, only 3.5 percent of journalists at 62 mainstream papers were Hispanic. At the *Light,* the 23 Hispanic journalists ranked third only to the *Los Angeles Times* (55) and the *Miami Herald* (27). On a percentage basis, the *Light* outranked all newspapers with about 18 percent staff representation. It also was one of the only papers in the country to have an open editorial board that included community members.

Hearst CEO Frank Bennack is a native San Antonian who worked his way to publisher from the advertising sales staff. He maintains close family and social ties there, but he made his decision based on deliberations among three people, all based in New York; not even community leaders were made aware until after the deal was struck. Murdoch's purchase of the *Express-News* in 1973 was his first market on American soil. Murdoch showed remarkable loyalty to his employees, taking them out of the purchase negotiations and insisting they be retained.

But Hearst and Murdoch faced the dilemma of preserving a voice for the disfranchised with at least a short-term prospect of losing more money. The Justice Department, meanwhile, was charged with mediating the dilemma in a manner that primarily limits economic harm, exercising its authority under anti-trust law that predates the Sherman Act of 1890 and has its roots in the Constitution's commerce clause.

The publishers in San Antonio, following the lead of their counterparts in Dallas two years before, took a newly blazoned trail, which permitted a market-dominant paper to purchase a competing but "failing" newspaper, close it and thereby capture the market. And on January 27, 1993, the *Light* went out in San Antonio, placing that city in the vast majority of American cities with a single newspaper.

## Micro Issues:

1. When a community is served by only one newspaper, what additional responsibilities, if any, does that newspaper incur?
2. Newspapers have been called an "unregulated monopoly," in most U.S. cities. What is the government's proper role in trying to keep competing newspapers alive in major U.S. cities?
3. What measures should a broadcast outlet take to assure that its staff is representative of the community?

## Middle-range Issues:

1. Should the fact that the *Light* was serving the Hispanic community better than the competition have been a factor in which newspaper remained after the merger?

2. Should the fact that the *Light* was a better newspaper by objective measures than the competition have been a factor in which newspaper remained after the merger?

## Macro Issues:

1. Is a community better served by one financially healthy newspaper or by two newspapers that are losing money?
2. Both of the newspapers involved in this case were owned by a chain. What does a corporate chain owe a community where it publishes a newspaper?

## CASE VII-F
## Calvin Klein's Kiddie Porn Ads Prick Our Tolerance
VALERIE LILLEY
*Kansas City Business Journal*

As if a pantiless Brook Shields cooing, "Nothing comes between me and my Calvins," weren't enough. As if displaying a nipple to sell millions of dollars of Obsession perfume wasn't pushing tolerance to its edge, Calvin Klein pressed further. His 1996 television and magazine advertisements showing young people posed in provocative positions had some critics calling them common child pornography and prompted an FBI investigation.

"It was the portrayal of youth that was part of people's rage," said Katie Ford, chief executive of Ford Models Inc. in a *Wall Street Journal* article. "I think obviously a line was crossed because it created such an uproar. That's not a personal opinion, but it seems to be America's opinion."

The ads were shot in an environment right out of a cheap back room or basement. The print ads feature unknowns such as Delancey Berzin, a 14-year-old male, who was paid $1,000 to pose topless in Calvin Klein jeans, according to the *Philadelphia Inquirer.* One male model unbuttoned his pants to reveal his underwear looking as if he were in the midst of undress. Another young man is stripping off his shirt looking vulnerable, and yet another photograph shows a young woman, lying spread-eagled on a bench with her denim mini skirt yoked up revealing her underwear-covered crotch. She wears an innocent expression while she teases a piece of hair.

The sleazy effect was intentional. The $6 million campaign was shot by Stephen Meisel, who built his career on photographing seductive greats such as Madonna's 1992 book, *Sex.*

Klein did get one thing out of the campaign: free publicity. *Washington Post* columnist Bob Garfield described it best. Klein releases his ads and "lobs them into the firetrap of the media culture. The ladder trucks and pumpers of journalism race to the scene, bystanders run to see what the commotion is about and, as they stand in their nightclothes gawking, appalled but somehow also titillated by the conflagration, Klein strolls by and sells them $100 million worth of pants."

Klein said placing the kiddie porn stigma on his clothes was not his intention. In a full-page *New York Times* advertisement, Klein said the ads' message was intended to show "that young people of today, the most media savvy yet, have a real strength of character and independence. They have a strong defined line of what they will and will not do."

The campaign was withdrawn in August of 1996 after a public outcry. The main force behind the dissent was the Rev. Donald Wildmon, founder of the conservative American Family Association. He urged retailers to boycott the ads and threatened to have AFA members picket the stores if they didn't comply.

Perhaps one of the problems in pushing public taste is that Klein used young males in these exploitative roles. In the ads that ran on MTV, an older male voice

*AP/WIDE WORLD PHOTOS*

asked youthful-looking men, "You got a real nice look. How old are you?," "You think you could rip that shirt off you?" and "That's a nice body . . . do you work out?"

Society has long accepted this use of young women in this role, but boys are still off-limits. "To get sexy little guys gazing moistly at the camera, that gives everyone a terrible shock because boys are not to be used in this way," said Anne Hollander, author of *Sex and Suits,* in a *Washington Post* article.

Yet, minor-aged models who do seductive shoots do so willingly. Model Rainer Hammer, 15, who wants to pose for Klein and has already been photographed by Meisel, the campaign's photographer, is typical of the would-be models. She built up a portfolio of pictures of her in shackles and underwear. She has posed with a boy in a bed for Replay jeans. Wearing jeans, he lay on top of her and slightly lifted up her white undershirt. "I know the models in the Calvin Klein ads, and they don't care," she told the *Wall Street Journal.* "To us it's acting."

## Micro Issues:

1. Do the ads described meet your definition of kiddie porn?
2. Do the ads described meet your definition of bad taste?

## Middle-range Issues:

1. Has Klein been able to manipulate the media with his shocking commercials? Is it possible that free publicity was the intent of this modest budget ad campaign?
2. What should be the proper media response to those who use shock tactics to try to garner publicity?

## Macro Issues:

1. How do you respond to the claim that the commercials were shocking because boys were placed in vulnerable positions? Would the commercial have generated as much publicity if all the models had been female?
2. These commercials were accepted by major media outlets. What duty does a medium have to reflect the mores of the culture in which it operates?

## CASE VII-G
## Punishing the Messenger: The Tobacco Industry and the Press
STEVE WEINBERG, Associate Editor, *Columbia Journalism Review*
*University of Missouri—Columbia*

When ABC News, under the cloud of a $10 billion libel suit, apologized to Philip Morris in August 1995 for an award-winning investigation entitled "Smoke Screen" most journalists were stunned. The network's action damaged the credibility of a top-notch news organization, perhaps undermined investigative reporting as a journalistic genre, and encouraged lingering questions about the impact of the bottom line on corporate decision making regarding news stories.

The two-part investigative piece reported by Pulitzer prize winner Walt Bogdanich stated that tobacco companies, including Philip Morris and others, added nicotine to cigarette tobacco with the purpose of keeping smokers hooked on the drug. The story itself had been exhaustively researched for more than a year, and all of the sources but one—Deep Cough—had agreed to go on-the-record with their comments. In the process of researching the story, Bogdanich learned that, during the manufacturing process, nicotine is actually removed from tobacco at one point only to be added back into the tobacco later.

Less than a week before the show aired on the news magazine "Day One," the U.S. Food and Drug Administration issued a letter stating that the FDA believed there was mounting evidence that nicotine is "a powerfully addictive agent" and that "cigarette vendors control the levels of nicotine that satisfy this addition" (Weinberg 1995, 27).

Spokespersons for the tobacco industry were quoted in the segments, and Philip Morris, just days before the show was to air, sent ABC news a two-paragraph statement that said, in part, "Nothing done in the processing of tobacco or manufacture of cigarettes by Philip Morris increases the nicotine in the tobacco blend above what is naturally found in the tobacco." The investigative report never made the allegation that nicotine levels were increased beyond those that occur naturally, rather it suggested the tobacco companies had the ability to remove some of the drug from cigarettes and had chosen not to do so.

Controversy erupted after the first part of the story aired on February 28, 1994. A second segment, which aired one week later, focused on the list of 700 cigarette ingredients the tobacco companies had supplied to the federal government. Thirteen of those ingredients are banned in food. Philip Morris was not mentioned at all in the second segment.

Journalists applauded the work. The coverage won a George Polk award and a DuPont/Columbia University award. Congressional hearings into the tobacco industry were called as a result of the story. One day before those hearings were to begin, Philip Morris sued for libel, asking for $5 billion in compensatory damages and

Adapted from the *Columbia Journalism Review,* November/December 1995. Used by permission.

$5 billion in punitive damages despite the fact that Virginia law capped punitive damage awards at $350,000. The story about the libel suit ran nationally, often without the notation about the award restriction. In addition, the tobacco giant gave every indication that it would pursue the suit vigorously, spending more than $1 million per month for more than a year on the litigation.

At ABC, newspeople saw what they perceived as an immediate chilling effect. The day Philip Morris filed the lawsuit, two independent producers were notified by a producer at ABC's program "Turning Point" that their documentary on the tobacco industry's advertising tactics and production transfers to overseas sites was being shelved, despite the outlay of about $500,000.

Legally, the going was equally difficult. Although the network gave every indication that it intended to fight and win the libel suit, discovery tactics by Philip Morris bedeviled the process. Documents that normally would have been public were marked as trade secrets, thus sealing them and making them impossible to report on. Worse yet, from the journalists' view, Philip Morris attempted to unearth Deep Cough's identity by subpoenaing records of reporter's phone bills, credit card purchases, and travel in an attempt to retrace the journalist's footsteps to Deep Cough's door. A judge initially approved of the subpoenas in the discovery process but later reversed himself after the network contested the decision.

As in many expensive lawsuits, talk about a settlement surfaced from time to time, starting in the summer of 1994, just three months into pretrial discovery—and just as rumors began that Disney might make ABC part of its entertainment empire. Insiders weren't surprised. But it wasn't until almost a year later, on June 30, 1995, that the *Wall Street Journal* reported that settlement talks had begun anew. By that time, and despite ABC's trial lawyers assurances, other lawyers and some ABC managers had decided that portions of the investigative report would not withstand trial scrutiny.

It turned out that the trial lawyers had been kept away from the settlement negotiations. In-house lawyers, who were joined in the final days by renowned First Amendment lawyer Floyd Abrams, worked with Philip Morris's litigators on the language of an apology to the two tobacco companies. Abrams had been involved in the case briefly, before the settlement talks began. The network's statement ultimately ran in more than 700 publications under the headline "Apology Accepted." Philip Morris dropped the suit.

The apology was clearly a victory for Philip Morris, but was it a sell out for ABC? If "Smoke Screen" contained one or more factual errors, it might be possible to consider the extremely limited language of the apology and the absence of any monetary awards (ABC did agree to pay the other side's legal fee, at least $15 million) a victory of sorts for the network. ABC's assertion in the apology letter that it stands behind the show's intended principal focus and the signing of the reporter and producer to new long-term contracts with substantial raises—even though both refused to sign the settlement agreement—are a vindication of sorts for the show.

ABC was purchased by Disney after the suit was settled.

Still, if the owners of ABC News care about good journalism they will follow the advice of *Newsweek* columnist Jonathan Alter:

"The 'Day One' story was of historic importance . . . ABC should delete the small portions it apologized for, and rebroadcast it."

As of this writing, no such broadcast has occurred.

## Micro Issues:

1. Should Deep Cough have been allowed to remain off-the-record?
2. What standards of evidence should journalists doing investigative work demand from their sources and documents?
3. How should other news organizations that covered the libel suit have reported it?

## Middle-range Issues:

1. Should journalists work out agreements about legal liability with their editors in advance of broadcast or publication?
2. Should the journalists have been willing to wait on the story and work with government regulators on the issue?
3. What professional values are served by stories such as "Smoke Screen."
4. Does reporting on undesirable products or issues—toxic waste or tobacco, for example—demand a different professional standard than reporting on city government?

## Macro Issues:

1. What is the responsibility of "corporate ownership" to encourage and protect investigative reporting?
2. Do journalists, who increasingly work for large corporations, have a responsibility to the public to find mechanisms to counter the demands of the bottom line?
3. Do journalists have a "watch dog" role when it comes to covering corporations and economically powerful interests?
4. Compare "Smoke Screen" to Upton Sinclair's classic *The Jungle*. Would such a treatment of the tobacco industry be possible today?

# CHAPTER VIII

## *Picture This: The Ethics of Photo and Video Journalism*

**At the end of this chapter, the student should:**

- **Understand the legal and ethical issues involved in photojournalism in the area of privacy.**
- **Be aware of the technology available to alter photos and the ethical and epistemological issues those possibilities raise.**
- **Be able to define and recognize *eyewash*.**

### Introduction

Perhaps the most instantaneous of all ethical decisions in the mass media is the one made by the photographer at the scene of a news story: Shoot or don't shoot? How a photographer prepares for such moments, and what decisions he makes when a questionable situation arises, is sometimes thought to be the only issue in photo and video ethics. However, a number of ethical issues surround the visual part of the business, many of them evolving rapidly with new technology. In this chapter we will discuss the following:

1. Balancing the right to privacy and newsworthiness;
2. Staging video and news photographs;
3. Changing images electronically;
4. Selective editing to support a point of view;
5. Using unrelated eyewash photography in news.

What do these issues have in common? Perhaps it is that they all seem to center on the twin themes of fairness and accuracy. However, once the problems are identified, the answers are not that simple. What is fair? What is accurate?

While each photographer and photo editor will have to answer these questions individually, perhaps some minimum standard can be established: No image used in the news, whether video or still photograph, is ethical unless it treats the subjects or topics fairly and attempts to present an accurate and unambiguous picture of reality.

We will examine the inherent problems of visual communication, then look at specific ethical issues.

216

"Your work sounds interesting." Francesca said. She felt a need to keep neutral conversation going.

"It is. I like it a lot. I like the road, and I like making pictures."

She noticed he'd said "making" pictures. "You make pictures, not take them?"

"Yes. At least that's how I think of it. That's the difference between Sunday snapshooters and someone who does it for a living. When I'm finished with that bridge we saw today, it won't look quite like you expect. I'll have made it into something of my own, by lens choice, or camera angle, or general composition of all of those.

"I don't just take things as given; I try to make them into something that reflects my personal consciousness, my spirit. I try find the poetry in the image."

*The Bridges of Madison County*
Robert James Waller

## Problems in the Process

Ages-old axioms assure us that "the camera never lies" and that "seeing is believing." Yet no photograph or videotape can be completely accurate, since the mechanics of photography demand that the lens and film make choices the eye is not required to make. These differences between the eye and the camera influence perception, as Arthur Berger points out in *Seeing Is Believing*. Because of the many variables in photography—camera angles, use of light, texture, and focus—Berger says a picture is always an *interpretation* of reality, not reality itself. He adds that a dozen photographers taking pictures of the same scene would produce different views of the reality of it. For instance, one photographer, Nat Fein, won the Pulitzer prize for photography while taking a picture of an event dozens of photographers were shooting—the retirement of Babe Ruth. By moving to the rear of his subject, Fein captured a different angle and told a different and more dramatic story with his photo.

Not only does the camera differ from the eye in its ability to manipulate angle, light, and focus, cameras also capture an isolated reality by presenting us with a slice of life, free from context. In *About Looking,* John Berger says:

> What the camera does, and what the eye can never do, is to fix the appearance of that event. The camera saves a set of appearances from the otherwise inevitable supersession of further appearances. It holds them unchanging. And before the invention of the camera nothing could do this, except in the mind's eye, the faculty of memory. (1980, 14)

Although the camera and the eye are vastly different in their functions and their abilities, most media consumers believe the photographs they see because most people assume their eyes don't deceive them. And in this unguarded assumption lies the possibility for manipulation and deception.

Compounding the reality problem is the importance of visuals to both the electronic and print media. No major story is complete without a photo or footage. In this rush to shoot compelling visuals to accompany a story, photojournalists must juggle deadline and competitive pressures with other, less tangible qualities, such as privacy.

## To Shoot or Not to Shoot?

Each day, before pictures are chosen, cropped, and placed in the paper by the appropriate editor, another important decision is made in the field by the photographer. Arriving on the scene of the newsworthy event, she must make several decisions. The most basic of these is whether to take the photo of a subject who is in no position to deny the photographer access to the photo. Often these vulnerable subjects are wounded, in shock, in grief. And in that newsworthy moment, the subject of the photograph loses a measure of control over his or her circles of intimacy. That control passes to the photographer, who must make a decision.

Goffman (1959) claims people possess several "territories" they have a right to control. Included in Goffman's list are two territories that are problematic to the visual journalist—the right to a personal space free from the intrusion (i.e., by a camera lens) and the right to preserve one's "information," such as a state of joy, grief, etc., from public view.

By its very nature, photojournalism is an intrusive and a revealing process—two violations of Goffman's sense of self. And in many cases, it appears that someone else's misfortune is good fortune for the photojournalist. One study (Junas 1980) found that more than half of the winners in top photography contests were pictures of violence and tragedy.

Inevitably, every photojournalist happens on an assignment that will intrude on a subject's privacy. Garry Bryant (1987), a staff photographer with the *Deseret News* of Salt Lake City, offers this checklist he goes through "in hundredths of a second" when he reaches the scene of events such as the ones that were just described:

1. Should this moment be made public?
2. Will being photographed send the subjects into further trauma?
3. Am I at the least obtrusive distance possible?
4. Am I acting with compassion and sensitivity?

To this list, however, Bryant adds the following disclaimer: What society needs to understand is that photographers act and shoot instinctively. We are not journalists gathering facts. We are merely photographers snapping pictures. A general rule for most photojournalists is: "Shoot. You can always edit later" (p. 34).

Many photojournalists have taken comfort in the "shoot first, edit later" arrangement that they hope will shift the ethical decision to a later, less frenzied moment. However, sometimes it is the *act* of shooting the photograph that offends the subject as much as the subsequent publication. One of the most memorable photos of the assassination of presidential candidate Robert Kennedy is a photo of Ethel Kennedy, his wife, attempting to block the lenses of photographers immediately after the shooting.

Many editors argue that decisions cannot be made concerning photos that do not exist. Not every picture of grief needs to be ruled out just because the subject is vulnerable. Newspaper readers and television viewers need to know that drugs kill and leave behind grieving parents and friends. Where to draw the line is a decision best made in the newsroom rather than at the scene. The photographer who attempts to perform a type of ethical "triage" at the scene of a tragedy might find his career in jeopardy if the assignment fails to capture the pathos of the event when all other photographers did. In addition, the photographer who fails to capture some of the event, for whatever reason, fails to capture some of the truth for the audience.

However, the window of time for deciding later is closing. Today's microwave technology means that the media can be "Live at Five" on the scene of a tragedy, broadcasting footage even before the immediate family is alerted. Scenes that might once have been edited as the story was compiled now go straight on the air. An important stage in the ethical decision-making process is bypassed when such stories are aired live.

How can the victims of these tragedies come to life as vulnerable humans with feelings to a professional who sees the world most of the time through a lens? That question was asked at a conference held on the campus of Texas Christian University in 1986. Entitled "Crime Victims and the News Media," the conference brought together victims of violent crime and the journalists who covered their stories. Participants said such meetings generate empathy. ABC's media critic Jeff Greenfield noted, "Once a journalist hears their simple, eloquent stories of what happened to them, he will never approach the story of a human tragedy in quite the same way."

Essentially, the photographer who is deciding whether and how to photograph a tragedy is wrestling with the dilemma of treating every subject as an end and not merely a means to an end. We can agree that powerful images of accident victims may cause some drivers to proceed more safely, but if that message often comes at the expense of an accident victim's privacy, is it a message that needs to be told? Bovée (1991), in an essay entitled "The Ends Can Justify the Means—But Rarely," offers this set of questions to help the photographer find the answer.

1. Are the means truly morally evil or merely distasteful, unpopular, etc.?
2. Is the end a *real* good or something that merely *appears* to be good?
3. Is it probable that the means will achieve the end?
4. Is the same good possible using other means? Is the bad means being used as a shortcut to a good end when other methods would do?
5. Is the good end clearly greater than any evil means used to attain it?
6. Will the means used to achieve the end withstand the test of publicity?

While application of this test might help the photographer make some decisions, the choices will always be tough. The line between newsworthiness and intrusiveness, between good pictures and bad taste is often blurry. Donald Gormley, general manager of the *Spokane Spokesman-Review,* offers some insight into the difference between photos that are universally offensive and photos that are simply tough to view.

> Compassion is not the same as good taste. If a reader knows the person pictured in a very dramatic photograph, he may find it offensive. That's a sin against compassion. If he is offended whether he knows the person or not, the sin is probably one against good taste. (1984, 58)

## Staging Photographs

Every photographer has had the feeling: you are about to capture that perfect moment on film, except _____. You can fill in the blank with any number of problems. For the photographer at a birthday party, the issue is inconsequential. You simply remove the offending child, relight the candles, or arrange the scene and try again. To the photojournalist attempting to convey the truth of a story, however, the issue is much more complex: to tamper with the subject is to rearrange reality.

The issue is not a new one. As early as 1876, an enterprising photographer staged a picture of his own death (Lester 1992). More than one hundred years later, the ethics of the issue of staging remain unresolved, even in major news organizations.

For instance, during the 1992 November sweeps period, NBC's magazine show "Dateline" aired an 18-minute segment on a faulty design of General Motors pickup trucks that concluded with video of a truck exploding into flame immediately after a side impact collision. More than 300 people had died in such collisions since GM had introduced the trucks. The story included gripping still photographs of charred bodies pulled from accident scenes, court documents from the many suits filed against GM over the truck's design, and videotaped testimony from independent auto safety experts and a former GM engineer, all saying that the corporation had known about the design flaw yet chose to do nothing.

However, NBC did not inform viewers that, in order to capture the closing video, "sparking devices" had been mounted on the test cars by the independent testing agency the network had hired as part of its investigation. Even with the addition of the sparking devices, only one of two test vehicles had exploded on cue and the fire had gone out almost immediately.

About two months later, a jury returned a $105 million damage judgment against the auto maker in a wrongful death suit litigated around the truck's design flaws. The NBC story had not been introduced in the court case. A week after the jury returned the verdict, General Motors filed a libel suit against the network, charging—among other things—that the network had staged the concluding video. In an unprecedented move, anchors Jane Pauley and Stone Phillips read a three-minute retraction of the original "Dateline" story, admitting that the network had

# Calvin and Hobbes

## by Bill Watterson

aired the concluding video even though it was staged. The NBC–General Motors confrontation proved to be the end for network news President Michael Gartner. He resigned less than a month later.

The NBC incident raises several questions. Is there a place for re-enactment in the news? If so, when? How should such photos and video be labeled? The issues are not trivial, nor are they resolved. In a poll conducted by the National Press Photographers Association, the number-one ethical problem reported by photojournalists was set-up shots.

The questions surrounding fakery and staging speak to the purpose of news photography. Two possible purposes exist: the "mirror" and the "window" photograph (Szarkowski 1978).

The mirror photograph attempts to subjectively recreate the world in whatever image suits the photographer. Anything can be manipulated: light, proportion, setting, even subject. On the other hand, window photographs should be as objective a picture of reality as the medium will allow, untouched by the bias of the lens or the photographer.

Each type of photography has a function. A large percentage of the government-commissioned Dust Bowl era photographs that have seared our memories of the Depression would fit into the mirror category. Photographers searched for settings, posed people, and shifted props to achieve the maximum effect.

On the other hand, the photos that show us the horrors of war and famine, and arouse public opinion, are windows, where the photographer captures the moment with no attempts to alter it. *The problem comes in the substitution of one for the other.* When a photograph mirrors a photographer's bias, yet is passed off as a window on reality, the viewer has been deceived.

## Electronic Manipulation

Another major ethical issue in visual reporting is manipulation. Again, the history of photo manipulation is long. It has included such crude drawing board techniques as scissors and paste, darkroom techniques such as "burning" and "dodging," and more recently, airbrushing.

Today, technology allows increasingly sophisticated changes to be made to an image after it has been captured. Video technicians using computers can add missing information or change existing information to meet the needs of the story, by adding or deleting dot-sized picture elements ("pixels"). Digital retouching of pixels has progressed to a point where photographs can be altered or synthesized without detection, with little formal training and with inexpensive computers and software.

Technology has, in fact, made the word photography—literally "light writing"—obsolete, as a lighted reality no longer must exist in order for a "photograph" to be created. Photos and video are now what Reaves (1987) calls a "controlled liquid," capable of being manipulated into a seamless, yet totally unrealistic image. What this technology will ultimately lead to, Reaves claims, is an epistemological shift away from photography as irrefutable evidence of a story to photography as changeable story illustration. Eventually, she argues, as the public realizes that photographs can be (and frequently are) electronically altered, photos could lose their "moral authority." Tomlinson (1988) adds that technology could render photos nonadmissible as legal evidence once they lose the assumption of validity.

With an overwhelming amount of technology available for enhancing photos, editors must consider the ethical ramifications of their use. However, they should be aware that the public may begin to question the truthfulness of photographic images as the use of computers to enhance and even create photographs becomes more widely spread and publicized.

The first popular attention to the possibilities of computer technology on photography outside the news business came in the publicity surrounding the blockbuster film *Terminator II*. In that film, a video technique called "morphing" was used to create a shape-altering villain to challenge Arnold Schwarzenegger character's return to the twentieth century. Within a few years morphing technology was affordable and its use was seen in media from movies to advertising.

Digital technology allowed for juxtaposition of images that previously had no relationship to each other. For instance, Diet Coke made ads featuring Paula Abdul and a variety of old film stars including Groucho Marx and Gene Kelly. Similarly, Budweiser recently inserted footage of the late movie actor John Wayne in a commercial for its beer.

## Selective Editing

Another ethical question centers on the video editing process: whether editing itself renders a story untrue or unfair. While this complaint is not new with television, the charges leveled against video editing are more vociferous, since editing for time considerations is a much more noticeable constraint than editing for space. Scenes aired out of sequence, answers dubbed behind questions that were not originally asked, and a preponderance of one view dominating the final cut at the expense of another view are some of the most frequently cited instances of *selective editing*.

Actually the term selective editing is redundant. All editing is selective. The issue is who does the selecting, and what predispositions do they bring to the process. Some observers have noted that a dual standard is emerging between words and photos. A strange ethical dichotomy has long existed in the business of creating and processing print news and the photos that accompany it. The writer is allowed to reorder facts and rearrange details into an inverted-pyramid story on the rationale that the reader wants the most important facts taken out of sequence, and even out of context, and placed first in the story for more efficient reading. The result is praised as good writing and is taught in every journalism program.

However, should a photographer attempt to do the same thing with a camera—rearrange reality to make a more interesting photo or videotape—the result is called "staged." Our unwillingness to allow visual journalists the same conventions as print journalists says something fundamental about the role of visuals in the news. Media tradition says that while the truth in a print story about an explosion can contain only the highlights, the truth of a photo about the same explosion should be kept in context.

Such an analogy to print is important. When a writer edits, the result is called focusing, and it is applauded. When a photographer or video editor does the same thing, he or she is open to accusations of distortion. That is because we evaluate news photos according to print standards: linear and logical. Yet video and photographs are neither. They have a quality Marshall McLuhan called "allatonceness" that we are not quite comfortable with as a technology. Just what the photographer can do with the visual truth the camera uncovers is still a topic of debate.

Some photographers argue that to take away the possibilities that computer technology allows is to put them at a disadvantage in trying to tell a story visually. Should a photographer attempt to rearrange reality to make a more interesting photo or piece of film, the photograph is denigrated as "staged." And if a computer is used to correct focus or remove distractions, the photograph is derided as being "manipulated." In either case, the photographer could face sanctions.

However, as long as readers hold the view that "seeing is believing," that view—whether based in reality or not—becomes a promise between the media and their audience that photographers and videographers should be hesitant to break. While many photojournalists argue that "seeing is believing" should have never been a cultural truism (see Lester 1992), others argue that we must work within our readers' or viewers' predispositions about the truth of what they see. Steve Larson, director of photography for *U.S. News & World Report,* summarized this viewer-based rationale:

> The photo is a record of a moment in time. We're on shaky ground when we start changing that. We must maintain this pact. Catching a moment in time has history. When you look at a Matthew Brady photo there is that sense "this really happened." I believe strongly that's where photography draws its power. (Reaves 1991, 181)

## Eyewash

Another ethical issue in photojournalism is the controversial use of stock photos or file footage to illustrate news stories. Such *eyewash* is used regardless of the context of the original photograph and sometimes without the consent of the subject (Tomlinson 1988).

For instance, an article on compulsive gamblers might show a woman enjoying herself on a sunny afternoon at the races. While her action is taking place in public view, she might or might not be a victim of the syndrome addressed in the article, although the casual reader might infer that she is, indeed, a compulsive gambler. In this context, the photo is serving the purpose of eyewash, decoration for a story that bears no genuine relationship to it.

Eyewash has had a brief history in the courts. A Washington, D.C. television station used a tight shot on a pedestrian facing the camera, chosen at random, to illustrate the "twenty million Americans who have herpes." The court ruled that the combination of the film and the commentary was sufficient to support an inference that the plaintiff was a victim of herpes, which she contended was not true.

However, not all plaintiffs are successful. One young couple photographed in a public embrace in the Los Angeles Farmer's Market later saw their private moment published in *Harper's Bazaar* illustrating an article on "Love Makes the World Go 'Round." The California Supreme Court noted that the couple had "waived their right of privacy" by their voluntary actions and said that publication of the photograph merely extended and increased the public who could view the plaintiffs in their romantic pose.

With the rulings of the courts ambiguous on the matter of eyewash, the media have created divergent policies to cover the issue. Some newspapers and television stations, for instance, will use no picture not directly related to the story. Others limit the use of file or stock footage to that which is clearly labeled. Others limit the shooting of eyewash only by insisting that it occur in public view.

The issue is exacerbated by the voracious appetite that both television and the print media have for visuals. Virtually all surveys have shown that the presence of a photo adds to the number of readers for a newspaper story, while television insists that viewers will watch "talking heads" for only a few seconds before diverting their attention elsewhere. The answer to the question "Have you got art?" often means the difference in running or killing a story. At other times, good visuals can get a story in the coveted first slot on the nightly news or the front page of the newspaper.

Given the importance of visuals to a story, it is not surprising that ethical lines blur. Coleman (1987) tells the story of his young son's falling off a horse and breaking his arm. A photographer friend took a picture of the boy "dirty, tear-stained, in great pain, slumped in a wheelchair with his arm in a makeshift sling" on his way to the operating room. About a year later, a textbook publisher ran across the photo and wanted it as an illustration for a book on child abuse. Coleman denied the request but added that the photo could have run with little or no repercussion if he had not been easily available for the publisher to ask. Had that happened, the public would have been deceived by a photograph of a boy who had been a victim of nothing more than a childhood accident.

## Conclusion

Visual ethics is emotionally charged and constantly changing with new technology. *What this means is that the consumer of news photography is being presented with a product that is sometimes too raw to be palatable and sometimes too polished to be believable.*

The problem lies in the nature of the photojournalist's job. On a day-to-day basis, photography can be a mundane and poor-paying job. When an opportunity for a gripping photo does arise, like word that police are searching for a drowning victim, the desire to break out of the daily grind can lead to one of the extremes—a photo that is too raw with emotion or a photo that is worked over electronically until it bears little resemblance to reality.

Photojournalists, therefore, should operate under this version of Kant's categorical imperative: Don't deceive an audience that expects your pictures to be an accurate representation of a particular quality of reality. The imperative allows for exceptions, depending on audience expectations.

Most editors and photographers agree that manipulation or staging of news photos is generally more culpable than manipulation or staging of feature photos. The photo editors of a picture book such as *A Day in the Life of America* operate under a different set of audience expectations than the photo editors of the *New York Times*.

While the editors of *A Day in the Life of America* were criticized for a highly manipulated cover photo, their critics were misdirected. In the photo, a cowboy was moved closer to a tree, and the moon was moved and enlarged so the cowboy appeared as a silhouette against a full moon. The cover was not meant to be an accurate representation of reality. It was merely illustrative of the contents inside the book, which, according to its editors, contained no other manipulated photos. Similarly, advertising and entertainment operate under yet another set of imperatives.

The reasoning for this multiple standard is a presupposition that *while art may be manipulated, information may not* (Martin 1991). Such a flexible standard would be allowed under a categorical imperative as a permissible act, provided that:

- The photographer's intent is to merely make the photo more aesthetically pleasing and not to deceive; *and*
- The intended audience recognizes the difference; *or*
- The difference does not make audience members think or act in a manner in which they might not otherwise have thought or acted.

Fortunately, only a small percentage of photos offend, and only a small percentage of photos are staged or electronically manipulated. However, photographers are dealing with a trust that readers and viewers have placed in them. If that trust is betrayed, it will be slow to return.

## Suggested Readings

Berger, Arthur Asa. 1989. *Seeing is believing.* Mountain View, CA: Mayfield Publishing Co.

Berger, John. 1980. *About looking.* New York: Pantheon Books.

*Journal of mass media ethics.* 1987, Spring-Summer. Special issue on photojournalism.

Lester, Paul. 1991. *Photojournalism: An ethical approach.* Hillsdale, NJ: Lawrence Erlbaum Associates.

———. 1996 *Images that injure.* Westport, CT: Greenwoood Press.

# CHAPTER VIII CASES

## CASE VIII-A
## Problem Photos and Public Outcry
JON ROOSENRAAD
*University of Florida*

Campus police at the University of Florida were called on a Saturday to a dorm to investigate "a large amount of blood on the floor of a women's bathroom," according to police reports. They determined that the blood "appeared to have been from a pregnancy miscarriage" and began searching the dorm area. Some time later a police investigator searching through a trash dumpster behind the dorm found bloody towels, plastic gloves, and a large plastic bag containing more towels and the body of a six- to seven-pound female infant.

Police discovered no pulse. Rigor mortis had set in. After removing the body from the bag, the police briefly placed the body on a towel on the ground next to the dumpster. The photographer for the student paper, the *Independent Florida Alligator,* arrived at this time and photographed the body and dumpster.

Later on Saturday, the eighteen-year-old mother was found in her dorm bed and taken to the university's hospital. The hospital exam revealed "placenta parts and the umbilical cord in her" and she was released later in good health. A local obstetrician contacted about the case said that judging by the size of the infant, it was likely a miscarriage and not an abortion. The infant was determined to be about seven months' developed.

The story began on the front page of the Monday issue, across the bottom of the page, under the headline, "UF police investigate baby's death at dorm." It jumped inside to page 3 and was accompanied by the photo.

It was a dramatic photo, contrasting two well-dressed detectives and one uniformed policeman with the naked body; contrasting the fragile human form with the harsh metal dumpster filled with pizza and liquor boxes. The photo was played seven by five inches.

The story was well written and the photo dramatic but likely offensive to many—potentially so offensive that the newspaper's staff debated most of Sunday about how to use it before the editor decided to run it. But in an unusual move, she wrote an editor's column that appeared on the opinion page of the same issue explaining why. It showed a scene one might visualize in a ghetto but not on a college campus. It showed that supposedly sexually educated and sophisticated college students of the 1980s still need help. The editor wrote:

> "Even with these legitimate reasons we did not run the picture on the front page. This is partially in response to our concern that we do not appear to be exploiting this picture to attract readers. . . . We also examined the photographer's negatives to see if there were any less graphic prints. . . . Is the message perceived by the reader worth the shock he or she experiences? After pondering what we feel is a very profound photo, we decided there is. This was a desperate act in an area of society where it is not expected. The picture shows it."

*Photo courtesy of the* Independent Florida Alligator. *Used by permission.*

The local daily covered the story Monday in a police brief. No photo ran.

It was determined that the body was from a miscarriage. The woman involved left school. The campus paper got several letters critiquing its coverage of the story. Many chose to criticize the editors for running the photo, while some praised the staff for pointing out the problem and for listing places on campus where sex and pregnancy counseling was available. Some letters did both.

An example of some of the outrage over the running of the photo by the *Alligator* came from a female student who called the coverage "the most unnecessary, tactless piece of journalism I've ever encountered." Another letter from a male student called the photo "in poor taste and extremely insensitive." The writer added, "There are times when good, sound judgment must override 'hot' copy."

Perhaps the most pointed comment came from a female writer who added twenty-four other names to her letter. The letter stated that "the incident *could* have been used to remind people that they need to take responsibility for their own sexuality. The story *could* have been used as a painful reminder that there are many uneducated, naive people out there who need help. But, unfortunately, the *Alligator* chose to sensationalize the story with a picture, completely nullifying any lesson whatsoever that might have been learned."

## Micro Issues:

1. Should the photographer have taken the picture?
2. Is this a legitimate story, and if so, does it belong on page 1?
3. If this was the only photo available, did the paper then have to run it?
4. Various letters to the editor called the photo "unnecessary," "tactless," and "insensitive." What would you say to those charges if you were on the staff?

## Middle-range Issues:

1. Does running the photo inside lessen any criticism of poor taste? Did its placement mitigate any ethical criticism?
2. If the staff was so unsure, was the editor correct in writing a same-day rationale for its publication?
3. Critique the reasoning stated by the editor in running the photo. What moral philosophy, if any, would lead one to agree with the action?

## Macro Issues:

1. Should a paper play a story and photo like this to crusade about a problem?
2. Is the perceived social value of such a picture worth more than the shock and criticism?
3. Was the writer correct in her assessment that the shock of the photo negated any good that might have been done by the story?
4. Should a campus newspaper have a different standard—of taste, play, news value—than a "regular" daily?

---

## CASE VIII-B
## Digital Manipulation of Photos with New Computer Technology
SHIELA REAVES
*University of Wisconsin, Madison*

You are an assistant feature editor who is trained in good graphic design and has a reputation for eye-catching layouts. Your newspaper has invested about two million dollars for the powerful new computer technology that is sweeping the print media. These computers give superb color production on tight deadlines. This is crucial for making news deadlines on breaking stories. An added advantage is the computers' ability to clone objects and move them. The changes are quick and easy. You can seamlessly combine photos to create exciting new graphics for your feature section.

The editors caution everyone never to alter news photographs. The editors acknowledge that feature stories often need to rely more on illustrations, which are OK to alter since most editors believe readers can tell the difference between news and illustrations.

You want to use a file photo of a U.S. senator for a feature story on his political career. However, the photo is badly flawed in composition. There is a flag that appears to grow out of the senator's head, and you know this is distracting for the reader. You know that the photographer was in a rush when she took the photo and did not have time to compose a better picture using the flag. You alter the photo to

*Original photo*          *Altered photo on computer*

*Shiela Reaves. Used by permission.*

*Original photo*

*Altered photo on computer*
*Shiela Reaves. Used by permission.*

clean up the background. You slightly enlarge the flag by 25 percent, move it to the right, and lighten the print. No one notices the change except the photographer, who admits it's a better composition.

You next use the computer to create an illustration for a story on adolescent dance fads. You prefer a file photo of three teens break dancing. However, the girl on the right is rather awkward in her movements. On the computer you digitally remove the girl and boom box. Next you digitally clone one of the dancers, flip his image, and paste him where the girl once stood to restore the horizontal format. You clean up distracting objects in the background in seconds.

When the feature illustration runs, you get a phone call from the teen's mother. She saw the original photo that ran five years ago in the news section. She is confused by your illustration. She wants to know what became of her daughter and how you mysteriously cloned her son so that he appears twice in the photo. Her question to you: "Does your newspaper do this to all your photos?"

## Micro Issues:

1. Do you explain to your reader the difference between news and feature illustrations? Is there a difference?
2. Do you apologize for using an old photo that apparently was still recognizable to some people?
3. Do you think it's allowable for newspapers to alter photos so long as the subject or the photographer gives permission?

## Middle-range Issues:

1. What are the limits of altering a photo on the computer?
2. Do you think that cleaning up bad composition in a feature portrait is allowable? How does cleaning up in this context differ from fakery?
3. Is there a difference between how photos should be handled in news sections and feature sections, or should both be treated with the same standards?

## Macro Issues:

1. If you can edit words, why can't you edit photos? What's the difference between cleaning up quotes for grammar and cleaning up a busy background in a feature portrait?
2. If readers come to doubt the authenticity of photos that appear in feature sections, will they doubt photos that appear in news sections?
3. Can readers readily distinguish the difference between illustrations and news photos?

# CASE VIII-C
## Military Censorship of Photographs
PAUL LESTER
*California State University, Fullerton*

The United States has been engaged in military conflicts both honorable and questionable. Inspired by the need to report each war to an anxious public, journalists have traveled to the front lines to produce stories and pictures both supportive and critical. As the informational and emotional power of visual images has become more understood, military strategists and politicians have instituted various forms of censorship of images in an attempt to protect their troops and to control public opinion.

Termed "Desert Storm" by the military and the "Gulf War" by the media, the clash with Iraq over Kuwait was an example of the often tenuous relationship between government officials and journalists. Hundreds of journalists throughout the world were in Saudi Arabia covering the fight, but only about 100 made up the official military press pool. With more than 500,000 American troops in the area and fighting erupting on several fronts, newspapers, for example, relied on only 16 journalists to cover every ground unit in the country. Although most reporters accepted the fact that a pool was necessary, many were frustrated by the military's slowness in transporting the pool members to troubled areas. Once there, pool members were accompanied by an ever-present military escort.

Department of Defense ground rules signed by all journalists prohibited reporting that would in any way endanger the troops. A journalist had to get approval before attempting any story. Once the piece was completed, the story and pictures were subject to U.S. and allied military censorship. Although there was no stated prohibition against showing wounded or killed soldiers, some journalists were wondering halfway into the war why they had not "seen one picture of bloodshed (or) anyone who's dead yet." Charges of "news management" and a "credibility gap" between official and pool reporter accounts surfaced. Claiming that press pool restrictions were too harsh, nine U.S. publications and novelists asked for a federal court injunction against the Defense Department's pool procedures.

The Gulf War was difficult to cover. It was primarily an air campaign waged in the middle of the night using fast-moving aircraft carrying computer-guided missiles with video cameras in their nose cones to signal the result of their prearranged mission. The Iraqi government was extremely hostile to journalists, only allowing a handful of correspondents to report from their side of the conflict. The isolated nature of the terrain was a further barrier to full-access coverage. It was simply not possible to conveniently drive across the huge desert seeking front-line firefights as in previous wars.

Besides, it was quite dangerous to try such a mission as Bob Simon and his crew from CBS discovered. Simon and his associates decided to drive to Iraq through the desert on their own because they were frustrated by the military's strict censorship controls over their actions. They were soon captured by Iraqi forces and

*David C. Turnley*/Detroit Free Press

detained until the end of the conflict. Despite these dangers and restrictions, CNN's coverage of the night bombing of Baghdad was particularly impressive and the subsequent damage to buildings in that ancient city reported by Peter Arnett—the only American correspondent able to report with his words and images from Baghdad.

As never before, technology played a significant part in fighting and reporting the war. Arnett and others were able to report from the far-off country because of the use of a portable satellite transmitter. Photographers were able to quickly send their images to their waiting editors because of digital cameras and transmitters. Nevertheless, most still photographers and videographers were frustrated by their lack of access to any real fighting scenes. They were left to cover noncombat scenes involving soldiers drilling. Once the ground war had commenced, a few journalists found themselves riding along with the tank units. But most of the fighting occurred at night making it extremely difficult to record action scenes. Most of the pictures out of the fighting areas in Iraq were of the long lines of Iraqi prisoners captured by military forces.

One highly emotional picture that did get through military censors was taken by *Detroit Free Press* photographer David Turnley. Turnley was riding with the 5th MASH medical unit inside Iraq. A fierce firefight had recently erupted between Saddam Hussein's Republican Guard and the 24th Mechanized Infantry Division.

Turnley's helicopter filled with medical personnel and equipment touched down about 100 yards from a frantic scene. An American military vehicle had just taken a direct hit. Soldiers on the ground were upset as they said it had mistakenly been struck by a U.S. tank. The wounded were quickly retrieved from the vehicle and carried to the helicopter. Sgt. Ken Kozakiewicz, suffering from a fractured hand, slumped into the helicopter. The body of the driver of Kozakiewicz's vehicle was placed on the floor of the helicopter inside a zippered bag. A medical staff member, perhaps thoughtlessly, handed the dead driver's identification card to Kozakiewicz. Turnley, sitting across from the injured soldier, recorded the emotional moment with his camera when Kozakiewicz realized that his friend was killed by the blast.

Later at the hospital, Turnley asked the soldiers their names. He also asked if they would mind if the pictures were published. They all told him to get the images published.

The rules of combat enforced by the military required that Turnley give his film to military officials for approval for publication. A day after the incident, Turnley learned that his editors had not yet received his negatives from the Defense Department officials. Military officials insisted that they were holding on to the film because the images were of a sensitive nature. They also said that they were concerned about whether the dead soldier's family had been informed of his death. Because of Turnley's argument that the family must have been informed by then, the officials released his film.

His photographs were eventually published in Detroit and throughout the world. The picture of Kozakiewicz crying over the loss of his friend was called the "Picture of the War" on the cover of *Parade* magazine. Several months after the war, Turnley spoke to Kozakiewicz's father, who had been in one of the first American military units in Vietnam. Reacting to the censorship of images by military officials, David Kozakiewicz explained that the military was "trying to make us think this is antiseptic. But this is war. Where is the blood and the reality of what is happening over there? Finally we have a picture of what really happens in war." For David Kozakiewicz, showing his son grieving over the death of a fellow fighter gave added meaning to the soldier's death.

## Micro Issues:

1. Should the photographer have taken the picture?
2. Should the photographer have asked permission of the injured soldier to take the picture?
3. Does a picture of a grieving soldier belong on page one?
4. Should photographers be allowed to travel along with military personnel to the fighting fronts?

## Middle-range Issues:

1. Would criticism be lessened if the image was run small and on an inside page?
2. If the soldier is not from your newspaper's local area, why should the picture run?

3. How would you as an editor react to a reader's complaining that the picture demoralizes America's war effort?

## Macro Issues:

1. What moral philosophies influence an editor who uses the picture and a reader who complains about its use?
2. Does the military during a war have the right to censor images produced by a photographer?
3. Does "pool" coverage during a war offer the best solution for informing the public back home?
4. Should an editor wait to publish a picture of a dead person until relatives are informed? Why or why not?
5. Should journalists avoid taking and publishing images that criticize the nation's war effort?

## CASE VIII-D
## Faking Photos: Is It Ever Justified?

JAMES VAN METER, Freelance Photographer
*Bellingham, Washington*

Chris Jones, a reporter with a large, metropolitan daily newspaper, is told by a source that a computer software corporation is considering his city as a plant site. Jones calls to confirm the tip, and the corporation's public relations representative reads him the following statement:

> Our corporation is interested in purchasing the two-block area between Third and Maple Streets on Washington Avenue. The corporation believes the site would be to its advantage, with easy access from the interstate and the airport and adequate parking space. The plant would produce software material and offer ten new jobs to trained applicants. We are preparing to make a more than substantial offer to the landowner, Joe Sullivan. The corporation hopes to begin production on the plant three months from now, in March.

Jones notes in his story that the proposed site, commonly known as skid row, houses several run-down hotels, bars, and a homeless shelter.

One week later, Jones talks to Sullivan and the corporate representative again. He learns an offer was made to purchase the land, and although Sullivan is eager to accept, he will wait three days to give his response.

Jones's city editor makes a photo assignment, asking for shots of the homeless people who live in the two blocks. The city editor tells veteran photographer Steve Stone he needs strong, emotional pictures to run with a story about how the homeless shelter cannot afford to move to another location. The city editor also wants the photographs to run before Sullivan responds to the corporation's offer.

Stone spends an entire day walking up and down Washington Avenue, trying to get close enough to the people sleeping and eating on the streets. Yet they either cover their faces, walk away, or plead with him not to take their pictures.

During the morning of the second day, Stone manages to take some photographs, but after he develops them he discovers that his images did not capture the pain he felt when seeing firsthand how these people struggle to survive.

Under deadline pressure, Stone calls some of his friends and asks them to pose for him as homeless people. He takes his friends, dressed in torn clothes with black greasepaint smeared on their faces, into an alley near, but not on, skid row. Stone takes some created photographs and turns them into his editor minutes before deadline.

The city editor is so impressed with Stone's work that he decides to run one of the photographs on the front page the next day, with photo essays on two inside pages.

The day the photographs are printed, both the newspaper and the computer software corporation are flooded with phone calls protesting the plant site. Later that day, the corporate executives hold a press conference, saying they believe it would be best to look into other plant locations in the city.

*Photo by James Van Meter. Used by permission.*

Is it likely that such deception would work? Examine closely the photo of the man sleeping in the doorway of the church building that accompanies this case. He is a college student who volunteered to pose for the photographer. He is neither poor nor homeless.

## Micro Issues:

1. Should Stone have told his editor that he was having problems getting the right photographs before he set up the shots?

2. If you were Stone, would you have gone ahead and taken pictures of the homeless people despite their protests?
3. After letting the editors see the photographs, should Stone have told them how he took the photographs? Justify your answer.
4. What is the editor's obligation in framing the assignment?

## Middle-range Issues:

1. Because the photographs were an obvious factor in the corporation's decision to find another location for the plant, did the end justify the means?
2. Do you think the photographer allowed his personal feelings about the issue of the homeless interfere with his professional judgment?
3. Does the fact that the photos closely mirrored reality make a difference in whether the deception was ethically justified?
4. What do you see as the difference between asking a friend to help you fake the photo and directing a cooperative homeless person to pose for you? Is one any more truthful than the other?
5. What is the distinction between the faked photo and a print journalist who writes about a composite character?

## Macro Issues:

1. Does a photographer create a pseudo-event just by showing up with his camera?
2. Should a news photographer voice his personal opinion through his photographs? Explain your answer.
3. In this case, the photographer recreated a likely news scenario—a homeless man lying in a church entry. In 1992, NBC's "Dateline" recreated a fiery truck collision on camera by rigging the truck with incendiary devices before it was rammed by another vehicle. It is a fact that some homeless people sleep in doorways and some trucks explode on impact. Is there a difference in NBC's efforts to assure good video of a crash and this photographer's efforts to assure good photos of the homeless? If so, what are the differences? Are both equally culpable activities?

## CASE VIII-E
## "Above the Fold": Balancing Newsworthy Photos
## with Community Standards
JIM GODBOLD, Managing Editor
JANNELLE HARTMAN, Reporter
*Eugene Register-Guard, Eugene, Oregon*

*Author's note: On November 10, 1993, a nightmare unfolded in Springfield, Oregon, a quiet town adjoining the university community of Eugene, as Alan McGuire held his two-year-old daughter, Shelby, hostage in their house. By the end of the standoff both were dead and the media had captured some horrific photos.*

*Seven children had died as a result of child abuse in Lane County, Oregon in the twenty months prior to that day and the media had just witnessed the eighth. Jim Godbold, was the assistant managing editor of the* Eugene Register-Guard *at the time. The remarks below are from an interview with him months after the event.*

**Godbold:** The call came over the police scanner shortly after noon. We responded to a hostage situation, a man holding someone at knife point in a Springfield neighborhood. We knew it was probably 20 minutes from the *Register-Guard* in the best of possible circumstances so we really scrambled. Photographer Andy Nelson and police reporter Jannelle Hartman went as fast as they could to the area.

We got there when the police were trying to set up a perimeter to get people away from the area. It was real pandemonium right when Andy arrived. The situation didn't unfold for more than a few minutes before there was a burst of flame inside the house that caught the attention of the police officers and they immediately made the decision that they were going to have to go inside.

A group of officers ran at the door, and then all of a sudden Alan McGuire, the man who was in the house, came hurtling through the front window on fire. I am not even sure if police officers knew how many people were in the house at the time. His wife had escaped from the home. She had been held at knife point and bound, and she had somehow gotten out and she let police know that their two-year-old daughter Shelby McGuire was in the house.

Shelby was a hostage and being held at knife point. Police saw her and tried to set up a telephone line so they could negotiate with McGuire but the events unfolded rapidly and after Alan McGuire jumped through the front window police broke down the door. Two officers hauled McGuire's flaming body to the ground and tried to douse the flames with a garden hose. Inside the house one of the officers saw Shelby McGuire sitting upright on the couch. She had a plastic grocery produce bag over her head, and it apparently had been duct-taped in some fashion, maybe around the neck.

They immediately tore the bag away. A detective picked Shelby up and sprinted out of the house with her. It was at that moment that Andy Nelson snapped his picture of one of the officers with Shelby's body in his arms running out, two other officers standing on the side of the doorstep, another officer with a hose near Alan McGuire, and Alan lying on the ground. The flame's now out but the charred and still smoking body was present in the view finder as Andy snapped the picture.

At that moment the officer with Shelby McGuire, the two-year-old, began mouth-to-mouth resuscitation on the front lawn. Andy subsequently took a photograph of that.

*Photo courtesy of Eugene* Register-Guard. *Used by permission.*

Then they rushed both Alan and Shelby McGuire to the hospital. We did not know Shelby's condition. The police didn't respond about whether she was able to be resuscitated.

We have a standing policy at the newspaper that as a general rule we don't run photographs of dead bodies of children. That immediately triggered the kind of review that we would go through to determine where this particular incident was going to stand up on our policy, whether or not anyone was going to argue for publication or against publication.

We began to talk about the policy and the potential community reaction that we might face. The discussion was pretty brief. The photo was so compelling and the situation that it sprang from so horrifying that we began looking at the photograph and saying, "well, I don't know, but, look at what the photo has captured."

"People are going to be upset."

"This is potentially a photograph of a dead two-year-old child."

"Look at the concern and the expression on the police officers' faces. This is an example of what they deal with day in and day out. They are up against this kind of domestic violence hostage situation and people don't realize that."

*Photo courtesy of Eugene* Register-Guard. *Used by permission.*

So, the debate was intense, and yet pretty short. We prepared a selection of pictures, and we brought those to the then-managing editor Patrick Yak and made the case that this is going to be a tough photograph for us to run. This is going to be one that we are going to have to be prepared to defend. But we believe it's that kind of exception to the rule that we look for.

The public response to the publication of the Shelby McGuire photograph was unprecedented in my 22 years in journalism and unprecedented at this newspaper. I have not come across a case, having been shown a number of them subsequently, that is of the magnitude per capita of reader's response to a single photographic image. We received on the order of 450 telephone calls that began the moment people got the newspaper which started at 6 A.M. First they came into our circulation department. The circulation department switchboard became overloaded and gave them the main newsroom switchboard, which didn't open until 7:30. At 7:30 when they threw the switch all 20 of our incoming phone lines lit up, and the calls began to roll over into a holding pattern that had never been utilized by our switchboard before.

I was called at home by Al Gimmell, the corporate controller, who said, "We are inundated with telephone calls. We need some help." So I immediately came in to try to handle telephone calls and I tried to find the time in between phone calls to call other editors in but the calls were coming so rapidly that every time I hung up it rang again. When I picked up my voice mail message I had 31 unanswered messages, and that was probably 7:45 in the morning.

The range of responses weren't monolithic except in their anger. But the anger came from different places. For some people the anger came from a belief that we had simply stooped to a tremendously sensational graphic crime picture trying to sell newspapers. For others the anger came from the terrible sense of violation that the surviving mother and brother of Shelby McGuire would have to wake up in the morning after their ordeal and see this on the front page of the hometown newspaper.

Another component argued that this was wholly inappropriate for the kind of newspaper the *Register-Guard* has been and continues to be. That five-year-olds and six-year-olds were sharing the newspaper at the breakfast table and parents were finding themselves in a position of having to explain this horrifying incident and having the question "How is the little girl?" asked again. And there was also a range of response from people who were themselves victims of domestic violence or spouses of victims or had family members who were involved in it. For them it was a combination of anger and pain.

I spoke with literally dozens of people through tears. It was an emotional response that was overwhelming and people were extremely upset by the picture. Most asked the question "Why? I need to understand why the newspaper published this picture."

We were really I think at a loss initially to respond to that question. I think a lot of that had to do with being in a very real sense out of touch with a substantial number of readers. The kind of reaction that we had was not anticipated by anyone in the news department.

If we were presented with a similar situation and a similar photograph today we would absolutely not do it the way that we did it in the Shelby McGuire case. Thousands of our readers have defined for us a boundary in this community and for this newspaper that I don't think until we began to see it materialize we had any sense of exactly where it was.

# Micro Issues:

1. Look at the photos that accompany this text. The photo of the officer carrying out Shelby McGuire ran in full color above the fold, two-thirds of the page wide and six inches tall. Does a photo of that size over-sensationalize the story?
2. The photo of Sgt. Swenson's attempts to resuscitate Shelby ran below the fold in a small two-column photo. Why do you think the decision was made to run this photo smaller and lower?

# Middle-range Issues:

1. Does the fact that Shelby died influence your decision on whether to run the photos? If so, in what way?
2. Does the fact that at least one television station and the local Springfield newspaper were there with photographers influence your decision to run the photos? If so, in what way?

3. Does the fact that seven other children had died in Lane County in less than two years affect your decision to run the photos? If so, in what way?

4. The bi-weekly *Springfield News* chose to run a front-page photo of Alan McGuire falling out of the front window of his home, his badly burned flesh still in flames. However, they covered the front page with a wrapper that read "Caution to Readers" and explained the content of the stories and photos underneath the wrapper. Critique that approach to handling the story.

5. A local television station showed a few seconds of the scene described above after warning viewers of the violent nature of the video that followed. The station got fewer than 20 complaints. How do you explain the vast difference in the reaction to the broadcast and print photos?

## Macro Issues:

1. What are the privacy rights of:
   (*a*) Shelby McGuire?
   (*b*) Shelby McGuire's mother and her four-year-old brother?
   (*c*) Sgt. Swenson?

2. Critique the argument that these photos should be shown because they illustrate the type of tragedy that law enforcement officers are often called upon to handle.

3. Critique the argument that these photos should be shown because they illustrate the horror of domestic violence.

4. Critique the statement that "If we were presented with a similar situation and a similar photograph today we would absolutely not do it the way that we did it in the Shelby McGuire case." In your opinion is that based on sensitivity to reader concern or caving in to reader pressure?

## CASE VIII-F
## "Film at Ten": Handling Graphic Video in the News
SONYA FORTE DUHÉ
*University of South Carolina*

It was supposed to be a routine transport of an alleged kidnapper. WBRZ-TV had been following the story and was at the Baton Rouge Metropolitan Airport to get videotape of sheriff's deputies escorting Jeffrey Doucet back to stand trial.

FBI agents had arrested Doucet in California for the alleged kidnapping of 11-year-old Jodie Plauche. In February, Doucet, a karate instructor, allegedly kidnapped the boy in Baton Rouge and took him to California. A month later, Jodie was found unharmed when FBI agents arrested Doucet in an Anaheim hotel room.

East Baton Rouge Parish Sheriff's Department Major Mike Barnett and Deputy Bud Conner were escorting Doucet. WBRZ-TV was the only news crew waiting at the airport for Doucet's 9:17 arrival. Reporter Ed Buggs planned to insert the video of Doucet's arrival into a story for the ABC affiliate's 10 P.M. newscast—a story about the return of the alleged kidnapper.

As WBRZ-TV photographer Abram McGull videotaped the scene, Barnett walked about six feet into the airport terminal checking the area for suspicious characters. Then, Barnett signaled to Conner to bring the handcuffed Doucet forward. With Doucet on his right, Conner walked past a bank of public telephones. At that point, a man wearing blue jeans, a striped tee shirt, dark glasses, and a baseball cap turned from the wall phone where he was standing, aimed, and fired at Doucet's head. The man who pulled the trigger was Jodie's father, Gary Plauche.

The WBRZ news crew had witnessed and videotaped the event. The tape distinctly showed Plauche firing the gun and Doucet's head jerking as the bullet entered his skull. From there, the cameraman quickly focused on Doucet as he dropped to the floor. Next, McGull focused on the action in front of the telephones where Barnett and Conner grappled with Plauche. Barnett called the suspect by name, "Gary why, why Gary?" Finally, the two sheriff's officers grabbed the suspect's gun. From there, the cameraman zoomed into Doucet's face and open eyes as blood gushed from his head.

The next pictures showed Conner kneeling over Doucet as Barnett held Plauche in the background. Both men yelled almost synonymously, "Call the sheriff's office, call the sheriff's office, call an ambulance!" A policeman then walked into the scene and radioed emergency medical services for help.

By this time, Conner was crouched over Doucet's body. The videotaped action now showed Plauche being handcuffed. Next, Conner is shown delicately slipping Plauche's gun into Barnett's coat jacket. McGull then videotaped a wider scene where Conner paced around Doucet's body as it lay still on the floor—his head surrounded by a pool of blood.

Reporter Buggs immediately called his newsroom for help from News Director John Spain. At the time, Spain was attending a local theatrical production a few blocks from the station. After being paged, he told the news team at the airport to

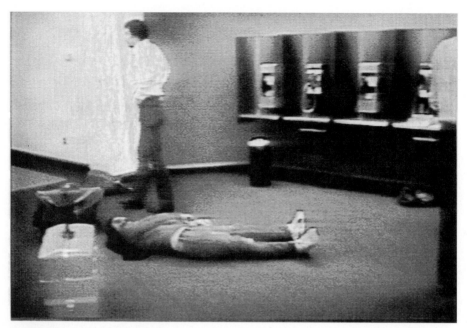

send back the video via their microwave truck and proceed as quickly as possible to the station.

The story led the ten o'clock newscast. WBRZ anchorman Jay Young said good evening and introduced Buggs who was sitting beside him. Young said, "A Baton Rouge man arrested for the recent kidnapping of an eleven-year-old boy has just been gunned down at the Baton Rouge Metropolitan Airport minutes ago as detectives brought him back from California. "Eyewitness News" cameras were rolling with reporter Ed Buggs as the shooting rang out. Ed, a dramatic, a tragic, and, of course, a bloody event."

Buggs responded, "And I think, Jay, that what rests most in my mind as I try to calm down, as well as news photographer Abram McGull, is the fact that it was so unexpected. We were in the airport for the arrival this evening of a 25-year-old karate instructor. He was arriving back in Baton Rouge. Local authorities were bringing him back. He has been indicted by a local parish grand jury on charges of aggravated kidnapping. What you are about to see is some very graphic film."

Talking over the videotape of Doucet walking into the airport, Buggs told the story of the night's shooting. The tape showed Doucet walking down the hall with Conner. The tape continued to roll with the suspect firing the deadly shot, the struggle to control the suspect, and then Conner kneeling over Doucet's body. At this point, editing of the videotape begins to take place.

As Buggs explained, Doucet was on a transfer flight from California, the video shows police handcuffing Plauche. That scene continued as Buggs said, ". . . the gunman who was standing there by the telephones you see was in such a position that you did not have to go through security guards to carry a weapon." Here the shot changes. Buggs shows a wide shot of Conner pacing around Doucet. The viewer could see Doucet's entire body on the ground with his head in a pool of blood. The picture then zooms back to Plauche. The reporter is now back on camera introducing the story that was supposed to air originally on Doucet's return.

## Micro Issues:

1. Should the photographer have kept taking the videotape after the shooting occurred? Why?
2. Should any of the videotape have aired on the news? If so, how much?
3. Since the station's microwave truck was at the airport, should the reporter have gone live to tell the story for its 10 P.M. newscast?
4. If police confirm Plauche learned about Doucet's arrival from a WBRZ employee, should that employee be fired?

## Middle-range Issues:

1. Does a disclaimer for the graphic video ethically allow its use?
2. Should a person lying in a pool of blood ever be shown on television news? If so, what are some of the scenarios when you would allow it?
3. Was it okay to air the videotape and tell the story without knowing whether Doucet's relatives had been notified?
4. Should stations in other markets air the film? Why?

## Macro Issues:

1. Should the videotape be used in subsequent newscasts?
2. What responsibilities do newspeople have regarding source confidentiality?
3. Is it ethical to use police sources to break a story?
4. Will running this videotape prevent Plauche from getting a fair trial in East Baton Rouge Parish?

## CASE VIII-G
## Horror in Soweto
SUE O'BRIEN
*The Denver Post*

On September 15, 1990, freelance photographer Gregory Marinovich documented the killing, by a mob of African National Congress supporters, of a man they believed to be a Zulu spy.

Marinovich and Associated Press reporter Tom Cohen spotted the man being led from a Soweto, South Africa, train-station platform by a group armed with machetes and crude spears. Marinovich and Cohen continued to witness and report as the man was stoned, bludgeoned, stabbed, doused with gasoline and set afire.

It was one of 800 deaths in two months of black factional fighting as rival organizations vied for influence in the declining days of apartheid.

The graphic photos stirred intense debate among editors. In one, the victim, conscious but stoic, lies on his back as a grinning attacker poises to plunge a knife into his forehead. In the final photo of the series, the victim crouches, engulfed in fire.

As the series was transmitted, several member editors called up to question what the photographer was doing at the scene—could he in any way have stopped the attack? In response, an advisory went out on the photo wire, saying Marinovich had tried to intervene and then, when told to stop taking pictures, had told mob leaders he would stop shooting only when they "stopped hurting that man."

Decisions on what to do with the photos varied across the country, according to a survey. If any pattern emerged, it was that newspapers in competitive markets such as Denver, Minneapolis-St. Paul, and New York were more likely to go with the harsh graphics.

The burning photo was the most widely used, the stabbing the least. Several editors said they specifically rejected the stabbing as too extreme. "It showed violence and animalistic hatred," said Roman Lyskowski, graphics editor for the *Miami Herald.* Another editor, who agreed that the stabbing was much more disturbing than the burning, said he recalled immolation pictures from the Vietnam era. "That's not as unusual an image as that knife sticking right out of the skull."

When the Soweto series cleared at the *Miami Herald,* the burning photo was sent to Executive Editor Janet Chusmir's home for her approval. At her direction, the immolation picture ran on the front page, but below the fold and in black and white. The detail revealed in color reproduction, Chusmir and her editors agreed, was too graphic.

At the *Los Angeles Times* and *Dallas Morning News,* however, the burning photo ran above the front-page fold—and in color.

The *St. Paul Pioneer Press* chose the stabbing for front-page color. "I look at the moment that the photo freezes on film," said News Editor Joe Sevick. "Rarely do you see a photo where a knife is about to go into somebody." The photo ran in color on the *Pioneer Press* front page, accompanied by the story Cohen had written

AP/ WIDE WORLD PHOTOS

on the attack and a longer story on the South African government's attempt, announced that day, to crack down on black-on-black violence.

In Denver, at the *Rocky Mountain News,* Managing Editor Mike Madigan wanted to run a comprehensive package on the Soweto story. The tabloid's only open page was deep in the paper, but a Page-3 box referred readers to the story with a warning the photos were "horrific and disturbing." Inside, stories on the attack and government crackdown and an editor's note on Marinovich's intervention accompanied three photos: the victim being led away from the train station, the stabbing, and the burning.

Most papers that ran the more challenging photos involved top management in the decision. Frequently, top editors were contacted by telephone, or came in from home, to give the photos a final go-ahead.

In most newsrooms, the burning or stabbing photos made it to the news desk for approval or rejection. But there, they sometimes were killed abruptly. "The editors at that point said no," one picture editor reported. "They would not take the heat."

Several editors deferred to the so-called "breakfast test." "The question is, 'Which of those photos would help tell the story without ruining everyone's breakfast?'" asked Rod Deckert, managing editor of the *Albuquerque Journal.* One edi-

*AP/WIDE WORLD PHOTOS*

tor said his paper is especially likely to de-emphasize disturbing material in the Sunday paper, which children often read with their parents.

But many editors who rejected the more brutal pictures said the "breakfast test" is irrelevant. "If you're putting out a paper in New York and don't have something that's going to cause some discomfort over breakfast, then you're probably not putting out the full paper you should," said Jeff Jarvis, Sunday editor at the *New York Daily News.* "I don't think the breakfast test works for the '90s."

Others cited distance tests. Some newspapers, in deference to victims' families, are less likely to use death photos from within their own circulation areas. Another editor, however, said his paper is *less* likely to run violent photos unless they are local and have a "more immediate impact on our readership."

Newspapers also differed widely on how they packaged the Soweto story. Some accompanied a photo series with the Cohen and crackdown stories, and a note on Marinovich's intervention. Some ran a single photo, often the burning, with only a cutline and a brief reference to the train-station incident in the "crackdown" story. Two respected big-city dailies, which omitted any reference to the Soweto attack in their accompanying stories, ran cursory cutlines such as: "Violence continues: A boy runs away as an ANC supporter clubs a Zulu foe who was beaten, stabbed and set ablaze."

Although 41 papers used at least one of the Marinovich photos, only four—the *Charlotte Observer, Akron Beacon-Journal, The Rocky Mountain News* (Denver), and *USA Today*—told the story of Marinovich's attempt to halt the attack.

Among collateral considerations at many news desks was the coverage of South African troubles that had gone before. At least one editor said the Soweto photos, which followed several other beating and killing photographs from South Africa that had been used earlier in the week, were "just too, too much."

With only three exceptions, editors said race did not figure in their considerations. One white editor said the fact that both attackers and victim were black deprived the series of clarity: "You don't have a sense of one side against another. You don't have a sense of right or wrong." Two editors who identified themselves as African-American, however, argued for aggressive use of the photos. Both work in communities with significant black populations. "I think black readers should be more informed about this," one said. "Across the board, black Americans don't realize what's going on with the black-on-black violence."

Front-page placement and the use of color frequently triggered reader objections, but the adequacy of cutline information and accompanying copy also appear significant. The *Albany Times Union* was flooded by phone protests and subscription cancellations. Two other papers perceiving significant reader unrest—the *Dallas Morning News* and *Los Angeles Times*—ran the burning photo on their front pages in color. But each of the three papers also ran the front-page photos with only cutline accompaniment, referring readers inside to the stories that placed the images in context.

In retrospect, *Rocky Mountain News'* Madigan said he was very pleased with the final Soweto package and readers' reaction to it. "It wasn't so much the idea that, 'Yeah, we ran these really horrific pictures and, boy, it knocked people's socks off.' I don't think that was the point. I think it was more the way we handled it," he said. "Just one word or the other can make a terrific difference in whether the public starts screaming 'sensationalize, sensationalize,' or takes it as a thoughtful, important piece of work, which is what we were after."

## Micro Issues:

1. In all but the most important stories, would you support a ban on dead-body photos in your newspaper or newscast?
2. Some editors believe it is their ethical duty to avoid violating readers' sense of taste or compassion. Others argue that it is their duty to force society to face unpleasant truths, even if it means risking reader anger and rejection. Whose side would you support?
3. Many readers suspect that sensational photos are chosen to sell newspapers, or capture rating points, by appealing to morbid tastes. Do you believe they're right?

## Middle-range Issues:

1. Editors sometimes justify running graphic photos by saying they can provide a "warning bell," alerting people to preventable dangers in society. What values might the Soweto photographs offer readers?
2. Is the desire to avoid offending readers an ethical consideration or a marketing consideration?
3. Is it appropriate to base editorial decisions on what readers are likely to be doing at home: to edit newspapers differently, for instance, if they are likely to be read at the breakfast table, or present newscasts differently if they are to air during the dinner hour rather than later in the evening?
4. As an editor, would you be more likely to run a photograph of someone being murdered if the event happened in your own community, or if it happened thousands of miles away and none of your readers would be likely to know the victim or his family?
5. Is there ethical significance in
   (*a*) whether a violent photo is run in color or black and white, or
   (*b*) whether it is run on the front page or on an inside page?

## Macro Issues:

1. Is aesthetic, dramatic, or photographic value ever reason enough to run a picture, regardless of how intrusive it may be or how it may violate readers' sensitivities?
2. Is it your responsibility as an editor to find out if a photographer could have saved a life by intervening in a situation, rather than taking pictures of it? Is that information you need to share with your readers?
3. Is it your responsibility as an editor to find out if the presence of the camera at the scene in any way helped incite or distort the event? Is that information you need to share with your readers?
4. When dramatic photographs are printed, how important is it for readers or viewers to be told all the background of the story or situation?

# CHAPTER IX

## *Ethics in Cyberspace: New Questions and New Roles*

**By the end of the chapter, the student should be able to:**

- **Understand the role of copyright law in ethical decision making about Internet content.**
- **Develop professional strategies for using the Internet as a reporting tool.**
- **Delineate two important policy issues the Internet raises for journalists.**

### Ownership on the Information Superhighway: What's Yours, What Isn't

In October of 1995, the *New York Times* found itself under siege from a distinguished group of authors, all of whom contributed occasionally to the paper. More than 300 writers and scholars, among them Norman Mailer, Alice Walker, Garry Trudeau, Kurt Vonnegut, Barbara Raskin, Roger Rosenblatt, Ben Bagdikian and Carolyn Bird, signed a petition protesting the *Time*'s newly implemented policy requiring writers to surrender syndication, electronic and other secondary rights to their work after articles were published in hard copy in the *Times*.

In an internal memorandum that became public in August 1995, the *Times* had announced it would require its freelancers to sign "work-made-for-hire" contracts. "The position on this is unambiguous: if someone does not sign an agreement, he or she will no longer be published in the newspaper." The writers responded that the memorandum was a historic break with publishing tradition where freelancers had been allowed to retain copyright to their own work.

What was really at issue, of course, was money. The freelancers wanted to be paid for the original publication of their efforts and for all subsequent publication of their work—regardless of medium. The *Times,* which was struggling to develop an Internet presence and to make money from that effort, was attempting to cut both costs and subsequent legal problems by demanding copyright ownership of its organizational contribution to the Information Superhighway. Since the *Times,* like all other news organizations, had been unable to turn the Internet into a profit center, it sought to reduce some expenses by curtailing its payments to freelancers. The writers, in turn, wanted the Internet to be governed by the same professional norms that

253

*Ed Stein. Reprinted courtesy of the* Rocky Mountain News.

had governed the print media—in other words, the writer retains the copyright and each user must pay for the privilege of reproduction.

Welcome to the brave new world of electrons. Today's brave new world, like Orwell's vision of *1984,* revolves around the use and manipulation of information. Put more concretely, the possibilities of computers linked to the Internet emphasize questions surrounding ownership and appropriation. What makes those questions urgent is the almost unanimous agreement that current interpretations of copyright law will have to be scrapped or fundamentally altered to deal with the possibilities the Internet raises. And, in the absence of the minimal standards that the law provides, ethical thinking may be the clearest guide to journalists braving the information highway in the twenty-first century.

## Copyright Law: Hints But Not Help

United States copyright law as it has evolved over the past 200 years can be boiled down into two succinct concepts. The first is that the courts have repeatedly ruled "you can't copyright an idea." As Justice Louis Brandeis observed, "The general rule of law is that the noblest of human productions—knowledge, truths ascertained, conceptions and ideas—become voluntary communication to others, free as the air to common use" (International News Service v. Associated Press, 248 U.S. 215, 250 (1918).

What can be copyrighted, however, is the particular execution of an idea. Mozart could not copyright the order of the keys on the harpsichord; but he could copyright the particular order of notes played on that instrument—the execution of an idea—in "The Magic Flute."

Court decisions surrounding this issue have hinged on whether the expression of an idea is novel and concrete enough to warrant protection, the second basic concept of copyright law. This "novel and concrete" approach to ideas is rooted in the seventeenth and eighteenth-century notion that ideas are like private property and, like private property, are worthy of protection. An entire line of cases involving television and radio formats has developed essentially through regarding particular formats and plot lines as concrete expressions of ideas that can be copyrighted. One legal scholar has noted that the essential feature of this branch of copyright law is "the right to determine what shall be done with an idea."

The courts currently protect ideas that are bound through contracts—what is called an expressed contract theory. A contract may be expressed through money changing hands or a promise to disclose the idea to a third party (for instance, a publisher's promise to publish a novel). Even if an idea is obtained fraudulently, the courts have been willing to protect its originator. The courts also protect ideas under what is called implied contracts. A freelancer submitting an article to a magazine in the hopes that it will be published is functioning under an implied contract that the publisher will consider the article but not steal it. Finally, the courts have developed a doctrine designed to impede unjust enrichment. Under this view, ideas should be protected because, to fail to do so, would allow one person or organization to enrich themselves while failing to compensate the original developer of the idea. For instance in 1990, humorist Art Buchwald was awarded $900,000 when the courts found that his idea for the movie *Coming to America* had been developed into a successful film without any compensation to him.

These legal theories developed before computers had the capacity to change all information into "1s" and "0s" and to reorganize it accordingly. The courts would normally consider a photograph a concrete expression of an idea. But what happens when the photograph has been cut into pixels, the individual pixel's color changed, the shape of the pixels reorganized—say from a camel to an elephant—and then the resulting image, which now looks a great deal like an elephant and lacks a negative to indicate that it was once a camel, is downloaded onto a Web site that belongs to your news organization?

Is the execution of the idea that the photograph represents the property of the photographer who shot the original image, the property of the multi-media author who took the photograph of the camel and changed it to an elephant, or the property of the news organization which ultimately distributed it—as electrons—on a Web site? Is there an express or implied contract in any of these actions? Does the creator of the elephant image owe royalties or acknowledgement to the creator of the camel? Is putting something on a Web site the same thing as publication?

Since few entrepreneurs are making any money from the Web itself (as opposed to the software to access it), can there even be such a thing as unjust enrichment? Do these issues persist after death? For example, who gets paid for, and who holds the copyright to, an image of television star Lucille Ball who, years after her death, is electronically reproduced and inserted into a 1996 television ad for Service Merchandise? Furthermore, what if the creator of the ad could prove that the image of Ms. Ball was created out of a group of uncopyrighted pixels? Who then would own the Ball image? On such complex issues, the courts have been silent.

In addition to what may be copyrighted, the Internet also raises questions of when. Say you work for a traditional medium—NBC television—which also has an Internet presence. Further, say an important and timely story breaks hours before the traditional nightly newscast. Do you as a journalist first air the story on your 24-hour Internet publication (thus gaining a professional scoop but a lesser audience) or do you wait to insert your story in the traditional news cycle, thus sacrificing some timeliness and perhaps some exclusivity?

In March of 1997, the *Dallas Morning News* first reported its story of the alleged confession of Timothy McVeigh on its Internet site. McVeigh was awaiting trial on charges in the Oklahoma City bombing when the newspaper reported first on its web site and the next day in its news pages that McVeigh had confessed to his lawyers. The news of the story spread quickly and led to an unprecedented number of "hits" on the *Dallas Morning News* Web site.

Historically, when one medium, for example radio, has surpassed another, say newspapers, in an important dimension such as timeliness, both mediums have evolved to take advantage of their unique strengths. Thus, as broadcasting developed, that medium tended to emphasize immediacy while print emphasized depth. At this juncture, it is unclear how the use and development of the Internet will influence these trends. Common ownership muddies the professional waters even further. Thinking about copyright has always included an element of "this came first," but that issue was defined in terms of weeks or years rather than nanoseconds.

However, some legal scholars have asserted that the legal view of copyright protection is rooted in ethical thinking. While recognizing that "the moral rights between persons which pertain to their ideas is a matter on which even the boldest and most confident writers on property have shown uncommon caution" (Wengraf, 1989 137–138), some legal philosophers have suggested that the moral right to property emerges through the connection between private property and the fundamental human right to liberty. In this view, property enables people to act freely, an ethical value.

Others have lodged the philosophical questions that the Internet raises more firmly in the intersection of the concepts of truthtelling and deception. "One way or another, a photograph provides evidence about a scene, about the way things are, and most of us have a strong intuitive feeling that it provides better evidence than any other kind of picture. We feel that the evidence it presents corresponds in some strong sense to reality, and (in accordance with the correspondence theory of truth) that it is true because it does so" (Mitchell 1995, 25).

The ability to digitize information challenges our intuitive assumptions about a variety of things—everything from the "reality" that a picture represents to the external symbol systems that words and images together create. Digitization enables media designers to confound the external referent as never before. Students at the turn of the century will recognize that John Wayne's image has been digitized and electronically inserted into a Coors ad. But students 20 years from now may not recognize the original John Wayne, may not know that he was a film star, and may not be aware that he has been dead for decades. They will have "lost" the external referent to the image. One consequence of that loss is that the Coors commercial may not be as meaningful, or seem as clever, to students of the next generation. But, there are other, more sinister possibilities, such as the twisting and destruction of meaning, that Orwell raised in *1984*.

Ethical thinking combined with sound professional practice can provide some paths out of this virtual swamp. The first, and probably the most basic maxim, arises from the habits of sound professional performance. Cite the source of your information—or your electronic bytes. After all, journalists are required to note the originators of their information when reporting on documents or interviews. Multi-media designers should be subject to the same standard, just as music arrangers (as opposed to composers) or screenwriters currently are.

If noting the originators of your information creates problems, as it did for the *New York Times* in 1995, then be willing to accept those problems as the price of using the information. In an ethical sense, such a professional standard allows you to achieve two results. In the Judeo-Christian tradition, you have avoided theft—an ethically culpable act. And, you have also fulfilled the ethical duty of beneficence, sharing credit with the originator of your information. While beneficence is something that is not traditionally associated with journalism it describes one of the positive aspects of the journalist-source relationship. In our experience in this world of bits and bytes, application of a maxim of "cite the source of your bytes" will prejudice you to the development of original and creative work. And, using your own stuff, and not someone else's, improves performance.

The second maxim which emerges from a discussion of deception is this: information that has the capacity to deceive the rational audience member as to its origin, original referent, or source must be regarded as suspect. While journalistic discussion of deception has generally focused on practices used to obtain stories, we believe the concept also applies to the relationship between the journalist and his audience. The issue is whether using digitized information is intended to mislead the audience. Thus, an October 1996 cover of *Life* magazine which combined more than 400 previous covers into an image of Marilyn Monroe does not intend to deceive the audience because the editors clearly explained what they are doing. But lifting an image from one Web site, downloading sentences from another, and combining them for your own news story without citing your original sources is an attempt to deceive both your editors and your audience.

While both plagiarism and forgery are clearly deceptive practices (Bok 1983, 218), the Web, with its nearly infinite possibilities as a source of information, has highlighted the need for journalists to take care. Even in a new era of pixels and bytes, journalists must maintain old-fashioned credibility with our audiences about the sources of our information and the means and methods of gathering that information.

## Sources: New Technology But Continuing Issues

New technology often raises old ethical issues but with additional permutations. Because the computer substitutes virtual interaction for the face-to-face variety, journalists using the Internet as a medium to conduct interviews or obtain data must take additional precautions to authenticate not just information but also sources. Sourcing via the Internet graphs new questions onto older ones.

Contemporary journalistic thinking about the role of news sources assumes an active audience. The notion is that readers and viewers may better understand and evaluate journalistic accounts if those stories identify journalists' information sources. Identification often goes beyond a mere name and address: journalists may provide background so audience members understand why a person or document is cited. The professional standard is that sources should be named and that journalists must have compelling reasons for withholding a source's identity.

Furthermore, granting anonymity is a mutual agreement between reporter and source, not a unilateral understanding imposed on one party by the other. Anonymous sources are expected to be the exception rather than the journalistic rule. Professional mores dictate that, should a reporter decide to grant anonymity, she does not have to divulge the source's identity to editors, other supervisors, or, in rare instances, the courts.

Like many contemporary professional practices, sourcing is not firmly rooted in journalistic history. In the era of the partisan press, story sources were most often the printers who controlled the presses. Further, printers were paid for their efforts by political partisans. Historians suggest that reader understanding of sources in the revolutionary era parallels contemporary understanding of a signed editorial.

Even the traditional practice of interviewing, now considered commonplace, was controversial at its inception. The critics claimed that interviewing would destroy reporting. Critics argued that, if journalists adapted this reporting technique, they would slip into a moral morass, fall prey to aggressive exploitation and manipulation and would no longer serve the public. One *New York World* correspondent referred to the practice as a "modern American inquisition." In 1869, the *London Daily News* castigated those journalists who were practicing this new form of reporting saying they brought the profession of journalism "into contempt." Editors and publishers feared then that reporters' use of the interview would lessen the control of the editor over the reporter.

Reporters' power grew with the use of the interview because they could select which quotations to use and determine which comments to include. As the journalistic practice of the interview developed concurrent with the rise of the professional ideal of objectivity, identifying news sources became accepted professional practice (Schudson 1995, 1978).

The role that sourcing plays with readers and viewers also has been questioned in mass communication research. One of the most widely accepted findings in the field is that audience members tend to disassociate the source from the message, what is known as the "sleeper" effect (Lowery and DeFleur 1988). Studies confirm that most people tend to retain the fact of what is said while forgetting the context in which they "heard" it. Practitioners, from Nazi master propodandist Goebbels through contemporary political consultants, have intuitively understood this human tendency to disassociate the source from the message. But, readers and viewers are morally autonomous actors. Identifying news sources allows audiences to evaluate those reports in terms of both content and a source's motives for divulging information.

The motives for providing and withholding information are sometimes central to political coverage, and political reporters have added an element of elasticity to the practice of anonymous sourcing.

The phrase "not for attribution" means journalists may quote what is said but agree to veil the source. Thus, the attribution "a high, White House source" may mean anyone from the President himself to cabinet officers to other, well-connected administrative appointees. The phrase "on background" means journalists should consider the information given as an aid in placing facts in context. Background information also may be used as part of a sourcing trail: journalists in possession of background information may use their knowledge to try to get other sources to provide them with the same information on-the-record.

Journalists continue to debate allowing sources to go "off-the-record" or "on deep background." A strict interpretation of these synonymous phrases means that the journalist who accepts such information may not quote the specific source and, in addition, may not use his knowledge to pry the same information from other sources. This stringent interpretation has meant that editors have instructed reporters to literally leave the room when a source asks for such anonymity. Journalists have spent time in jail rather than reveal a source's identity. Less stringent interpretations suggest that journalists who accept information off-the-record may not name or in any way reveal the identity of the source but may use the information itself to leverage similar or related information from other sources.

Until quite recently such agreements were arrived at through face-to-face conversation and negotiation. However, the advent of the Internet and the ability of journalists to lurk at many places on the Information Superhighway has stripped many interviews of their context and non-verbal cues that have traditionally signalled whether information is on- or off-the-record. Such agreements most often focused on the willingness of the source to be identified. But the Internet can alter this view. Journalists surfing for story sources or leads must be careful to identify themselves professionally on the Internet when they begin "conversing" with another Internet user. Some publications, for example the *Wall Street Journal,* maintain an informal policy that requires reporters to identify themselves as reporters when they begin their Internet conversations so there is less confusion about the role the journalist plays. The reasoning behind such requirements is that people, in this instance people who are telepresent through the Internet, need to know that they are dealing with a journalist working in a professional capacity when they respond to questions either about story ideas or Internet content.

Such professional identification—the Internet version of identifying yourself at the beginning of a telephone conversation—also raises additional professional issues. For example, it is possible for competitors, who also may be surfing the Net, to learn about the direction of a story or even of its specific content during the reporting process. This increases the chance that other news organizations will learn about stories or angles they have missed some time before actual publication. While this sort of competitive consideration has always influenced journalism, the Internet makes it easier and faster to learn what other news organizations are doing. However, most professionals agree that identifying yourself as a journalist is just as important when working on the Net as it is in face-to-face situations. Since journalists are well aware of the pitfalls of being deceived by a source, "wired" reporters should be more than sensitive to these problems when they become the party to the conversation with the power to deceive.

Whether it's in-person or through fiber optics, journalists who cover police, the courts and other areas of public life often develop informal agreements with frequent sources about when and how information may be attributed. Such relationships are necessary but risky. Many journalists have had to decide whether they will "burn a source"—reveal the identity of a source who has been allowed to remain veiled in earlier stories—for a particularly important story. Burning a source means terminating a relationship that worked well for both parties. It is considered a form of promise breaking.

Keeping the trust between reporter and source intact is one reason that larger news organizations often will send an investigative reporter to cover a particularly sensitive story that arises on another reporter's beat. Sending an investigative reporter allows the beat reporter's sourcing agreements to remain undisturbed, insuring a continuing flow of routine information while the investigation continues.

There are significant ethical justifications for using anonymous sources. They are:

• Preventing either physical or emotional harm to a source;
• Protecting the privacy of a source, particularly children and crime victims;
• Encouraging coverage of institutions, such as the U.S. Supreme Court or the
    military, which might otherwise remain closed to journalistic and hence
    public scrutiny.

It is this final justification that is used most frequently by journalists who cover institutions such as the Supreme Court or the military that have historically functioned in secret. Reporters maintain that only when sources are allowed to remain anonymous will they provide newsworthy information that would otherwise place their careers or their physical safety at risk.

## Policy Options: The Role of the Profession

The Information Superhighway, unlike some media technologies such as the printing press, was initially developed by the government for political reasons. The original Internet was a computer network designed first to support the military and then, in the 1960s, reorganized to allow scientists working primarily at universities and government laboratories to communicate quickly and easily among each other worldwide. This system remained confined to the intellectual and military elite until the early 1980s when the Internet, as we now know it, began to take shape.

This unusual history—a mass medium which was "invented" to support government policy—has made the Internet a difficult fit both for academic study and journalistic necessity. Unlike the printing press, which began as a private invention and remained private property, the Internet has historically owed a great deal to the government both in conceptual and financial terms. Because journalists never were part of the early history of Internet development, the notion of using the Internet as a profit-oriented mass medium is a very recent invention. Grafting a concept of mass communication into a system designed to support government-supported interpersonal interaction is fraught with the potential to raise some difficult questions. We will focus on two of them.

## Who Should Have Access to the Internet?

The contemporary conceptualization of the Internet, developed under the leadership of Vice President Al Gore (himself a former journalist), has urged that the government support a system that will link three areas of American life: schools (from kindergarten through university), hospitals and libraries. This proposal, which has yet to be funded but will cost in the billions, is rooted in both practical politics and ethical theory.

The political aspects are fairly straightforward: by linking schools, hospitals and libraries, the government is supporting an infrastructure that will promote education and learning and thus strengthen the economy through providing a better educated work force. A better educated work force is also generally considered a more efficient one, thus making American workers more competitive worldwide as well as driving down production costs domestically. A better educated populace, of course, also has military implications: it enables the military to draw from a more qualified pool of recruits who are being asked to operate increasingly more complicated weapons. Thus, the reasoning goes, the federal government fulfills its constitutional responsibility to protect Americans from international as well as domestic threats by supporting a system that will promote the country's growth and development in many obvious and subtle ways.

Linking hospitals, of course, is also viewed as one way to simultaneously improve the quality of health care for many Americans while holding down medical costs. Again, the reasoning is that private, for-profit medicine would not be as likely to connect all hospitals; through government support the projected benefit can be distributed throughout American society. It is of no small political import that Speaker of the House Newt Gingrich, an acknowledged conservative when it comes to the issues of when the federal government should intervene in the lives of American citizens, has supported this view of the Internet.

But this conceptualization of the Internet is also founded in ethical theory. As you may remember from the discussion of utilitarianism in chapter 1, the notion of the greatest good for the greatest number has profoundly democratic implications. Wiring schools and libraries should, in theory, provide access to the Internet for every American. Indeed, some libraries in California have experimented with "Internet addresses" for the homeless. Universal access to the Internet through education also would follow Rawls's theory—it would allow the maximization of freedom (access) while protecting weaker parties (people of color, the poor) who might not have access to many other goods in American society but can use the Internet as a way to better their individual and potentially collective lots in life.

Of course, journalists and journalism have not been included in this conceptualization. Yet, many journalists have argued that access is only part of the picture—it does people little good to access information if they can't make sense of it. Some scholars have suggested that, as the Internet develops, journalism itself will change from a profession that primarily gathered facts—something anyone can now do on the Internet—to a professional that places those facts within a context and makes them meaningful. If the development of the Internet does indeed encourage professional development along these lines, then ethical thinking would demand that access to news coverage be distributed as widely as possible among the population and that it remain economically affordable.

That stance, of course, puts journalists at odds with all those segments of American society who view the Internet as another potential profit center, including the multi-national corporations for which increasing numbers of journalists now work. Insisting that affordable news become part of the policy making that is currently swirling around the Information Superhighway would challenge the long-standing American tradition of regarding journalism and government as irreconcilable adversaries. Yet, ethical (and in some ways political) thinking would seem to suggest that making news coverage accessible to every American via the Internet has significant potential benefits for the individual and society at large. It also would make journalists and the government partners, a true philosophic shift in the conceptualization of a "free" press. Finally, such a partnership would demand that journalists themselves take an active part in developing and implementing legislation that will affect their working lives. Such a change in attitude also would require a philosophical shift, one that places journalistic responsibility to political society on an even plane with worker responsibility to profitable media industries.

## The Fragmentation of Political Culture

Nicholas Negroponte, the head of MIT's Media Lab and an Internet guru of some note, has since the early 1980s subscribed to a unique publication, the *Daily Me.* Negroponte programmed his MIT computer to develop a daily newspaper based on his information needs and desires as well as past information preferences. The *Daily Me,* for example, carries a great deal of news about computers and universities and relatively less news about sports, American politics, the environment, etc. Negroponte, acknowledging that he had a good chance of missing stories that he either should know about or would be interested in that would fall outside his desired categories, programmed his computer to select 10 percent of the *Daily Me*'s content literally at random.

Negroponte believes that all of us will have the capacity to develop a *Daily Me* from the vast collection of information now on the World Wide Web sometime early in the next century. And, while journalists acknowledge that newspapers and magazines produced in such a fashion will give the reader more editorial control, they are worried about the impact of such enhanced selectivity on the larger political culture.

Of course, reader and viewer selectivity is nothing new. How many people do you know who always read the sports page and never anything else? If most contemporary newspaper readership surveys are correct, about 35 percent of regular newspaper readers fit this profile. Or take the reverse problem. What if something new—say the emergence of a potentially deadly virus—is noted by doctors but is given little media attention. How will you know to tell your *Daily Me* that, instead of looking at the *New York Times,* the better sources are the alternative press in the gay community in San Francisco and New York? This was exactly the case from 1981 through 1986, when many major publications, including the *New York Times,* refused to carry front-page stories about the AIDS virus at the same time the gay press was covering the epidemic.

The Internet, by placing responsibility squarely on the shoulders (or at least in the computers) of users, has the potential to fragment American culture even more deeply than is the current case. Caucasians, for example, could select news about the O. J. Simpson case only from certain media outlets, thereby missing much coverage of the fact that their African-American fellow citizens view the trial quite differently. Political conservatives could read only certain points of view; many others would choose to read nothing about politics altogether. At some point, Americans may lose the shared political vocabulary and experience that is the foundation for representative, democratic government.

It is even more unclear what journalists themselves can do to alter this potential trend. News organizations are experimenting with interactive stories, individual editions tailored to particular groups of subscribers (say those who are interested in the stock market), special networks, like CNN's airport channel (that carries information for the business traveler but no news of airline crashes) and 24-hour news channels. But, no one yet knows what will work, what readers and viewers will accept, and what the impact of these changes will be on the larger political culture. What is clear is that journalists need to develop a better sense of how their work helps people make sense of their political, economic and social lives. The Internet has pointed out as never before the need for journalists to connect themselves to readers and viewers or face the consequences of being considered irrelevant and annoying. If there was ever a goad to improved professional performance, the Internet may be providing it.

## Suggested Readings

Grossman, Lawrence K. 1995. *The electronic republic: Reshaping democracy in the information age.* New York: Viking.
Negroponte, Nicholas. 1995. *Being digital.* New York: Alfred A. Knopf.

# CHAPTER IX CASES

## CASE IX-A
## Digital Sound Sampling: Sampling the Options
DON E. TOMLINSON
*Texas A&M University*

**Authors' note:** *At the time of this writing you could hear audio clips of the two versions of "Alone Again, Naturally" on the Internet at*

http://www.benedict.com

Hit records are hard to come by. No one *knows* which song the audience will find irresistible. As a result, record producers and recording artists are continuously in search of that elusive "magic" factor.

As a genre of music, "rap" is no different. In fact, rap producers and artists have been quite innovative in their searching. One innovation now commonly used in rap music is digital sampling. Using sophisticated computer technology, a part or parts of a previous sound recording can be "lifted" for use in a new recording. It can be music alone, or words alone, or both. Likely, the sampled recording is fairly old and was once quite popular.

Rap artists commonly use digital samples around which to build new songs. Such was the case of rap artist Marcel Hall, known professionally as "Biz Markie," who lifted three words and the accompanying music from a 1972 pop hit called "Alone Again Naturally" by Britisher Raymond "Gilbert" O'Sullivan. The sampled words and music were the title and "heart" of the song, what musicians refer to as the hook.

Using the sampled material as a framework around which to build, Biz Markie wrote a "new" song called "Alone Again," which was released in 1991 by Cold Chillin' Records. Permission to use the sample in the "new" song had not been received from copyright owners of the sound recording or the underlying musical composition.

The owners of the underlying musical composition and the O'Sullivan sound recording of the song sued, claiming copyright infringement. They asked a federal district court in New York City to grant them an injunction requiring Cold Chillin' to remove the song from distribution. The request was granted in late 1991.

Copyright law is implicated when a digital sample from a previous sound recording is used in a new work. Two separate copyrights are involved. First, a music publishing company (or companies) would own the copyright to the underlying musical composition and, second, a recording company (normally) would own the copyright to the sound recording itself. For example, Warner Brothers and Kicking Bear music publishing companies own the copyright to the 1970s crossover hit "Lyin' Eyes," written by Don Henley and Glenn Frey. Asylum Records owns the copyright to the sound recording the Eagles made of the song.

Should a rap artist sample the line "I guess every form of refuge has its price" from the Eagles version, Warner Brothers Music's and Kicking Bear Music's copyright in the underlying composition would be implicated as would Asylum's copyright. Copyright law would require appropriate permissions and compensation.

Copyright law is actually an exception to the First Amendment. Centrally, what the First Amendment does is prohibit the government from interfering in the expression of its citizens, such as expression by song. Copyright law, however, grants ownership rights in such expression and requires anyone wishing to use the copyrighted song of another to get the permission of the copyright owner to do so. Permission usually involves some sort of compensation. If permission is not received by the rap artist or the rap artist's record company, the courts will, if requested, disallow the continuation of the expression (the selling of CDs, for instance).

Because copyright law, therefore, implicates the First Amendment, there is a tension between the two ideas. Some people believe that copyright law is wrong when it, in effect, prevents new expression to be borne from old expression. Apparently, some in the rap community feel this way.

From an ethics perspective, if you do not believe there should be any ownership of previous expression, you likely would have no moral qualms about sampling previous sound recordings for non-permitted and non-compensated use in a new work. If, on the other hand, you do believe that some ownership rights should exist, you might find yourself on the horns of a dilemma when you consider digital sampling of a previous sound recording.

So, without regard to any *legal* implications, when a rap musician wants to sample from a previous sound recording, the artist faces these options.

1. The artist simply could use the sample without any kind of permission, believing that *no* ownership rights should exist in any previous expression because the notion of *free* expression, taken literally, would obviate ownership.
2. The artist could use the sample without any kind of permission on the basis that the amount of sampling done was minimal and, therefore, not a real or substantial copying of the previous expression.
3. The artist could use the sample without permission on the basis that the particular sample used was not the hook.
4. The artist could seek permission to use the sample from the owner of the sound recording but not from the owners of the copyright on the basis that the sound recording itself seems more like property than does the underlying musical composition.
5. The artist could seek permission to use the sample from the owner of copyright but not from the owner of the sound recording on the basis that the copyright itself is the fundamental element to be protected while the sound recording is simply one interpretation of the song itself.
6. The rap artist could argue that the use of the sample in the new work could make the previous sound recording popular again, thereby earning royalties for the owners of the sound recording and the underlying musical composition that they would not otherwise have earned.
7. The rap artist could argue that no permission or compensation should be required because the new work is evolutionary or derivative of the previous work, as opposed to being a copying of most or all of the previous work.

## Micro Issues:

1. Without regard to law, does the non-permitted and non-compensated use of a digital sample from a previous sound recording amount to stealing from the owner of the sound recording? From the owner of the copyright or the underlying musical composition?
2. Should it matter that only a slight amount of material was sampled from the previous sound recording?
3. Should it matter that the hook wasn't the sampled element?
4. Should both the owner of the sound recording *and* the owner of the underlying musical composition be compensated?

## Middle-range Issues:

1. Were there any alternatives to the non-permitted, non-compensated use of the digital sample?
2. Does copyright deny people the opportunity to hear and experience new art that is in part derived from previous art? If so, should it?

## Macro Issues:

1. Should all expression be absolutely free from interference by the government?
2. If there were no protection at all for the ownership of expression, would there be much new expression, especially in relation to music?
3. Do your answers change if what is sampled are words from a book?

## CASE IX-B
## Ethics on the Internet: Abiding by the Rules of the Road on the Information Superhighway
BRUCE LEWENSTEIN

*Cornell University*

ComNet is a commercial online service with a wide range of options available to its subscribers. These include databases, e-mail capabilities and forums for discussion of many topics. Some of these forums are available to all subscribers, while others require a separate sign-up system and are available only to registered users. In the case of JourForum, a discussion group for journalists, only working journalists may post or read messages to the group. Working journalists are defined as those employed by newspapers, magazines, or other legitimate publications; those whose names appear on the masthead of a regularly published magazine; those who belong to one of several professional organizations (such as the Society of Professional Journalists or the American Society of Newspaper Editors); or those who prove their legitimacy by presenting clips of their published work. ComNet is available both through direct modem connection and through the World Wide Web on the Internet.

Subscribers to ComNet agree to abide by the service's "Rules of Behavior," which include prohibitions against objectionable or lewd language, illegal activity and "abuse of the service." Journalists signing up for JourForum are reminded of these rules, and requested to use only their true names, as well as limiting their discussion to issues directly related to journalism. No specific statements are made about whether JourForum (or other parts of ComNet) are on- or off-the-record. Mark Morceau is the "moderator" of JourForum—its creator and, through contractual arrangements with ComNet, the person responsible for ensuring that uses of JourForum abide by ComNet's rules.

In a new message to the JourForum, Miriam Zablonsky identifies herself as the editor of a newsletter about "alternative" (nontraditional) medical treatments. She presents many details about a new drug treatment for AIDS, including information about the research leading to the treatment. She wonders why the media has failed to cover the story, she says.

In a response, Harry Lee, a reporter for an online magazine about medicine, suggests that the media usually cover medical stories only after they appear in medical publications such as *The New England Journal of Medicine.*

Zablonsky goes ballistic. In a long, biting, bitter message, she complains about a major medical journal that, she says, refuses to publish information about the new treatment. She calls the editor of the journal, Katherine Kelly, "a fat, sexist, lying slob." Kelly is a well-known commentator on the excesses of tabloid journalism (especially its coverage of medical topics); her columns are often accompanied by her photo, showing a slim, stylish beautiful woman of 42.

A flood of messages appears, condemning Zablonsky's comments. To each one, Zablonsky responds with long, rambling diatribes about conspiracies of "them" (unspecified) to control the world, about the deep distrust that a journalist should have toward all major institutions, and about her own unwillingness to change or even compromise her positions, no matter what information is presented to her.

At this point (less than a day after the original message from Zablonsky), Mark Morceau posts a message reminding Zablonsky of ComNet and JourForum's rules about objectionable language and abuse of the service (including posting long messages on topics that aren't germane to journalism). In addition, he asks her to apologize to Kelly and to avoid libelous statements in the future.

Zablonsky refuses, citing (among other arguments in another long, rambling message) her rights to free speech and freedom of the press.

Morceau tells Zablonsky that JourForum is not a publication, and so is not subject to rules of free press. It is, he says, more akin to a private club, which can enforce rules on its members. He points to the requirement that contributors belong to professional journalism organizations as one of the ways that JourForum maintains its limited membership. (Zablonsky once worked for a daily paper, and she maintains her membership in SPJ).

If JourForum is a private club, responds Zablonsky, what she said isn't libelous, because the club isn't a public place or publication. (All of these messages, as with all JourForum messages, are publicly posted so any subscriber to JourForum can view them.)

The next day, Katherine Kelly joins the online discussion. She threatens to sue Zablonsky, claiming that she has been libeled in a public forum. The international community of journalists with access to JourForum is so large that it cannot be considered a "private" club, she argues. Any one of those subscribers can read this forum, she reminds Zablonsky, making it equivalent to a trade paper or magazine. It is as public as any traditional publication, Kelly argues. Moreover, she says, in a landmark decision in June 1996, a federal appeals court described online forums as one of the most important contributions to free exchange of ideas since the development of the printing press. Clearly, Kelly says, the canons of a free press—including the responsibility of avoiding libel—apply to online forums.

Cynthia Smith has been following the online discussion. She finds the issues of potential censorship, free press and free speech fascinating. She writes an article about the fracas for her own newspaper's weekly "News from Cyberspace" page. That page appears on Thursdays in the business section of the paper; it is also available in the newspaper's online edition. In her story, Smith includes quotes from Morceau, Zablonsky, Kelly and other members of the forum; the quotes are not taken from interviews, but from the messages those people had posted online.

When Smith's story appears, she is accused (in another round of postings in JourForum) of violating the expectation that many journalists had that their words in the online forum were "off-the-record," and so would not be quoted.

## Micro Issues:

1. Can Zablonsky be sued for libel? Should she be sued for libel?
2. Should Smith have asked for permission to quote?
3. Does Morceau have the right to control what material appears in JourForum?

## Middle-range Issues:

1. Does it matter if Smith's article appeared only in the traditional paper format, only in an online supplement to the newspaper, or in a separate online magazine that does not have ties to a traditional format publication?
2. Is there a moral difference between Zablonsky's potentially libelous statements and Smith's potential violation of the standards of on- and off-the-record?

## Macro Issues:

1. Is JourForum a public or private place? What difference would it make if any ComNet subscriber could read messages in JourForum, though only registered members could post messages there? [Compare JourForum to the floor of a convention, where members of the press are often identified with badges so that speakers know they are talking to a reporter.]
2. Under what circumstances does a reporter need to identify himself or herself? At what point do "private" conversations become open to reporting by others?
3. Are online publications subject to different rules than traditional publications? If so, how do you distinguish between the rules that apply to publications that appear only online and those that appear in both online and offline versions? Does it matter if the online and offline versions are different or edited differently?

## CASE IX-C
## Cry Wolf: *Time* Magazine and the Cyberporn Story

KARON REINBOTH SPECKMAN
*Truman State University, Kirksville, Missouri*

A July 1995 *Time* magazine cover story entitled "On Screen Near You: Cyberporn" claimed pornography on the Internet was "popular, pervasive and surprisingly perverse." The magazine based its story on a study by "a research team" who "conducted an exhaustive study of online porn."

The article in *Time* claimed that on Usenet newsgroups where digitized images are stored, 83.5 percent of the pictures are pornographic. The finding alarmed both computer free speech defenders and government censorship advocates. What *Time* didn't tell its readers was that the "research team" was one person—a Carnegie-Mellon University undergraduate named Martin Rimm—and that Rimm had struck an agreement with *Time* that no outside experts could review the study because Rimm had an exclusive agreement for full publication with *Georgetown Law Journal.*

Adding to the cover story's alarmist tone was *Time*'s cover showing a young child staring wide-eyed with gaping mouth into a computer screen. The most sensationalist artwork was reserved for the inside—a full-page photo-illustration of a naked man "mating" with a computer. Another full page contained a drawing of a computer screen with a lollipop beckoning a small child and a sinister person standing behind the computer.

Critics reacted swiftly to the story and the "exhaustive" study on which it was based. They said *Time* author Philip Elmer-DeWitt interpreted the study incorrectly and violated many rules of journalism. Some of the criticisms from Donna Hoffman and Thomas Novak, Vanderbilt management professors and experts in surveying Net usage, were:

1. *Time* said, "There's an awful lot of porn online." But *Time* neglected to say that much of Rimm's study was of files on exclusively adult bulletin board services (BBS), most not connected to the Internet.
2. *Time* said that "917,410 sexually explicit pictures, descriptions, short stories, and film clips" were "surveyed." Yet those files were from adult-oriented BBSs, not Usenet or the Internet. Plus all text and audio files were deleted from analysis leaving only the actual number of descriptions of images studied to be 292,114. Rimm downloaded 3,254 available images but only analyzed 2,830 images due to technical difficulties.

   Hoffman and Novak also noted that while 917,410 pornographic files were found on adult BBSs, only 2,830 potentially pornographic images were found over a four-month period on the Usenet. Out of the 11,576 World Wide Web sites examined in December 1994, only nine Web sites (eight one-hundredths of one percent) contained material that could be classified as R- or X-rated adult visual material. *Time*'s statement that there is an "awful lot of porn online" was labeled by Hoffman and Novak as "blatantly misleading and irresponsible."

3. *Time* said that 83.5 percent of images in Usenet groups were pornographic. What Rimm actually said was, "Among the pornographic newsgroups, 4,206 images posts were counted or 83.5 percent of the total posts." Still Rimm did not provide a listing of the names of the groups so these could not be verified.

4. *Time* said, "There is some evidence that . . . the 1.1 percent . . . women (on BBSs) are paid to hang out on the chat rooms and bulletin boards to make the patrons feel more comfortable." Rimm provided no evidence for that claim.

5. *Time* said the images appeared on a "public network accessible to men, women, and children." Rimm provided no evidence of how much material from the adult BBSs makes its way to the Internet.

6. *Time* said, "Only about 3 percent of all the messages on the Usenet newsgroups [represent pornographic images], while the Usenet itself represents 11.5 percent of the traffic on the Internet." *Time* did not take the interpretation to its logical conclusion that less than half of 1 percent (3 percent of 11 percent) of the messages on the Internet are associated with newsgroups containing pornographic imagery. Much of the material in the newsgroups is text files only with comments by Usenet readers.

7. *Time* said, "The Carnegie-Mellon report will affect . . . the cyberporn debate" and "conservatives . . . will find plenty" of "ammunition." Yet, the report was not subjected to the rigors of peer review and was completed while the author was an electrical engineering undergraduate.

Rimm began the study about pornography on BBSs in early 1994. During this time, he also wrote a paperback called *Pornographer's Handbook: How to Exploit Women, Dupe Men and Make Lots of Money.* Rimm gave the software that he mentioned so prominently in his academic study to the BBS operators in exchange for their cooperation and files. It is doubtful that the operators knew that they were part of the study but instead believed they were receiving marketing help from Rimm.

Eventually Rimm convinced *Georgetown Law Journal* to publish his study "Marketing Pornography on the Information Superhighway" and pitched the study as an exclusive cover story to Elmer-DeWitt. Rimm had secured a secret agreement that only editors directly involved in the publishing of the study could see it. Rimm effectively sidestepped any peer review—the usual operating procedure for scientific studies—by pitching to a student-published, non-peer-reviewed law journal, as most law reviews are.

Rimm needed people to endorse his study to add credibility. His method for getting this support was telling people how his study matched their own agendas, said Mike Godwin, online counsel to the Electronic Frontier Foundation. Rimm also used the tactic of telling people his study matched their agendas when eliciting support from three law professors—Anne Branscomb, Catharine MacKinnon, and Carlin Meyer—who wrote commentaries to follow his article in the *Georgetown Law Journal.*

In early June 1995, Rimm's study arrived at *Time*. Elmer-DeWitt was busy editing another *Time* cover story, but four reporters helped him on the cyberporn story. One of the reporters talked to Vanderbilt's Hoffman, who warned the reporter about the study's flaws. Hoffman then e-mailed Elmer-DeWitt about her concerns. Even the top level of *Time* editors voiced concerns about the study, but Elmer-DeWitt was anxious for a scoop and ignored early warnings that the study was faulty to gain a coveted cover story and a promotion. He also was eagerly anticipating his vacation.

*HotWired* writer Brock Meeks said, "At this point, [Elmer-DeWitt] has too much invested in the story. Somehow he ignores the lingering doubts and presses forward with the writing." Perhaps Elmer-DeWitt believed his own press. *Time*'s president told readers in the July 3 "To the Readers" that "[Elmer-DeWitt] was unusually adept at cutting through the considerable hype and confusion that surround this baffling new medium. . . . it was Elmer-DeWitt's reputation for clear and accurate discussion of complex topics that led an interdisciplinary group of researchers to offer their study of online pornography first to *Time*" (Long 1995, 4).

*Time* then offered Ted Koppel and "Nightline" an exclusive to the story with another secret deal saying "Nightline" couldn't give the study to anyone else for review. "Nightline" scheduled Ralph Reed of the Christian Coalition to appear on the show with Godwin (Godwin 1995). During the "Nightline" taping, Godwin told an ABC reporter that there were problems with the study.

Meanwhile, not all was quiet on the Information Superhighway. The cover story became the focal point of a fiery discussion and attempt to uncover the truth on The Well, an online service used by leading journalists and media experts. On June 25, the message posted to the topic "Newsweeklies" on The Well was that the *Time* article was available on America Online.

Other media outlets such as CNN, AP, and UPI reported on the study without checking the facts. *Newsweek* gave Rimm's study one paragraph in its July 3 cyberporn study but said that Rimm concentrated mostly on adults-only bulletin boards. Using the *Time* story for support, Senator Grassley (R-Iowa), played to the June 26, 1995 C-Span camera: ". . . I have introduced S.892, entitled the Protection of Children from Computer Pornography Act of 1995 . . . Georgetown University Law School has released a remarkable study conducted by researchers at Carnegie-Mellon University. . . . I want to emphasize that this is Carnegie-Mellon University. This is not a study done by some religious organization analyzing pornography that might be on computer networks. . . . the university surveyed 900,000 computer images. Of these 900,000 images, 83.5 percent of all computerized photographs available on the Internet are pornographic."

David Kline, a business columnist for *HotWired* said, "[*Time*] failed to conduct journalistic due diligence on its cyberporn 'exclusive.' This is especially troubling given that *Time* surely knew its story would directly affect the prospects for pending legislation that could alter national policy regarding electronic free speech for decades to come" (Kline 1995).

## Micro Issues:

1. What steps should Elmer-DeWitt have taken to check on his source?
2. Should *Time* have agreed to an exclusive agreement with Rimm?

3. What was the purpose of *Time*'s exclusive agreement with "Nightline"? What then was "Nightline's" responsibility to its viewers regarding sources and exclusive agreements?

## Middle-range Issues:

1. What is a media organization's responsibility to slow down and check the facts when it fears another outlet may scoop it on the story?
2. How does a journalist draw the line between being cooperative with a source and siding with a source?
3. How could a media organization avoid the pitfalls outlined in this case with an "exclusive" story? What should *Time* have told its readers about the "exclusive" agreement? Where should those explanations be placed—beginning of article, end, corrections?
4. How is this story an example of "pack journalism"?
5. Critics say serious media outlets are joining the trend of tabloid journalism, which includes not thoroughly checking sources, using inflammatory illustrations or headlines, and focusing on salacious details. How is this case an example of tabloid journalism?

## Macro Issues:

1. New technology often brings fear until it is accepted. What is the responsibility of media to discuss all issues of those fears without alarming the public?
2. What is a reporter's responsibility when covering stories that have the potential to impact public policy?
3. What is a reporter's responsibility to the total "package" of a story—that is, cover art, photo illustrations and headlines?
4. Conflict is usually listed as a traditional news value. How can media outlets adhere to that traditional news value without sacrificing the ethical news value of accuracy, tenacity and equity?
5. In this case, computer experts used the computer itself as an alternate media form to discredit a story in traditional media. How has the computer changed traditional media's influence and how people get their information? Does the computer have the same potential for harm as the traditional media if care is not taken in sourcing, checking facts, etc.?

## CASE IX-D
## Filmmaking: Looking through the Lens for Truth
KATHY BRITTAIN MCKEE
*Berry College, Mt. Berry, Georgia*

"Who Shot JFK?" asked the headline in the cinema section of the December 23, 1991, issue of *Time* magazine. The story coincided with the release of *JFK,* director Oliver Stone's $40 million film that promoted a conspiracy theory of John Kennedy's assassination.

The screenplay centers on New Orleans District Attorney Jim Garrison's unsuccessful attempt to prosecute New Orleans businessman Clay Shaw for conspiracy in the murder. Garrison was the only U.S. legal official to try someone for suspected involvement in the assassination. Garrison even appears in the film, in the role of former U.S. Supreme Court Chief Justice Earl Warren.

Scenes for the film were shot in Dallas, New Orleans and Washington, D.C., at the actual sites of the assassination and the trial. Stone interposed real documentary footage and photographs (including the Zapruder film of the actual assassination) with new scenes shot in black and white, making it virtually impossible for viewers to detect the difference between the actual 1963 scenes and the re-enactments.

Stone told interviewer Richard Heffner that his technique was like sending "splinters to the brain." He added "We have 2,500 cuts in there, I would imagine. We're assaulting the senses. We admire the MTV editing technique and we make no bones about using it. We want to . . . get into the subconscious . . . and seduce the viewer into a new perception . . . of what occurred in Texas that day."

Heffner concludes that much of the criticism leveled at Stone was because he represented a new type of historian, "fully determined to have his own way with the pictures inside our heads."

Stone was criticized for casting box-office hero Kevin Costner as Jim Garrison. The role Costner plays is very different from the real-life person, both in terms of characterization and action. Stone told an interviewer in the December 13, 1991, *Newsweek:* "Filmmakers make myths. They take the true meanings of events and shape them. . . . I made Garrison better than he is for a larger purpose."

The film is roughly based on Garrison's book *On the Trail of the Assassins* and Jim Marrs' book *Crossfire: The Plot That Killed Kennedy.* But Stone says he also relied on the work of other researchers and theorists to concoct the conspiracy theory that underlies the film's plot. Stone openly advocates the theory throughout the film.

In the interview in the promotional press kit for the film, Stone explained the purpose for the film he called "one giant jigsaw puzzle," saying, "I think we're trying to create an alternate myth to the Warren Commission, to kind of explore the true meaning of the shooting in Dealey Plaza, what the murder of John Kennedy meant to his country, why he was killed." Later in the interview, he added: "I think in the Warren Commission, they smell a rat. I think they're going to like this movie, and I hope to God it will come to be seen by the young as an alternative explanation to JFK's death."

The film's mixture of conspiracies sharply contrasts with the findings of the Warren Commission empaneled by President Lyndon Johnson seven days after the November 22, 1963, assassination. The panel spent nearly 10 months compiling a 26-volume document that concluded that Lee Harvey Oswald acted alone when he killed the president and seriously wounded then-Texas governor John Connally with one bullet.

Thirteen years later, a government investigation did suggest that a conspiracy could have been involved in the assassination plot. The Congressional committee's investigation spanned more than two years, from September 1976 into December 1978. Its seven-page report concluded that while Oswald was implicated in the murder, others were also involved. The committee did not, however, indict or name anyone.

Stone's film, however, does point fingers at suspected conspirators, ranging from the CIA to the military, relying on a created character known as 'X' to reveal the plot to Garrison. In an interview in *Time,* Stone said he believes the film was not required to be historically factual. "Whenever you start to dictate to an artist his 'social responsibility' you get into an area of censorship. I think the artist has the right to interpret and reinterpret history and the events of his time. It's up to the artist himself to determine his own ethics by his own conscience."

Stone's film was sharply attacked before and after its release. Tom Wicker of the *New York Times,* who had covered the assassination for the paper, wrote in a December 15, 1991, column, "He uses the powerful instrument of a motion picture, and relies on stars of the entertainment world, to propagate the one true faith—even though that faith, if wisely accepted, would be contemptuous of the very Constitutional government Mr. Stone's film purports to uphold." *Newsweek* called the film "heretical history" but praised Stone for his courage: "two cheers for Mr. Stone, a troublemaker for our times."

## Micro Issues:

1. Should a filmmaker inform audiences that portions of a film are documentary and others are not?
2. How closely should a film that is based on a specific historical incident stick to the facts?
3. Should the filmmaker alert the viewer that certain characters within a historical film have been dramatized or that they are fictional composites?
4. Should a filmmaker deliberately seek to be persuasive or to advocate a political position in a history-based film?

## Middle-range Issues:

1. What are an audience member's responsibilities? Are those responsibilities different when watching a film than when using news media?
2. Should filmmakers be allowed to alter historical fact for a higher purpose? What about writers and editors in other media?

# Macro Issues:

1. Is film an appropriate forum for government criticism and debate? What standards should such filmmakers employ in terms of audience awareness and historical accuracy?
2. What standards of truth should entertainment meet? Are there different standards of truth for different media? Are there different types of truth?
3. Do artists have an obligation to arouse public criticism and debate? Should artists have a standard of social responsibility, and if so, what should that standard be?
4. Is mythmaking a legitimate purpose for a filmmaker?

## CASE IX-E
## The Madonna and the Web Site: Good Taste in Newspaper Online Forums
PHILIP PATTERSON
*Oklahoma Christian University*

***Authors' note:*** *At the time of this writing, the image described below could be viewed on the World Wide Web at*

http://www.lccl.com

*Students wishing to see the image in question can look there for a full-color picture.*

In late 1996, a 40-foot tall reflection appeared on a Clearwater, Florida, office building window. The multi-colored image, apparently caused by sunlight reflecting on the water-stained glass, appeared to be a woman with a halo around her head. The image quickly began drawing crowds of people to the site. Visitors to the image, which became known as the "Rainbow Mary," quickly transformed the area into a shrine leaving gifts, flowers, candles and rosaries during their pilgrimages to the site. News organizations from across the nation covered the phenomenon bringing national attention to Clearwater.

As the phenomenon began to attract attention, it became a topic in an online forum page of the *St. Petersburg Times* Web site. The *Times* posting rules are simple: make your point without using profanity or hateful language. However, the Madonna topic illustrates that there's often a line of distinction in determining what's offensive.

What follows is a copy of the *St. Petersburg Times* Web publications forum participation rules and a posting that addressed the Madonna phenomenon in a way that one *Times* staffer found offensive.

## The Rules:

The *St. Petersburg Times* World Wide Web site is a cyber-location open to visitors of all ages, backgrounds and beliefs. The use of vulgar, obscene, pejorative or hateful language is not allowed. We reserve the right to remove any material that violates these rules. Please conduct yourself accordingly. Because of the very nature of the Web, it is impossible to monitor all postings. But, if you see something that offends you, let us know through e-mail by clicking here:

Comments @SPTimes.com

The *St. Petersburg Times* provides this platform for its visitors' use. We do not in any way guarantee the accuracy, truthfulness or quality of the postings made by visitors to this site. Any concern over the truthfulness or quality of these postings should be addressed to the author of the material in question.

## The Posting:

The venomous Catholics and other assorted Bible-thumpers who have been sending hate mail to Mary Jo Melone [a *Times* columnist who questioned the phenomenon] are perfect examples of the pathetic and rotten side of modern superstition, otherwise known as organized religion. While some well-intentioned believers are extolling the virtues of communal prayer in front of a large streaky window, other self-righteous zealots are snarling at a columnist for daring to ridicule the utterly ridiculous.

As a fervent advocate of the freedom of religion, I must say that people should be allowed to gather and worship as they choose, so long as they are not infringing upon the rights of others. But as a fervent advocate of free speech, I must also voice my honest opinion that the window-worshippers are gullible fools who wallow blindly in the anachronistic Judeo-Christian mythology, and they've become a damned nuisance.

Religious freedom does NOT mean that non-believers are forbidden from criticizing or poking fun at a church (or at a profiteering cult that masquerades as a church, despite the threatening assertions of the $cientologists and their lawyers). Blasphemy is a right in this country, thank you.

As a nation, though, we tend to be very sensitive to religious beliefs. We are so sensitive, in fact, that the city of Clearwater is willing to spend thousands of dollars to shepherd the clueless across a busy highway to pray to the Virgin Mother of Light Refraction, rather than wash the bloody windows.

What's next? I suspect that dull-eyed $cientologists will soon be flocking to the men's room of the Carrollwood Bennigan's . . . there's a urinal cake in there that's a dead ringer for (the late Scientology founder) L. Ron Hubbard.

After a *Times* Web publishing staff member read the last paragraph and complained, it was deleted on the basis of offensive content. Soon afterwards, the following posting was received from the author of the original posting.

## The Second Posting:

Webmaster and Editor:

I find it rather curious and somewhat objectionable that the last line of my post to the virgin mary forum was censored. The final paragraph originally read:

"What's next? I suspect that dull-eyed $cientologists will soon be flocking to the men's room of the Carrollwood Bennigan's . . . there's a urinal cake in there that's a dead ringer for L. Ron Hubbard."

Everything after "What's next?" was cut, despite the fact that no "vulgar" language was used. Furthermore, the final sentence served a definite purpose in making my point: the worship of inanimate objects was taken to a ludicrous extreme, and a base, ignoble object was used to illustrate the absurdity of the practice.

Although the edited section was insensitive to $cientologists, the virgin nuts, and Bennigan's (and indeed a rather rude thing to say about a urinal cake), it is not the most insensitive sentiment expressed in my post or in many others that I read. The humor and ridicule of the statement is a valid expression of my opinion; it is not threatening or obscene, and it should have a place in such a public forum, regardless of whatever objections you may have received.

I must respectfully request that the post be returned to its original state.

Three days later the same correspondent posted this message on the *Times'* forum.

## Third Posting:

*shaking head in amusement* A few points to make here, folks . . .

1. In our chaotic world of dazzling hues, shapes, and images, many natural phenomena QUITE OFTEN take on many different familiar forms. Have any of you blind-faith lemmings ever heard of a guy named Rorschach? I didn't think so. Suffice to say that the image on the building is a giant, communal Rorschach inkblot, and about 500,000 people around here have failed the test miserably. Just because a given pattern resembles something familiar does not make it a holy miracle, whether it is a stain on a window or a stain in a urinal.
2. Is a thing inherently good, just because it brings people together in prayer? No. Hell, no. The catholic church has been responsible for millions of slaughtered lives throughout the world, and throughout human history. Perhaps you've read about a little phase called the Spanish Inquisition? "Yes, but," the lemming whine goes, "the church gives people hope and brings them together in PRAYER! So it must be good!" Right. The church causes some people to pray, it causes others to attempt to impose their will on other individuals' thoughts, speech, actions, and their very lives. It's a rotten institution that some people can squeeze some good out of, once in a while.
3. Freedom of religion does not mean that the state is required to support and encourage the idiocy that we're seeing at [the intersection of] Drew and 19. Quite the opposite, in fact, if you consider the separation of church and state. The city of Clearwater is required to allow people of religious faith to worship in their own fashion, in their own houses of worship, as long as their religion does not directly infringe upon the rights of others. FACT: The Seminole Finance Corporation could (a) clean or replace the windows, or (b) clear all the idol-worshippers from this property, whenever the hell it felt like it. FACT: None of the idol-worshippers has a First Amendment right to be on the property. FACT: They are a goddamn nuisance, tangling traffic, sucking life out of the businesses in the area, and giving Clearwater a bad name. Now, citizens of this free country can make a pilgrimage to whatever pathetic site they wish, but the company or the city could certainly remove the cause of the pilgrimage, and be perfectly within their rights.

According to Paul Jerome, Web publisher for the *St. Petersburg Times,* such messages put the newspaper in both a legal and ethical bind. If the newspaper's staff monitors the e-mail and censors it—it becomes the publisher of the page and is legally responsible for the postings on it. However, the newspaper retains the right to remove objectionable material from the site, even though such actions might place it in the legal role of publisher of the forum.

"We try to avoid meddling in online user's dialogue, but we feel a great sense of responsibility to standards of taste and decency. So we occasionally excise or remove in its entirety any posting that falls below the standard," said Jerome.

Tim McGuire, editor of the *Minneapolis Star Tribune* newspaper and also the head of the *Star Tribune*'s new media efforts, speaks for many editors of online sites when he says that monitoring the online chat rooms is a necessary part of a newspaper's role.

" 'Hear no evil, see no evil, speak no evil' is reprehensible to me. If it's coming through our site, we want to take responsibility. That's what we do for a living. The only thing we bring to this game is our brand name and our credibility. If we blow it, we're no different than the 19-year-old kid who uses the f-word every other word on his site," McGuire says.

## Micro Issues:

1. Was the last paragraph of the original posting sufficiently offensive to meet the *Times'* standard for removal?
2. Critique the *Times'* policy of letting the readers be the initiators of complaints about Web postings. Did they violate that policy in this instance by listening to one of their own employees who complained about the "urinal cake" paragraph?
3. Since the nature of the Web makes it almost impossible to monitor all postings, should any postings be monitored or should the newspaper simply tell the public that the chat room or bulletin board is offered as a service and leave it at that?
4. Consider the third and final Web posting. Is it offensive enough to remove under the *Times'* policy? Also, at what point, if any, do you cut off a user for monopolizing the conversation in a chat room or on a bulletin board?

## Middle-range Issues:

1. In what ways does a chat room or bulletin board on a newspaper's Web site resemble the "Letters to the Editor" page or column? In what ways are they different?
2. Are the differences significant enough to warrant treating them differently in policy or should they be treated the same? Justify your answer.
3. Critique the statement by Tim McGuire about the *Star Tribune*'s policy. Will such a policy lead to fewer voices being heard on the newspaper's Web site?

## Macro Issues

1. What should be the standard for statements removed from a newspaper's public forum on the Web? Who should decide how the standard is enforced?
2. What should be a newspaper's policy about the following types of postings on the newspaper's Web site?
   (*a*) Information the newspaper knows or believes to be wrong, such as a writer who denies that the Holocaust ever happened;

    (*b*) Information that could be harmful, the electronic equivalent of "yelling fire in a crowded theater";

    (*c*) Information that could be hurtful, including sexist, racist, homophobic or other offensive language.

3. Justify your decisions above with your notion of the responsibility of a newspaper in a democratic society.

# CHAPTER X

## *The Ethical Dimensions of Art and Entertainment*

During the twentieth century, the predominant use of the media shifted from the distribution of information to entertainment and the popularization of culture. In this chapter we will examine the ethical issues that arise from the field of aesthetics. We will apply these principles, plus some findings from social science, to the art and entertainment components of media industries, focusing on the responsibilities of the public as well as the creators of mediated messages.

**By the end of the chapter the student should be able to:**

- **Understand the link between aesthetics and excellent professional performance.**
- **Explain Tolstoy's rationale for art and apply it to issues such as stereotyping.**
- **Understand the debate over the role of truth in popular art.**
- **Explain the prosocial responsibilities of the entertainment media.**

### An Ancient Misunderstanding

Plato did not like poets. The ancient Greek's reasoning was straightforward. Poets, the people who dream, were the potential undoing of the philosopher king. They were rebels of the first order; insurrectionists on the hoof. He banned them from the Republic.

But, Plato's skepticism about the role of art is alive in contemporary culture. Few weeks elapse without a news story about an artist or entertainment program that has offended. You are probably familiar with at least some of the following:

- Attempts to ban books such as *Catcher in the Rye* or *Lady Chatterley's Lover* from public and/or school libraries for being too sexually explicit;
- The controversy over government funding of art that some claim is obscene;
- The furor over "raptivists" such as Tupac Shakur whose violence-prone lyrics seemed to mirror his life and death.

Such a response to works of art, whether it is by public officials or individuals, is essentially Platonic. Like Plato, those who would restrict the arts do so because they mistrust the power of the artist to link emotion and logic in a way that stimulates a new vision of society, culture, or individuals.

## Of Tolstoy and Television

Tolstoy was the sort of artist Plato would have feared. In his famous essay "What Is Art?" Tolstoy argued that good art had one dominant characteristic: it communicated the feelings of the artist to the masses in the way in which the artist intended.

> "To evoke in oneself a feeling one has once experienced and having evoked it in oneself then by means of movements, lines, colors, sounds or forms expressed in words, so to transmit that feeling that others experience the same feeling—that is the activity of art. . . . Art is a human activity consisting in this, that one may consciously by means of certain external signs, hand on to others feelings he has lived through, and that others are infected by these feelings and also experience them."

Tolstoy's application of his own standard—one which sounds remarkably like artistic social responsibility—was so demanding that he rejected the works of both Shakespeare and Beethoven as being incapable of being understood by the masses. While you may not agree with all of Tolstoy's specific applications, we believe his philosophical rationale has much to recommend it.

Tolstoy's rationale is particularly pertinent to photographers and videographers who, through their visual images, seek to arouse emotion as well as inform. The haunting pictures from Somalia and Ethiopia provided a spur for international concerns. Dramas, the AIDS quilt, and obituaries of famous artists who have succumbed to AIDS have all aroused both our intellect and our emotions regarding the disease. They invite action. Television and film documentaries have made viewers more aware of the plight of the mentally ill and homeless, raised important public policy questions, and occasionally made us laugh, through a unity of purpose and craft.

Such work reminds readers and viewers of the moral impetus of art by putting us in touch with characters and situations more complex than our own lives. By thinking about these fictional characters, we enlarge our moral imaginations. Both artists and journalists can provide such a stimulus, although it will not be reflected in every song, story, or film.

Unfortunately, Tolstoy's assertion that great art is defined by how it is understood by an audience also includes a genuine dilemma. There are those who, given even Tolstoy's life experiences, could not articulate the deep truths about human nature Tolstoy wrote about in *War and Peace.* Worse yet, we might not be able to sell those insights to a sometimes lukewarm public, or to produce them on demand for an hour a week, 36 weeks a year. The result might be popular art that loses its critical edge and takes shortcuts to commonplace insight.

In fact, some mass communication scholars have argued that the unstated goal of popular art is to reinforce the status quo; popular culture, they say, blunts the individual's critical thinking abilities.

Storytellers have a history as popular artists, and the mass media have become the primary cultural storytellers of the era. Jacques Ellul (1965) in *Propaganda* argues that in a modern society, storytelling is an inevitable and even desirable tool to stabilize the culture. To Ellul, this "propaganda of integration" is not the deliberate lie commonly associated with propaganda, but the dissemination of widely held mores to the culture at large. This is precisely where the entertainment media get their power—not in the overt programming messages, but in the underlying assumptions that (if unchallenged) will become widely held societal values.

Many observers complain that the media reinforce the status quo by constantly depicting certain groups of society in an unflattering and unrepresentative way, presenting a distorted picture of reality to the reader or viewer. For example, when was the last time you saw an Arab on television as anything other than a terrorist or religious fanatic? Or a beautiful, blonde woman who also happened to be an engineer? Depictions and omissions such as the ones above reinforce cultural stereotypes and offend the groups involved. They also leave the media in the position of constantly having to explain why the media world is so different from the real world.

At least some such distortion is the natural outcome of compression. Just as substances such as rubber change form when compressed, so do media messages. Given only thirty seconds to register a message in a commercial, an advertising copywriter will resort to showing us the stereotype of a librarian, a mechanic, or a pharmacist. Using stereotypes as a form of mental shorthand is a natural way media work and was noted as early as 1922 by Walter Lippmann in his classic work, *Public Opinion*. Lippmann said that for economy of time and maintenance of the status quo, we hold to stereotypes by defining first and seeing second. Soon, we expect reality to imitate art.

Mass communicators know the power of stereotypes and deeply held notions and use them. According to advertising guru Tony Schwartz (1973), advertising messages are often constructed backwards. The communicator actually starts with what the receiver knows—or believes he knows—and then constructs a message that fits within that reality. Schwartz calls it hitting a "responsive chord." It works the same in entertainment. If you need a pimp to further the plot and time is tight, dress an African-American male appropriately and let the audience fill in the details. If you need a terrorist, anyone of Arab descent will usually do. The audience gets the idea of a pimp or a terrorist, but another idea has been planted as well—the racist notion that most pimps are minorities or that all Arabs are terrorists. While these images suit the artist's purposes, they are problematic.

Some scholars have made a more universal argument. Meyrowitz (1985) argues that television has become a "secret-revelation machine," bringing behaviors once confined to the "backstage" to the screen. The result is a loss of faith in institutions such as government, religion, and parenthood, with a resulting loss of stability. This loss of stability, Postman (1986) claims, can happen in one of two ways. In the Orwellian concept (found in *1984*) culture becomes a prison; in the Huxleyan concept (found in *Brave New World*) culture becomes a burlesque. Postman believes we are in more danger of the latter. Television is a threat to society precisely because most of its messages are so common yet people take them so seriously. Fore (1987) ar-

# Calvin and Hobbes

## by Bill Watterson

gues that every culture reveals itself through its underlying assumptions—the decisions it makes about what to value, how to solve problems, who is powerful, and what is taboo. In earlier cultures, these values were transmitted around the campfire; in our society, they are transmitted via television to a viewer who is separate from feedback and outside points of reference. These conditions, Fore argues, make the viewer subject to "a tunnel vision that encourages unquestioning acceptance of the world view he or she sees on the screen" (Fore 1987, 4).

The unquestioning acceptance of an unchanging reality is the antithesis of the effect Tolstoy intended art to produce. In Tolstoy's vision, art introduces the reader or viewer to the novel with such power and depth that what is novel can become known and what is known can become understood.

## Elements of Contrast between Elite and Popular Art

In the past 150 years philosophers, sociologists, and artists have debated the meaning of art. Prior to the Industrial Revolution, art was something only the well educated paid for, produced, and understood. Mozart had to capture the ear of the Emperor of Austria to get a subsidy to write opera. Such "high" or "elite art" provided society with a new way to look at itself. Picasso's drawings of people with three eyes or rearranged body parts literally provided Western culture with a new way of seeing. Michelangelo's paintings and sculpture did the same thing in the Renaissance.

But patronage had disadvantages. The patron could restrict both subject matter and form. Gradually artists discovered that if they could find a way to get more than one person to "pay" for the creation of art, artistic control returned to the artist. The concept of "popular art" was born.

Scholars disagree about many of the qualities of elite and popular art; some even assert that popular art cannot truly be considered art. While both kinds of art are difficult to define, the following list outlines the major differences between popular and elite art and culture.

1. Popular art is consciously adjusted to the median taste by the artist; elite art reflects the individual artist's vision.
2. Popular art is neither abstruse, complicated, nor profound; elite art has these characteristics.
3. Popular art conforms to majority experience; elite art explores the new.
4. Popular art conforms to less clearly defined standards of excellence, and its standards are linked to commercial success. Elite art is much less commercially oriented; standards of excellence are consistent and integrated.
5. Popular artists know that the audience expects entertainment and instruction; elite artists seek an aesthetic experience.
6. The popular artist cannot afford to offend a significant part of the public. The elite artist functions as a critic of society; the work challenges and sometimes offends the status quo.
7. Popular art often arises from folk art; elite art more often emerged from a culture's dominant intellectual tradition.

# Truth in Art and Entertainment

No question in the field of aesthetics is more thoroughly debated with less resolution than the role of truth in art. Most philosophers seem to agree that artists are not restricted to telling the literal truth. Often artistic vision can reveal a previously undiscerned truth, a new way of looking at the world or understanding human nature that rings deeply true.

But, just how much truth should the audience expect from entertainment? And, how entertaining should the audience expect truth to be? There are several opinions. At one point on the continuum is the argument that there is no truth requirement at all in art. At another point on the continuum is the belief that one person's truth should be established as the accepted truth for all. This imposition of a specific moral, as opposed to ethical, "truth" is common to all cultures and political systems. Plato in *The Republic* had Socrates argue against allowing children to hear "casual tales . . . devised by casual persons." Its result, when applied to the mass media, is usually some form of licensing or censorship. In American society, that battle historically has raged over library books.

Classics such as *Huckleberry Finn, Of Mice and Men, The Grapes of Wrath,* and *The Merchant of Venice* are but some of the long-revered and award-winning works that now face censorship by various school systems. The American Library Association reports that incidents of book banning rise each year and now reach more than one thousand reported instances annually, with little or no impedance from the courts. In 1982, the U.S. Supreme Court allowed a lower court ruling to stand that forced the Island Trees, New York, school district to re-examine a list of books considered objectionable (most of them by minority writers or about minority experiences) and to justify the censor's motives, but since that time, the High Court has not heard another book-banning case.

While books are important because they form the most permanent part of our cultural and intellectual web, television has been the medium that has been the most frequent contemporary target of censorship and protest. The protests began early in the medium's history. The 1951 airing of the show "Amos 'n' Andy" was condemned by the National Association for the Advancement of Colored People for depicting "Negroes in a stereotyped and derogatory manner." In 1964 the United Church of Christ set a legal precedent when it successfully challenged the license renewal of WLBT in Jackson, Mississippi, on the grounds that the owners had blatantly discriminated against African-Americans.

In the '60s, '70s and '80s a variety of special interest groups used more subtle methods to influence entertainment programming. Some, such as the Hispanic advocacy group *Nosotros,* worked closely with network bureaucracies, previewing potentially problematic episodes of entertainment programs, often altering program content before it reached the airwaves. Other advocacy groups employed strategic campaigns with advertisers and affiliates to influence the airing of certain episodes of popular shows or to make certain that some characters which certain segments of society might find objectionable remained scripted in prime time.

The networks opted for a policy of balance, believing that co-option was superior to confrontation and that muting criticism in advance would have a positive impact on the networks' image and the bottom line. Yet, *New York Times* television critic, Jack Gould, framed the problem of artistic accountability in the early days of the ascendancy of advocacy groups: Such agreements ". . . hold[s] latent dangers for the well-being of television as a whole. An outside group not professionally engaged in theatre production has succeeded in posing its will with respect to naming of fictional characters, altering the importance of a leading characterization and in other particulars changing the story line" (Montgomery 1989, 21). For the artist, network attempts to "balance" competing advocacy group interests had come close to recreating the patronage system, albeit a far more sophisticated one.

The struggle over censorship, which some label as disagreement over taste, becomes even more acute when governmental sponsorship is at stake. Some argue that because tax dollars are extracted from all, the programs they fund should be acceptable to all. Federal support for programs such as the National Endowment for the Arts were repeatedly questioned in Congress in 1992 after conservatives objected to funding for such artists as photographer Robert Maplethorpe, whose blend of homoerotic photos and traditional Judeo-Christian symbols offended many. Eventually, the criticism was a factor in the resignation of NEA's director, Robert Frohnmeyer.

The government also censors in other ways. Infinity Broadcasting has been fined several hundred thousand dollars for disc jockey Howard Stern's on-air profanity and offensive racial slurs. Stern himself became offended, saying that the FCC's action amounted to an enforcement of political correctness in a country which values free speech. Those who supported the FCC's action noted that Stern most often castigated people and groups who were already among society's most disadvantaged and who were among the least likely to be able to produce alternative programming.

The debates over freedom and censorship continue. Perhaps the only solution is found in the words of U.S. Supreme Court Justice William O. Douglas when he said, "If we are to have freedom of mind in America, we must produce a generation of men and women who will make tolerance for all ideas a symbol of virtue."

## Entertainment Disguised as News

In his ingenious satire, *Network,* the late writer-director Paddy Chayefsky envisioned a time when the lines would be blurred between entertainment and news, rendering them indistinguishable. By the late 1980s, television was proving him right. However, Chayefsky was wrong in one detail. News did begin to take on the look of entertainment, as he predicted it would; however, he did not predict that entertainment would also begin to look increasingly like news. Consider these television shows:

"America's Most Wanted," re-enactments of crimes with photos or line drawings of the suspects, in which the audience is encouraged to help by calling in tips for police. Another in the genre is "Unsolved Mysteries."

"Inside Edition," is a voyeuristic look at stories dubbed "too hot to handle" for traditional network news. Others of the breed have included "A Current Affair," and "Hard Copy."

"COPS," a look at actual police as they perform their duties, has spun off imitations, such as "Rescue 911."

Currently, at least twenty such shows are in production simultaneously. Whether called "trash television," "tabloid TV," or "infotainment," by critics, they are hot with local television programming executives. Such shows provide relief from returns of situation comedies and the sameness of game shows, draw large ratings and often come prepackaged with ads embedded in them, making them attractive to station owners.

The blending of art and entertainment is not restricted to the small screen. Films such as *Nixon* and *Hoffa* reflect a particular artistic vision based on fact. *Hoffa* director Danny DeVito sought to make an entertaining film that, while it actually portrayed the major facts of the teamster leaders's life, took symbolic liberties with many events and people. DeVito told the "Today" show audience in early 1993 that what he sought was entertainment—"not sitting down and reading a book."

Though these films and the reality-based television shows differ in format and content, they are alike in invoking the license allowed entertainment programming while retaining the authority of fact—a risky combination. By blending information and entertainment into an internally coherent package, the possibility for abuse of an unsuspecting audience exists. To understand how this can happen, we must look to the mass-communication theory of *uses and gratifications.* Phrased simply, the theory says audience members will use the media to gratify certain wants and needs. People bring something to the message, and what they bring affects what they take away.

For example, seeking news and information is a common use of the media, with an expected gratification of getting information necessary for citizenship. Entertainment is another common media use, with its own expected gratification. Trash television, in keeping the look of news yet airing the content of lowbrow entertainment, may be produced to entertain but often has had the unintended "use" of informing. The problem arises when the information such entertainment programming provides about important institutions in American culture such as the court system or medical practice, or important political figures such as Malcolm X and Jimmy Hoffa, is fundamentally flawed.

*This confounding of expected and unintended uses and gratifications is important.* As *New York Times* columnist A. M. Rosenthal (1989) states, tabloid television shows are tantamount to buying news "off the shelf." He adds that stations buying such programs should add the disclaimer, "We did not put this stuff in the bottle, whatever it is."

With a look of authority (an anchor's desk, a courtroom, a police precinct) and the hype of their importance (i.e., 200 lives saved so far!), these shows appear to be useful for acquiring information, thus gratifying the human need to know. However, by invoking their license as entertainment, such shows are free to bypass accuracy, fairness, balance, and other standards normally associated with news and to focus on more sensational elements to gather larger ratings. For instance, in 1989 CBS moved one prime-time show, "Yesterday, Today and Tomorrow," with its re-enactments of news events, from its news division, where such re-enactments were banned, to its entertainment division, where the practice was allowable. Eventually, after much criticism and poor ratings, the show was dropped. In 1996, one television program re-enacted O.J. Simpson's civil trial because cameras weren't allowed in the courtroom.

In these shows, what is now being gratified is not the *need* to know, but the *want* to know in a way that some viewers might not even recognize it. In a recent Times Mirror poll, about half of the respondents said they believed "America's Most Wanted" was a news show, while only 28 percent said that it was entertainment (Thomas 1990). The result could be a population that gets its news from a program like "A Current Affair." In the words of one woman interviewed by the *Dallas Morning News* (Wicker 1990) about marital relationships, "I only believe what I see on 'Oprah.'"

## Aesthetics Is an Attitude

Artists see the world differently. While most people perceive only what is needful for a particular purpose, the artist works with what some philosophers call an "enriched perceptual experience." This aesthetic attitude is one that values close and complete concentration of all the senses. An aesthetic attitude is a frankly sensual one, and one which summons both emotion and logic to a particular end.

For example, the theatre audience knows that Eugene O'Neill's plays are "merely" drama. But, they also provide us with an intense examination of the role of family in human society—an experience that is both real and personal to every audience member. Such intense examination is what gives the plays their power to move.

We believe that the makers of mediated messages, whether they are the executive producers of a television sitcom or the designers of a newspaper page, share this aesthetic impetus. These mass communicators are much like architects. An architect can design a perfectly serviceable building, one that withstands the elements and may be used for particular purposes. But a great building—St. Paul's Cathedral in London or Jefferson's home at Monticello—does more. They are a tribute to the human intellect's capacity to harmoniously harness form and function.

In fact, philosophers have argued that what separates the commonplace from the excellent is the addition of an aesthetic quality to what would otherwise be a routine, serviceable work. These qualities of excellence have been described as:

- An appreciation of the function realized in the product;
- An appreciation of the resulting quality or form;
- An appreciation of the technique or skill in the performance.

These three characteristics of aesthetic excellence characterize excellence in mass communication as well.

Take the newspaper weather page. Before *USA Today* literally recalibrated the standard, weather pages were generally restricted to the upper right-hand quadrant of the second page of a newspaper section. They were printed in black and white, in columns of tiny type. Newspaper editors believed that most people weren't interested in the weather—unless it was weird—and designed their pages accordingly.

*USA Today* editors, on the other hand, understood that their readers agreed with the observations of political columnist Molly Ivins: when people aren't talking about football, they talk about the weather. The editors devoted more space to it and printed it in color. They added more information in a more legible style and form. In short, they gave newspaper weather information an aesthetic quality. While much about *USA Today* has been criticized, its excellent weather page has been copied.

Although mass-communication professionals are infrequently accused of being artists, we believe they intuitively accept an aesthetic standard as a component of professional excellence. As philosopher G. E. Moore noted in his book *Principia Ethica:*

> "Let us imagine one world exceedingly beautiful. Image it as beautiful as you can; put into it whatever on this earth you most admire: mountains, rivers, the sea, suns and sunsets, stars and moon. Imagine these all combined in the most exquisite proportion so that no one thing jars against another, but each contributes to increase the beauty of the whole. And then imagine the ugliest world you can possibly conceive. Imagine it just one heap of filth, containing everything that is most disgusting to you for whatever reason, and the whole, as far as may be, without one redeeming factor. . . .
> Supposing (all) that quite apart from the contemplation of human beings; still it is irrational to hold that it is better that the ugly world exist than the one which is beautiful." (Moore 1903, 83)

Substitute film, compact disc, poem, news story, photograph, or advertising copy for Moore's word "world" and we believe that you will continue to intuitively agree with the statement. While we may disagree on what specifically constitutes beauty in form and content, the aesthetic standard of excellence still applies.

## The Prosocial Effects of Media Entertainment

Philosopher John Dewey noted, "Aesthetic experience is a manifestation, a record and celebration of the life of a civilization, a means of promoting its development, and is also the ultimate judgment upon the quality of a civilization." If such is the case, then the entertainment media have much to contribute to the healthy side of the ledger. Some are detailed here:

One of the biggest entertainment events of the 1980s was the "Live Aid" concert held on two continents simultaneously to benefit those starving in the Ethiopian famine. Engineered by English singer Bob Geldof, the concert and its subsequent album sales raised more than $100 million in relief funds and an untold amount of awareness of the extent of the sub-Saharan famine.

Other entertainers picked up on the concept and in quick succession, though with more modest success, came:

• USA for Africa, a group of American superstars who joined together to record "We Are the World," with proceeds donated to African relief;
• Farm Aid, a concert of country and western singers, with profits going to America's drought-stricken farmers;
• Comic Relief, a comedy marathon by top-name comedians, with the profits helping the homeless;

- The Amnesty International worldwide rock tour in 1988 featuring Bruce Springsteen, Sting, Peter Gabriel, Tracy Chapman, and others, with proceeds funding human rights causes around the world;
- "For the Children," a CD featuring such artists as Paul McCartney, Springsteen, Sting, Barbra Streisand and James Taylor recorded in 1991 raised more than $3 million for the Pediatric AIDS Foundation in its first twenty-four months.

Other entertainers have maintained a lifelong association with a single cause, lending credibility and recognition to worthy organizations such as UNICEF (Danny Kaye), the Muscular Dystrophy Association (Jerry Lewis), animal rights (Betty White), and world hunger (Harry Chapin).

Not every effort is quite so elaborate, yet many are equally effective. Paul Simon's "Graceland" album sold millions of copies and won a Grammy award in 1986, while focusing the world's attention on apartheid in South Africa and the plight of African-Americans here. The 1996 movie *Ghosts of Mississippi* showed the nation that America had once been guilty of many of the same attitudes, and the work of Spike Lee in the 1989 film *Do the Right Thing* showed us that those attitudes might not be entirely in the past. MTV, often criticized for the sex and violence content of its programming, sponsored the Rock Against Drugs (RAD) program in the late 1980s, and Rock the Vote in 1992 and 1996. The latter included new programming about the 1996 election aimed at young people as well as mobilizing messages urging the MTV generation to get involved in the political process.

Television entertainment programming is worthy of praise in several areas. "The Burning Bed" addressed the problem of violent relationships, while "Something about Amelia" frankly discussed the tragedy of incest. Critically acclaimed programs in recent years have examined the possibility of nuclear holocaust and the plight of abused children, rape victims, the adult mentally handicapped, and other vulnerable segments of society. In addition, phenomena such as teenage suicide and Alzheimer's disease have been made more real to millions of Americans through docudramas. Media activist Elizabeth Thoman has called such prime-time television the major "continuing education" available to many adult Americans to help them learn to cope with contemporary crises (Thoman 1987).

Television helps kids, too. Shows such as "Sesame Street" and "Barney" have helped kids to acquire reading skills and learn how to get along. PBS's "Ghost Writer" promotes literacy for older children.

Norman Cousins, former editor of the *Saturday Review,* even claims physiological healing powers of the media. He claimed to have cured a collagen disease that had paralyzed most of his body through a self-prescribed routine of massive injections of vitamin C and laughter, in part induced by old film comedies (Cousins 1974). While it might be stretching the prosocial benefits of media entertainment to claim that the media can have medicinal power, entertainment can be meritorious. And meritorious programming need not be dull or commercially unsuccessful. The popular "Friends" provides television's most realistic look yet at the complex role of relationships in our lives.

Perhaps the most important positive effect is the media's ability to pull people away from the routine of everyday life and provide an outlet for escape. In an interview on the PBS series "The Promise of Television," former CBS news commentator Bill Moyers said:

> The root word of television is vision from afar, and that's its chief value. It has brought me in my stationary moments visions of ideas and dreams and imaginations and geography that I would never personally experience. So, it has put me in touch with the larger world. Television can be a force for dignifying life, not debasing it. (Moyers 1988)

Though Moyers's comments were made specifically about television, the same argument can be made for a good book, a favorite magazine, music, or a film. And whether the media are a force for dignifying humanity or debasing it is largely in the hands of those who own it and work in it.

## Suggested Readings

Leibert, Robert M., Joyce N. Sprafkin, and Emily S. Davidson. 1982. *The early window: Effects of television on children and youth.* New York: Pergamon Press.

Medved, Michael. 1992. *Hollywood vs. America.* New York: HarperCollins Publishers.

Montgomery, Kathryn C. 1989. *Target: Prime time. Advocacy groups and the struggle over entertainment television.* New York: Oxford University Press.

Palmer, Edward L., and Aimée Dorr, eds. 1980. *Children and the faces of television: Teaching, violence, selling.* New York: Academic Press.

Postman, Neil. 1986. *Amusing ourselves to death: Public discourse in the age of television.* New York: Penguin Books.

Tolstoy, Leo. "What is art?"

# CHAPTER X CASES

## CASE X-A
## Hate Radio: The Outer Limits of Tasteful Broadcasting
BRIAN SIMMONS
*Cascade College, Portland, Oregon*

Trevor Van Lansing has what some would call the greatest job in the world. He is employed by KRFP-AM, an all-talk-format radio station in a large city in the West. His program airs weekdays from 3:00 P.M. to 7:00 P.M., and he is currently rated number one in his afternoon drive-time slot. Van Lansing is, quite simply, the most popular radio personality in the market. He is also the most controversial.

Each afternoon Van Lansing introduces a general topic for discussion and then fields calls from listeners about the topic. However, Lansing's topics (and the calls from his listeners) revolve around a recurring theme—the world as viewed by a Caucasian, Anglo-Saxon, Protestant who also happens to be vocal, uncompromising, and closeminded.

A sampling of his recent programs typifies his show. On Monday, Van Lansing discusses a woman in a small Indiana town who quits her job in a convenience store to go on welfare because there is more money to be made on the federal dole than in the private sector. Says Van Lansing, "All these irresponsible whores are the same. They get knocked up by some construction worker, then expect the taxpayers to pay for them to sit around the house all day and watch Oprah Winfrey."

Callers flood the airwaves with equally combative remarks in support of and opposition to Van Lansing's comments. On Tuesday, the topic of racial discrimination (always a Van Lansing favorite) comes up. According to Van Lansing, "Those Africans expect us Americans to make up for two hundred years of past mistakes. Forget it. It can't be done. If they are so keen on America, let them compete against Caucasians on an equal basis without the 'civil rights crutch.' "

When one African-American caller challenges Van Lansing's thinking, the host responds, "Why don't you tell your buddies to work for what they get like us Caucasians? All you do anyway is steal from the guys you don't like and then take their women."

Wednesday finds Van Lansing lashing out against education: "The problem with today's schools is that our kinds are exposed to weird thinking. I mean, we tell our kids that homosexuality is OK, that we evolved from a chimp, and that the Ruskies are our friends. It all started when we elected women to school boards and started letting fags into the classroom. It's disgusting."

Thursday features an exchange between Van Lansing and an abortion-rights activist. At one point they are both shouting at the same time, and the airwaves are peppered with obscenities and personal attacks. By comparison, Friday is calm, as only a few irate Jews, women, and Mormons bother to call in.

Critics have called Van Lansing's program offensive, tasteless, rude, racist, obscene, and insensitive. Supporters refer to the program as enlightening, refreshing, educational, and provocative. The only thing everyone can agree on is that the show is a bona fide moneymaker. Van Lansing's general manager notes that the station's ratings jumped radically when he was hired, and that advertising revenues have tripled.

In fact, Van Lansing's popularity has spawned promotional appearances, T-shirts, bumper stickers, and other paraphernalia, all designed to hawk the station. "Sure, Trevor is controversial, but in this business, that's good," says KRFP's general manager. "Van Lansing is so good that he will make more money this year than the president of the United States. Besides, it's just a gimmick."

Does Van Lansing see a problem with the content and style of his program? "Look," he says, "radio is a business. You have to give the audience what they want. All I do is give them what they want. If they wanted a kinder, gentler attitude, I would give it to them." He continues, "Don't get mad at me. Thank God we live in a country where guys like me can express an opinion. The people who listen to me like to hear it straight sometimes, and that's what the First Amendment is about, right?"

Finally, Van Lansing points out that if people are really offended by him, they can always turn the dial. "I don't force these people to listen," he pleads. "If they don't like it, let them go somewhere else."

Others disagree. The National Coalition for the Understanding of Alternative Lifestyles, a gay- and lesbian-rights group, calls Van Lansing's show "reprehensible." "Trevor Van Lansing is hiding behind the First Amendment. What he says on the air isn't speech; it's hate, pure and simple," says the group's director. "His program goes well beyond what our founding fathers intended."

Adds a representative of the National Organization for Women, "Van Lansing is perpetuating several dangerous stereotypes that are destructive, sick, and offensive. Entertainment must have some boundaries."

## Micro Issues:

1. Would you be offended by Van Lansing's program? If so, why?
2. Would Van Lansing's program be less offensive if the station aired another talk show immediately after his which featured a host holding opposite views?

## Middle-range Issues:

1. Who should accept responsibility for monitoring this type of program? Van Lansing? The radio station, KRFP? The FCC? The courts? The audience?
2. What, if any, are the differences between Van Lansing's *legal* right to do what he does and the *ethical* implications of what he does?
3. Legal scholar Mari Matsuda (1989) has called for a narrow legal restriction of racist speech. She notes, "The places where the law does not go to redress harm have tended to be the places where women, children, people of color,

and poor people live" (Matsuda 1989, 11). She argues that a content-based restriction of racist speech is more protective of civil liberties than other tests that have been traditionally applied. Could such an argument be applied to entertainment programming?

## Macro Issues:

1. Are entertainers relieved of ethical responsibilities if they are "just giving the audience what they want?" Do Van Lansing's high ratings validate his behavior, since many people are obviously in agreement with him?
2. How does Van Lansing's narrow view of the world differ from a television situation comedy that stereotypes blondes as dumb, blue-collar workers as bigoted, etc.?
3. Van Lansing says that it's great that a guy like him can have a radio show. Is tolerance one of the measures of a democracy? If so, are there limits to tolerance, and who draws those lines?
4. How should democratic societies cope with unpopular points of view, particularly as expressed through the mass media? Does a social critic still have an important role, even if that criticism is unpopular?

## CASE X-B
## How To Remember Malcolm X
DENNIS LANCASTER
*West Plains News Leader,* West Plains, Missouri

Historian Michael Kammen writes in *Mystic Chords of Memory* that "we arouse and arrange our memories to suit our psychic needs." A culture's memory, he adds, "which contains a slowly shifting configuration of traditions," is "always selective and is so often contested."

Film director Spike Lee, known for his controversial portrayals of Black America, says his purpose in creating the epic 1992 film *Malcolm X* was "to open up the history book" on the assassinated activist. In doing so, Lee has provided an informative and entertaining yet mediated version of Malcolm X to a generation who knows very little of this man. The problem is that while it is impossible to offer a portrayal that generates a complete understanding of any individual, Lee often diverts from the accepted facts about Malcolm X, whose controversial life and legacy would seem, in this day, to demand an even closer attention to the "historical truth." The result is twofold: a figure is enshrined more than ever by memory's mythic mists and an art form is allowed to become a new generation's sole understanding of reality.

How close, then, should historical dramas created primarily for mass entertainment attend to the facts? Should filmmakers selectively arrange, rearrange, and distort history to suit the needs of the story, their aesthetic and social views, and/or a culture's "psychic needs"? Are falsehoods more dangerous when paired with accurate, truthful information? If the only reality presented is a mediated reality, then is constructing that reality ethical, especially when certain facts are misrepresented? Are there any acceptable reasons for revisionistic histories? And, finally, whose truth is Truth?

Parts of the *Malcolm X* film, based on the *Autobiography of Malcolm X* by Alex Haley, are not true to the facts, according to Bruce Perry's *The Life of a Man Who Changed Black America,* a book critically praised for its "more complex portrait" of Malcolm X. These alleged falsehoods include: the perpetuation of the "myth" that Malcolm's mom was a "strong but loving, protective mother" when she actually "ruled her children with an iron hand"; the portrayal of his mother as a "gun-toting" woman who fended off a band of Ku Klux Klansmen when the incident, according to his mother and aunt, never occurred; the creation of a hero out of Malcolm's "brutal," "skirt-chasing" father, Earl Little; the contradictory story of how Earl Little was burned out of his home, allegedly beaten, and subsequently killed when laid in the path of a streetcar; and the seemingly exacerbated retelling of Malcolm's life of violence and crime. Lee also used a fictional character to lead Malcolm to Islam instead of his own brother and sister, as described in both Haley's and Perry's books. In fact, nothing is said of Malcolm's sister (half sister really) Ella Little whose influence on him and his thinking was enormous.

Lee said his intention was to "not tear down Malcolm; for us, this is an act of love." Changing names and dates of events, Lee says, was not distortion.

". . . we're not making a documentary; we're making a drama. You can't include everything; some things you switch or turn around." The film's producer, Marvin Worth, who knew Malcolm X, says "Everybody's got their own version of Malcolm X. He was one of the most misunderstood people in history. We're not playing games with making up our opinion of the truth," noting the script's adherence to the Haley book and the writers' use verbatim of Malcolm's speeches.

Entertainment writer David Ansen asserts that Lee is not a historian but a consummate "showman" and knows how to entertain his audience, noting that the filmmaker devotes over a third of the movie to Malcolm's "wild early years." The artist in Lee wants to give us the man as well as the myth—"the inner evolution that is Malcolm's real and haunting story," he adds.

But does being a showman give license to distort? No, some of Lee's critics say, indicating Lee's stretching of the truth goes too far. Lloyd Rose says, "No one can argue that facts aren't primary in attempting to get hold of history." Perry writes: "Lee's film is well made and entertaining, but it is fatally flawed from the standpoint of biographical and historical accuracy. His Malcolm is largely a myth." Writer and Black activist Amiri Baraka says Lee "is able to manipulate popular imagery" in the pursuit of artistic but nationalistic ends, maintaining that, "We will not let Malcolm X's life be trashed to make middle-class Negroes sleep easier."

Baraka, perhaps the most vocal of Lee's critics, adds: "Malcolm X's life is not a commercial property. It can't be claimed by a petit bourgeois Negro who has $40 million," referring to Lee's accumulated wealth and to the merchandising of the Malcolm X name, a systematic selling of a cultural image via baseball caps and T-shirts.

In fact, many critics of the film and of Lee's directing-storytelling style have accused the filmmaker of "participation in a 'retrograde' movement" to rehistorize the memory of Malcolm X to serve Lee's own purposes. These presumed purposes range from the negative—pure profit motives and the enhancement of Lee's celebrity status—to the more positive—legitimatizing an authentic African-American hero and answering the call to "lay claim to an intelligent black culture."

As artist, Lee has been praised for his positive portrayal of African-American life and his ability to confront issues that no other filmmaker has been bold enough to tackle. His strength is in inviting the black audience "to discover the pleasures of seeing its usually hidden and segregated social and cultural world exposed to the legitimating power of celluloid. It is comforted by Lee's ability to construct recognizable images of racial community, particularly where the forms of solidarity in cinematic circulation are scarce outside the movie theater." His aim, it seems, is community-building within the African-American culture and the breakdown of stereotypes within America. To do this, Lee has "consistently put images or dialogue on film that have flooded the viewer with the remembrance of things past or recognition of things present."

In an interview with *Artforum,* Lee asserts that "I want people to be all fired up for this. To get inspired by it. This is not just some regular bullshit Hollywood movie. This is life and death we're dealing with, this is a mind set, this is what Black people in America have come through."

## Micro Issues:

1. How closely must a film based on a specific historical character stick to the known truth about the character?
2. Should the filmmaker alert the viewer that certain events within a historical film have been dramatized or that they are fictional?
3. Should a filmmaker deliberately advocate a political position in history-based film?

## Middle-range Issues:

1. What are the audience member's responsibilities when watching a film that purports to be a true account of history?
2. Should filmmakers be allowed to alter historical fact for a higher purpose? What about biographers? Creators in other media?

## Macro Issues:

1. Is film an appropriate forum for discussion of the civil rights movement?
2. What does the filmmaker owe to an audience that may have no firsthand awareness of the historical premise of the movie?
3. What standards of truth should entertainment meet? Are there different standards of truth for different media?
4. In an issue as complex as the civil rights movement, is there more than one version of truth?
5. Is the creation of a legend, whether with truth or with fiction, a legitimate purpose for a filmmaker?

## CASE X-C
## Beavis and Butthead: The Case for Standards in Entertainment
PHILIP PATTERSON
*Oklahoma Christian University*

In October of 1993, five-year-old Aaron Messner set fire to his family's trailer in Moraine, Ohio, killing his two-year-old sister. According to press reports and the local fire chief, the boy had been influenced by the pyromaniacal antics of MTV's Beavis and Butthead.

The Messner tragedy made headlines across the nation and brought Beavis and Butthead into the national limelight. However, the controversy over MTV's most popular show surfaced much earlier.

Beavis and Butthead is the creation of a former self-professed "awkward, miserable" adolescent, Mike Judge. Judge served as producer, animator and voice for the show in its early days. He says that the two losers depicted on the show were modeled after kids he knew in junior high, and not unlike the ones he sees today.

Judge told an interviewer for *Texas Monthly* magazine that he considers "Beavis and Butthead" to be "lowest common denominator humor." He thought of the concept after noticing "Everything I saw on TV was so politically correct. I just had this urge to be offensive and juvenile."

From its debut in March of 1993, the show hit a national nerve. Soon words such as "butt-munch" and "fartknocker" had made the popular culture lexicon. The annoying heh-heh-heh laugh was everywhere. The show garnered ratings four times higher than the typical MTV music video.

"Beavis and Butthead" focused on typical adolescent talk and humor. Girls were "chicks" to be scored on, though neither Beavis nor Butthead seemed capable. Bathroom humor abounded. A study by one *Rolling Stone* writer found that an anal reference was made every 16 words in the script.

The show had both critics and fans. *Time* magazine called it possibly "the bravest show ever run on television." *U.S. News & World Report* likened it to the "death knell of civilization." Psychologist and media figure Joyce Brothers praised it; South Carolina Senator Ernest Hollings condemned it. Pulitzer prize-winning columnist Anna Quindlen weighed in with a column wondering why a five-year-old was watching MTV alone.

Some advertisers avoided the program, but parent corporation Viacom stuck with MTV's highest rated show. Just prior to the debut of "Beavis and Butthead," MTV accounted for 22 percent of Viacom's revenues. Now the new show was the hottest item in Viacom's most profitable subsidiary.

But the show that could get away with ridiculing the explosion of the Space Shuttle *Challenger* found itself in deeper trouble when first one real-life tragedy then another were blamed on the antics of its characters. Within a few months, four fires, a cat killing, and the throwing of a bowling ball off a highway overpass on to a car which killed an eight-month-old girl were blamed on "Beavis and Butthead" and reported nationally. A causal link was denied by MTV in all the cases, and indeed the evidence in the bowling ball incident was particularly weak. But "Beavis and Butthead" was now vulnerable to criticism from the mainstream press.

MTV responded by eliminating the 7 P.M. (EST) airing of "Beavis and Butthead," moving the show to 10:30 and 11:00 P.M. at the same time arguing that less than 10 percent of the audience was under the age of twelve. The recurring motif of fire was also eliminated from the program, and a disclaimer warning viewers not to model Beavis and Butthead's behavior was added. In a statement issued about the changes, MTV said:

> While we do not believe the "Beavis and Butthead" cartoon was responsible [for the Messner tragedy], we feel the steps we are taking are the proper ones. "Beavis and Butthead" is made for the teenagers and young adults who make up the overwhelming majority of its audience. These viewers see the cartoon for what it is—an exaggerated parody of two teenaged misfits whose antics take place in a cartoon world . . . antics [the viewers] know are unacceptable and not to be emulated in real life. Nevertheless, we have decided to bend over backward as responsible programmers.

## Micro Issues:

1. Part of the behaviors of the two characters in "Beavis and Butthead" included sniffing paint thinner and using an aerosol can and lighter to create a blow torch. Should one assume that in an audience of millions that at least a few will try to emulate this behavior? Should that matter?
2. Can an advertiser reasonably expect to convince a "Beavis and Butthead" viewer to consume a certain beverage or buy a certain item? If so, what does that say about whether the show can alter a child's behavior in other areas of life?
3. Did MTV do the right thing by shifting the time the show aired?
4. Is the presence of a disclaimer urging viewers not to imitate the acts seen on the screen sufficient?

## Middle-range Issues:

1. Satire has been around for centuries. Jonathan Swift once wrote "A Modest Proposal" suggesting that Irish Catholics should fatten their babies for consumption by the English. Some readers thought he was serious. Would that classic work pass the political correctness test today? Should satire be exempt from the traditional standards of what is acceptable in a society?
2. To what extent are the media responsible for the level of violence in our society?

## Macro Issues:

1. One of the functions of media is to hold a mirror up to a society. Is part of the criticism of "Beavis and Butthead" that the adults who see it don't like the reality that it reveals?

2. Who is ultimately responsible for what children should see on television:
   (*a*) The media?
   (*b*) The government?
   (*c*) Parents?
3. If a product is defective, the manufacturer can be held liable under the doctrine of "strict liability" for the damage it causes. Should the media be held to the same standard as, for instance, pharmaceutical manufacturers, as some argue, since both produce a product to be "ingested"? Is it possible for a media message to be "defective"? If so, what should be the remedy?

## CASE X-D
## Schindler's List: The Role of Memory
LEE WILKINS
*University of Missouri—Columbia*

In 1982 director Steven Spielberg purchased the rights to Australian novelist's Thomas Kenneally's retelling of the story of the "Schindler Jews," a group of about 1,100 Krakow, Poland, residents who survived the Holocaust because Czech businessman Oskar Schindler was willing to cajole, bribe and bully the Nazis for their lives. Today, Schindler, a Roman Catholic by birth, is known in Israel as "righteous person"; he is the only Nazi buried in Jerusalem's Mt. Zion cemetery.

By 1992 when Spielberg did begin work on the film, both he and the world had changed. Bosnia was in the midst of "ethnic cleansing" as were nations in Africa and in the Far East such as Nepal. Some polls indicated that more than half of the American teenagers living in that decade had never heard of the Holocaust; about 23 percent of the American public at the time maintained the gassing of 6 million Jews plus 5 million other "undesirables" in Germany and its occupied territories never happened.

"I think the main reason I wanted to make this film was as an act of remembrance," Spielberg told the film editor of the *Atlanta Journal and Constitution.* "An act of remembrance for the public record. Maybe it won't be seen by gallons of people who see my other movies, but it might be the kind of movie shown one day in high schools. I also wanted to leave this story for my children. I wanted to leave them a legacy of their Jewish culture."

What Americans, as well as Spielberg's children will see is a three-hour-and-15-minute examination of the conscience of Oskar Schindler, who entered World War II on the side of the Nazis intending to make a profit. He hires Jews to work in his enamelware factory because they work for less than slave wages. Initially, he befriends the Nazis and the SS to help expedite his purchase and takeover of the plant. Later, after the Nazis have first ghettoized and then attempted to exterminate the Jewish population of Krakow, Schindler uses his personal charm, his connections and most of his war-amassed wealth to have "his" Jewish workers first labeled as essential to the German war machine and later moved from Germany and into Czechoslovakia for safekeeping. None of the bombs manufactured at Schindler's plant ever exploded.

Spielberg shot the film in black and white on location in Poland. Much of the movie has a documentary feel; cinematography is at eye level, and critics noted that it was often Spielberg himself who focused the hand-held camera. Hitler appears only once—in a photograph on someone's desk. And, by centering on Schindler, Spielberg captured the conscience of an uneasy hero.

As Kenneally's book indicates, Oskar Schindler was a complex man. He managed to maintain outward friendships with many Nazis whom he despised. He was a sensualist who enjoyed good food, expensive possessions, and carnal knowledge women who were not his wife. Spielberg's film, which was rated R, depicted all of this, including scenes of lovemaking that involved full, frontal nudity and more distant shots of concentration camp existence in which Jewish inmates were required to run naked in front of their guards to determine who remained well enough to work and who was sick enough to be murdered.

Perhaps the most disturbing element of the film was Spielberg's portrait of the violence imbedded in Hitler's "final solution" and of the banality of evil (Hannah Arendt's phrase used to describe convicted war criminal Adolph Eichman) that individual human beings can come to represent. That sundered humanity is symbolized by Amon Goeth (played by Ralph Fiennes), the amoral and some suggested sociopathic commandant of the labor camp from which many of the people who worked for Schindler escaped. Whether it is the Nazis hunting the Jews who remain in hiding in the Krakow ghetto or Goeth's randomized murder of the men and women who lived in his camp as before-breakfast sport, the violence in the film is devastating not just for its brutality but also for its casualness.

When Spielberg's mother told him making "*Schindler's List* would be good for the Jews," Spielberg responded that "it would be good for all of us."

Critics, who had a difficult time accepting that the same man who directed *Jurassic Park* could also produce *Schindler's List* in the same year, praised the film for its aesthetic qualities and for its retelling of the story of the Holocaust in such a powerful fashion. The film also brought Spielberg multiple Oscars, an award that had eluded him despite his enormous popular success. After the film's release, President Bill Clinton said that every American should see it.

Rita Kempley writing in the *Washington Post* saw more than a superficial resemblance between Schindler and Spielberg. "And Schindler, played with élan by (Liam) Neeson, is really a lot like Spielberg himself," she wrote, "A man who manages to use his commercial clout to achieve a moral end."

## Micro Issues:

1. Should a film like *Schindler's List* receive the same R rating as films such as Demolition Man?
2. What is the appropriate role of a film critic for films such as *Schindler's List?* Should different standards be used to evaluate this film than some other Spielberg successes such as *E.T.* or *Jaws?*
3. Would you allow a child under 17 to see this film?

## Middle-range Issues:

1. Should news accounts focus on events such as the ethnic cleansing in Bosnia with the goal of changing public opinion?
2. Are docudramas that focus on social issues such as spouse abuse or child molestation the appropriate mechanism to engage the public in debate or discussion about such serious questions?

3. Some people have argued that certain historical events such as the Holocaust or the recent genocide in Rwanda should never be the subject of entertainment programming because entertainment can never capture the true horror of what has happened. How would you evaluate such an assertion?

## Macro Issues:

1. Compare the moral development of Oskar Schindler in the film *Schindler's List* with that of the main characters in a film such as *Gandhi*.
2. John Dewey wrote about "funded memory," by which he meant how a culture remembers and reconstructs its own history. What is the role of entertainment programming in funded memory? What should be the role of news programming in such cultural constructions?
3. Tolstoy argues that good art communicates the feelings of the artist to the masses in such a way that others may experience the same feeling as the artist. How does this film accomplish that purpose?

## CASE X-E
## Joe Klein and the Authorship of *Primary Colors:*
## Stranger than Fiction
LEE WILKINS
*University of Missouri—Columbia*

*Primary Colors* hit the book stores in January of 1996, just as the Presidential race was heating up. In an industry where timing and word of mouth are crucial to commercial success, the satirical account of the 1992 Bill Clinton presidential campaign had a more unusual edge. The writer was that well-known author, "anonymous," whose pen name has been quoted in literary circles for more than 500 years. "Anonymous" has been exposed, in previous literary eras, as Jonathan Swift (who wrote under the name Isaac Bickerstaff) and Charlotte Brontë (Curer Bell) to name just two. While the book's content varied from the sleazy to the salacious, the real furor was the media race to unmask the author.

Book sales were brisk. As the *Buffalo News* noted, "Many Americans bought *Primary Colors* precisely because they thought they were getting the inside scoop on the campaign from someone intimately involved in the action. Using the 'Anonymous' authorship fed the erroneous idea that the book came from an observer too close to the Clintons to admit writing the book."

Readers who made it through the volume were treated to intimate moments that depicted a president who had a great deal of trouble keeping the fly of his pants zipped and a First Lady who slept with White House staffers. The overall tone was that of badly executed satire arising from the personal disillusionment of someone closely connected to the Clinton campaign. The author clearly admired Hillary Clinton and just as clearly found her husband wanting in the area of political leadership.

Speculation as to authorship began immediately. The *Washington Post* even ran the odds, with front-runners Garry Trudeau (creator of Doonesbury), campaign consultant Mandy Grunwald, White House aide George Stephanopoulos or novelist Christopher Buckley leading the pack. *Newsweek* columnist and CBS political commentator Joe Klein's chances were placed at less than 50 to 1. All involved, including Klein, denied authorship. Sales, inspired by the media frenzy over authorship, soared. By the time royalties, paperback and foreign rights, and movie rights were acquired, "Anonymous" could certainly consider himself a member of the upper class. The book is expected to earn at least $6 million, perhaps a great deal more.

But the mystery began to unravel in the late spring. By that time, a copy of the manuscript surfaced with handwritten notes. The *Washington Post* hired the former chief document examiner for the Chicago Police Department to inspect samples of both Klein's handwriting and the manuscript notes. The expert pronounced the samples identical. Next the book itself was subjected to a computer analysis and compared with Klein's other work. The evaluation remained consistent: Joe Klein was the author.

Throughout the spring, however, Klein continued to publicly deny authorship. What was not known at the time but which became public later was that Klein had told a *Newsweek* editor, Maynard Parker, that he had written the book. However, Parker allowed the magazine to proceed with an article speculating on the book's authorship including Klein's denial, which Parker knew to be untrue. Klein also denied that he was the author to his bosses at CBS, a denial that was aired on the network.

Finally, on July 17, 1996, the *Washington Post* got Klein to admit that he had written the book. At a press conference the same day, President Clinton was repeatedly questioned about whether he knew that Klein was the author; Clinton denied knowing that Klein had written the book. One week later, *Newsweek* suspended Klein for lying about writing the book; he was reinstated at the magazine on August 5 to cover the Presidential election. On July 25, Klein either was fired or resigned from his work at CBS. And, on October 25, Klein announced that he was leaving *Newsweek* to write for *The New Yorker* magazine.

In writing about the events in *Newsweek,* Klein admitted that, once book sales took off, he just "went with the flow." The recipient of two National Magazine Awards and an *American Journalism Review*'s Best in the Business Award for political coverage, Klein continued to assert that *Primary Colors* was a work of fiction whose characters just "took off" on their own as he was writing the book. "I had no idea where the plot was going. The whole thing just exploded out of me."

Many of his journalistic colleagues were less kind. "Obviously, I'm very troubled any time anyone is less than honest with me and less than honest with the American public," the president of CBS news told critics. An editorial writer for the *Buffalo News* put it this way:

> "But the real victims of this indefensible scam are American readers. They bought a book promoted under false pretenses, and they may now have a hard time believing honest journalists who write things they really should have confidence in." (*Buffalo News,* July 24, 1996, p. 2B)

## Micro Issues:

1. Should Klein have denied that he was the author of *Primary Colors?* What potential harm could come from the action?
2. Should Klein's *Newsweek* editor have stopped the magazine's coverage of the authorship issue since he was privy to the truth?
3. Should the *Washington Post* have devoted scarce investigative resources to covering the authorship story? Why?

## Middle-range Issues:

1. Since objectivity dictates that political journalists have to muzzle their opinions about candidates, is there ever an appropriate forum for expressing those views?
2. Will Klein be able to continue working as a credible political journalist? Analyze the question from the view of the readers, the candidates and Klein's new colleagues at *The New Yorker?*

3. Is political reporting's fascination with the "inside information"—a trend begun by Theodore H. White in his *Making of the President* series—responsible for much of the furor surrounding *Primary Colors?*

## Macro Issues:

1. Should readers (and other journalists) have realistically expected Klein's book to mimic an actual presidential campaign?
2. Compare *Primary Colors* with Robert Penn Warren's classic *All the King's Men,* a fictional account of the career of Huey Long. What questions about politics and political character do the books share? What does fiction allow an author to explore that traditional journalism does not?

# CHAPTER XI
## Becoming a Moral Adult

Most college undergraduates think of graduation as the completion of an educational process. They view it as an end to a 16-year effort, and the beginning of that scary time in life when their preliminary commitments to work, other people, and lifestyle will be tested in the "real world."

We suggest an alternate view, at least for ethical development. We'd like to suggest that your personal process of becoming an ethical person has now begun. Whether it has been through reading this book, taking a class in ethics, or making ethical choices in your life, what you understand about ethics now—and the choices you make—are a reflection of the person you are at this moment. The person you will be when you are 30 or 40 will have added insight. Growth may change your decisions. This process is not only inevitable but also desirable.

This chapter is designed to provide you with an overview of some psychological theories of moral development. It attempts to allow you to plot your own development not only in terms of where you are but also in terms of where you would like to be.

**By the end of the chapter you should:**

- **Know the stages of moral development as described by Piaget and Kohlberg.**
- **Understand the ethics of care.**
- **Understand the stages of adult moral development.**

## Basic Assumptions about Moral Development: The Rights-based Tradition

People can learn to develop morality just as they can learn to think critically (Clouse 1985). Scholars base this assertion on the following premises.

First, *moral development occurs within the individual.* Real moral development cannot be produced by outside factors, nor can it be produced merely by engaging in moral acts. People develop morally when they are aware of their reasons for acting a certain way.

Second, *moral development parallels intellectual development.* Although the two may proceed at a slightly different pace, there can be little moral development until a person has attained a certain intellectual capacity. For this reason, we exempt children and people of limited mental ability from some laws and societal expec-

tations. While one can be intelligent without being moral, the converse is not as likely.

Third, *moral development occurs in a series of universal, unvarying and hierarchical stages.* Each level builds on the lower levels, and there is no skipping of intermediate stages. Just as a baby crawls before walking and babbles before speaking, a child must pass through the earlier stages of moral development before advancing to the later stages.

Fourth, *moral development comes through conflict.* As moral development theorist Lawrence Kohlberg notes (1973, 13), "A fundamental reason why an individual moves from one stage to the next is because the latter stages solve problems and inconsistencies unsolvable at the present developmental stage."

The two developmental psychologists who are the most cited experts in the field did their work decades and continents apart yet came to remarkably similar conclusions. Jean Piaget conducted his research in Switzerland in the 1940s by watching little boys play marbles, and in the 1960s Lawrence Kohlberg studied Harvard students. Together they have produced many of the most provocative insights in the rights-based tradition. They are often called "stage theorists" for their work in identifying and describing the stages of moral development.

**TABLE 11.1     Piaget's Stages of Moral Development**

Piaget's moral development stages cleave along the following lines: source of authority, applicability of rules to all, internalization of rules.

**EARLY DEVELOPMENT** (before age 2)

• Interest in marbles is purely motor, i.e., put the marbles in your mouth.

**FIRST STAGE**—egocentrism (years 3–7)

• Children engage in "parallel play"; there is no coherent set of rules accepted by all.

• The moral reasoning is "I do it because it feels right."

**SECOND STAGE**—heteronomy (years 7–8)

• Children recognize only individual responsibility; obedience is enforced through punishment.

• Each player tries to win.

• Rules are regarded as inviolate, unbreakable, handed down from outside authority figures, usually older children.

• The children do not understand the reason behind the rules.

**THIRD STAGE**—autonomy (begins about age 11)

• Children internalize the rules; they understand the reasons behind them.

• They develop an ideal of justice and are able to distinguish between individual and collective responsibility.

• They ensure fair play among children.

• Children can change the rules in responses to a larger set of obligations.

• Authority is internal.

• Children understand universal ethical principles that transcend specific times and situations.

# The Work of Piaget

Swiss psychologist Jean Piaget turned his attention to children's moral development in the 1930s. He watched as boys between the ages of three to 12 played marbles and he later tested his assumptions about their playground behavior in interviews. Table 10.1 outlines the basics of Piaget's theory.

The youngest children under age seven didn't really play a game of marbles at all. They made up their own rules, varied them by playmate and game, and delighted in exploring the marbles as tactile objects. Their view of the game-playing universe was centered exclusively on what each individual child wanted.

Piaget found that younger boys (from 7 to 8) played marbles as if the rules had been taught to them by their parents or other authority figures and as if violations of those rules would result in punishment. The boys believed the rules were timeless and that "goodness" came from respecting the rules. Boys in this stage of moral development believed, "Right is to obey the will of the adult. Wrong is to have a will of one's own" (Piaget 1965, 193).

Children progressed to the next stage of moral development when the boys began to develop notions of autonomy. As they became more autonomous, the children began to understand that there was a reason behind the rules, and that the reasons (i.e., fair play and reciprocity) were the foundation of the rules themselves. Children in this stage of moral development understood that the rules did not originate from some outside authority figure but rather received their power from the group consensus because the rule itself promoted fair play and equality.

These children had internalized the rules and the reasons behind them. Understanding the rules allowed the boys to rationally justify violating them. For example, children in this stage of moral development allowed much younger children to place their thumbs inside the marble circles, a clear violation of the rules. But the younger boys' hands were smaller and weaker, and by allowing them a geographic advantage, the older ones had—in contemporary language—leveled the playing field. They had ensured fairness where literally following the rules would have made it impossible.

Although Piaget worked with children, it is possible to see that adults often demonstrate these stages of moral development.

Take the videographer whose primary motivation is to obtain a great shot, regardless of the views of those he works with or his story subjects. This journalist operates within an egocentric moral framework that places the primary emphasis on what "I" think, "my" judgment, and what's good for "me."

Beginning journalists, the ones who find themselves concerned with the literal following of codes of ethics, may often be concerned with the "heteronomy" stage of development. This journalist knows the rules and follows them. She would never accept a "freebie" or consider running the name of a rape victim. It's against organizational policy, and heteronomous individuals are motivated largely by outside influences.

Just as the boys at the highest stage of moral development were more willing to bend the rules to ensure a fair game for all, journalists at the final stage of moral development are more willing to violate professional norms if it results in better journalism. The journalist at this stage of moral development has so internalized and universalized the rules of ethical professional behavior that he or she can violate some of them for sound ethical reasons.

Proceeding with a story that is unpopular, expensive, or out-of-the-norm could be considered an example of journalism at the highest level of Piaget's schema. For instance, the Pulitzer prize-winning series by the *Des Moines Register* regarding the rape, recovery, and trial ordeal of a rape victim who volunteered to have her story told is an example of journalism that breaks the mold and goes far beyond the norm of stories of its type. Also indicative of this level of journalism is the painstakingly detailed series of articles written by two enterprising *Detroit Free Press* reporters who read volumes of the federal tax code and found it to be loaded with one-of-a-kind tax loopholes for individuals and businesses with political connections.

However, people seldom remain exclusively in a single stage of moral development. New situations often mean that people, including journalists and their sources, "regress" temporarily to a previous stage of moral development until enough learning can take place so that the new situation is well understood. But, such regression would not include behaviors that would be considered morally culpable under most circumstances, for example, lying or killing, despite the new context.

## The Work of Kohlberg

Harvard psychologist Lawrence Kohlberg mapped six stages of moral development in his college-student subjects. Table 10.2 outlines Kohlberg's stages of moral development, divided into three levels.

Kohlberg developed a lengthy set of interview questions to allow him to establish which stage of moral development individual students had achieved. He asserted that only a handful of people, for example, Socrates, Gandhi, Martin Luther King or Mother Teresa, ever achieved the sixth stage of moral development. Most adults, he believed, spend the greater portion of their lives in the two "conventional" stages. They are motivated by society's expectations.

Doing right, fulfilling one's duties, and abiding by the social contract are the pillars upon which the stages of Kohlberg's work rests. Under Kohlberg's arrangement, justice, and therefore morality, is a function of perception; as you develop, more activities fall under the realm of duty than before. For instance, reciprocity is not even a goal for students in the earliest stage, yet it is an essential characteristic of people in stage six. Conversely, acting to avoid punishment is laudable for those in the first stages yet might not be as praiseworthy for someone who is operating on universal ethical principles. The further up Kohlberg's stages students progressed, the more they asserted that moral principles are subject to interpretation by individuals and subject to contextual factors.

Kohlberg's stages are descriptive and not predictive. They do not anticipate how any one individual will develop, but suggest how most will develop. In addition, there is a difference in moral reasoning and moral behavior. They are correlated but not totally overlapping phenomena. Kohlberg focused not on the goodness of moral decisions, but the adequacy of the cognitive structures underlying them.

Kohlberg's formulation has much to recommend it to journalists, concerned as they are with concepts such as free speech, the professional duty to tell the truth, and their obligations to the public and the public trust. However, Kohlberg's work was not without its problems. At least two aspects of his research troubled other moral development theorists.

Many scholars have argued that any generalizable theory of moral development should allow people who are not saints or religious leaders to attain the highest

---

**TABLE 11.2    The Six Moral Stages of Kohlberg**

**Level 1: Pre-conventional**

**Stage 1: Heteronomous morality** is the display of simple obedience.

**Stage 2: Individualism** is the emergence of the self-interest. Rules are followed only when they are deemed to be in one's self-interest and others are allowed the same freedom. Reciprocity and fairness begin to emerge, but only in a pragmatic way.

**Level II: Conventional**

**Stage 3: Interpersonal conformity** is living up to what others expect, given one's rule: i.e., "brother," "daughter," "neighbor," etc. "Being good" is important and treating others as you would have them treat you becomes the norm.

**Stage 4: Social systems** is the recognition that one must fulfill the duties to which they have agreed. Doing one's duty, respect for authority, and maintaining the social order are all goals in this level. Laws are to be upheld unilaterally except in extreme cases where they conflict with other fixed social duties.

**Level III: Post-conventional**

**Stage 5: Social contract and individual rights** is becoming aware that one is obligated by whatever laws are agreed to by due process procedures. The social contract demands that we uphold the laws even if they are contrary to our best interests because they exist to provide the "greatest good for the greatest number." However, some values such as life and liberty stand above any majority opinion.

**Stage 6: Universal ethical principles** self-selected by each individual guide this person. These principles are to be followed even if laws violate those principles. The principles which guide this individual include the equality of human rights and respect for the dignity of humans as individual beings regardless of race, age, socioeconomic status or even contribution to society.

---

stages of moral development. While it has been argued that only saints can be expected to act in a saintly manner most of the time, history is replete with examples of ordinary people taking extraordinary personal or professional risk for some larger ethical principles. Many scholars felt that Kohlberg's conception—unlike Piaget's-was too restrictive.

Still more troubling was how those students who were tested on Kohlberg's scale performed. In study after study, men consistently scored higher than women on stages of moral development. This gender bias in Kohlberg's work—coupled with other findings from development psychology—prompted discussion about a different concept of moral development, founded on notions of community rather than in the rights-based tradition. It is called the ethics of care.

## Parallel Assumptions about Moral Development: The Ethics of Care

The psychologists who are developing the ethics of care disagree with at least two of the fundamental assumptions underlying Piaget and Kohlberg.

First, while moral development occurs within the individual and parallels intellectual development, moral development does not always occur in a series of universal, unvarying, and hierarchical stages.

Second, moral growth emerges through understanding the concept of community, not merely through conflict.

The rights-based scholars believe that moral development emerges from a proper understanding of the concept "I." Proponents of the ethics of care say that moral development arises from understanding the concept of "we."

Carol Gilligan's (1982) work provides the clearest explanation of the ethics of care. Gilligan studied women who were deciding whether to have abortions. As she listened to them, she learned that they based their ethical choices on relationships. The first thing these women considered was how to maintain a connection. She argued that the morally adult person needs to learn how to speak two languages—the language of rights and the language of responsibilities. The moral adult is the person who sees a connection, and is willing to maintain the connection between the "I" and the "other." The women spoke in a "different voice" about their ethical decision making.

For example, the psychologist presented the women with Kohlberg's classic ethical dilemma: the case of the desperate man and the greedy pharmacist. In this scenario, a man with a terminally ill spouse doesn't have enough money to purchase an expensive and life-saving drug. When he explains the situation to the pharmacist, the pharmacist refuses to give him the medication.

Under Kohlberg's system, it would be ethically allowable for the man to steal the drug. However, women made this particular choice less often. Instead, they reasoned that the most ethical thing to do was to build a relationship with the pharmacist—to form a community in which the pharmacist viewed him/herself as an active part. In that situation, the women reasoned, the pharmacist ultimately would give the man the drug in order to maintain the connection.

Gilligan proposed that the women's rationale was no more or less ethically sophisticated than that expected under Kohlberg's outline. However, it was different, for it weighed different ethical values. Whether those values emerged as the result of how women are socialized in Western culture (an assertion that has often been made about Gilligan's work) or whether they merely reflected a different kind of thinking still remains the focus of heated academic debate. But, for our purposes, the origin of the distinction—and whether it is truly gender-linked—is not as important as the content of the thought itself.

Gilligan's notion of moral development is not neatly tied into stages and does not borrow as heavily from the tradition of logic and rights-based inquiry. Her closest theoretical counterpart is probably communitarianism with its emphasis on connection to community and its mandate for social justice.

If one were to carve stages from Gilligan's work, they would resemble:

- **First**—an ethic of care where the moral responsibility is for care of others before self;
- **Second**—an acknowledgement of the ethic of rights, including the rights of self to be considered in ethical decision making.

- **Third**—a movement from concerns about goodness (women are taught to believe that care for others is "good" while men are taught that "taking care of oneself" is good) to concerns about truth. It is at this stage of moral development where commitment to a universal ethical principle begins, with truth at the core of that universal principle.

A complete sense of moral development, Gilligan observed, requires the ability ". . . to (use) two different moral languages, the language of rights that protects separations and the language of responsibilities that sustains connection" (Gilligan 1982, 210).

Contemporary journalists have struggled with the issues of connection. Since much of our profession is based on an understanding of rights as outlined in various legal documents, ethical reasoning for journalists almost always assumes a rights-based approach. This historically well-founded bias, however, has led journalists into some of their more systematic and profound errors in decisions about privacy, attitudes of arrogance towards sources and readers, and an unwillingness to be genuinely accountable to anyone.

News organizations can work to sustain community. A good example is found in the "We the People, Wisconsin" civic journalism experiment in Wisconsin. A combined effort of the (Madison) *Wisconsin State Journal,* Wisconsin Public Television, Wisconsin Public Radio, Wood Communications Group and WISC-TV3, the project invited citizens to participate in the democratic process in a variety of non-traditional ways. Conceived during the 1992 presidential campaign, the project is credited as the longest continually running civic journalism initiative. Its first major event was a March 1992 debate between presidential primary contenders Bill Clinton and Jerry Brown. The production, though undermined by cancellations and technical challenges, won a regional Emmy, and a movement was born.

In the years since it began, more thousands of Wisconsin voters have been a part of "We the People, Wisconsin" town hall meetings with candidates, including one forum where candidates for the state Supreme Court argued their cases for election in a forum entitled "You Be the Judge." Thousands more have called in to talk shows held before or after the meetings or read the in-depth coverage of the issues that mattered most to the voters.

The estimated cost of the project in the first four years is about $425,000, with $265,000 of that being raised by Wood Communications Group, a public relations and marketing firm.

Dale Iverson, executive producer for Wisconsin Public Television and the moderator of the electronic meetings says of the project: "You know we're all familiar with the phrase 'photo op journalism.' Sometimes I've thought of this as 'citizen's op journalism.' That if you give the people the chance, the opportunity to be citizens, they take it" (Schaffer and Miller 1995, 18).

If journalism as a profession is to mature ethically, it must see itself as the vehicle to help people become the citizens they can be and to help reconnect and sustain communities that have become increasingly fragmented, often by the very media that should have brought us together. In an essay entitled "Whose Values," written in the wake of the L.A. riots following the Rodney King verdict, *Newsweek* author Joe Klein wrote:

> Television brought the nation together in the '50s; there were evenings when all of America seemed glued to the same show—Milton Berle, "I Love Lucy" and yes, "Ozzie and Harriet." But cable television has quite the opposite effect, dividing the audience into demographic slivers . . . Indeed, if you are a member of any identifiable subgroup—black, Korean, fundamentalist, sports fan, political junkie—it's now possible to be massaged by your very own television and radio stations and to read your own magazines without having to venture out into the American mainstream. The choices are exhilarating, but also alienating. The basic principle is centrifugal: market segmentation targets those qualities that distinguish people from each other rather than emphasizing the things we have in common. It is the developed world's equivalent of the retribalization taking place in Eastern Europe, Africa and Asia. (Klein 1992, 21–22)

If there is one common denominator from the vast variety of projects that claim to fall under the "civic journalism" umbrella in the late 1990s, it is the fact that almost all of them have as a goal to bring people back together and foster a sense of community using the media as a primary tool in the process. To that end, the movement is a laudable one.

## Where Do You Go from Here?

Perry (1970) postulates that one of the major accomplishments of college students is to progress from a simple, dualistic (right vs. wrong) view of life to a more complex, mature and relativistic view. Perry states that students must not only acknowledge that diversity and uncertainty exist in a world of relativism but must also make a commitment to their choices (i.e., career, values, beliefs, etc.) out of the multiplicity of "right" choices available. And ethical choices abound in mass media careers. For instance, even the daily routine of setting the news agenda is an ethical issue since those decisions are often made by Caucasian males for others who are unlike them in significant ways. Even word choice is an ethical issue. Why do we see stories about "working mothers," yet none about "working fathers?"

Unlike physical development, moral development is not subject to the quirks of heredity. Each individual is free to develop as keen a sense of equity as any other individual, yet few reach their full potential. In your attempts to "grow" ethically, Kohlberg (1968) has offered one observation: we tend to understand messages one stage higher than our own moral judgment stage. Through "aspirational listening," that is, picking an ethical role model on a higher level and observing that person, you can progress to a higher stage of moral development. This observation is not a new one. In fact, it dates to Aristotle, who suggested that virtues could be learned by observing those who possess them.

This book uses the case study method so that you may see ethical decisions that were made at higher and lower levels of moral reasoning and aspire to the former. Often in case studies, it is the reasoning behind the answer rather than the answer itself that is the best determiner of moral growth (Clouse 1985). *An important part of moral development is the recognition that motive, not consequence, is the critical factor in deciding whether an act is ethical.*

Elliott (1991) illustrates the difference in the following scenario. Imagine a situation where you were able to interview and choose your next-door neighbor. When you ask Jones how she feels about murder, she replies she doesn't kill because, if she got caught, she would go to jail. When you interview Smith, he says he doesn't kill people because he believes in the sanctity of life. It takes little reflection to decide which neighbor you would prefer. Elliott concludes:

> Ethics involves the judging of actions as right or wrong, but motivations count as well. Some reasons for actions seem better or worse than others. (p. 19)

In the prior illustration of the pharmacist, Stage Two and Stage Six individuals of the Kohlberg taxonomy might condemn the man who stole the drug, but for very different reasons. And it is in those differences that true moral development lies.

## Suggested Readings

Belenky, Mary F., et al. 1988. *Women's ways of knowing: The development of self, voice and mind.* New York: Basic Books.

Coles, Robert. 1986. *The moral life of children.* New York: Atlantic Monthly Press.

Gilligan, Carol. 1982. *In a different voice: Psychological theory and women's development.* Cambridge, MA: Harvard University Press.

Levinson, Daniel J. 1978. *Seasons of a man's life,* New York: Alfred A. Knopf, Inc.

# APPENDIX A

## Thinking about Ethics with Film
LEE WILKINS
*University of Missouri—Columbia*

The mass media have provided a forum of thoughtful comment about ethics in general and media ethics in particular through film. The fact that most of these titles are available on videotape gives you ready access to a wealth of thought-provoking dramas to illustrate the problems of media ethics. The following list will provide you with a starting point for learning and thinking about ethics, using film as a tool.

*Roshamon.* Although it isn't edited at the standard American pace of frantic, this classic film provides the viewer with a profoundly aesthetic discussion of truth and point of view.

*Gandhi.* A fine portrait of individual moral development, particularly if Gandhi himself does not become the focus of all of the discussion.

*The Killing Fields.* This film raises a number of important ethical issues, among them how much can a journalist ask a colleague to risk to cover a story, Western reporting on Eastern cultures, and the role of the American mass media in creating a global community.

*Absence of Malice.* It's hard to match Sally Field and Paul Newman for a good discussion of reportorial relationships, both in and out of the newsroom.

*The Year of Living Dangerously.* At the core of this film is the question of conflict of interest, particularly where political and military secrets are at issue.

*The Front Page.* Whether you prefer the thirties' original or the seventies' remake, Hildy Johnson is a good example of a bad example of the scoop mentality.

*Reckless Disregard.* This film is loosely based on the lawsuit between Carl Galloway and "60 Minutes," where the issues are ambush journalism and the ethics of video editing.

*Under Fire.* Can a journalist get so involved in a story that he or she alters the events being covered? A photojournalist in El Salvador confronts this question in an otherwise slow-paced movie with an impressive cast.

*The Mean Season.* Police reporters who become caught up in what they cover are common, and this film frames a discussion of issues surrounding objectivity and personal involvement.

*The Dead Pool.* Clint Eastwood would make the day of any journalism ethics professor with his treatment of the media in this otherwise violent and predictable film.

*The Candidate.* While the film itself indulges in some indiscriminate bashing of the American electoral process, it does include a good critique of horse-race political journalism.

*Sophie's Choice.* An agonizing study of the sins of omission as well as those of commission.

*To Kill a Mockingbird.* Even children can learn to make complicated ethical choices about issues such as racial injustice, loyalty and benevolence. While this superb film is not quite as good as the novel it's based on, it is a delightful portrait of how people can grow as ethical beings.

*The Right Stuff.* The film version of this Tom Wolfe best-seller includes episodes of pack journalism and celebrity journalism at their worst.

*The Lost Honor of Katherine Blum.* Invasion of privacy entwined with the political issues surrounding media coverage of terrorism make this film thought provoking. Get the German version and not the American remake.

*All the King's Men.* Everything's here, including some good insights into American history and some better insights into the relationship between politicians and their PR persons.

*The Front.* Woody Allen stars in this view of the McCarthy era and of the politics of art.

*Word of Honor.* This little-known film takes a sensitive look at a journalist who makes a promise and then must go to great lengths to keep it.

*The Deer Hunter.* This film has been the focus of much debate about the impact of violence in film. But on a more subtle level, it provides a penetrating look at individual moral development.

*The China Syndrome.* Jane Fonda's on-screen portrayal of Brenda Starr raises some important questions surrounding media coverage of technology and crisis.

*Broadcast News.* It's a wonderful film that raises several questions, including what constitutes journalistic training, what is allowable in video editing, and to what extent corporate profits interfere with the newsroom.

*All the President's Men.* There's the good guys (the fellows from the *Washington Post*) and the bad buys (the folks from the White House) trying to balance journalistic means and political ends.

*Witness.* This film, which featured a terrific performance by Harrison Ford, has been criticized for its less-than-accurate portrayal of the Amish. Just how far should entertainment alter a way of life for the sake of a good story?

*Network.* What happens when entertainment and news collide? Besides a bevy of Oscar-nominated performances, you'll discover a satirical answer that cuts entirely too close to the bone. It's the dark side of *Broadcast News.*

*A Cry in the Dark.* The issue here is trial by media. Meryl Streep plays a mother whose child was either murdered or carried off by a dingo, an Australian wild dog. Only the Australian press seems to know which.

*Roger and Me.* Made on a shoestring budget in 1989 by a self-taught, first-time filmmaker, this documentary made virtually every top-ten list with its simple message of corporate responsibility. PR majors should consider the message to corporate America. Journalism students should ponder how the media missed this story. Film students will want to argue over how close to truth a documentary must stick.

*The Public Eye.* This 1940s-style film focuses on photojournalism and a journalist, played by Joe Pesci, who believes that "everyone wants to have their picture taken." The "everyone" includes corpses, the critically ill, the grief-stricken, and Pesci's acquaintances and friends. Although ethics receives a broad-brush treatment, the film exposes the seamier side of photojournalism.

*Hero.* While this film, starring Dustin Hoffman, was a box office flop, the ethical issues it raises are both subtle and richly treated. On one level, the film is a commentary on news as narrative—and what can go wrong with a predictable script. On a second level, the screenplay is an essay on the relationship between virtue ethics and common humanity.

*Sneakers.* There has been a spate of techno-thrillers on the market in the past few years, but none is as well plotted as this film which links money, computers and communication. If you want to think about information as bytes, and control as who has access to the most sophisticated computers and programs, this film raises all the appropriate malevolent questions.

*Cry Freedom.* This story of a Caucasian editor's attempt to tell the world about South African leader Steven Biko documents some of the events leading to the profound changes in South Africa in the early 1990s. While the subtext is racism, students can also learn of the government-imposed restrictions that continue to face journalists in the developing world.

*Natural Born Killers.* As only Oliver Stone can, this film fuses media coverage of violence and celebrity and the real world events surrounding those questions. The film is violent, the content has been electronically molded to the point of artificial reality, and Stone's penchant for conspiracy theories flavors the plot as well as the cinematography. Nonetheless, the film provides an acid commentary on the blur between news and entertainment, particularly when people seek the limelight through violent acts.

*The Net.* Although not as thoughtful about the link between information and power as *Sneakers, The Net* provides a hyped-up vision of the downside of cyber-based community. Current technology does not make it possible to completely alter a person's "on paper" identity the way Sandra Bullock's character is altered in the film, but the sense of invasion of privacy and personal loss that is the emotional core of the film is a real ethical problem even though cyberspace remains in its infancy.

*Rising Sun.* The film version of the xenophobic Michael Crichton novel focuses on the power of altering electronic images while downplaying the more serious issues—the link between economic power and information control. The film provides a wonderful primer on what it is now possible to do with images, a computer and malicious intent.

*Quiz Show.* Probably the most thoughtful film in decades about the mass media as economic entities, director Robert Redford leaves the audience to ponder the fundamental question of the 1990s. If lies are told, and people destroyed, but the industry itself continues to make money, is anyone really going to care enough to change institutional behavior?

*The American President.* The story of a mass-mediated President who falls in love with an environmental lobbyist can serve as a thoughtful entre into the core of questions surrounding the private lives of very public people.

*Schindler's List.* President Bill Clinton said that everyone in America should see this film. As horror piles on horror, director Steven Spielberg never loses sight of the humanity of all involved.

*Up Close and Personal.* All the big ideas about broadcast journalism—how you get a job in the business, the roles of anchors, reporters and producers, etc.—are wrong in this film starring Robert Redford and Michelle Pfeiffer. But the subtle stuff is disturbingly right—how broadcast reporters and editors frame a news story, how the "star" syndrome and ratings drive broadcast news, and how a significant number of network employees are deciding to remain at the local level for both professional and personal reasons. It's the small picture within the larger picture that's worth examining.

*Courage under Fire.* It's been called the *Roshamon* of the 1990s, offering multiple versions of a friendly fire incident set in the Persian Gulf War. What is truth, what is lie, and what dies with the soldiers in the field are among the film's central questions. The feminist subtext adds some important insights into military life.

# APPENDIX B

## Novel Ideas about Ethics
STEVE WEINBERG
*University of Missouri—Columbia*

The following is a list of novels with journalists as protagonists who face ethical dilemmas in the course of the plot. They are selected from a collection of nearly one thousand journalism novels owned by the author.

*The Fly on the Wall* by Tony Hillerman. Statehouse reporter John Cotton must decide whether to become personally involved with a government bureaucrat who might hold the key to a contracting scandal that has already cost one snoopy reporter his life.

*Images* by Cara Saylor Polk. Ambitious television newswoman Marlena Williams has to decide whether it's legitimate to get big stories in a horizontal position.

*Dirty Laundry* by Pete Hamill. Cynical journalist Sam Briscoe wonders whether he can perform the best possible investigation when the murder victim is his former lover.

*Fellow Travelers* by Alex Beam. Novice Moscow correspondent Nick Perkins has to wonder about his objectivity as he falls in love with the vast country he is supposed to cover for his magazine.

*Floater* by Calvin Trillin. A jack-of-all-trades at a news magazine fools readers with his alleged omniscience as part of his job description.

*The Circus Master's Mission* by Joel Brinkley. White House correspondent Christopher Eaton battles his heart as an affair with a national security official embroils him in a dangerous international story.

*The Evening News* by Arthur Hailey. Network news anchor Crawford Sloane tries to figure out how to report the news fairly when the number-one story is the kidnapping of his family by terrorists.

*The White Hand* by Jean Warmbold. Magazine writer Sarah Calloway will lie and cheat and steal and sleep with sources to get a story. Once in a while, she even has minor qualms about her techniques.

*The Almighty* by Irving Wallace. Publisher Edward Armstead tries to determine how far he can go in manipulating news events so that his newspaper is out front.

*Changes* by Danielle Steel. Network anchorwoman Melanie Adams tries to balance career and home when she falls in love with a source who wants her to move to his city across the country.

*Hot Type* by Kristy Daniels. Newspaper reporter Troy Satterly tests the limits as she strives for the top rung in scandal journalism.

*Episode* by Richard Pollak. Investigation reporter Daniel Cooper wonders about the limits of working a murder story when he is the prime suspect.

# APPENDIX C

## From the Past: Historical Glimpses of Media Ethics

SUSAN WILLEY
*University of Missouri*

Media ethics has more than just philosophical history. It has a professional heritage as well. Compiled below are capsule summaries of a few of the more significant events in the history of media ethics. While some are referred to in the text, we include them because we believe it's important to students to understand our professional history so we don't repeat our professional mistakes.

## John Peter Zenger and the Case for Truth

In the early days of this country, the press operated much differently. Published tracts expressed strong partisan political opinions. Often reports focused on exposing the evil deeds of the government, or as writers of the time put it: "publick wickedness." In 1735, New York printer John Peter Zenger wrote several hard-hitting stories exposing the corruption in the Royal government party. He was soon jailed and brought to trial on the charge of seditious libel. The jury found him not guilty, believing that what he wrote was, in fact, true.

The case established a legal precedent—that truth is a defense against libel. It also shows the long-standing tension between government and the press. By 1768, the printers and publishers began printing numerous criticisms of British authority. One historian noted that the early press' efforts to reveal secret information shows how "revolutionary ideology was translated into a language ordinary citizens could use to make sense out of daily events." The work of these early journalists at "watching" the government soon became incorporated as part of the journalistic mission—the "watchdog" function of the press and led to the development of today's investigative journalism.

*From* Protess, David, et al. 1991. *Journalism of outrage: Investigative reporting and agenda building in America.* New York: Guilford Press, pp. 30–31.

## Thomas Jefferson and the Press

Despite his staunch defense of a free press, Thomas Jefferson was not exempt from scurrilous attacks from editors. Although most journalists remember his famous quotation: "Were it left to me to decide whether we should have a government without newspapers, or newspapers without government, I should not hesitate a moment to prefer the latter," his frustration with news reports intensified during his presidency. The partisan press frequently engaged in political print battles, mounting vicious attacks on political opponents. Once such war occurred between the *Jeffersonian Bee* and the *Federalist Wasp,* two newspapers in Hudson, N.Y.

In 1804, the *Wasp* published a story attacking Jefferson for having paid "the notorious scandalmonger James Thomson Callender," the editor of the *Richmond Examiner,* to deliberately write lies about George Washington, calling him "a traitor, robber and a perjurer." The *Wasp* editor was charged and convicted of libel. Appealing the case was lawyer Alexander Hamilton, Jefferson's arch rival. At this trial Hamilton argued that newspapers have the right to publish the truth, and that truth alone is a defense against libel. Despite his historic speech, Hamilton lost the case.

Although Jefferson admitted he had helped Callender financially, he said it was only from a sense of charity not from any service rendered. Callender, however, wasn't quite so charitable. Years later, after Jefferson refused to name Callender postmaster of Richmond, Callender responded viciously, initiating a series of scandalous attacks upon his former benefactor. The editor accused Jefferson of keeping "a black harem" at Monticello and of fathering several children from "a black wench." Today, some scholars believe that Callender invented the entire story.

This kind of press freedom took its toll on Jefferson who, during his second term in office wrote: "The man who never looks into a newspaper is better informed than he who reads them: inasmuch as he who knows nothing is nearer to truth than he whose mind is filled with falsehood and errors."

*From* Daniels, Jonathan. 1965. *They will be heard: America's crusading newspaper editors.* New York: McGraw-Hill, pp. 62–67.

*Also* Edwin, Emery, and Michael Emery. 1978. *The press and America: An interpretative history of the mass media.* 4th ed. Englewood Cliffs, NJ: Prentice-Hall, p. 87.

*Also* Bates, Stephen. 1985. *If no news, send rumors.* New York: St. Martin's Press, p. 180.

## "Spinning" the War between the States

When the Civil War began, the country's press was strong and flourishing. The war that divided the nation also split journalists and newspapers. The Civil War sparked high emotions. Never before had the country waged battles within the nation itself. In this time of uncertainty, President Abraham Lincoln and his Secretary of War Edwin M. Stanton decided they needed to control information and clamp down on the press. The military censorship was widespread in the North, especially after the administration discovered that Southern generals were reading Northern newspapers to obtain military strategy information.

From the president's and Stanton's perspectives, the danger to national security justified the efforts to suppress information. By 1862, Lincoln received Congressional approval to grant military supervision of all telegraph material that mentioned the war. The military also instituted newsgathering requirements—reporters' accreditation, for example—that remain in effect today.

Editors advised their audience about the tactics used by the military to interfere with the flow of news. Stanton created a system by which his staff monitored all Associated Press reports and made sure that important newspapers received exclusive war reports in exchange for favorable coverage. During the course of the war, Lincoln's administration shut down about 300 Northern newspapers for varying lengths of time. Numerous war correspondents and editors at influential papers in New York, Baltimore, Chicago and other locations were arrested.

In one incident two New York papers published a story fabricated by war correspondents. Stanton immediately called for the arrest and imprisonment of everyone involved including unsuspecting editors and telegraph operators, some of whom had no idea that report had been false. One media history scholar wrote that "Lincoln's legacy became a legacy of all-out war censorship." The information control methods used by Stanton became a foundation for techniques still used by the military today during times of national crisis.

*From* Emery, Edwin, and Michael Emery. 1978. The press and America: An interpretative history of the mass media, 4th edition. Englewood Cliffs, NJ: Prentice-Hall, pp. 160–178

## Horace Greeley and the Power of the Publisher

Horace Greeley founded the *New York Tribune* in 1841, but he wasn't satisfied with being only a journalist. He wanted to be a politician, too. By the time the Civil War began, Greeley found himself increasingly frustrated by the current administration's policies. He didn't like President Lincoln's leadership and was severely critical of him in his editorials. So far so good. That's journalism. But then Greeley took his political interest a step further and, on his own, approached the French government about trying to intervene to mediate an end to the war. When the war finally ended, Greeley continued to try his hand at politics while serving as publisher. In 1872, when he ran for the presidency against Republican Ulysses S. Grant, he did take a leave of absence from the newspaper, but was still criticized. One newspaper called his candidacy "a crime in journalism."

*From* Sieb, Philip. 1995. *Campaigns and conscience: The ethics of political journalism.* Westport, CT: Praeger, pp. 30–31.
*Also* Black, Jay, Bob Steele, and Ralph Barney. 1993. *Doing ethics in journalism.* Greencastle, IN: The Sigma Delta Chi Foundation and The Society of Professional Journalists, pp. 60–64.

## Yellow Journalism

The formidable newspaper publishers William Randolph Hearst of the *New York Journal* and Joseph Pulitzer of the *New York World* were often engaged in circulation "wars." These battles helped birth what is called the "yellow journalism" era of the late 1880s. These reports were characterized by sensationalism, exaggeration and flamboyant writing created specifically to stir up excitement and draw readership. In 1898, the *U.S. Maine* battleship exploded in Havana Harbor. The cause was unknown and the Spanish apologized. Soon after, Hearst began a campaign. He wanted a war, and with the power of the press behind him, he got one. He won public support by publishing stories and headlines designed to incite and inflame readers to pressure Congress to act. When Congress finally did declare war, Hearst's newspaper headline said it all: "How Do You Like the *Journal's* War?" it asked readers. About 400 Americans died and 3,700 were wounded in this brief episode in history. Hearst's biographer said the war coverage "still stands as the acme of ruthless, truthless newspaper jingoism."

*From* Sieb, Philip. 1995. *Campaigns and conscience: The ethics of political journalism.* Westport, CT: Praeger, pp. 11–12.

## Nellie Bly and the Journalism of Deception

News woman Elizabeth Cochrane, better known as Nellie Bly, was thrust into newspaper history with her first story assignment for the *New York World* in the midst of the yellow journalism heydays. In 1887, she devised an elaborate ruse to feign insanity in order to get herself committed to Blackwell's Island, an infamous asylum for the insane. Her mission was to remain undercover long enough to observe and experience the abuses thought to be rampant within the institution. The resulting stories not only drew great readership for Joseph Pulitzer's paper, but propelled Bly into a celebrity. Soon after, she wrote a best-selling book on her experience called *Ten Days in the Madhouse.*

It was the first of many of Bly's exploits marked by her use of deception to get the story. The issue of deceiving to get information remains a central one in journalism. In 1975, the *Chicago Sun Times* was denied a Pulitzer prize for the deception it used in setting up a phony bar—the Mirage Bar scam—to discover whether city officials were on the take.

*From* Kroeger, Brooke. 1994. *Nellie Bly.* New York: Random House, pp. 85–99.

## The "Muckrakers"

President Theodore Roosevelt first used the term "muckraker" in an April 14, 1906, speech at the laying of the cornerstone of the New House of Representatives Office Building. In using the term to describe journalists of the time, he was referring to a character out of John Bunyan's 1678 work *Pilgrim's Progress* in which Bunyan described the "man with the muckrake," who could look only downward toward the filth on the floor. Roosevelt decried journalists who focused on "only on that which is vile and debasing." Journalists such as Jacob Riis, Lincoln Steffens and Upton Sinclair "raked the filth" of the times, exposing the plight of the poor immigrants in New York and the outrageous working conditions of the meatpackers in Chicago. Their reports revealed injustices and prompted change.

    Politicians, such as Roosevelt, agreed that reform measures were needed, but they also heavily criticized the press for its sensationalized reports. The muckraking led to continued discussions about whether the press needs to be licensed or whether journalists can police themselves.

*From* Goldstein, Tom, ed. 1989. *Killing the messenger: 100 years of media criticism.* New York: Columbia University Press, p. 55.
*Also* Protess, David, et al. 1991. *Journalism of outrage: Investigative reporting and agenda building in America.* New York: Guilford Press, pp. 36–37.

## World War I and the Birth of Propaganda

The great propaganda campaigns of the World War I era were among the first times government used the media for personal gain. Journalists responded to President Woodrow Wilson's plea to support for America's entrance into the war by helping mobilize public opinion to support the war effort. Propaganda was rampant in Europe. The Committee for Public Information was created to handle this call to action, and many journalists became involved in this information effort to sway public opinion toward support of America's involvement. In fact, the CPI's wartime activities later led to the first generation of professional publicists.

    There was one problem. When the war ended, the propaganda did not. Media critics began to worry about the power of the media's message, especially if it were "tainted at the source." Media critic Walter Lippmann charged that "modern journalism put national interest ahead of the truth." The fear of propaganda also brought forth one of the first proposals for a national study on the media's newsgathering methods and the influence of propaganda. And, it was during the 1920s that Lippmann wrote his classic book *Public Opinion,* as a response to the media's role in public opinion formation in World War I.

*From* Marzolf, Marion Tuttle. 1991. *Civilizing voices: American press criticism 1880–1950.* New York, Longman, pp. 106–116.

## Press Coverage of the Russian Revolution

Can skeptical journalists be taken in by sources to the extent that reports present a skewered picture of reality? On August 4, 1920, press critics Walter Lippmann and Charles Merz published an article in The New Republic charging the New York Times with doing just that—misleading the public through biased and incomplete reporting. The two critics examined the newspaper's coverage of the Russian Revolution from March 1917 to March 1920. They concluded that the coverage failed to reveal Russia's military weaknesses and the reports in fact indicated the opposite— that the Russian Army was successfully quelling the revolutionary attacks. This Russian-favored optimistic reporting did nothing for the advance of truth-telling. The reporters continued to emphasize good-news reports when the Russians had a victory and de-emphasized—or omitted altogether—reports of the incredible successes of the revolutionaries.

The authors contended that journalists compromised their ethics and duty to tell the truth by pursuing favorable Russian sources during dinners and social gatherings and then assuring them of anonymity so no one could check them out. At the gatherings, journalists were spoon-fed heavy doses of propaganda favoring the Russians' cause.

*From* Goldstein, Tom, ed. 1989. *Killing the messenger: 100 years of media criticism.* "A test of the news," by Walter Lippmann and Charles Merz. New York: Columbia University, pp. 86–106.

## The Teapot Dome Scandal

*Denver Post* owners Frederick G. Bonfils and Harry E. Tammen were notorious for their sensationalized news reports from the time they purchased the newspaper in 1895. They not only pursued reckless yellow journalism tactics, they also were greedy. One writer called Bonfils "the stingiest, most grasping, and most unscrupulous blackmailer who ever worked the West." By the 1920s, the publishers were in full power, but their insatiable greed would be their downfall.

In 1923, the American Society of Newspaper Editors (ASNE) was formed. It adopted the "Canons of Journalism" to promote journalistic standards of truth-telling, fair play, accuracy and impartiality. A year later, Bonfils would come under full attack from the ASNE for accepting nearly $1 million in bribes from private oil companies. The Teapot Dome was a government-owned oil reserve field in Wyoming, but secret leases were being made to private oil companies through bribes given to Secretary of the Interior Albert B. Fall.

Instead of exposing this corruption, Bonfils wanted a part of the action. In exchange for money, Bonfils suppressed all the information from his reporters and refused to publish anything about the conspiracy. The situation not only became a national scandal, but also threw the ASNE into a dilemma of ethical standards enforcement. The membership demanded that Bonfils be punished for his actions. After five years of debating the issue, and under the threat of a lawsuit from Bonfils, the ASNE voted instead to only ask for voluntary compliance to the code rather than requiring disciplinary actions. In the late 1990s, journalists continue to debate whether enforcement of ethical code violations should include sanctions.

*From* Werner, M. R., and John Starr. 1959. *Teapot Dome.* New York: Viking.

## The Press and a Twentieth-Century American Hero

The press has always been fascinated with society's heroes, and certainly this was the case with Charles Lindbergh, Jr., the first man to fly solo across the Atlantic Ocean. Despite his attempts to maintain his privacy when he married, the press hounded him. While on his honeymoon, reporters followed him and his bride, renting boats and circling the Lindbergh's anchored vessel for more than eight hours trying to get a photo of the couple. One tabloid called Lindbergh "a Grade A celebrity" thereby making him a "public commodity" with little or no privacy rights. Reporters gathered at his home, and some attempted to bribe the servants to betray any secrets of the household. When his infant son was kidnapped, the press went wild. A Chicago lawyer called the reporters "an army of enthusiastic ghouls." Lindbergh blamed the press and its unceasing focus on him and his family for causing the kidnapping and murder of his son.

The press' unrelenting invasion of Lindbergh's privacy helped spur the adoption of canon 6 of the code adopted by the American Society of Newspaper Editors: "A newspaper should not invade private rights or feelings without sure warrant of public right as distinguished from public curiosity."

*From* Goldstein, Tom, ed. 1989. *Killing the messenger: 100 years of media criticism.* "The press and the individual," by George Seldes. New York; Columbia University Press.

## Triumph of the Will

Leni Riefenstahl was a German filmmaker who wanted nothing more than to produce quality artistic films. But in the Spring of 1934, Adolph Hitler ordered her to produce a documentary film of the growing power of the Third Reich. Riefenstahl at first declined, wanting to work on her own projects. Hitler finally convinced her to make the film, giving her some artistic independence and a promise—one that would not be kept—that she would not be ordered to make any more such films. Riefenstahl produced the film *Triumph of the Will.* The film brought her accolades for artistic depiction but condemnation for its lack of morality and its blatant propagandistic message.

The highly charged emotional film shows massive Nazi rallies promoting Hitler and the German people as the master race. Nowhere in the film is it mentioned that the Third Reich was killing millions of Jews. One critic said the film "represents the complete transformation of reality." She was arrested by the Allied Forces after the war but was eventually cleared of political charges by 1952. Some critics argue that Riefenstahl's political understandings were naive. Others charged her with moral degeneracy. In either case, after *Triumph of the Will,* she was never again recognized as a filmmaker. Her real penalty was in public shame and ostracism, forever to be known as the filmmaker who glorified Hitler.

*From* Barsam, Richard Meran. 1975. *Film guide to* Triumph of the Will. Bloomington, IN: Indiana University Press.

## McCarthyism and the Media

The 1950s are sometimes viewed with nostalgia, but the decade was also one of paranoia and propaganda. Republican Senator Joseph McCarthy saw communism as America's greatest threat and nearly everyone as a communist suspect. The "Cold War" with the Soviet Union created a feeling of public insecurity, and when McCarthy began charging that communists had infiltrated high government agencies, the nation panicked. The U.S. Senate held the "McCarthy hearings"—in which everyone from Hollywood actors to government officials were grilled about their possible communist-related activities. People were black-listed. Jobs were lost, reputations ruined, fear and fanaticism reigned.

Journalism fed the furor. During the 1950s, journalism was bound by its creed of objectivity. Daily, the presses churned out pages of stories about potential communist activities, and they printed the names cited by McCarthy in open Senate hearings. One senator observed that "the American style of objective journalism made McCarthy." By 1953, however, some editors became concerned. They had discovered that being objective does not necessarily mean being fair and truthful. McCarthy was eventually censured by the Senate. Journalism had changed. The tenet of journalistic "objectivity" was now questioned as an attainable or valued, reporting goal.

*From* Protess, David, et al. 1991. *Journalism of outrage: Investigative reporting and agenda building in America.* New York: Guilford Press, pp. 45–46.

*Also* Jamieson, Kathleen Hall, and Karlyn Kohrs Campbell. 1992. The interplay of influence: News, advertising, politics and the mass media. 3d ed. Belmont, CA: Wadsworth Inc., p. 57.

## Edward R. Murrow, the Conscience of Broadcast Journalism

Edward R. Murrow was one of the best-known television commentators in the 1950s. Both the public and his peers trusted him. Journalism historians call Murrow "the conscience of broadcast journalists."

In 1951, Murrow brought his "See It Now" radio show to television. This hard news program broke new ground and firmly established Murrow as an honest and sincere reporter. During the McCarthyism era, Murrow stood for a voice of reason as other journalists fed the fires of the "Red Scare" and Sen. Joseph McCarthy's paranoid crusade against communists. Despite political pressure on CBS, Murrow continued to fight against McCarthy and, in a March 1954 broadcast, charged the senator with exploiting the fears of the people for his own advantage. Critics called his program brilliant, saying it was the most imaginative and courageous show on television.

Yet, to the dismay of viewers and critics alike, the program was cancelled by CBS in 1958. In 1960, Murrow narrated his most famous and one of the most acclaimed television broadcasts, "Harvest of Shame," which showed the plight of the nation's migrant workers. One critic said the film was advocacy journalism at its best. But by this time Murrow was becoming disillusioned with television, the ratings' game and the focus on profits. He resigned as a broadcaster in 1961 to become director of the U.S. Information Agency under President John F. Kennedy where he stayed until illness forced him to resign two years later.

*From* Emery, Edwin, and Michael Emery. 1978. *The press and America: An inter-pretative history of the mass media.* 4th ed. Englewood Cliffs, NJ: Prentice-Hall, pp. 403–408.

*Also* Sperber, A.M. 1986. *Murrow: His life and times,* 4th ed. New York: Freundlich Books.

## The Quiz Show Scandals

When a New York City police officer won $16,000 on the television quiz show "The $64,000 Question" in 1955, more than 45 million television sets were tuned in. And when Columbia University professor Charles Van Doren—squeezing his eyes tightly shut and biting his fingers in deep concentration—attempted to answer a question on the quiz show "Twenty-One," millions of television viewers were on the edge of their seats. The popular program prompted a television critic to write that "a nation breathed each breath with Charles."

The son of a Pulitzer prize-winning poet, Van Doren was thought to be the smartest man in the world. He was on the cover of *Time* as "the wizard of quiz" and became a national idol, a press personality and a model for school children. The television quiz shows of the 1950s differed in style, but had one commonality: they were all crooked. Quiz show producers picked and chose who they wanted to win or lose and fed the winners the correct answers.

Van Doren's knuckle-biting was just an act, and his answers fraudulent. When producers found a popular contestant that brought in millions of viewers and ad revenue, they quietly paid the loser off and focused on coaching the new "winner." But one loser was angry at having to give up his winner slot to Van Doren and blew the lid on what is now known as the quiz show scandals. In a press interview, losing contestant Herb Stemple charged the producers with collusion and fraud, eventually launching a Congressional inquiry. The quiz show fraud struck at the heart of the nation and the people's trust. The scandals, as one critic wrote, were "a betrayal of truth for the sake of wealth and power."

*From* Karp, Walter. 1989, May/June. "The quiz show scandals." *American heritage,* pp. 77–88.

## The Sam Sheppard Trial

Journalists in the 1950s pegged the murder trial of Sam Sheppard as the "trial of the century." It gained such national attention that Hollywood produced a long-running series based on the case—"The Fugitive." Dr. Sheppard, a surgeon, was arrested for the bludgeoning death of his pregnant wife at their home in a Cleveland suburb. From the beginning, Sheppard proclaimed his innocence saying that the murderer was an intruder he had grappled with as he tried to escape.

The Cleveland newspapers pushed for Sheppard's arrest in bold front-page editorials and in headlines that said "Why isn't Sam Sheppard in jail?" The reports were biased against Sheppard and, when he testified at a coroner's inquest at a school gymnasium, the live broadcast turned into a melee. Crowds of reporters, photographers and citizens greeted Sheppard at the police station when he was arrested. The newspapers ran cartoons mocking Sheppard and printed unsubstantiated stories about how his wife lived in fear of him.

The trial was no different. Reporters crowded the courtroom. The newspaper printed the names of all the jurors, all but one of whom had read all of the newspaper stories. The jury was not sequestered until it began deliberations and more than 40 photos of the jurors appeared in the Cleveland newspapers. One juror even took some time out from the deliberations to satisfy a photographer's request to pose for a picture. Despite his continuous protests of innocence, Sheppard was convicted of the murder in October of 1954 and given a life sentence.

After spending more than 10 years in prison, Sheppard's family hired criminal lawyer F. Lee Bailey who was successful in challenging the conviction. The U.S. Supreme Court decided that, because of the press publicity, Sheppard had been denied the right to a fair trial. One justice wrote that the sensationalized press coverage created "a carnival atmosphere." As a result of the decision, Sheppard received a new trial where he was acquitted.

*From* Watkins, John J. 1990. *The mass media and the law.* Englewood Cliffs, NJ: Prentice-Hall, pp. 269–270
*Also* McCarty, James F. 1996, February 23. "Son's new evidence in Sheppard case is put before judge." *The Cleveland plain dealer,* p. 1A.

## Media Cooperation in the Bay of Pigs Invasion

When President John F. Kennedy called the *New York Times,* that day in 1961, he urged the editors not to publish the information they had compiled about the CIA's planned Bay of Pigs Cuba invasion. Kennedy cited national security reasons. The *Times* editors agreed and omitted certain elements from the story. Yet, after the fiasco of a failed invasion, the president changed his mind and told the newspaper that, had they printed the information, they might have saved the nation a "colossal blunder." Had the newspaper fulfilled its basic obligation of telling the truth the president might have gained insight from public opinion and history may have been changed. Compare the Bay of Pigs case with CNN's live coverage of the 1990-91 Persian Gulf War.

*From* Goldstein, Tom, ed. 1989. *Killing the messenger: 100 years of media criticism.* "National security and the Bay of Pigs invasion" by Clifton Daniel. New York; Columbia University, pp. 107–115.

## *United Church of Christ* v. *FCC*

In the 1960s the Reverend Everett Parker, a Mississippi minister, became concerned about what he was seeing on two statewide television stations. Not only were blacks underrepresented, but news about blacks and the emerging Civil Rights movement was distorted or omitted altogether. In 1964, Parker gathered 28 residents of Tougaloo, Mississippi at the local United Church of Christ. There they were trained in television monitoring techniques. They analyzed one week's programs aired by Jackson, Mississippi stations WLBT and WJTV, whose licenses were up for a three-year renewal by the FCC (Federal Communications Commission).

Under the leadership of the Office of Communications for the United Church of Christ, the citizens found solid evidence of racial discrimination in all areas of the broadcasts. The FCC, however, said citizen groups had no right of standing to pursue the issue. Parker was incensed. He said the ruling meant that citizens "are being told they had nothing to say about the allocation of a national public resource—a public communications channel . . ." The ruling essentially permitted the television stations to ignore responsibility to nearly half the population of the state.

The church filed an appeal, and in a 1966 landmark decision, then U.S. Court of Appeals Justice Warren Earl Burger ordered that the citizens' advocacy group had a right of standing, with a "genuine and legitimate interest" as a listening audience. the United Church of Christ decision remains a watershed event in public-interest communications efforts.

*From* Brotman, Stuart N.1986, March 31. "Keeping the public involved in broadcast licensing." *The national law journal,* p. 13.

## The Media and the 1960s Race Riots

Historians agree that the 1960s was a decade of turbulence and controversy. One of the issues was race relations. During that long, hot summer of 1967 riots broke out in urban ghettos across the country. The news coverage of those riots, or "civil disorders" as they were officially termed, was controversial. President Lyndon B. Johnson convened a special commission to investigate and analyze the media's performance. The Commission on Civil Disorders (Kerner Commission) concluded that, despite some inaccuracies, the media had generally made an effort to provide "a balanced, factual account" of the riots. However, the commission stated that the media's portrayal of violence was "an exaggeration of both mood and event."

The most damning finding against the media was in its failure to adequately report on "the causes and consequences" of the riots and the "underlying problem of race relations." The Kerner Commission noted that the media failed to devote sufficient resources to covering urban ghetto areas and it also failed to seek out, hire and train African-American journalists. This absence of the black perspective and voice within the media affected the overall coverage.

*From* Goldstein, Tom, ed. 1989. *Killing the messenger: 100 years of media criticism.* "The role of the mass media in reporting of news about minorities," by Commission on Civil Disorders. New York: Columbia University, pp. 200–227.

# The Pentagon Papers

In 1971, Daniel Ellsberg, a Defense Department consultant, leaked a copy of highly classified Defense Department documents on the history of the Vietnam War to a *New York Times* reporter. By March, the newspaper began its series on "The Pentagon Papers." The reports showed that government officials had lied to the American public about the war, and soon President Richard Nixon's administration obtained a court order prohibiting the *Times* from publishing any further installments. By June, the U.S. Supreme Court lifted the gag order, but by that time other newspapers across the country had taken up the story.

In addition to taking legal action against Ellsberg, Nixon created a special unit within the White House, a secret surveillance team called "The Plumbers." This group burglarized Ellsberg's office searching for information to discredit him. Later, the Plumbers would be responsible for a break-in of the Democratic National Committee headquarters at the Watergate Hotel in Washington, D.C., an action that would lead to further investigation and eventually to Nixon's resignation as president.

*From* Protess, David, et al. 1991. *Journalism of outrage: Investigative reporting and agenda building in America.* New York: Guilford Press, pp. 49–50.

# New Journalism

The "new journalism" of writers such as Thomas Wolfe and Norman Mailer in the twentieth century merged reporting techniques with strong narrative form and the use of dialogue. New journalism propelled non-traditional journalists to change their writing style from the traditional "inverted pyramid" arrangement to narrative and "storytelling." Yet some critics believe that Wolfe and others embarked upon a dangerous ethical game when they wove "factual" news items with fictional, storytelling devices. This hybrid, critics say, is neither truth nor fiction, but something in-between. In his 1980 article in *Yale Review*, critic John Hersey said, "There is one sacred rule of journalism. The writer must not invent. The legend on the license must read: NONE OF THIS WAS MADE UP." Consider the case of journalist Janet Malcolm, who fabricated a quotation for an article in *The New Yorker* and was later sued for libel. Although she admitted falsifying a specific quotation, a jury found in her favor saying there was no reckless disregard for truth.

*From* Goldstein, Tom, ed. 1989. *Killing the messenger: 100 years of media criticism.* "The legend on the license," by John Hersey. New York: Columbia University, pp. 247–267.
*Also Time,* November 14, 1994, p. 39.

# Checkbook Journalism

In the 1970s, after Richard Nixon became the first American president to resign from office, a CBS news executive had what he thought was a great idea. He wanted to try to schedule an interview with one of Nixon's top aides, H. R. Haldeman. Televising an interview with someone who had been one of the most powerful staff members of the Nixon presidency would have been a powerful scoop. Haldeman was known for his great disdain of the press, but after his conviction for his part in the Watergate cover-up, he unexpectedly agreed to be interviewed. There was a condition. He wanted to be paid. CBS agreed and paid him $100,000 drawing severe criticism from other journalists, who thought the practice unethical. Nine years later, bowing to competition pressures, CBS paid $500,000 to Nixon for an exclusive interview.

*From* Day, Louis A. 1991. *Ethics in media communications: Cases and controversies.* Belmont, CA: Wadsworth, Inc., p. 160.

# Daniel Schorr and the CIA Papers

CBS correspondent Daniel Schorr got an early taste of political involvement in 1971 when he discovered he was being investigated by the FBI allegedly because he was supposed to be under consideration for a sensitive government position. In fact, there was no such job. The facts were revealed during the Watergate hearings. President Richard M. Nixon had become enraged at Schorr's report that criticized him and charged him with lying about issues for political gain.

Ironically, a few years later Schorr would himself come under fire for lying. As a 20-year news veteran, Schorr had established himself as a notable journalist. In 1976, after obtaining a secret House intelligence report on the CIA's actions during the Vietnam War, Schorr declined on reporting some of the information on his CBS news program. The government then decided not to release the report, and Schorr determined he had the only copy. He wanted to get the report published, but CBS subsidiaries were not interested. Schorr approached the Reporters Committee for Freedom of the Press, which connected him with the *Village Voice,* which agreed to publish the report.

There were no monetary rewards for Schorr. Instead, a substantial payment was to be made to the Reporters Committee for Freedom of the Press. Schorr's name was to be kept confidential in the transaction. The problem came when Schorr lied about his actions. A *Washington Post* reporter asked Schorr if he was the source and Schorr not only denied it, but indicated that coworker Lesley Stahl was the source. Stahl threatened to sue and CBS was furious at what they believed was Schorr's unauthorized use of network property. Schorr was suspended from CBS and later resigned. When Schorr was subpoenaed before the House Ethics Committee and questioned about how he obtained the document in the first place, he refused to betray his source saying "to betray a source would be to betray myself, my career and my life."

*From* Lambeth, Edmund B. 1992. *Committed journalism: An ethic for the profession.* 2d ed. Bloomington: Indiana University Press, pp. 132–137.

*Also* Bates, Stephen. 1985. *If no news, send rumors.* New York: St. Martin's Press, pp. 166, 225–226.

# The Girls in the Balcony

In May of 1972, a meeting was held in the 14th floor boardroom of the *New York Times*. Female employees had asked for the meeting to discuss the great disparity between male and female employees in wages, promotions, assignments and representation. The women were charging the *Times*' management with blatant gender discrimination in all phases of its operation. The meeting created a tidal wave of resentment, anger and resolve that swept through the paper and resulted in numerous complaints filed two years later with the Equal Employment Opportunity Commission.

Despite solid documentation that the *Times* was discriminating against its female employees, management dug in its heels and refused to make any but token concessions to address the women's complaints. The newspaper increased its hiring of women, but refused to take action on the major grievances such as salary inequities and promotions. Statistical experts found that women at the *Times* earned $3,725 a year less than men who had similar educational credentials and similar seniority.

A class action lawsuit was filed. For four years, while the newspaper executives battled privately with the women who had filed, they publicly promoted the paper's anti-discrimination stance. By the fall of 1978, tension was thick as those involved with *Boylan* v. the *New York Times* prepared for trial. Instead, lawyers reached a settlement agreement that gave the women less than $1,000 each. In addition, the newspaper agreed to a court-monitored affirmative action plan.

The monetary award was disappointing and the *Times* made certain that the settlement's language noted that the newspaper did not admit to any discrimination employment practices. The settlement and affirmative action plan was unprecedented at the time. The lawsuit opened many editors' eyes to the disparate treatment and forced the newspaper to begin addressing the discrimination. It also paved the way for many women reporters, giving them an opportunity to show their abilities.

*From* Robertson, Nan. 1992. *The girls in the balcony.* New York: Random House.

## The Press and the Watergate Break-in

The June 1972 burglary of the Democratic National Committee headquarters at the Watergate Hotel in Washington, D.C. at first received little press interest. Police arrested five men as they attempted to plant listening devices in the Democratic chairman's office. But a reporter at the *Washington Post* published a story the next day that connected one of the burglars to the United States Central Intelligence Agency (CIA). For a time, the *Post* reporters were the only journalists who saw a deeper story, but soon more and more newspapers began their own investigations into what is now known as "Watergate." Competition helped keep the Watergate story alive.

Although President Richard Nixon gained a landslide reelection victory in 1972, the public and Congress soon began to lose confidence in his denial of wrongdoing in the Watergate affair. Under intense pressure, Nixon became the first American president to resign from office. Today, the term "Watergate" is synonymous for government officials' misdeeds and covert actions. While the media was a critical force in revealing the president's unscrupulous actions, some trace the erosion of public confidence in their government to this time in history and say it also marked the beginning of the people's mistrust of journalists. Critics complained that, bolstered by the success of Watergate, reporters became more aggressive, more elitist, less concerned with ethics and responsibility toward the citizens.

*From* Protess, David, et al. 1991. *Journalism of outrage: Investigative reporting and agenda building in America.* New York: Guilford Press, pp. 50–52.

## Listerine and the FTC

In 1977, after nearly 100 years of making deceptive claims, Listerine mouthwash was challenged in court by the FTC (Federal Trade Commission), and it lost. Contrary to its popular advertisements, the mouthwash *did not* prevent the common cold or sore throats, and the court ruled it was deceiving the public to claim so. The court upheld the FTC's requirement that, for the next $10 million in ads, Listerine had to include a corrective advertising stating that it, in fact, *did not* prevent colds or sore throats. Corrective advertising, one of the most severe of the FTC penalties is sometimes called the "scarlet letter" penalty, since the advertiser has to publicly proclaim its "sin" of lying in its future ads. Advertisers can skirt around the deception issue by making unbelievable claims such as the lonely Maytag repairman or by more subtle methods. Claims that a product is "really fine," "ultra soft," or "most beautiful" are subjective statements that are difficult to prove false or true.

*From* Jamieson, Kathleen Hall, and Karlyn Kohrs Campbell. 1992. *The interplay of influence: News, advertising, politics and the mass media.* 3d ed. Belmont, CA: Wadsworth, Inc.

## Janet Cooke and "Jimmy's World"

In 1981, Janet Cooke proposed a story to her editors at the *Washington Post.* She had heard of a seven-year-old heroin addict that she would write a feature about to talk about the larger issue of the pervasiveness of drugs in the poor neighborhoods of Washington, D.C. Given several weeks to work on the story, Cooke wrote an excellent tale. Unfortunately, it was precisely that, a tale. During the research period she had been unable to find the child and decided to simply make him up in an article entitled "Jimmy's World."

Cooke's deception began to unravel when the article won a Pulitzer prize and reporters began searching into Cooke's background and into the story she had written. What they found was a young woman who had lied about her education and experience to get her job at the *Post,* and furthermore, there was no Jimmy. The Pulitzer was returned, Cooke was fired, and the entire profession of journalism suffered a national embarrassment.

Many questioned how the *Post*'s editors could have allowed the hoax to get into print without Cooke being forced to tell an editor the location of the alleged boy. "*Post* editors simply failed to do their job," said Lee Hills, former chairman of Knight-Ridder. "They trusted a gifted liar; a kid from Ohio who had even faked her background to get her job only nine months before. Everyone in our profession was injured because it gave ammunition to critics who want the press controlled."

*From* Fink, Conrad. 1988. *Media ethics: In the newsroom and beyond.* New York: McGraw-Hill, pp. 70–71.

# BIBLIOGRAPHY

Alderman, E., and C. Kennedy. 1995. *The right to privacy.* New York: Alfred A. Knopf, Inc.

Anthan, G. 1990, February 25. "Farm column." The Gannett News Service.

Arendt, H. 1970. *The human condition.* Chicago: University of Chicago Press.

Aristotle. *The Nicomachean ethics.*

Axelrod, R. 1984. *The evolution of cooperation.* New York: Basic Books.

Bad Apple. 1989, May. *Consumer reports,* pp. 288–291.

Bagdikian, B. H. 1987. *The media monopoly.* 2d ed. Boston: Beacon Press.

———. 1990. *The media monopoly.* 3d ed. Boston: Beacon Press.

Barsam, R. M. 1975. *Film Guide to* Triumph of the Will. Bloomington, IN: Indiana University Press.

Beasley, M. H., and R. R. Harlow. 1988. *The new majority: A look at what the preponderance of women in journalism education means to the schools and to the professions.* Lanham, MD: University Press of America.

Beck, M. 1989, March 27. "Warning! Your food, nutritious and delicious, may be hazardous to your health." *Newsweek,* pp. 16–19.

Begley, S., and M. Hagar. 1989, January 30. "Dangers in the vegetable patch." *Newsweek,* pp. 74–75.

Bennett, L. 1988. *News: The politics of illusion.* Longman: New York.

Bentley, R. 1986, August 4. "Lessons sought from tragic events." *Bakersfield Californian,* p. 15.

Berger, J. 1980. *About looking.* New York: Pantheon Books.

Black, J., B. Steele, and R. Barney. 1993. *Doing ethics in journalism.* Greencastle, IN: The Sigma Delta Chi Foundation and The Society of Professional Journalists.

Bok, S. 1978. *Lying: Moral choice in public and private life.* New York: Random House.

———. 1983. *Secrets: On the ethics of concealment and revelation.* New York: Vintage.

Boorstin, D. 1962. *The image.* New York: Antheneum.

Bovée, W. 1991. "The end can justify the means—but rarely." *Journal of mass media ethics,* 6, pp. 135–145.

Braun, S. 1994, November 2. "Tuning out the hype and gore." *Los Angeles Times,* p. 1.

Brooks, D. E. 1992. "In their own words: Advertisers and the origins of the African-American consumer market." A paper submitted to the Association for Education in Journalism and Mass Communications, Montreal, Canada, August 5–8.

Brotman, S. N. 1986. March 31. "Keeping the public involved in broadcast licensing." *The national law journal*, p. 13.

Bryant, G. 1987, Spring-Summer. "Ten-fifty p.i.: Emotion and the photographer's role." *Journal of mass media ethics*, pp. 32–39.

Carey, J. W. 1989, Autumn. Review of Charles J. Sykes' "Profscam." *Journalism educator*, p. 48.

Carlson, M. 1989, March 27. "Do you dare to eat a peach?" *Time*, pp. 24–27.

Cassier, E. 1944. *An essay on man*. New Haven, CN: Yale University Press.

Christians, C. 1986. "Reporting and the oppressed." In *Responsible journalism*. D. Elliott. ed. Newbury Park, CA: Sage Publications, Inc., pp. 109–130.

Christians, C. G., J. P. Ferré, and M. Fackler, 1995. *Good news: Social ethics and the press*. New York: Longman.

Christians, C., J. Ferré, and M. Fackler. 1992. *A social ethics of news*. New York: Oxford University Press.

Christians, C., K. Rotzoll, and M. Fackler. 1987. *Media ethics: Cases and moral reasoning*. 2d ed. New York: Longman.

Clouse, B. 1985. *Moral development*. Grand Rapids, MI: Baker Book House

Coleman, A. D. 1987, Spring/Summer. "Private lives, public places: Street photography ethics." *Journal of mass media ethics*, pp. 60–66.

Commission on Civil Disorders. 1989. "The role of the mass media in reporting of news about minorities." In *Killing the messenger: 100 years of media criticism*. Tom Goldstein, ed. New York: Columbia University.

Cousins, N. 1974. *The celebration of life: A dialogue on immortality and infinity*. New York: Harper and Row.

Crouse, T. 1974. *The boys on the bus: Riding with the campaign press corps*. New York: Ballantine.

Daniel, C. 1989. "National security and the Bay of Pigs invasion." In *Killing the messenger: 100 years of media criticism*. Tom Goldstein, ed. New York: Columbia University.

Daniels, J. 1965. *They will be heard: America's crusading newspaper editors*. New York: McGraw-Hill.

Dates, J. L. 1990. "Advertising." in *Split image: African Americans in the mass media*. Jannette L. Dates and William Barlow, eds. Washington, D.C.: Howard University Press.

Davies, J. C. 1963. *Human nature in politics*. New York: John Wiley & Sons.

Day, L. A. 1991. *Ethics in media communications: Cases and controversies*. Belmont, CA: Wadsworth, Inc.

Deford, F. 1992, April 20. "Arthur Ashe's secret." *Newsweek*, pp. 31–32.

Dionne, E. J. 1991. *Why Americans hate politics*. New York: Simon & Schuster.

Eisenberg, E. M. 1984, September. "Ambiguity as strategy in organizational communication." *Communication monographs*, 51, pp. 227–242.

Elliott, D. 1986. "Foundations for news media responsibility." In *Responsible journalism,* ed. by D. Elliott. Newbury Park, CA: Sage Publications, Inc., pp. 32–44.

———. D. 1991, Autumn. "Moral development and the teaching of ethics." *Journalism educator,* pp. 19–24.

Ellul, J. 1965. *Propaganda.* Trans. by K. Kellen and J. Lerner. New York: Alfred A. Knopf.

Emery, E., and M. Emery. 1978. *The press and America: An interpretative history of the mass media.* 4th ed. Englewood Cliffs, NJ: Prentice-Hall.

Epstein, E. J. 1974. *News from nowhere.* New York: Random House.

Etzioni, A. 1993. *The spirit of community.* New York: Crown Publishers, Inc.

Fallows, J. 1996. *Breaking the news: How the media undermine American democracy.* New York: Pantheon.

Fenton, D. 1989, October 3. Personal conversation with the author."

Fink, C. 1988. *Media ethics: In the newsroom and beyond.* New York: McGraw-Hill.

Fischer, C. T. 1980. "Privacy and human development." In *Privacy: A vanishing value?* William C. Bier, ed. New York: Fordham University Press, pp. 37–46.

Fitzgerald, M. 1995, November 11. "Decrying public journalism." *Editor and publisher,* p. 20.

Fletcher, G. P. 1993. *Loyalty: An essay on the morality of relationships.* New York: Oxford University Press.

Fore, W. F. 1987. *Television and religion.* New York: Augsburg Publishing House.

Fry, D., ed. 1983. *The adversary press: A modern media institute ethics seminar.* St. Petersburg, FL: The Poynter Institute.

Fuss, P. 1965. *The moral philosophy of Josiah Royce.* Cambridge, MA: Harvard University Press.

Gans, H. 1979. *Deciding what's news: A study of CBS evening news, NBC nightly news, Newsweek and Time.* New York: Vintage.

Gerbner, G. 1987, Summer-Fall. "Television: Modern mythmaker." *Media and values,* pp. 8–9.

Gert, B. 1988. *Morality, a new justification of the moral rules.* New York: Oxford University Press.

Gilligan, C. 1977. "In a different voice: Women's conceptions of self and morality." *Harvard educational review,* 47, pp. 492–505.

———. 1982. *In a different voice: Psychological theory and women's development.* Cambridge, MA: Harvard University Press.

Godwin, M. 1995. "The shoddy article." JournoPorn on *HotWired* (Online). Available: World Wide Web

http://www.hotwired.com/special/pornscare/

Goffman, E. 1959. *The presentation of self in everyday life.* New York: Anchor.

Goldstein, T., ed. 1989. *Killing the messenger: 100 years of media criticism.* New York: Columbia University Press.

Goodman, E. 1991, March 2. "To libel lettuce." Syndicated column.

Gormley, D. W. 1984. "Compassion is a tough word." *Drawing the line,* pp. 58–59. Washington, D.C.: American Society of Newspaper Editors.

Grcic, J. M. 1986. "The right to privacy: Behavior as property." *Journal of values inquiry,* 20, pp. 137–144.

Gross, L., J. S. Katz, and J. Ruby, eds. 1988. *Image ethics: The moral rights of subjects in photographs, film and television.* New York: Oxford University Press.

Haddix, D. 1990, March/April. "Alar as a media event." *Columbia journalism review,* pp. 44–45.

Haiman, F. 1958. "Democratic ethics and the hidden persuaders." *Quarterly journal of speech,* 44, pp. 385–392.

Hanson, K. 1986. "The demands of loyalty." *Idealistic studies,* 16, pp. 195–204.

Heaton, T. 1994, June 20. "Family sensitive news debate a wake-up call." *Electronic Media,* p. 8.

Henry, W. H., III. 1994. *In defense of elitism.* New York: Anchor Books.

Hersey, J. 1989. "The legend on the license." In *Killing the messenger: 100 years of media criticism.* Tom Goldstein, ed. New York: Columbia University.

Hersh, S. 1991. *The Samson option: Israel's nuclear arsenal and American foreign policy.* New York: Random House.

Hess, S. 1981. *The Washington reporters.* Washington, D.C.: The Brookings Institution.

Heston, C. 1992, August 17. "Just a song?" *National review,* pp. 37, 53.

Hixson, R. F. 1987. *Privacy in a public society.* New York: Oxford University Press.

Hobbes, T. 1958. *Leviathan.* Reprints from 1651. New York: Bobbs-Merrill.

Hodges, L. W. 1983. "The journalist and privacy." *Social responsibility: Journalism, law, medicine,* 9, pp. 5–19.

————. 1986."Defining press responsibility: A functional approach." In *Responsible journalism,* D. Elliott, ed. Newbury Park, CA: Sage Publications, Inc., pp. 13–31.

Honaker, C. 1978, March. "Why your news releases aren't working." *Public relations journal,* pp. 16–19.

"How a PR firm executed the Alar scare." 1989, October 3. *Wall Street journal,* p. 9.

Hoyt, M. 1990, March-April. "When the walls come tumbling down." *Columbia journalism review,* pp. 35–40.

Jamieson, K. H. 1992. *Dirty politics.* New York: Oxford University Press.

Jamieson, K. H., and K. K. Campbell. 1983. *The interplay of influence.* Belmont, CA: Wadsworth.

————. 1992. *The interplay of influence: News, advertising, politics and the mass media.* 3d ed. Belmont, CA: Wadsworth, Inc.

Johannesen, R. L. 1990. *Ethics in communication.* Prospect Heights, IL: Waveland Press.

Joy, D. M. 1983. *Moral development foundations.* Nashville: Abingdon Press.

Junas, L. 1980, February 23. "Tragedy and violence photos dominate in news prizes." *Editor and publisher,* p. 17.

Kaid, L. L. 1992. "Ethical dimensions of political advertising." In *Ethical dimensions of political communication.* Robert E. Denton, ed. New York: Praeger, pp. 145–169.

Kant, I. 1785. *Groundwork on the metaphysics of morals.*

Karp, W. 1989, May/June. "The quiz show scandals." *American Heritage,* pp. 77–88.

Kessler, L. 1989. "Women's magazines' coverage of smoking-related health coverage." *Journalism quarterly,* 66, pp. 316–22, 445.

Klein, J. 1992, June 8. "Whose values?" *Newsweek,* pp. 19–22.

Kline, D. 1995, July 21. *"Time* magazine's bogus cyberporn cover and censorship." *San Francisco examiner,* p. A-21 (Online). Available: Nexus "Cyberporn and *Time* magazine."

Kohlberg, L. 1968, September. "The child as a moral philosopher." *Psychology today,* pp. 25–30.

———. 1973. "The contribution of developmental psychology to education." *Educational psychologist, 10,* pp. 2–14.

Kroeger, B. 1994. *Nellie Bly.* New York: Random House.

Kurtz, H. 1990, March/April. "Dr. Whelan's media operation." *Columbia journalism review,* pp. 43–47.

———. 1994. "Crime doesn't play: Family sensitive news program tone down coverage of violence." *Washington Post,* p. B1.

Lafayette, J. 1995, February 13. "Family sensitive news dips in ratings." *Electronic media,* p. 1.

Lambeth, E. B. 1986. *Committed journalism.* Bloomington,IN: Indiana University Press.

———. 1992. *Committed journalism: An ethic for the profession.* 2d ed. Bloomington, IN: Indiana University Press.

Lasch, C. 1979. *The culture of narcissism.* New York: Warner Books.

Lebacqz, K. 1985. *Professional ethics: Power and paradox.* Nashville: Abingdon Press.

Leiss, W., S. Kline, and S. Jhally. 1986. *Social communication in advertising: Person, products and images of well being.* New York: Methuen Publications.

Lester, P. M. 1992. *Photojournalism: An ethical approach.* Hillsdale, NJ: Lawrence Erlbaum and Associates.

Lester, P. M. 1996. *Images that injure.* Westport, CT: Greenwood Press.

Linsky, M. 1986. I*mpact: How the press affects federal policymaking.* New York: W. W. Norton.

Lippmann, W. 1922. *Public opinion.* New York: Free Press.

———. 1982. *The essential Lippmann.* Cambridge, MA: Harvard University Press.

Lippmann, W., and C. Merz. 1989. "A test of the news." In *Killing the messenger: 100 years of media criticism.* Tom Goldstein, ed. New York: Columbia University.

Long, E. V. 1995, July 3. "To our readers." *Time,* p. 4.

Lowery, S., and M. DeFleur. 1988. *Milestones in mass communication research.* 2d ed. New York: Longman.

Madison, J., A. Hamilton, and J. Jay. *The Federalist papers.*

Malcomb, J. 1989. "Reflections: The journalist and the murderer." *The New Yorker,* pp. 38–73.

Mander, J. 1979. "Four arguments for the elimination of advertising." In *Advertising and the public.* K. Rotzoll., ed. Urbana-Champaign: University of Illinois Dept. of Advertising, pp. 17–28.

Martin, E. 1991. "On photographic manipulation." *Journal of mass media ethics, 6,* pp. 156–163.

Marzolf, M. T. 1991. *Civilizing voices: American press criticism 1880–1950.* New York: Longman.

Matsuda, M. 1989. "Public response to racist speech: Considering the victim's story." *Michigan law review, 87,* pp. 2321–2381.

McCarty, J. F. 1996, February 23. "Son's new evidence in Sheppard case is put before the judge." *The Cleveland plain dealer,* p. 1A.

Medved, M. 1992. *Hollywood vs. America.* New York: HarperCollins.

Meislen, A. 1994, December 14. "Blunting TV new's sharp edges." *New York Times,* p. 20.

Merrill, J. C. 1974. *The imperative of freedom: A philosophy of journalistic autonomy.* New York: Hastings House.

Merritt, Davis. 1995. *Public journalism and public life.* Hillsdale, NJ: Lawrence Erlbaum Associates.

Meyrowitz, J. 1985. *No sense of place: The impact of electronic media on social behavior.* New York: Oxford University Press.

Mill, J. S. 1859. *On liberty.*

———. 1861. *Utilitarianism.*

Miller, E. D. 1994. *The Charlotte Project: Helping citizens take back democracy.* The Poynter Papers: No. 4. St. Petersburg, FL: The Poynter Institute.

Miller, K. 1992, December. "Smoking up a storm: Public relations and advertising in the construction of the cigarette problem, 1953–1954." *Journalism monographs, 136.*

Mills, C. W. 1956. *The power elite.* New York: Oxford University Press.

Mills, K. 1989, Winter. "When women talk to women." *Media and values, 12.*

Molotch, H., and M. Lester. 1974. "News as purposive behavior: On the strategic use of routine events, accidents and scandals. *American sociological review, 39,* pp. 101–112.

Mitchell, W. J. T. 1995. *Picture theory.* Chicago: University of Chicago Press.

Montgomery, K. C. 1989. *Target: Prime time. Advocacy groups and the struggle over entertainment television.* New York: Oxford University Press.

Moore, G. F. 1903. *Principia ethica.*

Moyers, B. 1988. "Quoted in 'The promise of television,' episode 10." Produced by PBS.

National Association of Broadcasters 1985. *Radio: In search of excellence.* Washington, D.C.: NAB.

Nelkin, D. 1987. *Selling science: How the press covers science and technology.* New York: W. H. Freeman.

Neville, R. C. 1980. "Various meanings of privacy: A philosophical analysis." In *Privacy: A vanishing value?* William C. Bier, ed. New York: Fordham University Press, pp. 26–36.

Newsom, D. 1993. *This is PR.* Belmont, CA: Wadsworth.

Nimmo, D., and J. Combs. 1985. *Nightly horrors: Crisis coverage in television network news.* Knoxville, TN: University of Tennessee Press.

O'Toole, J. 1985. *The trouble with advertising.* New York: Times Books.

Oldenquist, A. 1982. "Loyalties." *Journal of philosophy, 79,* pp. 73–93.

Olsen, Jack. 1985. *Give a boy a gun.* New York: Delacorte.

Oran, D. 1975. *Law dictionary for non-lawyers.* St. Paul, MN: West Publishing Co., pp. 330–331.

Palmer, E. L., and A. Door, eds. 1980. *Children and the faces of television: Teaching, violence, selling.* New York: Academic Press.

Patterson, P., and L. Wilkins. 1991. *Media ethics: Issues and cases.* Dubuque, IA: Wm C. Brown Publishers.

Patterson, T. E. 1980. *The mass media election.* New York: Praeger.

Patterson, T. E., and R. D. McClure. 1972. *The unseeing eye.* New York: G. P. Putnam's Sons.

Perry, W. O. 1968. *Intellectual development in the college years: A scheme.* New York: Holt, Rinehart and Winston.

Piaget, J. 1965. *The moral judgement of the child.* Translated by Marjorie Gabain. New York: Free Press.

Plato. *The republic.*

Postman, N. 1986. *Amusing ourselves to death: Public discourse in the age of television.* New York: Penguin Books.

Powell, T. F. 1967. *Josiah Royce.* New York: Washington Square Press, Inc.

Protess, D., et al. 1991. *Journalism of outrage: Investigative reporting and agenda building in America.* New York: Guilford Press.

Rainville, R., and E. McCormick. 1977. "Extent of covert racial prejudice in pro football announcer's speech." *Journalism quarterly, 54,* pp. 20–26.

Rather, D. 1987, March 10. "From Murrow to mediocrity?" *New York times,* Sec. I, p. 27.

Rawls, J. 1971. *A theory of justice.* Cambridge, MA: Harvard University Press.

Reaves, S. 1987, Spring-Summer. "Digital retouching: Is there a place for it in newspaper photography?" *Journal of mass media ethics,* pp. 40–48.

———. 1991. Personal correspondence to the author quoted in "Digital alteration of photographs in consumer magazines." *Journal of mass media ethics, 6,* pp. 175–181.

Rieder, R. 1996, July/August. "The admiral and the 'V' clips." *American journalism review,* p. 6.

Robertson, N. 1992. *The girls in the balcony.* New York: Random House.

Robinson, M., and G. Sheehan. 1984. *Over the wire and on TV.* New York: Basic Books.

Rogers, E. M., and S. B. Chang. 1991. "Media coverage of technology issues:

Ethiopian drought of 1984, AIDS, *Challenger* and Chernobyl." In *Risky business: Communicating issues of science, risk and public policy.* Lee Wilkins and Philip Patterson, eds. Westport, CT: Greenwood Press, pp. 75–96.

Rosen, J. 1995. "What should we be doing?" *The IRE (Investigative Reporters and Editors) Journal, 18,* pp. 6–8.

Rosenthal, A. M. 1989, October 10. "Trash TV's latest news show continues credibility erosion." Syndicated column by *New York Times* News Service.

Ross, W. D. 1930. *The right and the good.* Oxford, England: Clarendon Press.

Rothmeyer, K. 1991, September/October. "The media and the recession." *Columbia journalism review.* pp. 23–28.

Royce, J. 1908. *The philosophy of loyalty.* New York: The Macmillan Co.

Russell, B., ed. 1967. *History of Western philosophy.* New York: Touchstone Books.

Sabato, L. J. 1992. *Feeding frenzy: How attack journalism has transformed American politics.* New York: Free Press.

Safer, M. 1992, January 30. "Keynote address at the annual Alfred I. DuPont—Columbia University Awards ceremony."

Sandel, M.J. 1982. *Liberalism and the limits of justice.* Cambridge, MA: Harvard University Press.

Sanders, M., and M. Rock. 1988. *Waiting for prime time: The women of television news.* Urbana: University of Illinois Press.

Schaffer, J., and E. D. Miller. 1995. *Civic journalism: Six case studies.* St. Petersburg, FL: The Poynter Institute.

Schoeman, F. D., ed. 1984. *Philosophical dimensions of privacy: An anthology.* Cambridge, MA: Harvard University Press.

Schoenbrun, D. 1989. *On and off the air: An informal history of CBS news.* New York: E. P. Dutton.

Schudson, M. 1978. *Discovering the news.* New York: Basic Books.

————. 1984. *Advertising: The uneasy persuasion.* New York: Basic Books.

————. 1995. *The power of news.* Cambridge, MA: Harvard University Press.

Schwartz, T. 1973. *The responsive chord.* Garden City, NY: Anchor Press.

Seldes, G. 1989. "The press and the individual." In *Killing the messenger: 100 years of media criticism.* Tom Goldstein, ed. New York: Columbia University Press.

Sheehan, M., and Robinson, M. 1984. *Over the wire and on TV.* New York: Russell Sage Foundation.

Shilts, R. 1987. *And the band played on.* New York: St. Martin's Press.

Siberner, J. 1989, March 27. "The great global food fright." *U.S. news and world report,* pp. 56–59.

Sieb, P. 19. *Campaigns and conscience: The ethics of political journalism.* Westport, CT: Praeger.

Siebert, F. S., T. Peterson, and W. Schramm. 1956. *Four theories of the press.* Urbana: University of Illinois Press.

Silver, R. 1989, Winter. "The many faces of media women." *Media and values,* pp. 2–5.

Smith, C. 1992. *Media apocalypse: I don't know what comes here.* Westport, CT: Greenwood Press.

Sperber, A. M. 1986. *Murrow: His life and times.* 4th ed. New York: Freundlich Books.

Stein, M. L. 1986, June 21. "Covering a disaster story." *Editor & publisher,* p. 17.

Stone, I. F. 1988. *The trial of Socrates.* Boston: Little, Brown and Co.

Szarkowski, J. 1978. *Mirrors and windows.* New York: Museum of Modern Art.

Thoman, E. 1987, Summer-Fall. "How well does television handle social issues?" *Media and values,* pp. 20–22.

Thomas, B. 1990, January 19. "Finding truth in the age of 'infotainment.' " *Editorial research reports.* Washington, D.C.: Congressional Quarterly, Inc.

Tomlinson, D. 1989. "One technological step forward and two legal steps back: Digitalization and television newspictures as evidence in libel." *Loyola entertainment law journal, 9,* pp. 237–257.

Toufexis, A., and C. Garcia. 1989, March 6. "Watch those vegetables, Ma." *Time,* p. 57.

Toulmin, S. 1988, Summer. "The recovery of practical philosophy." *The American scholar,* p. 338.

Warren, J. 1989, March 26. "How 'media stampede' spread apple panic." *Chicago tribune,* p. 1.

Watkins, J. J. 1990. The mass media and the law. Englewood Cliffs, NJ: Prentice-Hall.

Weaver, D. H., and G. C. Wilhoit. 1986. *The American journalist: A portrait of U.S. newspeople and their work.* Bloomington: University of Indiana Press.

Weinberg. S. 1995, Nov/Dec. "ABC, Philip Morris and the infamous apology. *Columbia journalism review,* pp. 29–37.

Wengraf, A. 989. "Property and ideas," 13 Legal Stud. F. 341, 341–42.

Werner, M. R., and J. Starr. 1959. *Teapot Dome.* New York: Viking.

Westin, A. F. 1967. *Privacy and freedom.* New York: Atheneum.

Wicker, C. 1990, March 7. "Awhile back, everyone was doing it—but not anymore." *Dallas morning news,* pp. 1–2C.

Wilkins, L. 1987. *Shared vulnerability: The mass media and American perception of the Bhopal disaster.* Westport, CT: Greenwood Press.

Wilson, E. 1940. *To the Finland station.* New York: Doubleday & Co.

Woods, G. 1996. *Advertising and marketing to the new majority.* Belmont, CA: Wadsworth.

# INDEX